Understanding Organizational Behavior

Denis D. Umstot
University of
Puget Sound

WEST PUBLISHING COMPANY
St. Paul   New York   Los Angeles   San Francisco

COPYRIGHT © 1984 By WEST PUBLISHING CO.
50 West Kellogg Boulevard
P.O. Box 43526
St. Paul, Minnesota 55164

Printed in the United States of America

Library of Congress Cataloging in Publication Data

Umstot, Denis D.
    Understanding organizational behavior.

    Includes bibliographies and index.
    1. Organizational behavior. I. Title.
HD58.7.U47   1984   658.3   83–25956
ISBN 0-314-77850-0
1st Reprint—1985

To Mary,
my partner in this book and in life

CONTENTS

PART 3

The Interaction Between People

PART 4
The Total Organization

PREFACE

For several years after I began teaching organizational behavior my course critiques often included statements like: "The course was really interesting, especially when you consider the *boring* nature of the material." This recurring comment bothered me since I believe organizational behavior is inherently exciting and interesting. When I explored the reasons for such comments, students noted that while I made the lectures interesting, the text was dry, boring, and academic. A review of student ratings of texts seemed to confirm this finding—most texts were rated average at best.

While there seemed to be a number of reasons why students did not like the texts, the main concerns were lack of examples and reading difficulty. It seemed that even though my colleagues and I teach motivation, we were not writing texts to motivate students or positively reinforce the learning experience.

My goal has been to design and to write a book that will involve the reader in the material, hopefully creating interest, challenge, and motivation. The strategy to reach the goal is to relate theory to organizational practice on a continuous basis by providing examples of every concept and theory. In addition, the book is designed to be stimulating and positively reinforcing to read. It not only provides the theory needed to understand human behavior in organizations, but also attempts to provide perspectives that broaden the reader's outlook by exposure to a wide range of ideas, techniques, research, and controversies not always covered in an organizational behavior book.

■ Features

It has been a challenging task to design and write a book that attempts to achieve these goals. A number of features and strategies have been used to aid in this effort.

Examples   Every theory and concept is illustrated with at least one example. My most challenging task was to integrate an example into almost every paragraph. I found that it was far easier to merely describe a theory than to provide a relevant example of how it applied.

Theoretical Base   Theories and concepts were chosen for their explanatory power, validity, and relevance for practice. A wide variety of theoretical perspectives are used. Systems theory has been used in a number of instances to bring unity to diverse concepts and to show the interrelationship among organizational subsystems.

Research Basis   While this is not what is termed a "research-oriented text," it does have its foundations in state-of-the-art organizational research. Over 600 references (38% 1980 or later) are cited to provide a strong academic foundation. On the average, approximately one-third of the citations are research studies or reviews. The aim of this text is to inform the reader about what we *do* know about organizational behavior rather than to explain all the doubts and reservations about every theory and research study. This is not to say that research or theoretical criticism has been ruled out—it is still included whenever serious problems arise that need to be addressed.

Writing Style   An active, interesting style results in a book that is easy and perhaps fun to read but still rigorous in content. Difficult terms are defined in a clear, straightforward way with examples to help the reader link them to personal experiences and thus be more likely to retain the terms and ideas in long-term memory. A glossary is provided for easy review of definitions.

Perspectives   While the central core of organizational behavior theory is covered in the main text, there are numerous interesting side issues for both theory and practice that cannot be covered in depth or that diverge somewhat from the main theme or thrust of the chapter. Nevertheless, these Perspectives add richness, color, and interest to the study of organizational behavior. Thus, the chapters include a number of Perspectives to perk interest and to generate curiosity. They should be treated as topics that add breadth and diversity and are not necessarily directly linked with the main textual material.

Previews and Opening Cases   Each chapter opens with a set of preview questions or statements to serve as interest-arousers and an outline overview of what is to be covered. In addition, each chapter begins with a case that surfaces issues related to the topics covered in that chapter. Its purpose is to arouse interest and create an organizational example for use in much of the rest of the chapter.

Current and Authoritative Material   In addition to the essential theoretical foundation, there is a strong emphasis on current topics such as power, politics, stress, job design, organizational behavior modification, organization culture, and Japanese management topics. In addition, the book reflects the state of the art in research and theory with references being added right up to presstime.

Sexism   I have tried to use examples that display a balanced use of men and women in both traditional and nontraditional roles. In addition, there are a number of Perspectives that specifically address unique problems faced by women in managerial positions.

Cases   In addition to the opening case, each chapter contains at least two short cases that relate to the topic.

■ Organization

There are four parts to the book. It begins with an introduction that defines the field of organizational behavior and puts it into perspective with other organizational studies.

The second section deals primarily with individual behavior, including such fundamental topics as: personality, values and attitudes, perception, and motivation. Additional applied motivation topics include organizational behavior modification, reward systems, goal setting, and job design.

The third section is concerned with the interaction of people. Topics include communication, group dynamics, conflict, stress, power, politics, leadership, and decision making.

The final section focuses on the total organization with topics including organizational design and behavior, organizational change and development, and organizational climate and culture.

Generally, the chapters are designed to stand by themselves so that they may be read in any sequence desired, although the reader may have to refer to the glossary to define terms that were included in an omitted chapter. Two exceptions may be the chapter on motivation, which provides the theoretical foundation for applied motivation strategies, and group dynamics, which provides the fundamental concepts about group behavior.

Acknowledgements

I am very greatful for the intellectual stimulation and criticism provided by the reviewers. Don Hellriegel, Texas A&M,and John Slocum, Jr., Southern Methodist University, were particularly influential and helpful throughout all stages in the book's development. I would also like to thank the following reviewers who made valuable comments and suggestions that resulted in significant improvements in the manuscript:

Elmore R. Alexander, III, *Memphis State University*
David Balkin, *Northeastern University*
John Blasingame, *University of the Pacific*
George S. Bowling, *Northeastern University*
Anthony T. Cobb, *Virginia Polytechnic Institute & State University*
James C. Conant, *California State University—Fullerton*
Patricia Manley Feltes, *Mankato State University*
Bruce Fournier, *Wilfred Laurier University*
Henry M. Frechette, Jr. *Northeastern University*
Andrea Freling, *Ferris State University*
Don Hellriegel, *Texas A & M University*
Herb Johnson, *Sam Houston State University*
Donald L. Joyal, *Worcester State College*
Ray Montagno, *Ball State University*
Kevin Mossholder, *Auburn University*
Douglas W. Naffziger, *Western Illinois University*

James S. Overstreet, *Appalachian State University*
William E. Rosenbach, *U.S. Air Force Academy*
John Slocum, *Southern Methodist University*
William B. Snavely, *Miami University (Ohio)*
Duncan Spelman, *Bentley College*
Robert P. Vecchio, *University of Notre Dame*
Paul L. Wilkens, *Florida State University*

A special thanks goes to Mary Umstot, who read every word of the manuscript in all of its numerous drafts and galleys. She was a helpmate, friend, critic, and supporter throughout the four years it took to research and to write. In addition, she was responsible for the complex process of obtaining copyright releases. Without her help, it is doubtful that I could have written this book.

The University of Puget Sound was also very helpful. Tom Johnson, the Director of the School of Business and Public Administration, was always willing to provide support and assistance. The administrative assistance provided by Doris Anderson, Joan Johnson, and Anita Baisinger was also most helpful.

The editorial guidance, assistance, encouragement, and "reality checks" of Dick Fenton and Esther Craig helped mold a final product out of the earlier versions of this book. In addition, my thanks go out to Phyllis Johannesen, a former West editor, who shared my initial vision of the book and motivated me to actually undertake the project.

A final thanks goes to my good friend, Don Jenni, Department of Zoology, Universityof Montana. He was influential in encouraging me to design a book that would motivate students to read.

FEEDBACK IS DESIRED

I would greatly appreciate any suggestions for improving the book or correcting errors. In addition, I would like to find out how well the test bank in the Instructor's Resource Manual works for you. Address corrections or comments to:

Professor Denis Umstot
School of Business and Public Administration
University of Puget Sound
Tacoma, Washington 98416

Understanding Organizational Behavior

What Is Organizational Behavior?

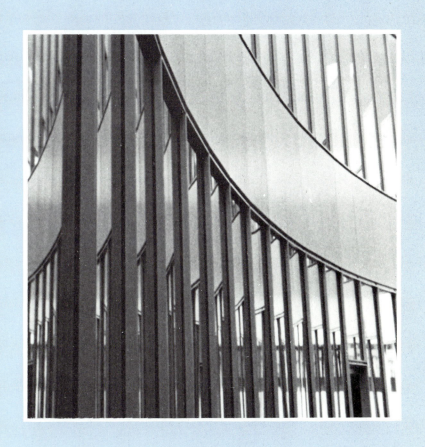

Introduction to Organizational Behavior

PREVIEW

- What is organizational behavior?

- Is there a best way to manage?

- Do you know the best techniques for learning a subject? This chapter will provide you with additional ideas.

- Which research strategy is better: natural observation, surveys, or experiments?

- How do you suppose Mark Twain used ants to conduct an experiment?

- Why is systems theory so important for preventing organizational failures?

Preview Case: Incidents in Organizational Behavior

The Nature of Organizational Behavior
- What is organizational behavior?
- What is an organization?
- The contingency approach
- Organizational structure, culture, and process
- *Perspective:* Learning Processes
- Organizational effectiveness

Research in Organizational Behavior
- Natural observation
- Survey research
- Experimental research
- *Perspective:* "On Experimental Design," by Mark Twain
- Evaluating Research

Organizations as Systems
- What is an organizational system?
- Environmental suprasystem
- An example of the systems approach

Overview of the Book

Summary
- Chapter review
- For discussion
- Key concepts and terms
- Suggested readings

Cases and Incidents
- Sam Holst, Manager
- Getting Started with Goal Setting

References

PREVIEW CASE: INCIDENTS IN ORGANIZATIONAL BEHAVIOR

Mike Sloane, heavy equipment salesman: "I'm always looking for a challenge. It seems that I'm not happy unless there are several big deals going at once." Mike is a crackerjack salesman, but would he make a good sales manager?

Susan Ling, supervisor: "It really makes me mad. No matter what I do my people only produce at their own leisurely pace. I know we could easily do one third more work if only my people were motivated. What can I do?"

Jake Olsen, foreman (to another foreman): "I just don't understand these new workers that personnel sent us. They were hired under our program to give disadvantaged workers an opportunity. The problem is that they just can't seem to get to work on time. I've started giving them a day off without pay as punishment, but things have gotten worse instead of better." Is a day off without pay a punishment or a reward for these workers?

Willard Aimes, management trainee: "But Mr. Johnson, I thought you said you wanted the reports by the end of the month, not the end of the week. I must have misunderstood."

Marsha Wagner, supervisor of the word processing center: "It's too bad Amanda quit. She was one of the best and fastest typists we've hired in a long time. Why she would put out almost twice the work of the other typists. But for some reason the others just didn't like her. I think they may have driven her off because she's so good." Do you think Amanda was really that much better or were the other typists "coasting"? Why didn't they like her?

Sandra Wool, chief of nursing for Sandhurst General Hospital: "We really have a serious problem here between the doctors and nurses. There always seems to be hard feelings between them and I'm afraid the patients suffer. The doctors complain that the nurses won't do what they are told and the nurses say the doctors act like 'little tin gods' and treat the nurses more like janitors than professionals." Is conflict such as this ever desirable?

Tony Ashly, fast-rising executive for Allstate Power Co.: "The way I get things done is through others. One strategy is to do favors for people. That not only makes them friends, but when I need something done I can always cash in a 'chit'." How important are power and politics to organizational life?

Chuck Hannick, chief of the plans division of the General Acceptance Corp., was standing at the main entrance to the plans building at 8:00 A.M. just waiting for someone to come in late. Sure enough, several did. He took their names and when he got back to his office he called their bosses and asked for a written explanation about why the people were late.

Jack Sloane, chief of manpower for Miser Corp. is discussing the results of his reorganization plan: "It was a disaster! No sooner had we announced the plan when we had almost a hundred grievances. In addition, several key managers said that they opposed the plan and would back the workers. I don't understand . . . the plan was so logical and such an improvement."

The incidents related above describe a variety of organizational behaviors that are encountered at one time or another by managers. They are only examples of the types of issues we will be addressing in this book. There is a great variety in human behavior that creates complexity, but this same variety also creates interest, stimulation, and challenge.

The purpose of this book is threefold: to help you understand the nature of human behavior in organizations, to provide some practical suggestions for improved people management, and to improve organizational performance.

In this introductory chapter, we will define the field of organizational behavior, describe how research is conducted to support our concepts, and provide an introduction to systems theory as a way of understanding the interrelated nature of organizations. The chapter concludes with an overview of the remainder of the book that provides the structure for future reading.

The Nature of Organizational Behavior

In this section we will define organizational behavior and discuss why it is important for managers. We will then discuss the ways in which organizational behavior can help people manage more effectively.

■ What Is Organizational Behavior?

The field of organizational behavior (often called OB or org behavior for short) is a relatively new field that has evolved from the older social sciences of psychology, sociology, social-psychology, anthropology, and political science (*see* Fig. 1.1). While the meaning of OB is still evolving,[1] we will define **organizational behavior** as the study of the human aspects of organizations, including individual behavior, group behavior, and their interaction with organizational structure, culture, and processes; with the goal of improving organizational effectiveness.

■ What Is an Organization?

Several aspects of the definition of OB need clarification. Perhaps the first one is to define an **organization** as a system that coordinates people, jobs, technology, and management practices to achieve goals. Organizational membership is made up of people, both individuals and groups, whose activities and jobs are structured and coordinated through management. Organizations also use technology—skills, information, techniques—to accomplish their goals or purposes. Finally, organizations work within some identifiable boundary; people can identify which elements fall within the boundary of the organization, such as its payroll or plant facilities, and which elements fall outside the boundary, such as the suppliers or customers.

■ The Contingency Approach

Certainly much of the effort in OB is aimed toward understanding and predicting how individuals and groups behave in different organizational circumstances. This often involves more than a simple cause and effect prediction, for different circumstances may result in different outcomes. For example, many people may seek more challenging, enriched, responsible

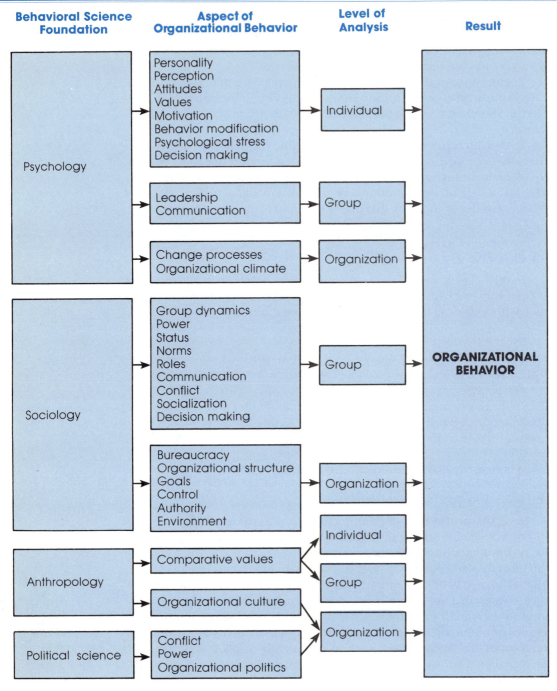

Figure 1.1. The field of organizational behavior.

Table 1.1 Organizational outcome questionnaire.[2]

Directions: Answer each question by answering *yes, no,* or *maybe/sometimes:*

	Yes	No	Maybe/Sometimes
1. Leaders should be equally concerned with their followers and the task.	_____	_____	_____
2. Satisfied workers are more productive.	_____	_____	_____
3. Employees would prefer exciting and challenging jobs.	_____	_____	_____
4. People want to participate in decisions that affect their job.	_____	_____	_____
5. Pay motivates people to work harder.	_____	_____	_____

jobs, but others may prefer jobs where they feel comfortable and do not have to stretch themselves intellectually. These two groups of people would not respond in the same way to a strategy that tried to change their jobs.

This process of determining the situational effects of OB is called the **contingency approach**.[3] Most OB outcomes, such as performance or job satisfaction, depend on the situation at hand. In other words, there is no one best way to motivate, communicate, lead, or design jobs. The best way will depend upon the situation. If you answered *maybe/sometimes* to all the questions in Table 1.1, then you understand that the contingency approach applies to each of them. Later in the book we will discuss what specific contingencies or situations are involved in each of these examples. While there is some controversy surrounding the overuse of the contingency approach,[4] it has served to improve our understanding and prediction of a number of organizational processes.

■ Organizational Structure, Culture, and Process

People do not exist in isolation in an organization; they interact with the structure, culture, and processes of the organization.

Organizational structure consists of the way tasks are broken down between people, the rules and procedures for accomplishing the task, and the authority and responsibility relationship that exists between people in the organization.[5] While structure impacts many different aspects of OB, it is treated as a separate topic in Chapter 15. Examples of structure would include job design and responsibilities, reporting relationships (Who is the boss?), and the laws that govern the organization.

Organizational culture, the topic of Chapter 17, is a broad integrating concept that includes such areas as the shared beliefs, philosophies, values, behaviors, and symbols that are characteristic of an organization.[6] Cultures spell out the informal rules that govern how people are supposed to behave. Tandem Computers, one of Silicon Valley's most successful companies, was founded on the belief that its greatest resource is people. This culture is widely shared and visible throughout the plant, as evidenced by the slogan, "It takes two to Tandem," the informality (no reserved parking places), and rituals and ceremony, such as the traditional Friday afternoon beer busts.[7]

1.1 Learning Processes

While the entire process of learning is rather complex, there are several concepts that can help improve your learning in organizational behavior or any other subject.[8]

Motivation. You must feel the need to learn. It helps to be interested and motivated. How can the information be useful to you? Examine your reasons for reading this book or taking a course. If you can recognize the positive benefits, then you are more likely to learn.

Feedback. You need feedback to correct erroneous perceptions and provide an evaluation of your progress. It is particularly useful if feedback can be given in a nonevaluative manner such as asking yourself questions about a topic to be sure you understand it or completing the case analysis at the end of each chapter. Exams and tests are also forms of feedback. As distasteful as they may be, they are useful motivators and useful sources of feedback.

Practice and repetition. The old saying, "practice makes perfect," has more than a grain of truth to it. Making an outline of the material you want to learn after you have read it helps imprint it on your mind. Frequent reviews are important for they help integrate the concepts and provide additional opportunities to record the information into your long-term memory.

Reinforcement. If you find learning the material is personally rewarding, you will be much more likely to retain it. One objective for this book is to try to make the material as interesting and rewarding as possible. Another important source of rewards is the chance to actually put the concepts to work in an organization. Try to use what you learn every chance you can—you will be surprised how much you retain.

Organizational processes involve studying how and why activities, results, or states happen—in other words, what steps take place in going from *a* to *b* to *c*.[9] Examples of processes might be the processes of motivation, communication, conflict, change, and others. We find examples of processes throughout the book. An example of a process might be the way we learn. The Perspective on Learning Processes provides some useful insights into this process.

■ Organizational Effectiveness

OB is aimed not only at improving your understanding of the way organizations behave, it is also directed toward improving organizational effectiveness. For example, in the opening incidents, a number of problems were raised:

1. How can we select people to get the best fit between the person and the job?
2. How do we motivate employees to perform better?
3. Can problems of stereotyping women and other minorities be overcome? How?
4. What is the most effective way to control or change behavior?
5. How can we get an informal group of employees to accept new members?
6. How may conflict be controlled or reduced?
7. What is the most effective way to supervise?
8. How can organizational change be accomplished?

Table 1.2 Organizational effectiveness criteria.

Productivity	Output of goods or services per worker
Quality	Defects per unit produced
Efficiency	Accomplishing the job with a minimum expenditure of effort and materials.
Job satisfaction	Degree of pleasant or unpleasant feelings toward your job
Attendance	Number of times and duration of employee absences
Turnover	Proportion of desirable employees who quit or leave
Quality of work life	Concern for individual well-being.

The answers to these questions and many more are the concern of OB because we want to be able to prescribe better ways to manage organizations. Some of the major organizational effectiveness outcomes that we are concerned with are shown in Table 1.2. We are concerned with multiple outcomes rather than each one alone. For example, we may wish to design jobs that simultaneously result in high productivity, high quality, and good job satisfaction.

Now that you have an overview of what OB is all about, we need to look briefly at the sources of our concepts and theories. The next section is concerned about research and OB.

Research in Organizational Behavior

In organizational behavior, we rely upon theories to help us understand and predict behavior. A **theory** tells us how concepts, variables, or things relate to one another.[10] For example, one relatively simple OB theory says that moderately difficult task goals, if accepted, improve people's performance.[11] This theory says that if we give people difficult goals they will work hard to reach them, provided that they accept the goals in the first place. Such a theory has obvious advantages for managers if it is true (the theory will be discussed in Chapter 7). It lets us know more about how motivation works, and perhaps more importantly, how to use the theory to change work behavior.

The way we test the usefulness of such a theory is through research, the topic of this section. We will cover three basic ways of conducting research: natural observation, survey research, and experimental research. Some understanding of these strategies is needed to evaluate how good the support is for a given concept or theory.

■ Natural Observation

When a researcher observes and records the natural environment and then analyzes and draws conclusions from these observations, **natural observation, observational research,** or **qualitative research** is being used. Although this strategy is the least rigorous of all the research methods, it can address very complex, broad problems and thus becomes quite valuable for looking at the broader aspects of OB. For example, how can we decrease organizational costs and at the same time improve quality of work life for organizational members? Or, how can we change the organization's culture? These questions are too broad to answer with other research strategies.

One form of natural observation often found in management is comments from successful or knowledgeable insiders called **authoritative opinions.** For example, Robert Townsend, the former Chief Executive of Avis Rent-a-Car company wrote a book called *Up the Organization*.[12] He gave advice based upon his experience, for example:

CONTACTS

A lesson very few have learned: If you want to approach the head of XYZ Corporation, call him cold. Tell him who you are and why you want to talk to him. A direct and uncomplicated relationship will follow.

The common mistake is to look for a mutual friend—or a friend's friend on his board, in his bank or investment bank or law firm—to introduce you. This starts all sorts of side vibrations and usually results in a half-assed prologue by the intermediary, who is apt to grind both edges of his own ax.[13]

Qualitative research may also be done by academically trained scholars, often with good results.[14] Authoritative opinions, such as those put forth by Peter Drucker, a famous writer on management topics, have been very influential among practitioners and academics alike.[15] The recent best-selling book by William Ouchi, *Theory Z*, is also an example of how authoritative opinions can be influential.[16]

Another form of observational research is the **case study**, in which the researcher describes what happened in a particular organization. Case studies are sometimes written by **participant observers**—academic researchers who join an organization as a member so as to observe in a natural way what is happening in the organization. For example, John Van Maanen actually joined a police force on a full and part-time basis for a number of years. While he observed a range of interesting behaviors, he also noted difficulties in remaining detached and objective and concludes that all such participant-observer research is based on a combination of "passion and judgment"; thus, it is impossible to fully assess its accuracy.

While observational techniques are not as rigorous as other research strategies because they are subject to biases of the observer, they often provide insights into important issues that would not have been addressed using other research strategies.

■ Survey Research

Survey research involves the use of questionnaires to gather data about anything that is of concern to the manager or researcher.[17] For example, many organizations regularly measure job satisfaction to find out how well employees like their jobs (*see* Chapter 3 for an example). In addition, you might be interested in finding out if employees are experiencing job stress, if they are satisfied with supervisory practices or pay, or if they desire some change in working hours.

Survey responses, which are usually obtained from either a sample or from all employees, may be analyzed in several ways. One way is to simply present the percentages who responded in a certain way or the average

Understanding Organizational Behavior

scores for each question. These types of analysis are called **descriptive statistics**. Another common strategy for analysis is to relate one variable (a factor that you wish to measure, such as job satisfaction) on the questionnaire with another one (such as job performance). This type of analysis is called **correlation**. An important consideration when using correlation is that you can only find out the degree of relationship between two variables; you cannot tell which one is the cause and which one is the effect.

An example of the use of survey research might be using a questionnaire to find out if there is a relationship between job satisfaction and attendance or absenteeism. Based on our knowledge of OB, we would expect the relationship to be moderately strong. To accomplish the research, let's assume that the firm has 200 employees and that a sample of fifty was taken. The job satisfaction scores are then calculated and correlated with the attendance records for each employee. A correlation coefficient is calculated that will range somewhere between −1.0 and +1.0. The closer the correlation to 1.0, either positive or negative, the stronger the relationship. The closer the correlation is to zero, the weaker the relationship.

The results of our research show a correlation of −0.45, which indicates a moderately strong relationship between job satisfaction and absenteeism—as a job satisfaction goes up, absenteeism goes down. This is the expected relationship and might be an indication that our efforts to improve job satisfaction are linked with lower absenteeism. But remember that the correlation relationship does not prove that lower job satisfaction causes absenteeism. Perhaps being absent causes people to like their jobs less rather than the reverse. Figure 1.2 is a graphic plot of the correlation scores.

Survey research is widely used for practical organizational purposes as well as for building and testing theory. It is relatively easy to do; and thus

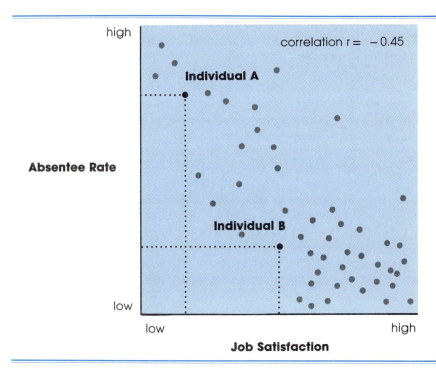

Figure 1.2.
Relationship between job satisfaction and absenteeism using hypothetical data.

costs are low. Problems center around the validity of the survey instruments and the problems in determining what is the cause and effect.

■ Experimental Research

Experimental research is powerful because it allows us to determine cause and effect relationships. In **experiments** the researcher creates a situation, manipulates events, and controls the research environment.[18] There are two basic settings for experiments: field and laboratory. **Field experiments** are conducted in real organizational settings, while **laboratory experiments** are conducted in settings contrived by the researcher. In OB research we see both settings used.

Take a field experiment as an example. Researchers wish to see if enriched jobs result in higher job satisfaction and productivity. A organization is located that is willing to participate in the experiment. The experimental design includes two groups: an experimental group and a control group. Be-

---

1.2 *"On Experimental Design" by Mark Twain*[19]

I constructed four miniature houses of worship—a Mohammedan mosque, a Hindu temple, a Jewish synagogue, a Christian cathedral—and placed them in a row. I then marked fifteen ants with red paint and turned them loose. They made several trips to and fro, glancing in at the places of worship, but not entering.

I then turned loose fifteen more painted blue; they acted just as the red ones had done. I now gilded fifteen and turned them loose. No change in the result; the forty-five traveled back and forth in a hurry persistently and continuously visiting each fane, but never entering. This satisfied me that these ants were without religious prejudices—just what I wished; for under no other conditions would my next and greater experiment be valuable. I now placed a small square of white paper within the door of each fane; and upon the mosque paper I put a pinch of putty, upon the temple paper a dab of tar, upon the synagogue paper a trifle of turpentine, and upon the cathedral paper a small cube of sugar.

First I liberated the red ants. They examined and rejected the putty, the tar and the turpentine, and then took to the sugar with zeal and apparent sincere conviction. I next liber-ated the blue ants, and they did exactly as the red ones had done. The gilded ants followed. The preceding results were precisely repeated. This seemed to prove that ants destitute of religious prejudice will always prefer Christianity to any other creed.

However, to make sure, I removed the ants and put putty in the cathedral and sugar in the mosque. I now liberated the ants in a body, and they rushed tumultuously to the cathedral. I was very much touched and gratified, and went back to the room to write down the event; but when I came back the ants had all apostatized and had gone over to the Mohammedan communion.

I saw that I had been too hasty in my conclusions, and naturally felt rebuked and humbled. With diminished confidence I went on with the test to finish. I placed the sugar first in one house of worship, then in another, till I had tried them all.

With this result: whatever Church I put the sugar in, that was the one the ants straightway joined. This was true beyond a shadow of doubt, that in religious matters the ant is the opposite of man, for man cares for but one thing; to find the only true Church; whereas the ant hunts for the one with the sugar in it.

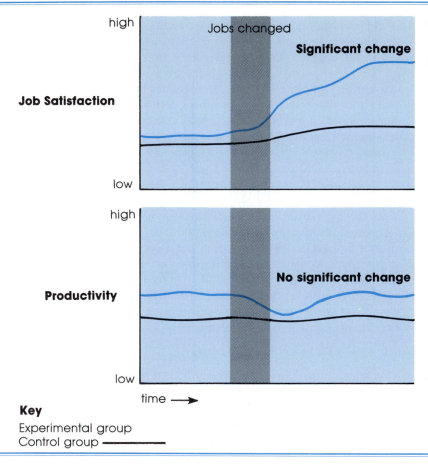

Figure 1.3. Results of an experiment on the effects of job enrichment on satisfaction and productivity using hypothetical data.

fore the jobs of the enriched group are changed, productivity and satisfaction of both groups are measured. Then the jobs of the experimental group are redesigned to be more enriched (interesting, meaningful, and challenging—*see* Chapter 7). No changes happen to the jobs of the control group. After the changes (called the experimental treatment), the results are measured to see what changes occurred in job satisfaction and productivity. It was found that redesigning jobs resulted in higher satisfaction, but there was no change in productivity (*see* Fig. 1.3).

Experiments offer us precision and control. They are the most rigorous of all research techniques and the only ones from which we can determine cause and effect relationships. However, experiments do not lend themselves to broad-based problems that cannot be manipulated (culture, for example). They may also be so controlled and rigorous that people in organizational settings may react adversely and cause distortions in the results.[20]

■ Evaluating Research

Critical evaluation of research requires considerable knowledge of research methods and statistics.[21] An important thing for managers to consider is that a number of different methods are appropriate for organizational research, but each has its problems. Observational techniques are good for

Introduction to Organizational Behavior

broad research issues; survey research offers inexpensive answers to theoretical and practical questions; and experiments offer the rigor and control to determine what factors are causal. Perhaps the ideal situation is when a number of different research strategies seem to converge in support of one theory.

Now that you have an overview of what organizational behavior is about and how we gather data to support OB theories, we need to examine one more important introductory topic—how everything fits together using the systems view of organizations. This is the topic of the next section.

Organizations as Systems

Even though we tend to separate the topics of organizational behavior into perception, motivation, communication, or group dynamics, in reality these topics interrelate and merge together. Every managerial analysis and decision needs to consider the impact on other parts of the organization. Managers need to question what will happen to other parts of the organization's structure, culture, or processes besides the one being changed. For example, if you are designing a new pay system, it may have impacts on motivation, organizational goals, leadership behavior, and quality of work life.

■ What Is an Organizational System?

One way to maintain a total organizational perspective while studying individual topics is to use a systems view of organizations. An **organizational system** is an organized, unitary whole made up of interdependent subsystems and delineated by identifiable boundaries from the environmental suprasystem.[22] Examples of organizational systems might be Rainier National Bank, Detroit General Hospital, Apple Computers, Boeing Aircraft Company, or Shakey's Pizzas.

Every system is made up of a number of **subsystems**, just as your body is made up of a number of subsystems, such as the circulatory system or the nervous system. The subsystems of an organization could be divided up in many ways. One way separates them into five major subsystems: technical, structural, goals and values, psychosocial, and managerial. Definitions for each of these subsystems are given below:[23]

☐ **Psychosocial subsystem**—The individual and group behavior of people working together.

☐ **Goals and values subsystem**—Values, or the broad general beliefs people hold, influence the goals and direction of the organization.

☐ **Technical subsystem**—The knowledge, processes, techniques, and facilities that are used to transform inputs to the organizational system into outputs.

☐ **Structural subsystem**—The structures, procedures, and rules in the organization serve to divide up the tasks and coordinate them. Some examples in this area include time schedules, job descriptions, work rules, communications procedures, and lines of authority.

☐ **Managerial subsystem**—The central roles of coordinating, planning, controlling, leading, and goal setting are accomplished by managers working in the managerial subsystem.

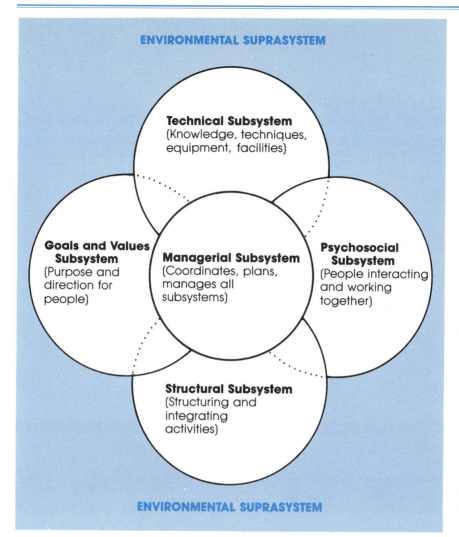

Figure 1.4.
Organizations as
systems.

ENVIRONMENTAL SUPRASYSTEM

Technical Subsystem
(Knowledge, techniques, equipment, facilities)

Goals and Values Subsystem
(Purpose and direction for people)

Managerial Subsystem
(Coordinates, plans, manages all subsystems)

Psychosocial Subsystem
(People interacting and working together)

Structural Subsystem
(Structuring and integrating activities)

ENVIRONMENTAL SUPRASYSTEM

□**Organizational system**—All of the above subsystems compose the organizational system. In other words, an organization is made up of goal-directed people, with values, operating within a structure and technology that allows them to accomplish the organization's purpose.

Figure 1.4 shows that each of the subsystems are interrelated and overlapping and that the managerial subsystem acts as the integrating force.

■ Environmental Suprasystem

Organizations are also part of a larger environmental suprasystem that includes such dimensions as customers, suppliers, competitors, politics, and economic conditions. (These topics are discussed in Chapter 15.) For example, an oil company doing business in the turbulent Middle Eastern environment faces considerably different environmental problems than does a major department store chain in the United States.

Introduction to Organizational Behavior   **15**

■ An Example of the Systems Approach

The Atlas Sign Company provides an example of how systems concepts apply to organizational behavior. The applicable systems concepts are noted in parentheses. The case concerns the Atlas Sign Company, owned by Jeff Baxter and his brother-in-law, Willie Sanchez, and located in a medium-sized town in northern Florida.

The company was founded in 1951 and had prospered. It specialized in leasing road signs for hotels, restaurants, motels, and other businesses (environmental suprasystem—customers). Businesses that wanted road signs contracted with Atlas on an annual basis to provide the signs (structural subsystem—procedures). Each customer approved a color sketch of the sign and the general geographical location of the sign (technical subsystem—design and placement). By 1958, Atlas had almost sixty employees organized into three divisions: construction, painting, and sales (structural subsystem—division of labor).

The construction division did all the heavy work including digging the holes for the signs, erecting the heavy telephone poles, and building the framing and sign faces (technical subsystem—design and building). The construction crews were generally a pretty tough, hard-drinking lot (psychosocial and values subsystems—macho values). Crews would work hard if they were supervised, but they would take every chance they could to "goof off" and had to be closely supervised by their foremen (psychosocial subsystem—group pressures).

The painters liked to think of themselves as artists and were quite temperamental, so these employees had to be handled with "kid gloves" (psychosocial and managerial subsystems—communication).

The salespeople were always trying to beat the company goals (psychosocial and goals and values subsystems—motivation). Unlike the construction crews, they required little supervision because their sales dollar values provided a direct measure of their work performance (structural and managerial subsystems—self-motivated).

(For the remainder of this case you may wish to check your ability to determine which subsystem or suprasystem is involved. Use a separate sheet of paper and preletter it a through j. Then following each letter write the subsystem(s) or suprasystem you think is applicable. More than one subsystem is often involved since they interact. Answers appear at the end of the references at the end of the chapter.)

Until the early 1960s everything went just fine for Atlas. However, a law passed by Congress was to have far-reaching effects on their future (*a*). An act was passed that required all roadsigns to be placed no closer than 600 feet from the highway. This made the current techniques of construction obsolete since much larger signs and lettering would be needed so that people could see them from the road (*b*). In addition, it raised the cost per sign astronomically.

At almost the same time another event went almost unnoticed—big chain motels were taking over the business once held by the big city hotels (*c*). And to make things even worse, these new chain motels were using centralized telephone reservation services that made the need for signs somewhat less important than it once had been (*d*). Thus, costs were going up and the number of customers was declining.

About this time Jeff and Willie should have reevaluated their direction (*e*) to see if there was some different product, such as neon signs, that they might pursue. However, they elected to continue using the same business techniques they had always used.

Their first step was to lay off employees. The first ten people were no problem since most of them were transitory. But then they had to lay off one of their long-time employees, Solomon Clark. Solomon had been a bit outspoken and had never gotten along well with his foreman or with the owners (*f*). Solomon went to the union with his grievance (*g*). Although the union had always been pretty weak, the firing gave them a rallying point, and they were able to call a general strike against Atlas (*h*). Since Jeff and Willie were violently anti-union (*i*), they held out for almost ten weeks before they finally gave in to most of the union demands including reinstating Solomon Clark (*j*).

Unfortunately, when the strike effects were combined with reduced sales and increased costs, Atlas Sign went bankrupt within six months—the owners lost everything!

As you can see there is a great deal of interaction between the subsystems, and it is not always clear which subsystem is the dominant one. In this case the environmental suprasystem was probably crucial. If the owners had paid more attention to what was happening in their industry, they might still be in business. The objective of this example is not to make you a systems expert but to alert you to the interactive nature of all of the material we will be covering in the book.[24]

Table 1.3 shows the topics of the book and the primary organizational subsystems that apply. Keep in mind that there is almost always an interaction between several subsystems.

Overview of the Book

We will begin our study with the nature of individuals who work in organizations. Personalities, values, attitudes, and perceptions of people influence much organizational behavior, including the important topic of motivation. In the first section of the book we will cover a number of interesting applied topics, such as managing one's impression, barriers to the advancement of women in organizations, personal characteristics of general managers, and a comparison of Japanese and American values.

Our next focus will be how to motivate employees. After learning some theories of motivation we will turn to several ways to apply motivation. The relatively new area of behavior modification will be added to the more traditional strategies of using pay, goals, and job design.

Once we have completed the individually oriented first section of the course, we will examine three important aspects of communication including interpersonal communications, listening behavior, and nonverbal communication. Communication, the link between individuals, will lead us into the next section of the book, which focuses on group behavior.

The study of group dynamics begins the interaction-between-people section. We learn a number of practical concepts for understanding group behavior and find out what it takes to make groups effective. The inevitable conflict that results when people and groups interact will be our next topic.

Table 1.3 Organizational behavior topics related to systems theory.

Chapter	Subject Matter	Primary Systems Relationships (*See* Legend for key)					
		Psycho-social	Goals and values	Technical	Structural	Managerial	Environmental
2	Personality	🟦	□			🟦	□
3	Values and attitudes	🟦	■			🟦	🟦
4	Perception	■	🟦			🟦	□
	Impression management	🟦	□	□		🟦	🟦
5	Motivation	■	🟦	🟦	🟦	■	🟦
6	Behavior modification	■	□		🟦	🟦	□
	Pay	🟦	🟦	□	🟦	🟦	
7	Job design	🟦	□	🟦	■	■	□
	Goal setting	🟦	■	□	■	■	□
8	Communication	■	🟦		🟦	■	🟦
9	Group dynamics	■	🟦		🟦	□	□
10	Conflict	🟦	□		🟦	🟦	□
	Competition	🟦	□		🟦	🟦	□
11	Stress	■	🟦		□	🟦	□
12	Power	🟦	□		🟦	■	🟦
	Politics	🟦			🟦	🟦	🟦
13	Decision making	🟦	🟦	🟦	🟦	■	🟦
14	Leadership	🟦	🟦	□	🟦	■	□
15	Organization design	🟦	□	🟦	■	■	□
16	Organizational change	🟦	🟦	🟦	🟦	■	🟦
	Organization development	🟦	🟦		□	🟦	□
17	Organizational culture	■	🟦		🟦	■	🟦
	Quality of work life	■	🟦		□	🟦	🟦

Legend: ■ High impact   □ Low impact   🟦 Moderate impact   Blank indicates very little impact

We will learn which resolution techniques to use. One outcome of conflict is often stress, a relatively new topic in OB that concentrates on recognizing and managing the factors that cause stress. Certainly no study of organizations would be complete without the study of power and politics in organizations. You will learn the concepts and tactics.

In the next topic of the section, you will find out how to use people for making effective decisions. We will cover when to use groups and when to avoid them. We will also cover several useful approaches to decision making. The final chapter in the section deals with leadership. You will find out what makes an effective leader and what strategies seem to work best.

The last section of the book deals more with organization-wide issues. Organizational design discusses the strategies for designing effective organizations and some of the common types of organizations. Our attention will then shift to organizational change—we will be concerned with ways to get ready for change and conduct it so it will be effective and lasting. We will also learn about an applied strategy for change called organization development. The final chapter in the book deals with the concept of organizational culture, climate, and quality of work life—critical management issues for the 1980s.

Chapter Review

■ The field of **organizational behavior** is derived from many disciplines. It is concerned with individual and group behavior and their interaction with structure, culture, and processes.

■ The **contingency approach**, used extensively in OB, involves study of how different circumstances and situations affect behavior.

■ **Organizational effectiveness**, a goal of OB, involves improving such factors as productivity, quality, efficiency, job satisfaction, attendance, retention, and quality of work life.

■ Theories of OB are supported by research. Three major approaches to research—natural observation, survey research, and experiments—provide most of the verification for theories. All of these strategies are important. **Natural observation**, whether it be expert opinion or case study, allows us to address broad, ill-defined areas. **Survey research**, which is relatively cheap and quick, allows us to find answers to specific questions and explore general relationships. **Experiments**, the most rigorous approach, offer an opportunity to assess causation and to exert control of what happens.

■ The **systems approach** gives us insights into how all aspects of an organizational system are interrelated. The subsystems are ways to envision an organization just as chapters in this book are ways to organize the total field of organizational behavior.

For Discussion

1. Based upon your organizational experience, think of an example of the contingency approach.
2. Using the learning processes outlined in the Perspective on Learning Processes, outline an effective strategy for conducting the organizational behavior class.
3. Is there one factor that is the key to organizational effectiveness? Explain why or why not.
4. How can one evaluate the quality and validity of the natural observation method of research?
5. Explain the meaning of a correlation between job satisfaction and turnover at -0.40.
6. Identify the advantages and disadvantages of each of the three major approaches to research.
7. Pick any organization with which you are familiar and describe it using systems concepts.

Key Concepts and Terms

organizational behavior
organization
contingency approach
organizational culture
organizational structure
organizational processes
learning processes

organizational effectiveness
qualitative research
survey research
experimental research
organizational systems and
 subsystems
environmental suprasystem

Introduction to Organizational Behavior

Suggested Readings

Cummings, L. L. (1981). Organizational behavior in the 1980s. *Decision Sciences* 12: 365–77.

Dubin, R. (1982). Management: Meanings, methods, and moxie. *Academy of Management Review* 7: 372–79.

Nadler, D. A., and Tushman, M. L. (1980). A model for diagnosing organizational behavior. *Organizational Dynamics* Autumn: 35–51.

Scott, W. R. (1981). *Organizations: Rational, natural and open systems*. Englewood Cliffs, N.J.: Prentice-Hall.

Sommer, R., and Sommer, B. (1980). *A practical guide to behavioral research*. New York: Oxford University Press.

CASES AND INCIDENTS

Sam Holst, Manager

Sam Holst, project manager for the new computer chip at Zoolite Electronics, is upset. Because of the traffic tie-up, he is five minutes late getting to the office. Several of the office employees who see him come in have rather strange looks on their faces. Probably because it was only yesterday that Sam was lecturing them about coming to work on time. Sam thinks to himself that he'll have to set the alarm fifteen minutes earlier.

As he passes his secretary's desk he notices that she is not there yet. Perhaps she too was caught in the traffic. After a few minutes at his desk trying to sort out his day and make his "to do" list, he receives a call from his secretary, Alice. She is in tears. Apparently there have been marital problems at home, and she and her husband are separating. She says she is just too upset to work this week and needs some time off to get herself together. What can Sam say? He knows that the big conference is coming up next week, and he really needs Alice to help him organize it. Sam tells her it is OK to take off, but realizes he's really in trouble.

Sam knows he will have to go to the administrative department to get a replacement for Alice. However, just last week he had a big run-in with Manley, the department head.

He'll really have to "eat crow" to get this favor from Manley.

The replacement secretary that Manley sends him is certainly no jewel. She is slow. She has to be told almost everything in great detail to do it right. Oh well, there is all week to get things ready for the conference. But wait. Mr. Robins, the production manager, is on the line and wants Sam to dry-run the presentation for the conference first thing in the morning, so there will be time to change anything that is not just right.

Now Sam has a real problem. He must have his presentation done and charts made by tomorrow morning. He decides that now is the time to call in some chips. George owes him a favor for the bonus Sam swung for him after the electronics module project. Sam calls George, who says, "Sure old buddy, I'll do the charts as a special favor, but I'll have to have them by 2 P.M. today or else they won't be ready for tomorrow morning."

The critical holdup is with Sam's own people—if only they were as motivated as he is. Sam remembers their sullen looks when he came in late this morning. This is a time when he needs an all-out effort from them, but with all the pushing and ranting that he has been doing lately, they probably won't budge without some type of reward. The only trouble is that Sam does not really control pay or anything like that. All he can do is explain the situation to them and hope they will put out for him.

Discussion questions
1. What subsystems apply to this case?
2. What research strategy would you use to evaluate the job satisfaction of Sam's workgroup?

Getting Started with Goal Setting

Sharon Lind, a recent graduate from a respectable business school, has just been appointed as the supervisor of the installation department for residential telephone installations. Her boss told her that she faces a real challenge because productivity of her new workgroup is down and absenteeism is very high. Sharon's boss gave her a free hand to improve the department.

Sharon had learned from her OB class that goal setting is an effective technique for motivation. She decided that she would use it to solve her problems. On her second day on the job she announced to the crew that they would each have a goal for the day to accomplish. These goals were set at 110 percent of the production of each person during the past sixty days. The reception to Sharon's edict was cool, but she was pleased that she was assertive and forceful and had everything under control.

The next day every single person in the department called in sick.

Discussion questions
1. What did Sharon do wrong?
2. How could she have used research to assess readiness for goal setting?
3. What research design would she use if she wished to evaluate the effects of her goal-setting program?

REFERENCES

1. For a discussion of definitional issues, *see* Cummings, L. L. (1978), Toward organizational behavior, *Academy of Management Review* 3:90–98.

2. Adapted from an idea of Pinder, C. C. (1983), Contingency quiz, in *Organizational behavior*, 3rd ed., ed. D. Hellriegel; J. W. Slocum, Jr.; and R. W. Woodman, p. 19, St. Paul, Minn.: West.

3. *See* Cummings, L. L. (1981), Organizational behavior in the 1980s, *Decision Sciences* 12:365–377; and Kast, F. E. and Rosenzweig, J. E., eds. (1973), *Contingency views of organization and management*, Palo Alto, Ca.: SRA.

4. For a critique *see* Schoonhoven, C. B. (1981), Problems with contingency theory: Testing assumptions hidden in the language of contingency 'theory,' *Administrative Science Quarterly* 26:349–377.

5. Payne, R. and Pugh, D. S. (1976), Organizational structure and climate, in *Handbook of industrial and organizational psychology*, ed. M. D. Dunnette, p. 1127, Chicago: Rand-McNally.

6. *See* Pettigew, A. W. (1979), On studying organizational cultures, *Administrative Science Quarterly* 24:570–581.

7. Deal, T. and Kennedy, A. (1982), *Corporate cultures*, Reading, Mass.: Addison-Wesley.

8. Burris, R. W. (1976), Human learning, in *Handbook of industrial and organizational psychology*, ed. M. D. Dunnette, pp. 131–146, Chicago: Rand-McNally.

9. *See* Schein, E. H. (1969), *Process consultation: Its role in organization development*, Reading, Mass.: Addison-Wesley.

10. Dubin, R. (1976), Theory building in applied areas, in *Handbook of industrial and organizational psychology*, ed. M. D. Dunnette, pp. 17–39, Chicago: Rand-McNally.

11. Locke, E. A.; Shaw, K. N.; Saari, L. M.; and Latham, G. P. (1981), Goal setting and task performance, 1969-1980, *Psychological Bulletin* 90:125–152.

12. Townsend, R. (1970), *Up the organization*, New York: Knopf.

13. Townsend, *Up the organization*, p. 22.

14. *See* Van Maanen, J.; Dabbs, J. M., Jr.; and Faulkner, R. R. (1982), *Varieties of qualitative research*, Beverly Hills, Ca.: Sage. *Also see* the December 1979 issue of *Administrative Science Quarterly*, which is devoted to qualitative research.

15. One of P. F. Drucker's recent books is (1982) *The changing world of the executive*, Truman Talley Books.

16. For references to Ouchi's *Theory Z* published by Addison-Wesley in 1981, *see* Chapters 3 and 17.

17. *See* Dunham, R. B. and Smith, F. J. (1979), *Organizational surveys*, Chicago: Scott, Foresman.

18. Fromkin, H. L. and Streufert, S. (1976), Laboratory experimentation; and Cook, T. D. and Campbell, D. T. (1976), The design and conduct of quasi-experiments and true experiments in field settings; both in *Handbook of industrial and organizational psychology*, ed. M. D. Dunnette, Chicago: Rand-McNally.

19. Original source unknown. Quoted from Scott, W. E. and Cummings, L. L. (1973), *Readings in organizational behavior and human performance*, Homewood, Ill.: Irwin, p. 2.

20. Argyris, C. (1968), Some unintended consequences of rigorous research, *Psychological Bulletin* 70:185–197.

21. For more information *see* Stone, E. F. (1978), *Research methods in organizational behavior*, Santa Monica, Ca.: Goodyear; and Emory, C. W. (1980), *Business research methods*, Homewood, Ill.: Irwin.

22. Kast, F. E. and Rosenzweig, J. E. (1979), *Organization and management*, 3rd ed., New York: McGraw-Hill, p. 18.

23. Kast and Rosenzweig, *Organization and management*.

24. For a more complete description of systems theory, *see* Kast, F. E. and Rosenzweig, J. E. (1972), General systems theory: Applications for organization and management, *Academy of Management Journal* 15:447–465; and Scott, W. R. (1981), *Organizations: Rational, natural and open systems*, Englewood Cliffs, N.J.: Prentice-Hall.

Answers to the systems example:
a. Environmental
b. Technical
c. Environment
d. Impact of technology on the environment
e. Goals and values
f. Psychosocial, managerial
g. Structural
h. Structural, goals, and values
i. Goals and values
j. Structural, managerial, and psychosocial

Individual Behavior in Organizations

PART

2

Understanding Individual Behavior

PREVIEW

- How good are you at empathizing? Did you know this skill is vital for managing people?

- Do you seem to turn into a different person when you are hot and irritable? Does your environment affect your personality?

- Which side of your brain is more dominant, the right or the left? Why is the answer important for management?

- How strong is your self-esteem? A questionnaire will provide a measure of its strength.

- Are there personality barriers that prevent the advancement of many women in organizations?

- What blend of achievement, power, and affiliation motives are related to managerial success?

- Are you an internalizer or an externalizer? Check your self-knowledge by completing a questionnaire.

- Why is participation in competitive games and sports a good preparation for top management?

PREVIEW CASE: JENNI PIKE'S CRISIS

Jenni Pike touched her throbbing forehead and thought to herself, "I can't take any more of this, it's driving me crazy. I'll turn in my resignation tomorrow. There has to be a better job than the one here at Interdivisional Enterprises."

Today had been another bad day for Jenni; one of many since she joined the Promotion Department after graduating from a school of business administration.

Jenni's job is to develop promotional ideas for presentation to the senior marketing staff. Although she had always thought of herself as a competent, intelligent person, she was beginning to wonder—since only one of her ideas had been approved by the senior staff during the past six months. Since Jenni has always been a high achiever, this lack of success has depressed her. She is beginning to doubt whether she is cut out for a promotion job.

Jenni blames some of her problems on her boss, Fritz Grubb, because he always seems to assign her to difficult products or markets with which she is unfamiliar with. For example, her latest product promotion was for electric garage door openers. Jenni knows nothing of garage door openers— she doesn't even have a garage.

And then there is the awful weekly senior staff meeting where Jenni must present her ideas. Most of the senior staff are men and seem to think that women do not really belong in a company specializing in building products. While they do not openly discriminate against her, she feels there is an underlying hostility and distrust for any of her ideas. Thus, she has to work twice as hard to sell something as a male would.

Several times the strain has just been too much. She has become enraged at one of the male staff and told him off. These episodes end in tears and a later counseling session with her supervisor.

"Yes", Jenni thought, "tomorrow I will get even. They won't realize how much I have contributed until I'm gone. Revenge is sweet."

How would you like to be in Jenni's position? Most of us would find it pretty uncomfortable. Although there are many complex forces at work in this case, one important theme is the interaction of the job, the social environment, and individual characteristics and traits—personality. The goal of this chapter is to better understand individuals: their self-concepts, their motives, and the roles they play. We will also study several approaches to personality traits.

Why Study Individual Behavior?

There are several reasons for the studying the different reactions, responses, and behaviors of people, (often referred to as **individual differences**). We need to develop a sense of empathy, and to improve our knowledge of personal problems that may interfere with work performance. We must also select and promote the right people.

■ To Develop Empathy

Most of us tend to be **egocentric** about what makes people behave the way they do. In other words, we tend to think others have the same feelings, attitudes, motivation, and perspective that we do. This is seldom true, even between close relatives or spouses. Thus, we are likely to make erroneous judgements and poor decisions because of this faulty way of thinking. **Empathy**, the ability to put yourself in the place of another, is a skill that is quite difficult to develop, but it is very useful for understanding organizational behavior. One of the purposes of this chapter is to help you develop a better sense of empathy.

■ For Selection and Placement

Since people are different, it follows that some will be more suited for a particular job or company than will others. For example, a person who likes to have everything organized and laid out by the supervisor may be quite unhappy in a job where there is a great deal of discretion and judgement involved. In a typical group of people, we might also find someone who feels frustrated and constrained if too much structure is imposed. Others might be completely indifferent. Managers must consider these differences if they want to be able to pick the right person to hire, promote, or transfer.

■ To Improve Counseling Effectiveness

One of the tasks of a manager is to counsel and help employees who are experiencing personal difficulties. While the manager is not a psychologist, there are many times when personal problems will interfere with getting the job done. Understanding individuals will help make you more effective at this task.

The Nature of Personality

In this section we will delve into the nature of personality, including the situational impact on personality. We will discuss the origin of personality, the self-concept, roles, and the social aspects of personality.

■ What Is Personality?

Personality is a stable set of characteristics and tendencies that determine our thoughts, feelings, and actions in combination with the social and biological pressures of the moment.[1] While we all know that people have different characteristics, abilities, and behavior patterns that reflect their personality, when we try to measure these differences we find they are often elusive. Part of the reason is that it is impossible to get "inside someone's head" to know what thoughts, feelings, and behavioral intentions actually exist—we must depend upon inaccurate self-reports and inferences based on the behaviors exhibited.

Another aspect of personality emphasizes the similarities among individual behavior rather than the differences. While we are all different in many ways, we also share with others many characteristics, abilities, and behavior patterns. One challenge to managers is to sort through the similarities and differences in the way people respond to organizational changes. For example, if we want to make people's jobs more responsible and interesting, then we must make sure that the people who must do the jobs have personality characteristics that fit this design. If many of them do not, our innovation is headed toward problems.

■ The Situation and Personality

The definition of personality also calls attention to the importance of the situation at the moment. People's personalities may show different forms depending upon the social or biological pressures that exist. For example, have you noticed how many college students exhibit much different personalities when they are in the presence of their parents than they do in the presence of their peers?

Organizational situations also create pressures on personality. For example, a normally congenial and friendly person may become quite hostile under the right environmental pressures. One incident occurred on a hot day last August when the air conditioner was broken. Jim, the supervisor of the drafting section, was hot and his clothes were soaked with perspiration. While he was normally quite easy to get along with, that day was different—he was very irritable and uncomfortable. Even the simplist tasks seem burdensome. Just when Jim was about to go outside and get a breath of fresh air, Duane (one of his subordinates) came in and began asking a lot of questions. As he listened to Duane's numerous questions he became more and more irritated. Finally, Jim was unable to control his temper any longer. He angrily swept some papers off his desk and shouted at Duane in a threatening and hostile manner. Duane beat a hasty retreat wondering what he had done wrong.[2]

While not everyone becomes more aggressive when they become hot and uncomfortable, many people do. Temperature is only one of many environmental and social pressures that may shape personality at any given moment.[3]

■ How Does Personality Develop?

Two major factors influence personality: heredity and social environment.

Heredity Provides a Starting Point
Heredity contributes the basic structure for everyone's personality. It determines sex, race, body type, motor skills, and capacity for learning. These characteristics influence our early life experiences and place constraints on our goals and aspirations. For example, a linebacker for the National Football League could not have become what he is without the hereditary potential for a large, muscular body. Likewise, a professional figure skater or ballet dancer must have some genetically acquired athletic coordination to excel. Even though heredity is important for providing the foundation for personality, the most influential inputs come from the environment.[4]

| 2.1 | *The Two Sides of the Brain* |

There are differences in many people based upon which hemisphere of the brain is dominant. Unless we have had a stroke, both sides of the brain operate in all of us. We alternate from one side to the other; however, most of us favor one side or the other and that influences our personality. People whose left brain dominates are more analytic, systematic, sequential, and verbal. When the right brain dominates, a person will be more intuitive, visual-spatial, sensuous, and holistic.[5] For left-handed people the hemisphere functions are usually reversed.

There are several implications for management.[6] People with a strong left-brain orientation may be good for analytical jobs such as planners, engineers, or accountants. On the other hand, top managers need a sense of the overall situation (the "big picture") and good intuition; they should be right-brain people. In addition, it appears that right-brain people are more effective as task force leaders because they pay more attention to making the group work harmoniously and effectively (*see* the group maintenance roles in Chapter 9). Another situation where the right-brain should be emphasized is in creative activities, such as formulating strategic goals, or developing innovative solutions to problems.

The relationship between brain functions and organizational assignment is still speculative. Little or no research has been conducted to support these relationships.

Social environment   The most powerful determinant of personality is the social environment.[7] As Figure 2.1 indicates, there are a number of social impacts on personality including family, educational experience, and peer interactions. Cultural factors, such as values, language, and religion, also have a strong impact on personality.[8]

■ Self-Concept: The Center of Personality

The self-concept is an extremely important aspect of personality because of its impact on an individual's emotions and behaviors. The **self-concept** is the "totality of the individual's thoughts and actions with reference to himself [or herself] as an object."[9] In other words, the self-concept is the concern we feel for ourselves as an individual. The self is made up of the same types of inputs as personality. It includes **social identity** based on things such as sex, age, race, and religion; and various **dispositions**, such as attitudes, values, preferences, and personality traits (intelligence, bravery).

The self-concept is linked with **self-esteem**—the positive or negative feelings about one's self. The questionnaire in Table 2.1 is a measure of self-esteem that you might wish to complete. People with a strong self-esteem generally feel good about themselves while people with a weak self-esteem are unsure of themselves and may be easily threatened. In the opening case, Jenni Pike felt a threat to herself after she continually failed to get her ideas approved. She coped with the threat by quitting.

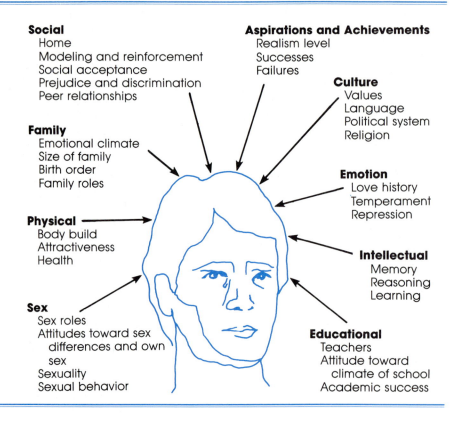

Figure 2.1. The determinants of personality.[10]

Social
Home
Modeling and reinforcement
Social acceptance
Prejudice and discrimination
Peer relationships

Family
Emotional climate
Size of family
Birth order
Family roles

Physical
Body build
Attractiveness
Health

Sex
Sex roles
Attitudes toward sex
  differences and own
  sex
Sexuality
Sexual behavior

Aspirations and Achievements
Realism level
Successes
Failures

Culture
Values
Language
Political system
Religion

Emotion
Love history
Temperament
Repression

Intellectual
Memory
Reasoning
Learning

Educational
Teachers
Attitude toward
  climate of school
Academic success

Table 2.1   The Rosenberg self-esteem scale.

Directions: For each question circle the answer that best represents your agreement or disagreement with the statement. *SA* means strongly agree, *A* means agree, *D* means disagree, and *SD* means strongly disagree.

1. On the whole, I am satisfied with myself.	SA	A	D	SD
2. At times I think I am no good at all.	SA	A	D	SD
3. I feel that I have a number of good qualities.	SA	A	D	SD
4. I am able to do things as well as most other people.	SA	A	D	SD
5. I feel I do not have much to be proud of.	SA	A	D	SD
6. I certainly feel useless at times.	SA	A	D	SD
7. I feel that I'm a person of worth, at least on an equal plane with others	SA	A	D	SD
8. I wish I could have more respect for myself.	SA	A	D	SD
9. All in all, I am inclined to feel that I am a failure.	SA	A	D	SD
10. I take a positive attitude toward myself.	SA	A	D	SD

Scoring: If you circled *SA* or *A* for questions 1, 3, 4, 7, or 10, give yourself a 1 for each *SA* or *A* response. If you answered *SD* or *D* for questions 2, 5, 6, 8, or 9, give yourself a one for each *SD* or *D* response. Your score will range from 0 to 10. Scores of 6 or below may indicate low self-esteem levels.

From *Conceiving the self*, by Morris Rosenberg. Copyright © 1979 by Basic Books, Inc. Reprinted by permission of the publisher.

Understanding Organizational Behavior

Another incident that illustrates this point is the case of Ellen, a competent computer operator. Through bitter experience, Ellen's boss found out that she had to be very careful about correcting Ellen's behavior. Almost every time Ellen is corrected for even the most minor mistake, she breaks out into an uncontrolled episode of crying. One possible explanation for this behavior is that Ellen has a weak self-concept and low self-esteem. She may be very unsure of herself and quite threatened whenever someone criticizes her. There is no way for us to know the actual causes of Ellen's problem. However, now that there is awareness that she appears to be particularly sensitive to criticism, her boss can be more careful in handling corrections.

■ Protecting the Self Through Defense Mechanisms

People use defense mechanisms to try to reduce their anxiety and frustration when there is some threat to their self-esteem. Defense mechanisms tend to deny reality, distort reality, or push things to the unconcious level. Table 2.2 shows some of the reactions people have when threatened or frustrated.

It is important for managers to realize that behavior does not always reflect the obvious. For example, a person who is angry at the boss may show it by viciously shouting at a coworker. This behavior might be interpreted by the manager as a weakness in getting along with coworkers, while the real problem may lie with the manager. (This is an example of the displacement coping mechanism.) Awareness of the existence of these coping mechanisms will help you more accurately interpret individual behavior.

Table 2.2 Psychological self defense: Coping mechanisms.[11]

Rationalization	Devising self-satisfying explanations for behavior that would otherwise be unacceptable. An example would be a sales person padding an expense account because "everyone does it."
Displacement	Transferring an emotional feeling for one person or thing to another person or thing. An example would be an angry outburst towards a subordinate as a result of a frustrating meeting with the boss.
Repression	Excluding a feeling, experience, or event from one's conciousness because it is psychologically disturbing. An example is an employee who "forgets" to list a job on her application blank after she was unfairly fired.
Withdrawal or flight	Leaving, either physically or psychologically, whenever a situation becomes threatening or frustrating. Examples would be the sulking salesman who has just lost a big sale or the indignant manager who quits after receiving a "less than perfect" performance appraisal.
Projection	A projection of one's own shortcomings to others without admitting that they are true of yourself. An example would be a unsuccessful person who is trying to block the promotion of others in the organization because "they are out to get me."
Negativism	Active or passive resistance or aggression. An example might be the assembly-line employee who is forced to work on Saturday and who sabotages the assembly line to get even.

■ Feelings About Self and Others—OK or Not OK

Another way to understand the self-concept is through **transactional analysis** (TA), developed by Eric Berne.[12] TA involves much more than feelings about one's self and others; it is a theory of personality and human behavior. In Chapter 8, we will discuss how TA can help us understand the communication process.

According to TA, the experiences that form people's personalities cause them to make decisions about themselves that result in their feeling comfortable in certain **psychological positions** (*see* Fig. 2.2). The positions are related to how they feel about themselves (**OK** or **not OK**) and how they feel about others (**OK** or **not OK**). Once a psychological position is taken, an individual will look for events, behaviors, feelings, and experiences that reinforce the position. Situations may also affect and change the psychological positions by triggering feelings and emotions within the self.

Psychological Positions

In organizations, psychological positions can be used in many ways as an aid to understanding people. For example, say you supervise an employee named Lee who is always making mistakes. He just does not seem to be able to do anything right. He is very apologetic about these errors, but they are still very annoying to you, and you give him a verbal reprimand every time it happens. While you have tolerated his behavior, it is getting to the point where you are thinking about firing him.

A TA analysis of Lee's behavior pattern indicates that he is probably operating in the "I'm not OK, you're OK" quadrant. He may actually be seeking negative strokes, perhaps because these were the kind of strokes he received as a child. Sometimes people get into repetitive patterns of behavior that reinforce their "not OK" feelings. In the next section we will discuss this issue.

TA Games

Lee's behavior may indicate that he is playing a TA game called "kick me." People who play "kick me" are attempting to reinforce self-negation and self-pity. They may say things like, "I could kick myself for

Figure 2.2.
Transactional analysis psychological positions.[13]

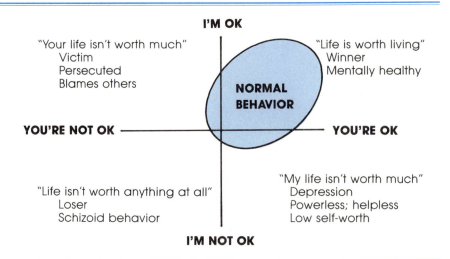

Understanding Organizational Behavior

doing that" or "Isn't it terrible what I did." They obviously do not feel OK about themselves, they have low self-esteem. **Games** are recurring patterns of behavior that are aimed toward some predictable outcome or payoff that is usually associated with not-OK feelings about one's self or others.[14]

Avoiding Games   The way to avoid being an unwitting participant in any game such as "kick me," is to withhold the negative payoff. When someone like Lee says "I wouldn't blame you if you were upset," you should be careful to avoid being upset and providing a negative stroke to the "kick-me" player. The kick-me game is only one type of organizational game that indicates a personality problem. Several others are summarized in the Table 2.3.

■ Role-Playing and Personality

Roles are sets of behaviors that are expected when a person occupies a certain position.[15] We play the role of the student (attentive, hardworking, intellectual), or we may play the role of a union member (ambivalent or hostile toward management, interested in pay and benefits, reluctant to learn new jobs). Some roles are easy to change as we change positions. Other roles, such as those associated with being a man or woman, form a central part of our personalities and are thus more difficult to change (*see* the Perspective: Individual-Level Barriers to the Advancement of Women in Organizations).

People Play Different Roles   People play a number of roles in organizations. They adapt their roles to different organizational situations. For

---

Table 2.3 Games people in organizations play.[16]

Yes, but	A very common game between the boss and subordinates and the line and staff people in organizations. Peole who play the game appear to be looking for suggestions, but are really trying to put down the suggester (to make him or her feel not OK).
If it weren't for you	A blaming game where people who feel inadequate blame others for their inability to perform (may involve people in the "I'm not OK, you're not OK" quadrant).
Blemish	The office nitpicker looks for some minor or insignificant flaw in someone else's work as an excuse for a put-down. If the blemish player is the boss, then it may result in considerable anger and frustration on the part of the subordinates. (The blemish player wants others to feel "not OK.")
Now I've got you, you S.O.B.	A player lies in wait for a mistake and then pounces with angry feelings of self-righteous indignation. Oftentimes, the victim may be set up by the player; for example, a boss may give incomplete instructions and then get angry when the project is done wrong.
Bear trapper	Baiting someone with false promises and then dashing their expectations is a common game played when trying to lure a new employee into the bear trapper's organization. It also commonly happens when someone has continually offered their assistance, but when it is really needed it is withdrawn.
Poor me	There are many versions of this game that all stem from feelings of "not OK" and signify that "I'm stupid." It may develop into the "kick-me" game discussed earlier.

2.2 Are Organizations and People Incompatible?

A number of people think that there may be a basic incongruity between people and organizations. Chris Argyris[17] has argued that organizations have a life of their own that is often diametrically opposed to the needs of their individual employees.

Organizations foster immaturity by designing specialized and fractionized work, giving orders, evaluating performance, and generally controlling all aspects of the work environment. Organizations often treat people like infants, who begin life by being dependent and submissive, possessing few abilities, and having a short-time perspective. Adults, on the other hand, strive toward independence and autonomy, developing their abilities and having a longer time perspective.

Since organizational practices and policies tend to foster dependency and immaturity, the needs of mature individuals are not met. The incongruency between an individual's needs and the formal organization causes individuals to experience frustration, psychological failure, a short-time perspective, and conflict. People tend to react to these experiences by leaving the organization (either psychologically or physically), fighting the organization (perhaps by joining a union), or by concentrating their attention on pay, benefits, and time off.

Argyris recommends dealing with the problem by designing organizations to take into account the needs of mature individuals. Jobs should be designed so that people can use their initiative and feel responsibility for work outcomes (job enrichment, the topic of Chapter 7, is one way to do this). In addition, managers should supervise in a mature way so that people feel they are treated as adults rather than children.

example, a manager will often seem to be level-headed, analytical, good-natured, and people-oriented when dealing with superiors. But to subordinates, that same manager may be a hot-headed, angry, authoritarian. Just like actors, some organizational members are much better than others at role playing. Alert observation of people in different situations and attention to inputs from other sources can provide a more accurate picture of the person.

Roles May Conflict   Sometimes one role will conflict with another and cause considerable discomfort. For example, a craftsman, such as a finish carpenter, may believe that the proper role to follow is producing top-quality, meticulous work. On the other hand, the supervisor may require high *quantity* of work with only minimal quality standards. Thus the role of the craftsman may conflict with the role of a good subordinate.

■ Summarizing the Nature of Personality

An individual's personality is made up of all the characteristics and tendencies that make a unique person. In addition, we usually share a number of personality traits in common with others. The situation at the moment may also influence which aspect of our personality surfaces. Our per-

---

| 2.3 | *Individual-Level Barriers to the Advancement of Women in Organizations* |

The difficulty of integrating women into organizational leadership positions is a many-faceted problem that involves issues at the societal, institutional, organizational, and individual level.[18] Several individual-level problems are highlighted in this perspective. Many have to do with roles.

Would you agree that the ideal woman is strong, assertive, powerful, ambitious, and able to produce results? Most people would not. In fact, a woman who displayed those behaviors might be labeled as "pushy."[19] In the United States the ideal woman is generally seen as less aggressive, less independent, less dominant, less active, more emotional and as having greater difficulty making decisions than the ideal man.[20] When women are viewed in this perspective, it is clear that they may wind up being criticized regardless of their actual performance.[21]

In addition, women are seen by themselves and men as being primarily responsible for the role of caring for children and home and are thus placed at a disadvantage since "their all" cannot be given to their job without sacrificing marriage and children.[22] Women may also prevent their success because they may accept nonline (jobs that are not central to the organization's purpose such as production and sales), dead-end, or underpaid jobs.[23]

Another problem is that women and men often avoid close working relationships because they are afraid of implications of sexual intrigue or innuendo.[24] This may mean that women are excluded from informal work groups and may thus be at a disadvantage.

---

sonality, which develops from heredity and social environment, forms during childhood and adolescence and is relatively stable throughout the rest of our life.

A central concept for understanding personality is the self-concept, which reflects our feelings of self-esteem and self-worth. We use defense mechanisms, such as rationalization, displacement, or withdrawal, to cope with threats to our self-esteem. Some people develop a poor self-concept and feel "not OK" about themselves throughout their lives. This may result in destructive psychological games.

Finally, we noted that the roles people play are influenced by their basic personality. Sometimes a role conflict may result that is harmful to the individual or the organization. (This topic is covered in Chapter 10.)

Personality and Behavior

Now we will turn to a review of several personality theories and concepts that are useful for understanding organizational behavior. Two major concepts will be covered: motives and locus of control. There are many other interesting and relevant personality issues since the field is rich in theory and research; however, space limits our coverage to those that seem most relevant to organizations.[25]

■ Motives of Individuals

One way of understanding individual behavior is to look at the motives or needs of individuals. A **need** is a tension created by some psychological or physiological deficiency that arouses an individual to try to satisfy that need. The **motive** process is dynamic—"it is an active, goal-directed sequence that begins with arousal and ends with some form of satisfaction."[26] In Chapter 5, we will discuss the relationship between needs and motivation. This chapter concentrates on the personality implications of various motive patterns. Three motive patterns or needs have particular relevance for understanding personality: need of achievement, need for power, and need for affiliation.

Achievement Motive

David McClelland has spent many years studying people who have high **achievement** needs, whom he calls *achievers*.[27] These achievers are very concerned with efficiency and getting things done. They take moderate risks and seek feedback on performance. They are concerned with excellence, doing well in competition, creating unique accomplishments, and getting feedback about how well they have done.

People who are high achievers often gravitate into sales. A sales job provides them with the challenge, risk, and the concrete feedback they need. An interesting problem sometimes results when the high-achieving supersalesperson is promoted to sales manager. The achiever will sometimes become quite unhappy in this supposedly better position, since individual achievement will no longer be possible, and other motives, such as need for power, become more important. The same thing may happen with a crackerjack engineer or scientist.

Power Motive

Higher level managers and leaders need to have a relatively high need for **power**, the desire to influence and control others.[28] Since a large part of a top manager's job concerns influencing, directing, and controlling others, it seems logical that a person with a high need for power would be more comfortable and effective in such a position. However, the power motive seems more effective when it is directed toward accomplishing organizational goals and not just personal gain.

Affiliation Motive

People with a high need for **affiliation** are particularly concerned with social relationships such as love, friendship, and approval of others. Too much of this motive apparently makes top managers less effective because they lack the courage to make difficult personnel decisions without worrying about being disliked.[29]

Implications of Motive Patterns

Motive patterns have important implications for personnel selection and placement. When selecting people for sales jobs, high achievement needs are desirable. For higher level management jobs, high power needs combined with a relatively low need for affiliation is a more appropriate combination. We must be aware that different demands and rewards may be associated with supervisory jobs. If these conflict with the motives of the individual, then unhappiness and frustra-

2.4 Motive Patterns and Long-Term Success in Management [30]

A study of managerial success within American Telephone and Telegraph Company over a sixteen-year period found that motive patterns were important correlates of managerial success.

The study was made of 311 entry-level managers whose careers were followed for sixteen years. At the end of sixteen years, there were 237 managers still remaining in the study. Sixty-one percent of the managers were in nontechnical fields, such as sales, customer service, administration, and personnel. Thirty-nine percent were in technical management fields, such as construction, maintenance, and installation.

The results indicated that nontechnical managers with moderate to high need for power, low need for affiliation, and a high need for self-control were more successful in terms of promotion within the company. At lower management levels, a high need for achievement was also related to success because promotion depends more on individual achievement. However, once the job becomes one of supervising others, achievement is no longer related to success. These patterns did not hold for technical managers. Their success seemed unrelated to motive patterns and more related to their technical competence.

tion may result. A research study supporting these conclusions is summarized in the Perspective: Motive Patterns and Long-Term Success in Management.

■ Locus of Control

Another aspect of personality that is important to organizations is the locus of control.[31] Before we begin our review you can test your locus by answering the questions in Table 2.4.

Did you score below 4 on the Rotter scale? Then you probably feel that you are the master of your own fate; that you can control what you do, where you live, and where you work. You are what Julian Rotter calls an *internalizer* or someone whose locus of control is internal.[32] If you scored above 5 you may feel that your fate is more a matter of luck or "whatever will be will be." You may feel that circumstances are more in control of your destiny. You may be an *externalizer*.

Internal and External Locus of Control   When something happens and it is attributed to luck, fate, chance, under the control of other powerful people, or unpredictable because of the complexity of the situation, then this belief represents an **external locus of control**. If what happens is attributed to a person's own behavior or characteristics, then the belief represents an **internal locus of control**.[33]

An example of external locus of control might be Arnie Chang, who just received a lower than expected performance evaluation and reacted like this: "Oh damn! Those fellows up in personnel have done it to me again by changing the form. If we had used the old system I would have gotten a

Table 2.4 Rotter internal-external control scale (abridged).

Directions: Circle the response *a* or *b* that best reflects your feelings about the statement.

1. a. Many of the unhappy things in people's lives are partly due to bad luck.
    b. People's misfortunes result from the mistakes they make.

2. a. In the long run people get the respect they deserve in this world.
    b. Unfortunately, an individual's worth often passes unrecognized no matter how hard he tries.

3. a. The idea that teachers are unfair to students is nonsense.
    b. Most students don't realize the extent to which their grades are influenced by accidental happenings.

4. a. No matter how hard you try some people just don't like you.
    b. People who can't get others to like them don't understand how to get along with others.

5. a. I have often found that what is going to happen will happen.
    b. Trusting to fate has never turned out as well for me as making a decision to take a definite course of action.

6. a. Becoming a success is a matter of hard work, luck has little or nothing to do with it.

    b. Getting a good job depends mainly on being in the right place at the right time.

7. a. When I make plans, I am almost certain that I can make them work.
    b. It is not always wise to plan too far ahead because many things turn out to be a matter of good or bad fortune anyway.

8. a. Who gets to be the boss often depends on who was lucky enough to be in the right place first.
    b. Getting people to do the right thing depends upon ability; luck has little to do with it.

9. a. Many times I feel that I have little influence over the things that happen to me.
    b. It is impossible for me to believe that chance or luck plays an important role in what happens to me.

10. a. What happens to me is my own doing.
    b. Sometimes I feel that I don't have enough control over the direction my life is taking.

Scoring: If you answered *a* to questions 1, 4, 5, 8, or 9, give yourself a 1 for each answer. If you answered *b* to questions 2, 3, 6, 7, or 10, give yourself a 1 for each answer. Now add up the total number of 1s. Your score should range from 0 to 10. A low score indicates a high internal locus of control while a high score indicates a high external locus of control. The average score for college students is about 4.

From J.B. Rotter, 1966, Generalized expectancies for internal versus external control reinforcement, *Psychological Monographs*, Vol. 80 (No. 609). Copyright 1966 by the American Psychological Association. Reprinted/abridged by permission of the author and the publisher.

good rating and been promoted." If, on the other hand, Arnie had reacted from an internal locus of control he might have responded like this: "I'm disappointed that my performance was not as good as it might have been. I will have to find out what I can do to improve it so I will be promotable."

Using Locus of Control   People with an internal locus of control are especially important in organizational positions that require initiative, innovation, and self-starting behavior, such as managers,[34] researchers, planners. If the task requires complex information analysis and processing, internalizers do the job better.[35] Internalizers are potentially more motivated than externalizers. If you planned to implement a pay system where people are paid "piece-rates" (pay for each unit produced within a given time), then internalizers would be preferable since they believe that the outcomes

Understanding Organizational Behavior

2.5 *Personal Characteristics of General Managers*

John Kotter conducted an in-depth research study of fifteen general managers of U.S. corporations with revenues ranging from around $100 million to $5 billion or more. They included a variety of industries ranging from high technology to banks, retailing, communication, and professional services. He found a number of common personality characteristics summarized below.[34]

Reprinted with permission of Macmillan Publishing Company from *The general managers* by John P. Kotter. Copyright © 1982 by The Free Press, a Division of Macmillan Publishing Company.

Basic Personality

Needs/Motives

- Liked power
- Liked achievement
- Ambitious

Temperament

- Emotionally stable and even
- Optimistic

Cognitive Orientation

- Above average intelligence (but not brilliant)
- Moderately strong analytically
- Strong intuitively

Interpersonal Orientation

- Personable, and good at developing relationships with people
- Unusual set of interests that allowed them to relate easily to a broad set of business specialists

Accumulated Information and Relationships

Information

- Very knowledgeable about their businesses
- Very knowledgeable about their organizations

Relationships

- Had cooperative relationships with a very large number of people in their organizations
- Had cooperative relations with many people in their industry also.

2.6 The Gamesman[37]

Based on a research study of managers in high technology corporations, Michael Maccoby classified people's personality and style into a number of categories; one of which is the gamesman. The **gamesman** is interested in challenge, competition and winning—life and work are just one big game to be treated with enthusiasm. The gamesman may say, "Winning isn't the only thing, it's everything."

The notion here is that some of the lessons learned from competitive sports also apply to organizations. For example, people who engage in sports learn to accept defeats or ego punctures without being psychologically threatened. Game players also learn to capitalize on an opponent's weaknesses and to use "end runs" rather than frontal attacks. Maccoby says the style of the gamesman fits a number of organizational situations:

■ When organizations are facing strong competition on an internal, national, and inter-national basis, the **gamesman** has the experience of coping with competition.

■ When innovation is needed to create and maintain an advantage over competitors, the gamesman has learned that this is the way to become a winner.

■ When interdependent teams are needed to discover, develop, and market new products, the gamesman's team experiences are essential.

■ When there is a requirement for fast-moving flexibility to meet changing schedules and deadlines and motivate people, the experience with games provides a solid foundation for coping.

A mature gamesman is probably the type of person to pick for leadership positions that require teamwork, flexibility, speed, and drive. However, when the task requires deliberate, thorough analysis—such as an engineering plan—the gamesman would not be a good choice as a leader.

are under their control.[38] Internalizers would also prefer more freedom from supervision than externalizers, and they would perform better with more personal control over their work environment.

■ Using Personality Concepts

Now that you have finished the chapter, you should have a much better sense of the nature of personality and why people differ. An important point to remember is that while personality is relatively stable, people can change their outward behavior because of the environment—people play different roles in different situations. The self-concept also provides a central concept for understanding why people experience depression and why they behave in ways to protect their self-esteem.

In addition, we have covered a number of characteristics of individuals that might make them more effective managers, such as a moderate to high power motive, a relatively low affiliation motive, and an internal locus of control. These personality concepts provide us with insights into ourselves and others.

Chapter Review

◼ The study of individual behavior is important because it is important to develop **empathy** so we are not **egocentric**. We need to be able to select and promote the right people, and managers need to be skilled at counseling.

◼ While personality is comprised of a stable set of characteristics and tendencies, the social and biological pressures of the moment affect how we behave.

◼ The **self-concept** is made up of our positive and negative feelings toward ourselves as an object; it represents our self-esteem. We use a number of different coping mechanisms to protect the self when it is threatened.

◼ One way to look at these positive and negative feelings about ourselves and others is to use **transactional analysis**, which categorizes behavior into a number of psychological positions based on whether a person feels *OK* or *not OK* about themselves and others. People often play **games** that reinforce their feelings that either they are not *OK* or that others are not *OK*. These games always have some type of negative payoff. Games can be stopped by withholding the negative payoff.

◼ There may be a basic incongruity between people and organizations. Organizations tend to foster immaturity by designing specialized work and generally controlling the work environment. Adults, on the other hand, strive toward independence, autonomy, and maturity. People may react by leaving or becoming hostile to the organization.

◼ People in organizations play different **roles** depending upon the situation. Some of these roles, such as being a man or a woman, are very deep seated and difficult to change. When roles conflict, it can cause considerable discomfort for the person.

◼ There are a number of individual-level barriers to the advancement of women in organizations. Some of the barriers concern role conflicts, such as homemaker versus career woman. Other barriers revolve on the tendency for women to accept nonline, dead-end jobs and the fear of sexual intrigue.

◼ **Motive patterns** provide insights into personality. People who are high achievers may be better assigned to sales or production, while people who have high power motives may make better managers.

◼ People can be divided into **internalizers** or **externalizers** based on their **locus of control**. Internalizers are generally the preferred personality type for organizations because they will be more self-motivated.

For Discussion

1. How stable is a person's personality? Has your personality changed in the past two years? How?
2. Describe some situational factors that may influence personality. Do any of these factors affect your personality?
3. What are the implications of the study of left-brain, right-brain for organizations?

Understanding Individual Behavior

4. Would a manager use different supervisory strategies for a person with a strong self-concept and one with a weak self-concept?
5. Using Figure 2.2 that describes the TA psychological descriptions, identify which games and coping strategies seem to fit in a given quadrant.
6. What does Argyris mean when he says that organizations and people are basically incompatible?
7. How may roles cause problems for managers?
8. McClelland highlights three important motives: achievement, power, and affiliation. Analyze which motives are more important to you. Does this profile fit that of a manager?
9. Why would someone with an external locus of control have a more difficult time being an effective manager?

Key Concepts and Terms

personality
left-brain, right-brain
   functions
self-concept
defense mechanisms
transactional analysis
psychological positions
games

role
motives and needs
achievement motive
power motive
affiliation motive
locus of control

Suggested Readings

Jongeward, D. (1976). *Everybody wins: Transactional analysis applied to organizations*. Reading, Mass.: Addison-Wesley.

Kotter, J.P. (1982). *The general managers*. New York: The Free Press.

Levinson, H. (1980). Criteria for choosing chief executives. *Harvard Business Review* Jul.-Aug.: 113–120.

Martin, P.Y.; Harrison, D.; and Dinnitto, D. (1983). Advancement of women in hierarchical organizations: A multilevel analysis of problems and prospects. *Journal of Applied Behavioral Science* 19: 19–33.

Nugent, P.S. (1981). Management and modes of thought. *Organizational Dynamics* 9: 44–59.

CASES AND INCIDENTS

The Crying Waitress

To visualize the pressures on service in Chandler's Restaurant, let us consider this statement by a 21-year-old [woman], who had had a year of experience in this restaurant. She put it this way.

You know, I was so mad! I finally broke down Tuesday and cried. That was really a terrible day. The guests were crabby, and I wasn't making any money, and we kept running out of food in the kitchen.

Once I went past one of my tables just when a new party was sitting down. One of the women picks up 50 cents and puts it in her pocket. She says, "Look, the people here must have forgot and left their money." I could have screamed, but what could I do?

Well the guests were yelling at me all day, trying to get my attention. Everybody had trouble. Sue cried too.

The waitress was asked if she could remember the particular incident that set the crying off.

Yes, it was like this. I was rushed, and I came in to the service pantry to get my hot plates. There were three hot plates standing up there on the counter, and, when I called my order in, the woman standing behind the counter just said, "Take them," so I put them on my tray and started out. I thought I was doing all right, but then Sue comes in. You see she had been stuck all day. She had orders for hot plates for her whole station all at once, and she couldn't carry it all out, so she left some of her hot plates at the counter and told the woman behind the counter to save them for her.

When she came back and saw the hot plates all gone with a long line of girls waiting to get them, she started to cry. Well, when I saw that the plates were really hers, I gave them right back to her, and a couple of other girls gave plates back to her, so she got her hot plates right back, and she didn't have to leave the floor.

But that upset me. You know, I was getting out of a hole with those hot plates, but then all of a sudden I had to give them up and get right at the end of a long line. I just started to bawl.

I had to go down to the rest room. Well, the way I am, I'm just getting over it when I think again what one of the guests said and the way they were acting, and then I get feeling sorry for myself some more, I start to cry all over again. It took me an hour to get back on the floor Tuesday.

Abridged from W.F. Whyte, *Industry and society*, pp. 127-29. Copyright © 1946 by McGraw-Hill, New York. Used with permission.

Discussion questions
1. What do you think caused the crying episode?
2. What level of self-esteem does the waitress have? Is this affecting her behavior?
3. What coping mechanisms is she using?

Barbara Herrick

She is thirty; single. Her title is script supervisor/producer at a large advertising agency; working out of its Los Angeles office. She is also a vice president. Her accounts are primarily in food and cosmetics. "There's a myth: a woman is expected to be a food writer because she is assumed to know those things and a man doesn't. However, some of the best copy on razors and Volkswagens has been written by women."

She has won several awards and considerable recognition for her commercials. "You have to be absolutely on target, dramatic and fast. You have to be aware of legal restrictions. The FTC gets tougher and tougher. You must understand budgetary matters: will it cost a million or can it be shot in a studio in one day?"

Men in my office doing similar work were being promoted, given raises and titles. Since I had done the bulk of the work, I made a stand and was promoted too. I needed the title, because clients figured that I'm just a face-man.

A face-man is a person who looks good, speaks well, and presents the work. I look well, I speak well, and I'm pleasant to have around after the business is over with—if they acknowledge me in business. We go to the lounge and have drinks. I can drink with the men but remain a lady. (Laughs.)

That's sort of my tacit business responsibility, although this has never been said to me directly. I know this is why I travel alone for the company a great deal. They don't anticipate any problems with my behavior. I equate it with being the good nigger.

On first meeting, I'm frequently taken for the secretary, you know, traveling with the boss. I'm here to keep somebody happy. Then I'm introduced as the writer. One said to me after the meeting was over and the drinking had started, "When I first saw you, I figured you were a—you know. I never knew you were the person *writing* this all the time." (Laughs.) Is it a married woman working for extra money? Is it a lesbian? Is it some higher-up's mistress?

I'm probably one of the ten highest paid people in the agency. It would cause tremendous hard feelings if, say, I work with a man who's paid less. If a remark is made at a bar— "You make so much money, you could buy and sell me"—I toss it off, right? He's trying to find out. He can't equate me as a rival. They wonder where to put me, they wonder what my salary is.

Buy and sell me—yeah, there are a lot of phrases that show the reversal of roles. What comes to mind is swearing at a meeting. New clients are often very uptight. They feel they can't make any innuendoes that might be suggestive. They don't know how to treat me. They don't know whether to acknowledge me as a woman or as another neuter person who's doing a job for them.

The first time, they don't look at me. At the first three meetings of this one client, if I would ask a direction question, they would answer and look at my boss or another man in the room. Even around the conference table. I don't attempt to be—the glasses, the bun, and totally asexual. That isn't the way I am. It's obvious that I'm a woman and enjoy being a woman. I'm not overly provocative either. It's the thin, good nigger line that I have to toe.

I've developed a sixth sense about this. If a client will say, "Are you married?" I will often say yes, because that's the easiest way to deal with him if he needs that category for me. If it's more acceptable to him to have a young, attractive married woman in a business position comparable to his, terrific. It doesn't bother me. It makes me safer. He'll never be challenged. He can say, "She'd be sensational. I'd love to get her. I could show her what a real man is, but she's married." It's a way out for him.

Or there's the mistress thing: well, she's sleeping with the boss. That's acceptable to them. Or she's a frustrated, compulsive castrator. That's a category. Or lesbian. If I had short hair, wore suits, and talked in a gruff voice, that would be more acceptable than I am. It's when I transcend their labels, they don't quite know what to do. If someone wants a quick label and says, "I'll bet you're a big women's libber, aren't you?" I say, "Yeah, yeah." They have to place me.

From *Working: People Talk About What They Do All Day and How They Feel About What They Do*, by Studs Terkel. Copyright © 1972, 1974 by Studs Terkel. Reprinted by permission of Pantheon Books, a Division of Random House, Inc.

Discussion questions

1. What types of role conflicts does Barbara face?
2. Does she see a threat to her self-concept? How is she coping?
3. How does locus of control apply here?

Analyzing Jenni Pike's Crisis

Refer back to the opening case for this chapter and explain how each of the following concepts apply:

1. Which side of the brain was Jenni more likely to favor? Why?
2. What methods was she using to protect her self-esteem?
3. Locate her in terms of the psychological position diagram shown in Figure 2.2.
4. Was Interdivisional Enterprises (Jenni's company) incompatible with her? Why?
5. What roles seem to be important to Jenni?
6. Does she face special problems because she is a woman?
7. Is Jenni an externalizer or an internalizer?

1. Maddi, S.R. (1980), *Personality theories: A comparative analysis*, Homewood, Ill.: Dorsey, p. 10. *Also see* Gough, H. (1976), Personality and personality assessment, in *Handbook of industrial and organizational psychology*, ed. M.D. Dunnette, Chicago: Rand-McNally.

2. Adapted from an incident reported by Baron, R.A. (1977), *Human aggression*, New York: Plenum, p. 125.

3. Terborg, J.R. (1981), Interactional psychology and research on human behavior in organizations, *Academy of Management Review* 6: 569–576. *Also see* Baron, *Human aggression* and Maddi, Personality theories; for detailed discussions of environmental and social inputs to personality.

4. Price, R.A.; Vandenberg, S. G.; Iyer, H.; and Williams, J.S., (1982), Components of variation in normal personality, *Journal of Personality and Social Psychology* 43: 328–340.

5. Ornstein, R.E. (1972), *The psychology of consciousness*, New York: Viking Press; and Springer, S.P. (1981), *Left brain, right brain*, San Francisco: W.H. Freeman.

6. This discussion is based on Mintzberg, H. (1976), Planning on the left and managing on the right, *Harvard Business Review* Jul.-Aug.: 49–58; and Nugent, P.S. (1981), Management and modes of thought, *Organizational Dynamics* Spring: 45–59.

7. Price, et al., Components of variation in normal personality.

8. Levine, R.A. (1973), *Culture, behavior, and personality*, Chicago: Adline Publishing.

9. Rosenberg, M. (1979), *Conceiving the self*, New York: Basic Books, p. 9.

10. Adapted from the concepts presented in Hurlock, E. B. (1974), *Personality development*, New York: McGraw-Hill.

11. Adapted and abridged from Costello, T.W. and Zalkind, S.S. (1963), *Psychology in administration: A research orientation*, Englewood Cliffs, N.J.: Prentice-Hall, pp. 148–149.

12. For a more thorough discussion of TA, *see* Eric Berne's books: (1961) *Transactional analysis in psychotherapy*, New York: Grove Press; (1972) *What do you say after you say hello*, New York: Grove Press; and (1964) *Games people play*, New York: Grove Press.

13. *See* Berne, *Games people play*.

14. Adapted from James, M. and Jongeward, D. (1971), *Born to win: Transactional analysis with Gestalt experiments*, Reading, Mass.: Addison-Wesley.

15. Graen, G. (1976), Role-making processes within complex organizations, in *Handbook of industrial and organizational psychology*, ed. M. D. Dunnette, pp. 1201–1246. Chicago: Rand-McNally.

16. Based on Berne, *Games people play* and Jongeward, D. (1976), *Everybody wins: Transactional analysis applied to organizations*, rev. ed., Reading, Mass.: Addison-Wesley.

17. Based on Argyris, C. (1957), *Personality and organization*, New York: Harper; and Argyris, C. (1973), Personality and organization theory revisited, *Administrative Science Quarterly* 18: 141–167.

18. Martin, P.Y.; Harrison, D.; and Dinnitto, D. (1983), Advancement of women in hierarchical organizations: A multilevel analysis of problems and prospects, *Journal of Applied Behavioral Science* 19: 19–33.

19. Martin, et al., Advancement of women in hierarchical organizations.

20. Broverman, I.; Vogel, S. R.; Broverman, D. M.; Clarkson, F. E.; and Rosenkrantz, P. S.; (1972), Sex-role stereotypes: A current appraisal, *Journal of Social Issues*, 28. 59–78.; and Aterborg, J. R. (1977), Women in management: A research review, *Journal of Applied Psychology* 62 (6): 647–664.

21. Martin, et al., Advancement of women in hierarchical organizations.

22. Martin, et al., Advancement of women in hierarchical organizations.

23. Stacey, M. and Price, M. (1981), *Women in politics and power*, London: Tavistock; and Martin, et al., Advancement of women in hierarchical organizations.

24. Quinn, R.E. (1977), Coping with cupid: The formation, impact, and management of romantic relationships in organizations, *Administrative Science Quarterly* 22: 30–45; and Martin, et al., Advancement of women in hierarchical organizations.

25. For a thorough review of personality theories and concepts *see* Bavelas, J.B. (1978), *Personality: Current theory and research* Monterey, Ca.: Brooks/Cole.

26. Bavelas, *Personality*, p. 61.

27. McClelland, D.C.; (1953), *The achievement motive*, New York: Appleton-Century-Crofts; and McClelland, D.C. (1965), Toward a theory of motive acquisition, *American Psychologist* 20: 321–33.

28. McClelland, D.C.; Atkinson, J. W.; Clark, R. A.; and Lowell, E. L.; (1975), *Power: The inner experience* New York: Irvington-Halsted-Wiley; McClelland, D.C. and Burnham, D.H. (1976), Power is the great motivator, *Harvard Business Review* Mar.-Apr: 100–110.

29. McClelland, D.C. and Boyatzis, R.E. (1982), Leadership motive pattern and long-term success in management, *Journal of Applied Psychology* 67: 737–743.

30. McClelland and Boyatzis, Leadership motive pattern and long-term success in management.

31. Spector, P.E. (1982), Behavior in organizations as a function of employee's locus of control, *Psychological Bulletin* 91: 482–497. Phares, E.J. (1976), *Locus of control in personality* Morristown, N.J.: General Learning Press, p. 45.

32. Rotter, J. B. (1966) Generalized expectancies for internal versus extrental control reinforcement, *Psychological Monographs* 80 (No. 609).

33. Rotter, Generalized expectancies, p. 1.

34. Miller, D.; Kets de Vries, M.F.R.; and Toulouse, J.M. (1982), Top executive locus of control and its relationship to strategy making, structure, and environment, *Academy of Management Journal* 25: 237–253.

35. Spector, Behavior in organizations as a function of employee's locus of control.

36. Kotter, J. P. (1982), *The general managers*, New York: The Free Press. For another perspective on personalities of chief executives, *see* Levinson, H. (1980), Criteria for choosing chief executives, *Harvard Business Review* Jul.-Aug: 113–120.

37. Maccoby, M. (1976), *The gamesman*, New York: Simon and Schuster.

38. Spector, Behavior in organizations as a function of employee's locus of control.

An Individual's Perspective: Values and Attitudes

CHAPTER 3

PREVIEW

- How does value programming happen?

- What values are important to you? Fill out the questionnaire and compare your values with others.

- Are you a Theory X manager or a Theory Y manager? Find out how these values affect organizations.

- Why would 11,500 air traffic controllers quit their jobs over a value issue?

- Do employees in Japan really have a job for life? Find out more about Japanese management practices.

- Is a "happy employee a productive employee"? Find out why this isn't necessarily true.

- Are most people dissatisfied with their jobs?

- What are some strategies for changing attitudes and behavior?

- What is cognitive dissonance and how can you use it?

Preview Case: Jack Blaylock's Lament

Values: The Broad Roadmap for Human Behavior
- What are values?
- How are values formed?
- Changes in values
- *Perspective:* Ethical values: Cheating, Lying, and Bending the Rules
- Human nature and management: Theory X and Y
- *Perspective:* What Would Make 11,500 People Quit Their Jobs?
- Resolving value conflicts

Cross-Cultural Values: Japan as an Example
- Paternalism
- *Perspective:* Lifetime Employment in Japan: Myths and Realities
- Hierarchy
- Implications for American managers

Attitudes and Organizational Behavior
- What are attitudes?
- Measuring attitudes
- Job satisfaction
- *Perspective:* Is Job Satisfaction in the United States Changing?
- Attitudes and behavior
- Job satisfaction and work behaviors
- *Perspective:* The Satisfaction-Performance Controversy
- Changing attitudes

Attitudes, Values, and Organizations: Some Conclusions

Summary
- Chapter review
- For discussion
- Key concepts and terms
- Suggested readings

Cases and Incidents
- The Graduates' Dilemma
- Negotiation Failure in Japan
- The Municipal Light Caper

References

PREVIEW CASE: JACK BLAYLOCK'S LAMENT

"**M**aybe it's time for me to retire," lamented Jack Blaylock, founder and chief stockholder of the Blaylock Venetian Blind Company. "It seems that everything is going wrong these days. When I first started the business in 1946, after I got out of the Army, it was rough financially, but at least then I didn't have any trouble with my employees."

"Yes, those were simpler times." As long as you took care of people and paid them regularly, they would really put out. And, if you wanted to fire someone, you just went ahead and did it. Today things are different. People don't work as hard as they used to and they seem to get upset when you try to look out for their interests.

"For example, back in the mid-sixties I used to take really good care of all 330-plus employees. I knew them all by name and usually knew their wives and children, too. We used to have regular picnics when everybody would come and have a good time. And if somebody got sick, I would make sure they were taken care of. Unfortunately, all that changed when the employees voted in the union in 1975. I was certainly upset that they would do that to me—especially after I had treated them like my own children. In fact, I got so mad that I fired the ringleaders, but the government folks wouldn't let me do that, so I had to take them back.

"Nowadays, people just don't seem to care whether they work or not. In fact, I've heard that some people make more from welfare than they do on the job. Back when I was younger and there was a depression on, you really worried about losing your job because if you did, you would have to go to the soup lines or sell apples to survive. And on the other hand, the boss was really the boss back then. If you didn't like somebody's work it was easy to give him his 'walking papers.' You can't do that any more. Now if you want to fire someone you have to have a lawyer. There are so many government regulations—grievance procedures, affirmative action—that you just don't boss your own business any more.

"But worst of all, I just don't understand the younger generation. The longer hair that most of the guys wear really gets my hackles up. If I had my way I would get some barber shears and cut it all off. Unfortunately, I tried to order people to wear short hair, but the union forced a wildcat strike. Seems like you just can't win.

"See why I think it's time to retire? I just don't seem to be able to run my own company any more."

Jack Blaylock is having a difficult time coping with value systems that differ from his. His employees' values often conflict with his and cause him a great deal of frustration and discomfort. Values and attitudes are important determinants of individual behavior. Values about people and work influence behavior in a variety of organizational situations. They are related to supervisory style and reactions of subordinates. They influence how successfully people can respond to changes in organizational conditions. The study of values is also particularly crucial for understanding cross-cultural differences—an increasingly important skill with the growth of international business.

In this chapter we will examine some of the impacts of values and attitudes on organizational behavior and what we might do to resolve value conflicts and to change attitudes.

Values: The Broad Roadmap for Human Behavior

■ What Are Values?

A **value** is a broad, general belief about some way of behaving or some end state that is preferable to the individual.[1] Examples of values might be: leading an exciting life, having a comfortably rich existence, being courageous, being honest and ethical, living in a peaceful world, having personal freedom, or being a top-notch business manager. Values guide actions and judgments in many different situations and beyond people's immediate goals to more ultimate end-states of existence.[2]

Values are a form of **belief**, or personal conclusions we have made about what is true or not true or what is beautiful and good about the world.[3] Beliefs are organized within our minds into a more or less organized system that we will refer to as a **value system**. Before proceeding with our discussion of values, you may wish to complete the questionnaire in Table 3.1 to find out what you value.

■ How Are Values Formed?

Values are formed in much the same way that personality is developed. The term **value programming** has been used to describe this formation process.[4] Figure 3.1 shows some of the sources of value programming. With such a wide variety of sources, we might expect that no two people would hold exactly the same values.

There is probably a great deal of similarity between the values of people of the same age, ethnic origin, geographic location, or family. One might even be able to generalize certain value orientations to people in certain age groups.[5] For example, those people who grew up during the great depression in the 1930's are sometimes obsessed with financial security and staying out of debt. In contrast, many people who grew up during the 1950's are generally less concerned about financial security, believing that installment loans and credit cards are a way of life. Obviously, not all people conform to these overly simplified generalizations; value programming is far more complex than this.

■ Changes in Values

While the values of most people tend to stabilize by the time they reach adulthood, the values of each generation undergo a never-ending change process from one generation to the next. Research by Daniel Yankelovich, a psychologist who specializes in conducting polls for government and industry, shows that people are questioning the Western passion for efficiency, cost effectiveness, and control by statistics. People are less interested in success in terms of material possessions, money, and status.[6] Instead, they are more interested in self-fulfillment, being creative, spending

Table 3.1 Rokeach value survey.

The following eighteen values are listed in alphabetical order. Your task is to arrange them in order of their importance to *you*, as guiding principles in *your* life. Place a 1 beside the item that is most important, a 2 next to the second most important item, etc., until you have reached number 18.

	A Comfortable Life a prosperous life
	An Exciting Life a stimulating, active life
	A Sense of Accomplishment lasting contribution
	A World at Peace free of war and conflict
	A World of Beauty beauty of nature and the arts
	Equality brotherhood, equal opportunity for all
	Family Security taking care of loved ones
	Freedom independence, free choice
	Happiness contentedness
	Inner Harmony freedom from inner conflict
	Mature Love sexual and spiritual intimacy
	National Security protection from attack
	Pleasure an enjoyable, leisurely life
	Salvation saved, eternal life
	Self-Respect self-esteem
	Social Recognition respect, admiration
	True Friendship close companionship
	Wisdom a mature understanding of life

After you have completed the survey, you may wish to compare your ranking with the average for a number of college students who have taken this survey. You will find these results at the end of the references in the back of this chapter.[7]

Adapted from Rokeach, M., "Beliefs, Attitudes, and Values," San Francisco: Jossey-Bass, 1968 & 1972. By permission of author & publisher. Copyrighted by Milton Rokeach, 1967, 1982. Permission to reproduce granted by publisher, Halgren Tests, 873 Persimmon Ave., Sunnyvale, CA, 94087.

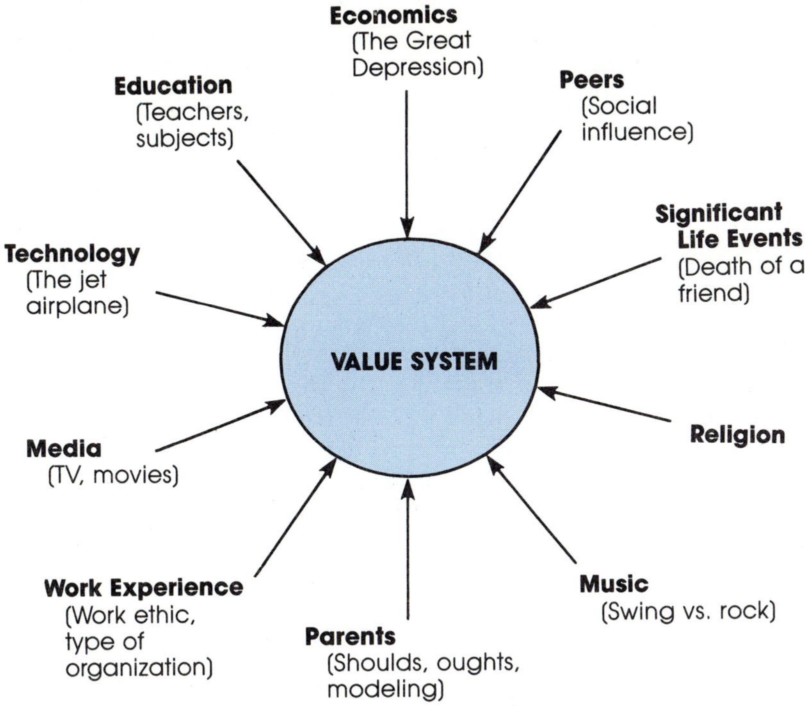

Figure 3.1. Sources of value programming.[8]

Education
(Teachers,
subjects)

Economics
(The Great
Depression)

Peers
(Social
influence)

Technology
(The jet
airplane)

Significant
Life Events
(Death of a
friend)

VALUE SYSTEM

Media
(TV, movies)

Religion

Work Experience
(Work ethic,
type of
organization)

Parents
(Shoulds, oughts,
modeling)

Music
(Swing vs. rock)

more time with friends, and enhancing self-understanding. He also found that people are becoming much more "liberated" in their view toward the division of labor between the sexes. Most respondents felt that the roles and aspirations of men and women need not be radically different.

The Desire for Self-Control   Another change with major implications for organizations, is that people are saying they are "entitled" to more "social rights," including a say in decisions that affect their jobs and a job that is pleasurable and satisfying. In other words, they are demanding psychological incentives as well as economic ones.[9] Henry Ford II summarized this point of view:

> *Throughout the world, ordinary people, especially young people, are deciding that they have had it with the way things are. They are no longer willing to put up with rules and conditions which make life more narrow and less satisfying than it could be. They want a voice in decisions which affect them. They are more concerned with quality of life and their relations with people than with the quest for status and possessions.*[10]

Coping with Value Changes   As values change, organizations must develop coping strategies. If people are more interested in job satisfaction, then job enrichment may be needed (*see* Chapter 7). If more leisure time is desired, then more flexible work weeks and longer vacations may be necessary. If employees are more concerned with fair treatment, then new

Ethical Values: Cheating, Lying, and Bending the Rules[11]

A survey of over 24,000 readers of *Psychology Today* (not a random sample) concerning their ethical behavior and values yielded some interesting results. The following shows the proportion of people who admitted doing these behaviors:[12]

■ Taken home office supplies or other materials in the past year   68%

■ Taken sick days from work although well enough to go in during the last year   47%

■ Tried to save money on tax returns by lying or withholding information (in the past five years)   38%

■ Made personal long distance calls at work in the past year.   37%

■ Cheated on an expense account in the past year   28%

Does this mean a great many people hold values that dishonesty is OK? While there is no direct answer in this research, the responses to a scenario of an everyday ethical problem—driving away after scratching another's car without telling the owner—provide some insight. Forty-four percent of the respondents said they would leave, but 89 percent said that it is probably unethical. Matters got even worse if the possibility of getting caught was nil—52 percent would leave. Thus, there seems to be a gap between values and behaviors in this case.

procedures may be needed to provide due process.[13] If people are less honest, then strategies are needed to protect the organization from loss.[14] Managers need to be sensitive to value changes so they can adapt.

■ Human Nature and Management: Theory X and Y

One aspect of a person's value system that is particularly important in organizational settings is the nature of a person's values concerning human nature. Many people tend to believe that people are basically competitive, hateful, unfriendly, lazy, and irresponsible while others are more optimistic and believe that people are industrious, responsible, cooperative, and friendly.[15] Before proceeding you may want to complete the questionaire in Table 3.2 to find out what your view of people is like.

What Is Theory X and Theory Y?   Douglas McGregor described two contrasting views of people held by industrial managers as **Theory X:** people are essentially like machines that are set into action by external forces and **Theory Y:** people are an organic system whose behavior is affected not only by external forces but by intrinsic ones.[16] Your scores on the X-Y Scale give a rough indication of your beliefs about the nature of people in work situations. A moderate to high score (5 or above) on the Y scale indicates tendency toward Theory Y while a moderate to high score on the X scale indicates a tendency toward Theory X. It is possible that you hold both Theory X *and* Theory Y views if you scored about equally on each scale. This indicates that our view of people is made up of many beliefs, some of which may even be contradictory. A more complete description of Theory X and Theory Y is provided in Table 3.3.

Table 3.2 Table 3.2. The X-Y questionnaire.[17]

Directions: The following are types of behavior that a supervisor (manager, leader) may engage in in relation to subordinates. Using the scale below as a guide, mark the number that corresponds to the way you would behave in in the situation described.

1	2	3	4	5
Make a great effort to do this	Tend to do this	Do not know what I would do	Tend to avoid doing this	Make a great effort to avoid this

_____ 1. Closely supervise my employees because to make sure they do the job right.
_____ 2. Develop goals for my subordinates and then leave them pretty much alone.
_____ 3. Look for ways to give my subordinates more responsibility.
_____ 4. Use punishment to correct undesirable behavior.
_____ 5. Encourage my subordinates to set their own goals and objectives.
_____ 6. Take over whenever there are indications that the job is slipping.
_____ 7. Allow subordinates to share in making important decisions.
_____ 8. Use rewards as a way to get people to work.
_____ 9. Give my subordinates as much freedom to do the job as possible.
_____ 10. Look for ways to give people more challenging and interesting jobs.

Scoring: If you answered 4 or 5 to questions 1, 4, 6, or 8 give your self a one for each answer and call it your Y subtotal. Then, if you answer 1 or 2 to questions 2, 3, 5, 7, 9, 10 give yourself a one for each answer and add it to your Y subtotal to get your Y score. Your Y score should total between 0 and 10. Continue scoring below.

Y Score = _____

Now if you answered 1 or 2 to questions 1, 4, 6, or 8 give yourself a one for each answer and call it your X subtotal. Then, if you answer 4 or 5 to questions 2, 3, 5, 7, 9, and 10 give yourself a one for each answer and add it to your X subtotal to get your X score. Your X score should also total between 0 and 10.

X Score = _____

Keep your X and Y scores in mind when reading the section in the text about theory X and Y.

Understanding Theory X and Y   The terms Theory X and Theory Y are widely used in most organizational settings, especially at managerial levels. The two views are not meant to be imply that Theory X is tough, demanding management while Theory Y is weak, permissive management. A manager holding Theory Y views may be just as demanding as a Theory X manager, although there will probably be differences in style and methods.

For example, a Theory X manager would employ much tighter supervision and control than would a Theory Y manager. There would be more tendency for the Theory X manager to behave in a distrusting, suspicious manner. Motivation would be through fear, imposed goals, and pay. A Theory Y manager, on the other hand, would be more likely to use participative goal setting and joint planning to give the subordinate direction. The Theory Y manager would trust the subordinate and grant quite a lot of freedom (within the limits of the goals). Motivation would be primarily through opportunities for people to grow, to learn, and to achieve.

An Individual's Perspective: Values and Attitudes

Table 3.3 Theory X and Theory Y views of human nature.

Theory X: The traditional view of direction and control.
1. The average human being has an inherent dislike of work and will avoid it if he can.
2. Because of this human characteristic of dislike for work, most people must be coerced, controlled, directed, and threatened with punishment to get them to put forth adequate effort toward the achievement of organizational objectives.
3. The average human being prefers to be directed, wishes to avoid responsibility, has relatively little ambition, and wants security above all.

Theory Y: The integration of individuals and organizational goals.
1. The expenditure of physical and mental effort in work is as natural as play or rest.
2. External control and the threat of punishment are not the only means of bringing about effort toward organizational objectives. Man will exercise self-direction and self-control in the service of objectives to which he is committed.
3. Commitment to objectives is a function of the rewards associated with their achievement.
4. The average human being learns under proper conditions not only to accept but to seek responsibility.
5. The capacity to exercise a high degree of imagination, ingenuity, and creativity in the solution of organizational problems is widely, not narrowly, distributed in the population.
6. Under the conditions of modern industrial life, the intellectual potentialities of the average human being are only partially utilized.

Adapted from D. McGregor, 1960, *The human side of enterprise*, pp. 33–34, 47–48. Copyright © 1960 by McGraw-Hill, New York. Used with permission.

PERSPECTIVE

3.2 | *What Would Make 11,500 People Quit Their Jobs?*[18]

In August 1981, 11,500 air traffic controllers walked off their jobs on an illegal strike against the Federal Aviation Administration (FAA). The strikers, who could only be employed by the FAA, knew that the President was determined to defeat the strike. Even when they were given an opportunity to return to their jobs, they did not. To find out why the controllers engaged in such seemingly irrational behavior, the Secretary of Transportation commissioned a research study.

The results of the study indicated that while there were a number of complex contributing factors, a central cause was the Theory X (autocratic) management style of the FAA. The research showed that the striking controllers were in the lower 6 percent nationally on the Theory X Scale—they were quite Theory Y oriented. In contrast to these mostly younger strikers, the supervisors split into two groups. Forty percent of the supervisors were very low on the X scale, while 50 percent of them were very high. Thus the difference in values between the controllers, who had a Theory Y orientation, and the senior supervisors, with a Theory X orientation, made a clash inevitable.

The study concludes that "organizational conditions and management practices [Theory X]—together with their end products of alienation, dissatisfaction, and stress, not peer pressure—caused 11,500 separate individuals to decide to strike."[19]

Understanding Organizational Behavior

How do you suppose employees react to these two contrasting management systems? For an example of how Theory X views caused serious organizational problems, *see* the Perspective, What Would Make 11,500 People Quit Their Jobs?

■ Resolving Value Conflicts

The conflict between FAA managers and striking controllers described in the Perspective is certainly an example of a value conflict. When values conflict, serious organizational repercussions can occur. Thus, dealing with value conflict is an important process.

Another example of value conflicts is Jack Blaylock's lament, related in the opening case of this chapter. Jack held paternalistic values; he believed that his employees should be treated just like he would treat his own children. But his employees did not seem to respond favorably to this type of treatment. In fact, we might expect many employees of the 1980's to value self-reliance, responsibility, autonomy and self-control. These values are in direct conflict with Jack's. In the confrontation, Jack lost—the employees voted in a union to protect them.

Dealing with Individual-Level Value Conflicts   Since an individual's values are deep-seated and hard to change, the best way of dealing with them is to live and let live. Unless there is some overwhelmingly strong reason for a value confrontation, why not let people have their own values. Even though you may like your own value set, there is no reason to think that only you have the only "straight line to the truth."

And yet sometimes a value conflict may have an important adverse impact on the organization or upon you as a person or manager. In that case, a confrontation is necessary. When confronting another, one good technique is to confront the other person with solid evidence that the conflict has some tangible effect on yourself or the organization.[20] If the person can see that it does, it is quite possible that he or she will understand your position and modify his or her behavior, if not basic value itself. If the other person does not see the tangible effect, the conflict will probably continue, or it must be resolved through force.

While force or power may be the only alternative for solving a value conflict, it is a dangerous strategy that may result in alienation and anger. Sometimes the individual and the organization both lose in this confrontation. (*See* Chapter 10 for more information on conflict resolution strategies.)

Dealing with Conflicts Between Groups of People   The controllers' strike described in the Perspective: What Would Make 11,500 People Quit Their Jobs? is an example of a widespread organizational-value problem. This type of value conflict is especially difficult to resolve. It may take major changes in people, structure, and personnel systems to resolve such system-wide values problems. Strategies may include problem solving (discussed in Chapters 10 and 13) and organization development (discussed in Chapter 16).

Cross-Cultural Values: Japan as an Example

Value differences become even more pronounced between different countries with varied cultural backgrounds. For illustration, we will briefly examine some Japanese values that result in quite different work behaviors—and often superior work performance—from that of American employees. Anthropologists, who have compared the two cultures, note a number of key differences between Japanese values and American values.[21]

■ Paternalism

The Japanese people tend to become very closely attached to the people in their work organization. They in effect become members of an organizational family. They form deep attachments to their work organization so that they become part of the organizational household. In addition, there is a normal parent-child relationship between the employer and the employee. The parent is seen as a person with ability, status, and personal attraction who looks after the weaker child. This relationship is seen as quite natural and desirable by both parties.

Out of these paternalistic organizational values grows the *lifetime employment* policy that is common to many, but not all, Japanese firms (*see* the Perspective, Lifetime Employment in Japan). The feeling often is that the "enterprise is the people" or "this is my company." In fact, the employer and employee are sometimes bound by ties as close and firm as those shared by husband and wife.[22] Paternalism and lifetime employment are two-way ties that meet the needs and values of both the organization and the Japanese people.

Jay Blaylock, in our opening case, might have been delilghted with these Japanese employees. Unfortunately, his younger American employees did not share the value that organizational paternalism is a desirable end state. In fact, they were concerned with just the opposite—individual freedom and self-control.

■ Hierarchy

One's position in the hierarchy depends mostly upon seniority; you have to wait your turn. The Japanese world is divided into three basic categories: seniors, juniors, and one's colleagues.[23] It is interesting to note that "colleagues" takes on a somewhat different meaning than in the United States. Colleagues are those people who graduated with you and entered business in the same year. Thus, as you can see, the system is very much seniority oriented.

While everyone takes their "proper station," the roles they play may be quite flexible. For example, in the Japanese decision-making system, most people in the organization, regardless of rank, have an opportunity to put their input into the decision. It would be quite proper for a junior manager, right out of business school, to make an input into a decision that would ultimately go to the chief executive of the company.

$\boxed{3.3}$ *Lifetime Employment in Japan: Myths and Realities* [24]

Many employees in Japanese business and industry have a guaranteed job once they are on the payroll, they have lifetime employment. While they are on the job, they have practically complete job security, which is endangered only in the event of a severe economic crisis or catastrophe. They also are paid on the basis of seniority with pay doubling about every fifteen years, regardless of the type of job. However, there are a number of people who do not enjoy lifetime employment:

■ Women are almost always considered "temporary" rather than "permanent" employees; so they are exempted from the benefits.

■ In many "traditional" Japanese businesses, such as workshop industries producing lacquer, pottery, and silk, workers are hired and paid by the hour.

■ Even in the "modern" industries there is a slowly shrinking, but substantial (perhaps 20%), body of employees who, by unilateral management decision, are considered "temporary" and remain in that category for many years.

■ Most people who have lifetime employment are forced to retire at age fifty-five with a relatively small pension. These people may then become temporary employees or open their own businesses.

■ Implications for American Managers

We have covered only a few of the many value differences between Japan and the United States. For almost any culture, differences exist that are important management considerations if you have to deal with that culture. For example, an American multinational corporation must carefully consider cultural values before operating in any foreign environment.[25] In addition, it is becoming more and more common for Japanese and other foreign companies to build subsidiaries in the United States. This means that many Americans may be working for Japanese bosses. Careful study of values will make managers more sensitive to motivation and leadership problems in such organizations.

Perhaps even more important is the lessons in management we might learn from the Japanese, for they have developed some extremely effective management strategies.[26] If we are to critically evaluate Japanese techniques for possible application in an American setting, then we need to be able to tell how values relate to management. For example, lifetime employment and paternalistic values allow Japanese managers more freedom to design costly training programs. Japanese firms place very strong emphasis on extensive (often three months long) training programs for new employees. They can afford to do it because they know that their employees will stay with them for a very long time. If we in the United States were to sink as much money into training new employees as the Japanese do, we might find it was quite costly because of our higher turnover rates.

The study of values is a key element in the process of understanding individuals, whether in the same or different cultures. In the next section

An Individual's Perspective: Values and Attitudes

we will discuss how attitudes emerge from values and how they influence our behavior.

Attitudes and Organizational Behavior

Attitudes are closely related to values and have a number of important organizational implications because they are often linked with job satisfaction, turnover, absenteeism, and other organizational behaviors. In this section we will discuss the meaning and measurement of values, their relationship to behavior, and how attitudes may be changed.

■ What Are Attitudes?

Attitudes are a tendency to react in some favorable or unfavorable way toward some object, person, group, or idea.[27] Attitudes differ from values in that they focus on a specific object, whereas values are very broad, general beliefs about some end state. Often, attitudes are an outgrowth of values. Examples of attitudes might be: typists are boring people, supervisors cannot be trusted, unions are bad, bankers are stuffy people (for more examples, *see* Table 3.4). Note the attitudes focused on typists, supervisors, unions, and bankers—all quite specific when compared to such values as honesty or an exciting life. Both attitudes and values tend to be implicit guides for action in that people often act in accordance with their values and attitudes.

Attitudes involve a preferential response tendency. We tend to feel satisfied or dissatisfied, positive or negative, favorable or unfavorable toward the object of our attitude. Each of the attitude examples in Table 3.4 shows this preferential response tendency: "I really love my job," or "This is a real rip-off." In organizational settings, attitudes tend to be centered around the job, supervisor, pay, benefits, facilities, promotions, coworkers, and other similar dimensions. Obviously, it is important for us, as managers, to find out the nature of people's attitudes and, if needed, attempt to change them to a more positive direction.

Table 3.4 Examples of attitudes.

Union representative	"You just can't trust management. My job is to push the union position regardless of its merit."
Office employee	"My boss just doesn't care about us. He will walk right past you in the morning without even saying hello. That really turns me off."
Military officer	"One of the best things about the military is that you get to meet so many new and interesting people."
Foreman	"Let's face it. You have to treat these workers like some faceless robots or they will take advantage of you."
Bricklayer	"I really love my job. I can look around town and see hundreds of buildings that were built with my own two hands. I wouldn't trade this job for anything."
Cook	"Hey man, this is a real rip-off. They expect us to do everything around here and then only pay us minimum wages."
Chief executive officer	"You've got to work through people to get the job done. We've got some of the most competent people I know. They can be trusted to do the job right."

■ Measuring Attitudes

Sometimes we can tell the attitudes or "feel the pulse" of an organization by simply listening and observing. This method may be good for small organizations, but when an organization gets larger there is always the possibility that a vocal minority may be the loudest source of information. Thus, there is a distinct possibility that such a sample may be biased and may not reflect the attitudes of the entire organization. More accurate information can be obtained through systematic use of attitude questionnaires.

Using Questionnaires to Measure Attitudes   Almost everyone has filled out some type of attitude survey. A pizza house wants to know if you like thick or thin crusts. A stereo designer wants to know if you like a black or gold front for your receiver. Likewise, organizations are interested in a number of issues. Do you like your job? Are you thinking about quitting? Is the pay reasonable? Do you get good food and service from the company cafeteria? Do you respect your boss? Do you like your coworkers? Are promotions fair? Organizations want to know the answers to these questions in order to evaluate the impact of system changes, to pinpoint the need for future changes, to evaluate the status quo over time, or perhaps just because someone simply wants to know. To get a feel for an attitude questionnaire, you may wish to fill out the one provided in Table 3.5.

Table 3.5 Job satisfaction scale.

Directions: If you are now working, respond to the questions in relation to the job you are doing. If you are not working, think of some job you have done in the past and respond in relation to that job. Indicate how satisfied you are with each aspect of your job listed below using the scale provided. Write the appropriate number in the space beside each statement.

1	2	3	4	5
Very dissatisfied	A little dissatisfied	Neutral	Somewhat satisfied	Very satisfied

_____ 1. The job itself.
_____ 2. The amount of pay and fringe benefits I receive.
_____ 3. The amount of personal growth and development I get in doing my job.
_____ 4. The kinds of things I have to do on this job.
_____ 5. The degree of respect and fair treatment I receive from my boss.
_____ 6. The degree to which I am fairly paid for what I contribute to this organization.
_____ 7. The amount of independent thought and action I can exercise on this job.
_____ 8. The overall quality of supervision I receive in my work.

Scoring: Compute four job satisfaction indices by combining these questions:

a. Add questions 1 and 4 to get
        General Job Satisfaction = _____
b. Add questions 2 and 6 to get
        Satisfaction with pay = _____
c. Add questions 3 and 7 to get
        Satisfaction with growth = _____
d. Add questions 5 and 8 to get
        Satisfaction with supervision = _____

Scores of 7 above indicate relatively high satisfaction while scores of 5 or below indicate low satisfaction.

Adapted from J. R. Hackman and G. R. Oldham, 1975, Development of the job diagnostic survey, *Journal of Applied Psychology* 60:159–170. Copyright 1975 by the American Psychological Association. Reprinted/adapted by permission of the author and the publisher.

An Individual's Perspective: Values and Attitudes

To do a thorough job of designing a **valid** (Does it measure what it is supposed to measure?) and **reliable** (Does it measure consistently?) questionnaire, you need an expert. However, there are a number of questionnaires that are already tested that measure such areas as job satisfaction, pay satisfaction, or attitudes toward supervisors.

■ Job Satisfaction

Since one of the attitudes that we most frequently try to measure is job satisfaction, we will take a closer look at this attitude. **Job satisfaction** refers to the degree of pleasurable or unpleasurable feelings that one has toward a job or job experiences.[28] A general job satisfaction scale such as the one in Table 3.5 represents a **global** or overall measure of job satisfaction. Other ways to ask global job satisfaction questions might be to ask people how much of the time they like their jobs, or to compare their jobs with others.

People who are satisfied with their jobs will make statements like this about their jobs: "I love it," "It's a great job," or "I wouldn't exchange this job for any other." People who don't like their jobs will say: "I really hate this job," "I would quit right now if I could," or "I never feel good about this lousy job."

Managers are also interested in specific job satisfactions such as satisfaction with supervision, promotion, pay, and growth. Questions can be designed to measure these attitudes and more. (Several of these scales appear in the instrument in Table 3.5.)

■ Attitudes and Behavior

Do Attitudes Predict Behavior?   Some experts say that attitudes predict behavior while others say they do not. Since an attitude is a predisposition to react, doesn't reaction mean behavior? While it usually it does,

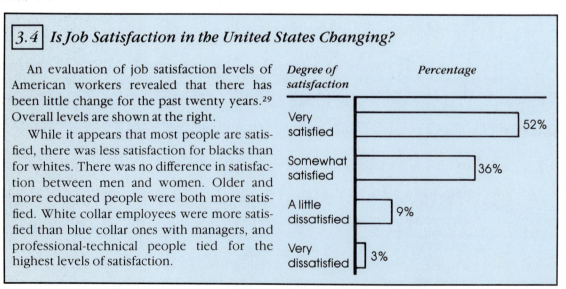

3.4 | *Is Job Satisfaction in the United States Changing?*

An evaluation of job satisfaction levels of American workers revealed that there has been little change for the past twenty years.[29] Overall levels are shown at the right.

While it appears that most people are satisfied, there was less satisfaction for blacks than for whites. There was no difference in satisfaction between men and women. Older and more educated people were both more satisfied. White collar employees were more satisfied than blue collar ones with managers, and professional-technical people tied for the highest levels of satisfaction.

Degree of satisfaction   *Percentage*

Very satisfied — 52%
Somewhat satisfied — 36%
A little dissatisfied — 9%
Very dissatisfied — 3%

the reaction could be internal within the person with no external behavior that shows. The cartoon in Figure 3.2 shows that even though a person may have unfavorable attitudes towards a job, behavior will depend upon what options are available. If you live in a small town with high unemployment, you may be much less likely to quit even when you are quite dissatisfied with your job. Another factor is that people hold many attitudes, some being stronger than others. Thus it is hard to tell which one or ones are driving behavior at a given moment.

■ Job Satisfaction and Work Behaviors

The most extensively studied job attitude is job satisfaction. Many researchers have searched for a link between job satisfaction and performance, reasoning that "a happy employee is a productive employee." However, the research results have been far from clear on this issue.[30] The Perspective: The Satisfaction—Performance Controversy explains this.

While the link with performance has been inconsistent, job satisfaction has been fairly consistently related to absenteeism (being absent from

WITH A LABOR SURPLUS

WITH A LABOR SHORTAGE

Figure 3.2. The situation impacts the relationship between attitudes and behavior.

From J. S. Keyes, Jr., 1950, *How to develop your thinking ability,* p. 135. Copyright © 1950 by McGraw-Hill, New York. Used with permission.

3.5 | *The Satisfaction-Performance Controversy*

Point—*Satisfaction Improves Performance*.

Many managers feel that a happy worker is a productive worker. Since both high satisfaction and high performance are desirable outcomes, then they ought to go together. One rather thorough research review found that there was frequent evidence that positive job attitudes are related to increased productivity.[31] Another review of the research[32] concludes that there is more evidence to support the satisfaction-improves-performance relationship than is often credited.

Counterpoint One—*Performance Improves Satisfaction*.

Another view is that when people perform well and they are properly rewarded, they will be satisfied.[33] One reason for developing this view is that a number of research reviews have found no relationship or a very weak relationship between satisfaction and performance.[34]

Counterpoint Two—*Both of the above? . . . Or, none of the above?*

Either approach may be working depending upon the situation.[35] A social exchange process may cause people who are satisfied to reciprocate by rewarding (through high performance) their benefactors. Or, perhaps satisfaction and performance are codetermined by a third variable—rewards; such as pay, recognition, and promotion.[36] Thus, counterpoint two indicates that the reward relationship may be the most crucial one.

work),[37] turnover (quitting the organization),[38] and retirement.[39] These behaviors are very important to organizational managers since the cost of absenteeism and turnover can be high. For example, if 5 percent of your workforce is consistently absent, you may have to hire additional people to fill their positions, and union contracts and federal laws may require you to pay the absent employees as well. Turnover is even more costly, especially if the job requires time to train a person to perform. Training costs and personnel system overhead costs make replacing people very expensive.

Job satisfaction may also be related to life satisfaction and physical and mental health.[40] Thus, job satisfaction is related to several important organizational behaviors.

■ Changing Attitudes

Managers of organizations are often interested in changing attitudes. A great deal of company effort is frequently put into this task. Unfortunately, not all these efforts are successful. Although attitudes are certainly easier to change than values, they are still relatively hard to influence or change. There are a number of attitude-change techniques available[41] including using group pressures (*see* Chapter 9), employing behavior modification and reinforcement strategies (*see* Chapter 6), and creating favorable images through impression management (*see* Chapter 4).

Cognitive Dissonance Theory   Dissonance theory concerns the way people organize their thoughts, beliefs, and attitudes. **Cognitive dissonance** exists when two attitudes, beliefs, values, or behaviors are in conflict because the opposite of one follows from the other.[42] The assumption behind dissonance theory is that people try to keep their thoughts internally consistent with their attitudes, values, and behaviors. If some event is psychologically inconsistent, then the resulting dissonance is usually quite uncomfortable for the individual, and thus every effort will be made to reduce the inconsistency.

An Example of Dissonance

A new employee, Sandra Ming, after trying for a very long time and with considerable effort to get a job at the Blaylock Venetian Blind Company, is finally hired. But she then finds that working for the company is not anything like what she expected it to be— the job is quite routine and boring, although the pay is good. After expending the effort to get the job and bragging about it to all her friends, she has to do something to resolve the uncomfortable feeling of dissonance. She could quit, but that could make her even more uncomfortable when she had to explain it to her friends. Sandra could also decide that the job isn't so bad after all . . . and, since it pays so well, it is now really great. In this case the dissonance resulted from the conflict between her attitude about the company before she was hired (very favorable) and the reality of the company after she was on board (boring job). She reduced the dissonant element (a routine and boring task) by concentrating on the consonant element (good pay).

Using Dissonance to Change Attitudes

To change attitudes using dissonance theory, one has to create a dissonant situation that will force or encourage the person to resolve the dissonance in favor of the attitude changer. Often it is possible to use a relatively small amount of force to get someone to change, called **forced compliance**. For example, studies have shown that by paying people relatively paltry sums to do something that they do not want to do, people may actually come to change their attitudes because accepting such a "cheap bribe" for doing the task is obviously inconsistent with their self-concepts. However, if the person is paid a relatively large sum, it can be rationalized that "everyone else would do the same" if they were faced with such a temptation. Thus the person would not find it necessary to change his attitudes.

The maximum amount of attitude change occurs when a moderate amount of pressure or force is used to obtain compliance (as illustrated in Figure 3.3). When employees are pressured to complete an unpleasant task by their manager, they will at first be quite negative toward the task. But if they eventually voluntarily comply with the wish of the mangager, they will experience cognitive dissonance. To resolve the dissonance they feel about having completed the action, they are likely to change their attitudes to become much more favorable. However, if too much pressure is used, or if the person is not given a choice of whether or not to comply, then attitude change will be unlikely.

How to Use Dissonance in Organizations

There are a number of instances in organizations where the forced compliance model is useful. Take, for example, the introduction of a new computer-based accounting system. Sometimes (especially with an older workforce) when such a system is introduced, employees resist it. They may have negative attitudes to-

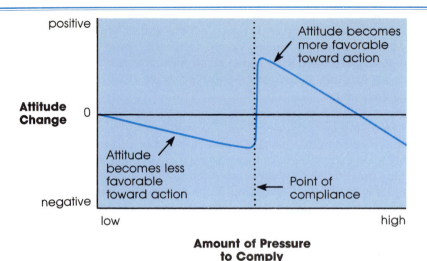

Figure 3.3. The relationship between force and attitude change.

positive

Attitude Change

0

negative

Attitude becomes more favorable toward action

Attitude becomes less favorable toward action

Point of compliance

low   high

Amount of Pressure to Comply

From T. R. Mitchell, 1982, *People in organizations*, p. 139. Copyright © 1982 by McGraw-Hill, New York. Used with permission.

wards computers, or they may think that computers will cost them extra effort. To use the forced compliance method, you would force them to use the new system by rewarding them with relatively small prizes, such as praise or a desirable new office gadget. By accepting such rewards for compliance, employees may actually change their attitudes toward the computer system. If you use heavy force, like threats of firing or docked pay, people will probably comply, but their attitudes will not change. We should remember that people can and do behave in ways that are opposed to their attitudes. Our goal is to change attitudes, not simply apply force.

Values, Attitudes, and Organizations: Some Conclusions

Values and attitudes are particularly important for understanding individual-level behavior in organizations because they affect the way people behave and the way they perceive the world. In the next chapter, we will examine perception and see how values and attitudes act as filters that determine where we direct our attention.

An understanding of values and attitudes gives us a framework for understanding how people feel about their jobs, their supervisors, their pay, and many other important organizational variables. If we understand the basic nature of values and attitudes, then we can measure them and possibly change them. This should lead to more precise management strategies and a more effective organization.

SUMMARY

Chapter Review

■ **Values**, broad, general beliefs about some end state, are formed in much the same way as personality. Values change quite a lot between different age groups, but individual values are relatively stable and difficult to change.

■ Managers' views of human nature are particularly important influences on their management style and their potential for clashing with the values of their subordinates. **Theory X** values revolve around views that people are basically lazy and that authoritarian styles are needed to control them. **Theory Y** values indicate a belief that man is responsible and mature and that a more participative style may be appropriate.

■ **Value conflicts** are difficult to resolve. If possible, the organization can be tolerant of deviant individual values. If a confrontation is needed, the deviant must see how values adversely affect the organization.

■ Values in other cultures, such as Japan, may be very different from those of the United States. Japanese values about the extended family make **paternalism** and **lifetime employment** the optimal way of managing Japanese organizations. The concept of seniority based on age is also quite different from western concepts of seniority. With international organizations proliferating, it is important to keep value differences in mind.

■ **Attitudes** involve the tendency to react in some favorable or unfavorable way. They differ from values because they are focused on a specific object while values concentrate on broad end states. Both attitudes and values are guides for individual action.

■ Attitudes are important for measuring the "pulse" of the organization on such issues as job satisfaction, supervisory satisfaction, pay system changes, or flexible working hours. One of the best ways to measure attitudes is by using published questionnaires that have been tested and validated.

■ Job satisfaction, or the pleasurable feelings one has toward the job, is a key attitude because it is related to a number of important organizational behaviors, including **absenteeism, turnover, and retirement**. However, job satisfaction is not consistently related to performance.

■ Attitudes do not always predict behavior because individuals have many complex attitudes, some even in conflict. Thus, when a decision is made, it is difficult to tell which, if any, attitude is governing behavior.

■ **Cognitive dissonance**, a theory of attitude change, exists when two attitudes or beliefs are in conflict because the opposite of one follows from the other. If you can get people to do something that conflicts with their attitudes, through either free will or **forced compliance**, they will be quite likely to change their attitude to get rid of their uncomfortable feelings of dissonance.

For Discussion

1. How are values related to personality, the topic of the last chapter?
2. What is the difference between beliefs, values, and attitudes?
3. Choose some person that is approximately twenty-five plus years older than you are. Compare similarities and differences in values between yourself and that person.
4. Describe a Theory X manager and a Theory Y manager. What would be the impact of each of these managers in a research lab? In a prison?
5. Do you think that the Japanese practice of "lifetime employment" is exportable to America? Explain your position.
6. What organizational advantages and disadvantages result from Japanese cultural values?

7. Conduct a miniresearch study on ten working people to find out how satisfied they are with their jobs. How do your results compare with those in the Perspective: Is Job Satisfaction in the United States Changing? How might you explain the differences?
8. What is the relationship between job satisfaction and performance?
9. Pick one of the attitude change techniques covered in the chapter and try to change someone's attitude. Did your strategy work? What problems were encountered?

Key Concepts and Terms

value	**attitudes**
value programming	**job satisfaction**
Theory X	**cognitive dissonance**
Theory Y	**forced compliance**
value conflicts	

Suggested Readings

Bem, D. J. (1982). *Attitudes, beliefs, and human affairs*. 2nd ed. Belmont, Ca.: Brooks-Cole.

Bowers, D. G. (1983). What would make 11,500 people quit their jobs? *Organizational Dynamics* Winter: 5–19.

Greene, C. N. and Craft, R. E., Jr. (1977). The satisfaction-performance controversy—Revisited. In *Organizational behavior: A reader*, eds. H. K. Downey, D. Hellriegel, and J. W. Slocum, pp. 187–201. St. Paul, Minn.: West.

Hatvany, N., and Pucik, V. (1981). Japanese management practices and productivity. *Organizational Dynamics* Spring: 5–21.

Yankelovich, D. (1981). New rules in American life: Searching for self-fulfillment in a world turned upside down. *Psychology Today* 15: 35–37cf.

CASES AND INCIDENTS

The Graduates' Dilemma

Jammie and Bill have been constant companions over the past six months—they are deeply in love. They met in an organizational behavior class and have hit it off ever since. After their graduation in June, they plan to be married.

But they have encountered one problem. There is a conflict about what positions Jammie and Bill should accept. Jammie's combination of undergraduate chemical engineering and master of business administration has made her particularly attractive to a number of major corporations. The best offer she has received is for an exciting position with a major oil company headquarters in New York City. The pay is quite good, almost $40,000, with a certain raise if she works out.

Bill, on the other hand, has an undergraduate degree in philosophy. In spite of his M.B.A., he still does not have many job offers.

In fact, the only decent offer he has received is from a publishing house in St. Paul. The salary will be $16,000. Jammie has also had an offer from a chemical firm in Minneapolis with a starting salary of $24,000. While she is impressed by both companies, the one in New York is much more exciting.

Bill is afraid that if they go to New York he will have to rely entirely on Jammie. The idea of becoming a "house husband" does not appeal to him.

Discussion questions
1. How should Jammie and Bill resolve this dilemma?
2. What value issues are involved?
3. Would it make any difference if Bill were the engineer with the New York job offer?

Negotiation Failure in Japan

A large American electronics distributing company had identified a potential market for a new type of test equipment being manufactured in Japan. They anticipated that the product would be very successful. After preliminary contacts with the Japanese manufacturer, they dispatched a team of four managers to Tokyo to negotiate a contract for $8 million worth of test equipment. Even though both sides were interested in a successful conclusion to the negotiation, it failed. Here is a partial summary of what happened:

When the Americans arrived, they immediately opened the conference by suggesting that everyone be called by their first names, a practice common within their firm. In addition, they pressed the person who was the leader of the Japanese negotiation team for immediate decisions on various parts of the contract (Tokyo is a costly city to visit and the American team was anxious to conclude negotiations as fast as possible).

Negotiations dragged on for several weeks with the American team becoming increasingly frustrated because of the delays. Finally, after three weeks, they presented the Japanese team with an ultimatum—either sign a contract or they would find another supplier. The Japanese were offended by this move and elected not to sign the contract even though it would have been quite beneficial to them.

Discussion questions
1. What value issues seem to be involved here?
2. How might the American team have reacted so that a more favorable outcome would result?

The Municipal Light Caper

The following article appeared in the *Hamilton Harbinger* newspaper:

NEWMAN SUSPENDS 16 AT MUNICIPAL LIGHT

PRIVATE DETECTIVES TURN UP "ABUSES"

City Light Superintendent Charles Newman disclosed yesterday he has suspended 16 field employees and reprimanded 2 for abusing coffee break periods.

Newman said he hired a private detective firm to shadow Municipal Light crews for one week after getting complaints from citizens that some men were taking extended coffee breaks at their Hamilton cafés.

The investigation also turned up possible abuses of coffee break times by "15 to 18" employees of the Hamilton Engineering Department, according to George Everest, principal assistant city engineer for operations.

However, Everest said he cannot say if there are any actual violations in his department until he has had each reported case checked out. This is being done now.

The three cafés involved, Everest said, are near 2d Avenue and Barstow Street, 7th

Avenue N.E. and Interlake Way, and N. 34th Street and Stevens Way N.

Newman said two Municipal Light employees were suspended for 10 days without pay, five were suspended for 2 days and nine for one day. Two others received letters of reprimand.

The superintendent said at least one of the disciplined employees also was disciplined in a similar investigation three years ago, for the same thing.

Everest said his department also has to discipline employees from time to time for coffee break time abuses.

The private detective agency placed the three locations under surveillance during the work week of October 30 through November 3 and made its reports according to vehicle license numbers.

The private eyes timed the length of time crews spent in the cafés. Normal time allowed for coffee breaks is 15 minutes in the forenoon and afternoon, Everest said.

Newman said: "We talked to our people involved and they admitted the abuses. The severity and frequency of the violations varied."

Newman stressed that the infractions involved only a small minority of Municipal Light workers and "I continue to be amazed at the dedication of 99 percent of our employees."

He said those abusing lunch or coffee break periods not only are gypping the city—"they also are cheating on their fellow employees."

"I will not stand for this."

He said most of the violators "had been around for a while." He said that if any "extenuating circumstances" turn up later, the disciplinary actions will be rectified.

"We're not against coffee breaks—just the abuse of them," Newman declared. Although the place has been disguised, this incident really happened.

From F. E. Kast and J. E. Rosenzweig, 1976, *Experiential exercises and cases in management*, p. 341. Copyright © 1976 by McGraw-Hill, New York. Used with permission.

Discussion questions

1. What values do you think the City Light Superintendent holds? Is he a Theory X or Theory Y manager?
2. How do you think his actions affected the employees?
3. Do you think the attitude of the employees toward management changed?
4. What impact do you think the action will have on performance?

REFERENCES

1. This definition is similar to the one used by Rokeach, M. (1968), *Beliefs, attitudes, and values,* San Francisco: Jossey-Bass, Inc., p. 124.
2. Rokeach, *Beliefs, attitudes, and values*, p. 160.
3. Rokeach, *Beliefs, attitudes, and values*, p. 1.
4. Massey, M. E. (1980), *The people puzzle: Understanding yourself and others* Reston, Va.: Reston.
5. Massey, *The people puzzle*.
6. Yankelovich, D. (1981), New rules in American life: Searching for self-fulfillment in a world turned upside down, *Psychology Today* 15(4):35cf.
7. For a more thorough assessment of your personal values, *see* Simon, S. B.: Howe, L. W.: and Kirschenbaum, H. (1972), *Values clarification: A handbook of practical strategies for teachers and students*, New York: Hart.
8. Adapted from Massey, *The people puzzle*.
9. Yankelovich, New rules in American life.

10. Ford, Henry, II (1970), *The human environment and business,* New York: Weybriaght and Talley.

11. Based on Hassett, J. (1981), But that would be wrong . . ., *Psychology Today* 15(11):34cf.

12. From Hassett, But that would be wrong . . ., p. 41.

13. *See* Ewing, D. W. (1982), Due process: Will business default?, *Harvard Business Review*, Nov.–Dec.:114–122.

14. *See* the summary of a study by Cherrington, D. J. and Cherrington, J. O. (1981), How to keep them honest, *Psychology Today* 15(11):50cf.

15. Knowles, H. P. and Saxberg, B. O. (1971), *Personality and leadership behavior*, Reading, Mass.: Addison-Wesley.

16. McGregor, D. (1967), *The professional manager*, New York: McGraw-Hill, pp. 79–80.

17. Based on the concepts of Theory X and Theory Y presented in McGregor, D. (1960), *The human side of enterprise* New York: McGraw-Hill.

18. Bowers, D. G. (1983), What would make 11,500 people quit their jobs?, *Organizational Dynamics*, Winter:5–19.

19. Bowers, What would make 11,500 people quit their jobs?, p. 17.

20. *See* Gordon, T. (1977), *Leadership effectiveness training, L.E.T.*, New York: Wyden.

21. For an analysis of Japanese culture, *see* Nakane, C. (1970), *Japanese society*, Berkeley, Ca.: University of California Press. For a sociological analysis of Japanese society in comparison to the United States, *see* Vogel, E. F. (1979), *Japan as number 1: Lessons for America*, Cambridge, Mass.: Harvard University Press.

22. Nakane, *Japanese society*.

23. Nakane, *Japanese society*.

24. There are many recent articles on Japanese management. I recommend Hatvany, N. and Pucik, V. (1981), Japanese management practices and productivity, *Organizational Dynamics* Spring:5–21; and Drucker, P. F. (1981), *Behind Japan's success, Harvard Business Review* Jan.–Feb.:83–90. For an earlier review, *see* Drucker, P. F. (1971) What we can learn from Japanese management, *Harvard Business Review* Mar.–Apr.:113cf.

25. Harris, P. R. and Moran, R. T. (1979), *Managing cultural differences*, Vol. 1 Houston: Gulf.

26. *See* Pascale, R. T. and Athos, A. G. (1981), *The art of Japanese management: Applications for American executives,* New York: Simon and Schuster; and Ouchi, W. G. (1981) *Theory Z: How American business can meet the Japanese challenge*, Reading, Mass.: Addison-Wesley.

27. Rokeach, *Beliefs, attitudes and values;* Bem, D. J. (1982), *Attitudes, beliefs, and human affairs*, 2nd ed., Belmont, Ca.: Brooks–Cole.

28. Locke, E. A. (1976), The nature and causes of job satisfaction, in *Handbook of industrial and organizational psychology*, ed. M. D. Dunnette, p. 1300, Chicago: Rand-McNally. *Also see* Wanous, J. P. and Lawler, E. E., III, (1972), Measurement and meaning of job satisfaction, *Journal of Applied Psychology* 56(2):95–105.

29. Weaver, C. N. (1980), Job satisfaction in the United States in the 1970s, *Journal of Applied Psychology* 65:364—367. For another view about changes, *see* Cooper, M. R.; Morgan, B. S.; Foley, P. M.; and Kaplan, L.

B. (1979), Changing employee values: Deepening discontent?. *Harvard Business Review* Jan.–Feb.:117–25.

30. Locke, The nature and causes of job satisfaction.

31. Herzberg, F.; Mausner, B.; Peterson, R. O., and Capwell, D. F.; (1957) *Job attitudes: A review of research and opinion*, Pittsburg: Psychological Service of Pittsburg.

32. Organ, D. W. (1977), A reappraisal and reinterpretation of the satisfaction-causes-performance hypothesis, *Academy of Management Review* 2(1):46–53.

33. Porter, L. W. and Lawler, E. E., III, (1968), *Management attitudes and performance*. Homewood, Ill.: Irwin.

34. Greene, C. N. and Craft, R. E., Jr. (1977), The satisfaction-performance controversy—revisited, in *Organizational behavior: A reader*, ed. H. K. Downey, D. Hellriegel, and J. W. Slocum, pp. 187–201, St. Paul, Minn.: West.

35. Organ, A reappraisal and reinterpretation of the satisfaction-causes-performance hypothesis.

36. Greene and Craft, The satisfaction controversy—revisited.

37. *See* Steers, R. M. and Rhodes, S. R. (1978), Major influences on employee attendance: A process model, *Journal of Applied Psychology* 63:391–407; and Watson, D. J. (1981), An evaluation of some aspects of the Steers and Rhodes model of employee attendance, *Journal of Applied Psychology* 66:385–89.

38. Mobley, W. H. (1982), *Employee turnover: Causes, consequences, and control*. Reading, Mass.: Addison-Wesley.

39. Schmidt, N. and McCune, J. T. (1981), The relationship between job attitudes and the decision to retire, *Academy of Management Journal* 24:795–802.

40. Locke, The nature and causes of job satisfaction.

41. *See* Zimbardo, P. G.; Ebbesen, E. B.; and Maslach, C. (1977), *Influencing attitudes and changing behavior*, 2nd ed. Reading, Mass: Addison-Wesley; and Bem, Attitudes, beliefs, and human affairs.

42. Festinger, Leon (1957), *A theory of cognitive dissonance*, Evanston, Ill.:Row, Peterson.

Rokeach Value Survey, Table 3.1:
Rankings based on the responses of
college students in 1983.

Value	Ranking
Self-respect	1
Family security	2
Happiness	3
True friendship	4
Freedom	5
Wisdom	6
Sense of accomplishment	7
Inner harmony	8
Comfortable life	9
Exciting life	10
Mature love	11
World at peace	12
Salvation	13
Pleasure	14
Social recognition	15
Equality	16
World of beauty	17
National security	18

Perception: What Is Reality?

PREVIEW

- Why is it that two people can observe the same event and see entirely different things?

- Why do we see some things but ignore others—why do we selectively perceive?

- How can stereotypes act as invisible barriers to achieving equal treatment for blacks, Hispanics, women, and other minorities?

- What is the self-fulfilling prophecy and how does it work?

- Why does the halo effect cause so many problems in performance appraisal?

- Does the way you dress really make a difference in how well you succeed in organizations?

Preview Case: The Choice

The Perception Process
- What is perception?
- The perceptual process
- The sensing systems
- The psychological filters
- Person factors that can cause selective perception
- *Perspective*: The Self-Fulfilling Prophecy
- Object factors that cause selective perception
- The perception process in review

Problems in Perception
- Stereotyping
- *Perspective*: A Stereotype that Backfired!
- Problems with stereotyping
- Self-fulfilling stereotypes
- The halo effect
- Controlling the halo effect
- Reducing halo: A pessimistic conclusion
- *Perspective*: Managerial Myopia: Self-serving Biases

Impressive Management
- Ingratiation: Getting people to like you
- *Perspective*: How to Win Friends and Influence People
- Dress and impressions
- Dress for success
- Uniforms and authority
- *Perspective*: How Top Executives Describe Successful Dress
- Verbal and nonverbal impressions
- Implications of impression management

Perception and Organizations: Some Conclusions
- Employee's perceptions
- Performance evaluation
- Interviewing
- Organizational impression management
- Perception and motivation

Summary
- Chapter review
- For discussion
- Key concepts and terms
- Suggested readings

Cases and Incidents
- Sean O'Flaretty
- Stanley's Overcoat

References

PREVIEW CASE: THE CHOICE

Lacy Vanscott, who has been the Assistant Secretary of Defense for Electronics for six months, felt he was finally getting the hang of the job. When the secretary had called him at Xeron Electronics and asked him to take the job he had been flattered.

Lacy thought to himself: "Who would have believed that the Army Lieutenant of only twelve years ago would now be the Assistant Secretary! Obviously, I made the right decision to get out of the service and get my masters in electrical engineering from M.I.T. And, the fact that the Secretary and I were both undergrads at Yale didn't hurt either."

Lacy leaned back in his high-backed executive chair, lit up his pipe, and returned to his current major problem—choosing someone to head the Satellite Communications Division, called SCD for short. Ever since last week when John Oshiyama announced he was leaving for Howard Aerospace Industries, Lacy knew he would have a problem picking John's successor. Each of the three SCD branch chiefs seem well qualified. Herb Zawalski is a concientious, low-key individual who Lacy does not know much about. Dave Sands is a sharp-dressing, alert, high-visibility person who is always "Johnnie on the spot." The third possible choice is Wilma Marlow, who seems to be quite competent in spite of the rumor that she is the "token women" in SCD management. Whom should he choose?

Lacy turns his chair around and gazes out the window at the Potomac River. He is almost distracted by the sailboat gently moving up the river, but he forces himself to concentrate on the selection problem.

"Dave always seems to come to my mind first whenever I think of someone to promote. Why? Dave always looks competent and self-assured. He wears the right clothes—you know, dark grey pinstripes, with vest, dark tie and wing-tipped shoes. Dave also makes it a point to come around and talk about sailing at the beginning of each week. He is also a Yale graduate, although I can't remember his major. But, what about his performance? Well, I don't remember very much good or bad so I have to assume he runs a "tight ship." On the other hand, I do remember hearing about some grievances filed by some of his employees—disgruntled troublemakers, no doubt. Overall, it's sure hard to shake my very favorable impressions of Dave."

Actually, Dave's department is always on the verge of collapse. He is gone much of the time talking sailing with other enthusiasts. When he is there, he is openly ignored because of his lack of technical expertise and his general incompetence as a supervisor. He was a zoology major and seems to have little interest or talent for electronics. He responds to the slights from his people by blaming all his problems on his incompetent employees. He feels that he is quite competent, but he has been stuck with a bunch of dunderheads. He hopes that he will get the promotion because he can get away from these troublesome employees and, perhaps secretly, he can spend more time concentrating on sailing.

Understanding Organizational Behavior

Lacy continues his line of thought: "Now Herb, he's something else. He looks like he buys his suits from the bargain basement and in the summer he even wears an open shirt. He certainly doesn't project an executive image. Also, I don't see Herb as often. He never stops by for a social chat like Dave does. On the other hand, Herb's division is the most complex in SCD and he seems to handle all the problems quite well. He has an engineering degree from one of the far western state universities and, I believe, an MBA from one of the local night schools."

In reality, Herb is a very concientious and competent manager and engineer. His people respect him and will go out of their way to do things for him. Herb is so concerned with getting the job done that he does not find much time for small talk. Neither is he very interested in clothes. He would probably wear the same suit all week if his wife did not remind him to change. Herb perceives Dave as an incompetent supervisor and cannot imagine working for him.

And then Lacy turns to his last alternative: "What about Wilma? If I don't choose her, will she complain to the equal opportunity people? I'd sure hate to go through one of those messy investigations. And let's face it, Wilma's just too pushy. She would have everybody up in arms within a month. Although I've never heard anything bad about her management, I'm sure she would be very hard on her subordinates. Also, I can't forget that time about two months ago when she called me, in an obviously emotional state, and asked for a couple of days off for personal reasons. I think she might just break down when the pressure gets tough. We need someone that is stable in such an important position."

But in reality Wilma is a quite competent candidate. She is no more pushy than men who have similar positions. Her people respect her and certainly "put out" the work for her. She is also technically competent with a dual major in electrical engineering and management. The only unprogrammed time she has had to be absent in the last three years was when her mother died. She had been quite close to her and had been pretty broken up.

A few days later Lacy faces the deadline for a decision: "Well, I guess I'm going to have to 'bite the bullet' and make my decision. The way I see it the only real choice is Dave. Herb's appearance and lack of sociability make him unsuitable for a high-level position. Wilma, being a woman, is just too emotional for the position. That pretty much leaves Dave as the only choice.

Within the next three months Herb and Wilma left the federal government for lucrative jobs in private industry. Dave stayed on until the next big satellite communications program fell flat on its face. When he left he found a good position with an advertising firm on Madison Ave.

The accuracy and soundness of Lacy's decision to promote Dave depended upon the accuracy of his perception of Dave, Herb, and Wilma. Because we have more accurate information about the three candidates, we know that Lacy made a mistake. But as far as Lacy is concerned, he made the best decision possible using information and observations that were quite accurate and real to him. Thus, a very key aspect of perception is that *reality is in the mind of the perceiver.*

In this chapter, we will discuss the perception process, including factors within the person and the object being perceived that cause selective perception. Then we will turn to two major problems that may be associated with perception: stereotyping and the halo effect. We will also discuss ways that people manage others' perception of them using impression management. Finally, we will highlight several organizational implications for perception including performance appraisals and interviews.

The Perception Process

There are many sorts of stimuli out there in the environment. The way we make sense of all that data is through the perceptual process. In this section we will find out how the perceptual process works for individuals, and then we will turn to the effects of the object and situation on what is perceived. We will see why there are so many opportunities for us to **selectively perceive**—to see only a part of the total existing situation or environment.

■ What Is Perception?

Perception is the process of organizing and interpreting environmental inputs that are obtained through our senses.[1] The overabundance of information in the environment means that we must filter and interpret it so that it makes sense. In our opening case, Lacy was perceiving different types of information about each of his three candidates for promotion.

■ The Perceptual Process

Perception is both a physiological and a psychological process. Signals from the environment are filtered and picked up by the senses. They then pass through a master filter where the brain decides to attend to them or not. If there are too many signals or inputs, the brain may say "overload!" and simply ignore the input. However, if the signal catches the brain's attention, the signal will be further processed by the psychological filters. If the signal makes it all the way through the filtering process, then the perception will register and may result in some new attitude, behavior, feeling, or reaction. Figure 4.1 illustrates how the filtering process works.

■ The Sensing Systems

The initial input to the sensing system is through the body's five basic sensing systems: visual, auditory, taste-smell, touching (technically referred to as haptic), and orienting. Each of these systems is briefly defined below.[2]

1. **Visual**. Observation through our eyes allows us to gather information about the size and shape of people and objects. It allows us to see events, places, and things. It allows us to read. Lacy was relying primarily on the visual system when he formed an opinion about Herb from his dress.[3]
2. **Auditory**. Listening to voices and sounds is one of the most important sensing systems.

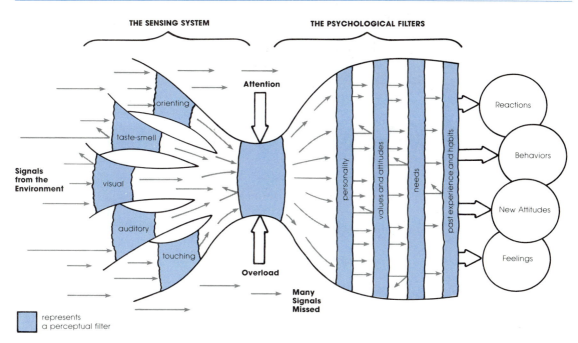

Figure 4.1. The perceptual filtering process.

3. **Taste-smell**. This sense allows us to determine the nature of odors and the composition of foods and liquids.

4. **Touching**. The feel of heat, cold, slippery, coarse, smooth, irregular, hard, soft provide us with additional information about the environment.

5. **Orienting**. This system has to do with the body's equilibrium. The inner ear (vestibular organ) maintains the body's sense of equilibrium. It tells us if we are accelerating, going up or down (as in an elevator), or being pushed. This system is particularly subject to distortion and thus, people in some lines of work must be keenly aware of the problems with this system. (For example, airline pilots are taught to pay attention to their instruments in bad weather, not the feeling in the pit of their stomachs that is created by their vestibular organs.)

■ The Psychological Filters

Even if our physiological senses were extremely accurate—and they are not—we have a number of **psychological filters** that are related to our personality, values, attitudes, needs, and past experiences. These filters change, distort, or block the sensory inputs. Although Figure 4.1 shows a sequence of psychological filters starting with personality and ending with past experience, there is no sequential order to the filtering process. Any one of the filters may operate as the primary one at a given time. The result of filtering is that many signals are missed or only partially perceived.

Perception: What Is Reality?

Personality, Values, and Attitudes   What would an authoritarian manager with Theory X values (*see* Chapter 3), perceive if he or she happened to find an employee reading a book on communication during the regular workday? Would the employee be perceived to be goofing off on the job and deserving of a reprimand? Or, would the employee be perceived as someone who is trying to improve and thus should be praised? We would predict that the Theory X manager would react in the former way—the positive aspects of the employee's behavior would not be seen. A Theory Y manager, in contrast, would be more likely to perceive the situation positively.

Needs   When you are hungry you can smell food for several blocks. When you are full you may not pay any attention to food smells. Thus your needs at the moment have a strong influence on what you perceive. If you have a strong need for esteem and praise, you will be particularly attuned to the behavior of your boss on this dimension—you are not likely to miss an instance of either praise or criticism.

Past Experience and Habits   Have you encountered the signal before? For example, a foreman who constantly rides his workers may reach a point where the workers tune out the foreman's comments entirely. Another case might be an overly conscientious school principal who calls frequent fire drills. The students and teachers may become so accustomed to the drills that when a real fire occurs, they may not respond quickly.

■ Person Factors That Cause Selective Perception

Since we cannot attend to every possible sensory input, our mind only selects or allows certain inputs to predominate at any one time—a process called **selective perception.** There are two major thrusts to selective perception: factors within the person doing the perceiving and factors within the object being perceived. Many of the reasons for person-factor perceptual distortions are caused by the filtering process we have just described. We will provide some examples of person factors and show how expectations can be a major factor in what we perceive. Then in the next section we will discuss how factors relating to the object or environment influence perception.

Before proceeding with the discussion of selective perception, test your perception by counting the number of *F's* in the statement below:

Finally, we have an example of finished research that is the result of years of scientific study combined with the experience of a lifetime.

How many *F's* did you count? Three? Four? Most people who have not done the exercise before find four; however, the correct answer is eight! If you counted less than eight, you were probably selectively perceiving the statement without the four instances where the word **of** appears. Most people read right over such words as *of* and *the* without even perceiving them.

Another example of selective perception is when you are driving your car to work along a familiar route, the sense of driving the car and the motion of the car become almost nonexistent. Instead of attending to your driving, you may be perceiving how good the latest *Earth, Wind & Fire* tape sounds on your new car stereo system.

The phenomenon of selective perception can be of advantage in some work situations. For example, a very boring assembly-line job can be made tolerable if the perceptual system can be made to block out the unpleasantness of the task. This is often done by adding other sources of sensory input, such as piped-in music or allowing a group of workers to socialize together. The CB radio has provided truckers with this type of alternative sensory stimulation.

Expectations   Sometimes we hear only what we expect to hear because of what is called a **preparatory set** or **expectancy**. Our previous experience or a strong desire to see something come true causes us to distort the inputs to fit the pattern we want to occur. An interesting example of expectations is the story of Craig Branson, an up-and-coming young manager with a medium-sized computer firm.[4] Craig learned about this form of perceptual distortion quite painfully.

Craig had been commuting back and forth on weekends between New York, his home base, and Pittsburgh, a temporary base, with the company picking up his expenses. When he was married, he asked his boss if he could bring his wife to Pittsburgh at company expense. His boss said: "Sure, company policy permits you to turn in expenses for you and your new wife up to the average amount you have been spending on hotels, planes, and other reimbursable expenses."

<hr>

PERSPECTIVE

4.1   *The Self-Fulfilling Prophecy*

One powerful impact of expectations and perception is the **self-fulfilling prophecy** or **SFP**.[5] A SFP may occur when our expectations about ourselves or others cause us to behave in such a way that our expectation actually comes true. Our initial expectation may be either true or false. There is considerable evidence that this effect does in fact exist.[6]

The SFP process begins when the perceiver forms some type of expectancy about the behavior of himself, herself, or another person. An expectancy is formed based on a limited sample of behaviors such as the ones described in our opening case. Once the expectancy is formed the behavior of the perceiver will be influenced by the expectancies. If a person is expected to perform poorly, the behavior will encourage that poor performance. If the expectations are for superior performance, then the perceiver will encourage this type of behavior.

Nonverbal cues (facial expressions, body posture, tone of voice) are particularly important factors for reinforcing the expectancy and creating the SFP.[7] Subconscious signals often are primary factors in the process.

Organizational implications for the SFP are great. It a boss has high expectations regarding a person's performance, then it may in fact be superior. An interviewer who expects a person to perform well because of his or her educational background may be eliciting an SFP.[8]

Craig was elated. He figured that when he turned in his expenses for an amount equal to the average of his past total expenses, he would be able to bank most of his salary. All went well for about a month until Craig's boss noticed the same high amount of expenses on the voucher. He called Craig and chewed him out for padding his expense account saying, "It can't possibly cost you that much to live! I'm bringing you back to the home office until you learn not to fudge your expense account."

Craig had made a mistake when he perceived the boss' statement as "the average amount of your past expenses," rather than "*up to* the average amount of your past expenses." The boss had expected that during an extended stay the expenses would go down while Craig thought this was an opportunity to make some additional money legally. Craig heard what he wanted to hear because of his set of expectations.

■ Object Factors That Cause Selective Perception

Why do we notice some objects and entirely miss others? Basically, it all boils down to the "standout effect." For something or someone to be perceived it has to come to our attention. Some of the characteristics of objects that tend to subdue or bring things to our attention are covered in the following paragraphs.

Novelty   Something that is different is perceived more easily than something that is familiar. For example, a single problem incident, such as catching an employee smoking pot on the job, might be more easily perceived and remembered than the normal good performance of the employee.

Contrast   This close relative of novelty exists when something or someone stands out against the background. In organizational settings, contrast is sometimes desirable and sometimes not so desirable. Safety signs should be designed with bold, contrasting letters and colors; otherwise, they will just blend with the environment and not be seen. (This may happen anyway because they are too familiar.) Another example of contrast is the Transamerica building (called the Transamerica Pyramid) in San Francisco, shown in Figure 4.2. Its contrasting pyramidal shape causes it to stand out. Transamerica makes very effective use of this contrast in their advertising.

Size and Intensity   Remember Jeff Baxter, owner of Atlas Sign Company, whom we discussed in Chapter 1? He knew that the bigger the sign and the bigger the lettering, the more likely people were to see it. He also knew that when he used bright, intense colors like red and orange, people were more likely to pay attention. A status-seeking corporate president might ride in a silver Rolls Royce limousine that combines both size and intensity. The size and intensity of architecture is often used to get people's attention.

Similarity   We also tend to try to fit the environment into a scheme with which we are familiar. We may *group* things or people together even if they do not belong together. We may perceive a person much differently if

Figure 4.2. The Transamerica Pyramid.

Photo courtesy of Transamerica Corporation, 600 Montgomery St., San Francisco, CA, 94120.

he or she is a union member then we would if he or she was a member of management. Often, people are grouped into stereotypes because of ethnic background, color, or sex (to be discussed in the next section). While grouping sometimes causes problems, it is also a way of remembering and coping with the environment.

Proximity This is another form of grouping where people or things are put together because of their physical or time proximity. People in a particular department, such as accounting or sales, are seen as relatively similar because of their proximity. Temporal or time proximity can also cause perceptual distortion. For example, shortly after a new manager is hired, sales start a downward trend. The new manager could have been the cause, but there are also a number of other explanations, such as a change in market conditions.

■ The Perception Process in Review

There is a great deal of complexity in how we perceive the world around us. The process is made up of two general types of factors: those within ourselves, called person factors, and those contained by the object we are perceiving, called object factors. The person factors are made up of our sensing system, our psychological filters, and our expectations. The object factors involve such characteristics as novelty, contrast, size, intensity, similarity, and proximity. A central issue to remember is that what people perceive is reality to them even though the objective situation may be quite different from their perceptions.

In the next section, we will turn to several major organizational problems that arise from the perception process.

Problems in Perception

In the previous section, we noted a number of places in the perception process where distortion and selectivity can arise. Although perceptual distortion often serves a positive purpose for the individual by simplifying the environment, it may cause problems for the organization. Two of the most important and far-reaching perceptual problems, stereotyping and the halo effect, are discussed in this section.

■ Stereotyping

A **stereotype** is a generalization about a class or group of people. "Stereotypes are not necessarily incorrect, illogical, or rigid . . . although they may be less verifiable than generalizations about impersonal categories such as dogs or molecules."[9] Stereotypes may also be seen as oversimplified pictures of reality that make it easier for us to interpret and understand our complex world.[10]

When we generalize about women, blacks, old people, hippies, redheads, Germans, or Jews, we are stereotyping. Most people, except the "Archie Bunker-types" (a stereotype itself), seem to have a rather flexible approach to stereotyping. In other words, if they find an exception to their stereotype, they will accept that deviation but continue to hold the general stereotype. For example, if a stereotype is held that women are more likely to be passive and submissive, and then there is an encounter with an active and aggressive woman, she will probably be seen as an unusual exception—the one in a hundred that does not fit the rule. The overall stereotype usually remains unchanged. Thus, stereotypes are particularly difficult to change even in the face of evidence that they are inaccurate.

■ Problems with Stereotyping

Remember in the opening incident when Lacy saw Wilma as being too "pushy" and emotional? His stereotypic view of women was probably distorting his perception of Wilma. On the other hand, the stereotype of a well-dressed Yale grad may have worked in Dave's favor to get him the promotion.

Stereotypes often involve hidden prejudice that gets in the way of organizational affirmative action programs. (Affirmative action programs are designed to insure that women and other minorities, who have been discriminated against in the past, have at least an equal opportunity for all hiring, promotion, and pay decisions.) If Wilma had wanted to, she might have filed an affirmative action complaint against Lacy, although this is seldom done at higher managerial levels because even if she won, it would then be difficult if not impossible for her to work effectively with Lacy.

Decisions based on imperfect or even invalid stereotypes often cost organizations more than they realize. The departure of Herb and Wilma from the Department of Electronics proved very costly in terms of lost talent, leadership, and experience. And if Dave is really as incompetent as he seems, then the failure of the satellite communications system might also be attributable, at least in part, to the error in perception.

| 4.2 | *A Stereotype that Backfired!* |

This is a true story based on an experience of a high-ranking female procurement executive with the United States Air Force. Here is how she relates the story of a stereotype that caused considerable embarrassment to one of her male contacts:[11]

The automatic assumption of the female as a sex object can backfire. I had an inside chuckle once at the embarrassment of a man as a direct result of his own actions. I passed him in the stairwell in my office building. He was a stranger, and he leered at me and made a personal remark meant to be overheard, which I ignored.

Now, understand that I don't mind such things as being whistled at on the street by truck drivers or other similar little goodies. I'm old enough that I consider it a distinct compliment. But this man was clearly mortified when we later met in the conference room where I was chairman of a group which was hearing his company's plea for a subcontract adjustment of several million dollars.

■ Self-Fulfilling Stereotypes

Another rather insidious possibility is that if a manager believes strongly enough in a stereotype, then it may become a *self-fulfilling* prophecy (*see* the Perspective: The Self-Fulfilling Prophecy) for the people involved—they may come to actually come to behave in the way the stereotype predicts.[12] The **self-fulfilling stereotype** process works in much the same way as the self-fulfilling prophecy—the generalized beliefs and attitudes that form our stereotypes reinforce our own behavior and the behavior of the target of our stereotype so that actual behavioral outcomes are consistent with the stereotype.

One way the self-fulfilling process works is that people tend to notice, observe, and remember the characteristics that fit the stereotype, while ignoring those that do not. Thus, selective perception tends to maintain the stereotype and cause self-fulfilling behavior.[13]

An example of this behavior might be a supervisor who treats black employees as if they were less competent than whites (because of a racial stereotype or prejudice). This unfavorable stereotype may mean that blacks are unwittingly given less challenging work experiences and thus are not as well rounded as their white peers. Since less is expected of them, they may even perform at a lower level, thus confirming the stereotype.

■ The Halo Effect

When someone is good in one area and on the basis of this strength is then assumed to be good in all areas, then the person is said to wear a halo. The term **halo effect** means that a general impression permeates evaluations in other areas; or that a person is rated the same in many areas because

Perception: What Is Reality?

of one overall feature that is perceived to be related to these areas.[14] In practice this means that individual rating categories tend to be distorted because of the halo effect.

Take, for example, the opening case where Dave's sociability may have created a halo effect that resulted in Lacy's decision to promote Dave. Another form of halo effect is created when a person who is once rated outstanding continues to be rated outstanding in spite of a decline in performance. (In the section on impression management we will cover some strategies for harnessing this bias to your advantage.)

The halo effect works in reverse, too. If a person is once labeled as a poor performer or troublemaker, it is difficult to overcome that unfavorable image.

■ Controlling the Halo Effect

In performance appraisal, in promotion decisions, and in selecting new employees, it is important to control the halo effect. There are a number of methods including specifying performance criteria, increasing rater familiarity with the ratee, using multiple raters, and by training for raters.[15]

Establishing Performance Criteria One of the best ways is to clearly specify what behaviors and performance criteria an individual must meet. For example, Lacy might have established something like the following criteria for the selection of the Satellite division chief:

1. Effectively supervises employees.
2. Maintains costs within budget.
3. Makes accurate decisions.
4. Communicates effectively with Congress.
5. Is technically competent in satellite technology.
6. Is a good team member.

Increasing Rater Familiarity The more the supervisor knows about the subordinate's behavior, the more accurate the ratings are likely to be. In our opening case, one of the major problems was that Lacy did not know either Herb or Wilma and thus made erroneous ratings of their overall behavior based on a very limited and distorted sample of their performances.

Use Multiple Raters When possible, using several people who are familiar with a person's performance to rate that performance can reduce halo.[16]

Improve Training for Raters While the evidence is weak that training can reduce rating distortions, two techniques appear promising.[17] Supervisors could keep a diary that details the day-to-day performance of subordinates so that they would have a detailed factual reference for rating. Another strategy is to train supervisors to be critical. Most of us would prefer to rate someone leniently to avoid unpleasant confrontations.

4.3 | *Managerial Myopia: Self-Serving Biases*

A perceptual distortion that is related to both stereotyping and the halo effect is the tendency to generalize based on incomplete and biased information. When managers allow this bias to enter their decision processes, they are said to have **managerial myopia**, or a view of the future that is blurred because of their self-serving biases. The results of a research study into the effects of biases on managers' predictions of organizational growth concluded that: "self-serving biases are a wide-ranging phenomenon that can affect managerial decision making through the process of overly optimistic planning."[18]

Interviews were conducted with forty-eight presidents of manufacturing firms to find out how accurately they predicted the firm's future performance relative to competition.

Fifty-six percent of the executives predicted they would do better than their actual performance while only 8 percent predicted they would do worse than they actually did—in other words, there was a strong tendency to overpredict performance. Thirty-five percent of the presidents accurately predicted their performance.

The researchers conclude that managers perceive themselves to be more capable than they really are, and this bias affects their ability to realistically predict organizational performance.

Using another concept from the chapter, the self-fulfilling prophecy, one might ask if it is more desirable for a manager to be optimistic and overconfident or to be accurate and realistic?

■ Reducing Halo: A Pessimistic Conclusion

In spite of our desire to reduce the halo effect, few strategies seem to have much power. Since there are multiple opportunities for perceptual distortion during the rating process, we may continue to expect a fairly high degree of inaccuracy. Prevention of the halo depends on awareness. Managers must ask themselves: "Does this person actually behave the way that I am rating him or her? Have I observed his or her specific behavior for this factor? What is his or her actual performance level?"

Impression Management

So far we have been discussing the problems with perceptual distortion and filtering. Now we will turn to the application of perception techniques to control the image we project of ourselves. **Impression management** is the process of controlling the images and perceptions that others form about us.[19] Another way of thinking about the concept is to use the terms self-presentation or self-projection, since impression management has to do with the ways we present ourselves to others. This self-presentation process is an integral part of our self-concept and personality (*see* Chapter 2).

All of us have engaged in some type of impression management. For example, have you ever cut your hair or worn a nice suit to get a good job?

Favorable and accurate impressions are very important for organizational success. In our opening case, Herb's casual dress was certainly a major reason why he did not get selected for the promotion. Even if you do not want to use impression management—some people think it's manipulative—you should be aware of others that are employing the techniques. Knowledge of impression management might have prevented a mistake like promoting Dave.

In the remainder of this section, we will cover three major aspects of impression management: ingratiation, appearance and dress, and nonverbal impressions.

■ Ingratiation: Getting People to Like You

The word *ingratiation* has a somewhat negative connotation even though the techniques are widely used. **Ingratiation** means that an individual is making a conscious effort to increase another person's liking for him or her.[20] If it is done with sincerity and finesse, ingratiation can be very effective for both persons. However, if it is obviously motivated only by the desire for personal gain, such behavior is considered to be manipulation and is detested by most people. Yet the target of the ingratiation may be quite flattered and may respond positively toward the ingratiator, even though aware of the strategy.

There are a number of tactics used to increase liking.[21] In addition to those listed below, you might refer to some of those listed in the Perspective: How to Win Friends and Influence People.

1. Use *flattery*, compliments, and other techniques that enhance the self-concept of the other person.
2. *Conform* to the other's opinions, judgments, and behaviors. Remember that we tend to like those who are similar to ourselves.
3. Present and *describe yourself favorably*. Present a favorable self-image. But beware of too much self-praise; modesty may be a more effective strategy.
4. *Render favors* to the other person. Gifts and rewards to others tend to increase their liking for you.

■ Dress and Impressions

Clothes are one of the most important factors in impressions. Every day when you arrive at the workplace, your clothes are the first thing others notice. Even in a brief encounter, we normally observe what the other person is wearing and make judgments about that person and treat him or her according to how we react to the apparel.

One important aspect of personal appearance is whether it is appropriate or inappropriate for the situation at hand. Sports clothes in an office may be just as inappropriate as a wool suit on the tennis court. If a person is wearing entirely inappropriate clothes, we may form our strongest impression based primarily on the clothes. The cartoon in Figure 4.3 shows how much impact inappropriate dress can have.

It was interesting to observe the change in President Carter over the first three years of his term. At first, he was very informally dressed, some-

4.4 │ *How to Win Friends and Influence People*

Impression management is not new. Almost fifty years ago Dale Carnegie published a best-selling book, *How to Win Friends and Influence People*, that contained these six rules:[22]

1. Become genuinely interested in the other person.
2. Smile.

3. Remember that a person's name is to that person the sweetest and most important sound in any language.
4. Be a good listener. Encourage others to talk about themselves.
5. Talk about things that interest the other person.
6. Make the other person feel important—and do it sincerely.

times in open shirts and sweaters. Later, when he felt a need to change his image, he began wearing conservative, dark suits with conservative shirts and ties. He apparently believed that the conservative image made him appear more "presidential."

President Reagan, on the other hand, always seems to wear clothes that fit the situation. In Washington, he wears finely tailored dark suits, while on his ranch he dresses in informal western style. His appearance always seems appropriate.

Figure 4.3.
Inappropriate dress may decrease your effectiveness.

"If it please Your Honor, I would like to point out again that I am not the defendant but the defendant's counsel."

Drawing by Modell; © 1972. The New Yorker Magazine, Inc.

■ Dress for Success

John Molloy's book, *Dress for Success*, and his syndicated news columns on dress are extremely popular in many organizational circles. An example of the type of advice given by Molloy is as follows.[23]

> *No question, then: The tie is a symbol of respectability and responsibility; it communicates to other people who you are, or reinforces or detracts from their conception of who you should be. While the most appropriate tie, worn correctly, naturally cannot insure your success in business or in life, it certainly can—and should—give the right signals to keep you from being regarded as a no-class boob.*

We find more and more people looking like the conservative, successful business executive that he describes. Molloy's emphasis, based on research (*see* the Perspective: How Top Executives Described Successful Dress for an example of his somewhat unconventional research), is to describe effective dress, not what is good or bad taste in dress. His assumption is that if you are perceived to be powerful, successful, and attractive, then you will enhance your chances of promotion and corporate success. More recently, Molloy also published another book entitled, *The Woman's Dress for Success Book*,[24] aimed at aspiring female executives. Other studies, although few in number, tend to confirm Molloy's views on dress and impressions.[25]

■ Uniforms and Authority

When someone is dressed in a uniform, such as a policeman or military person, they are much more likely to be obeyed. A research study showed that 83 percent of the people obeyed a person in a guard uniform while only 46 percent obeyed the same person dressed in civilian clothes.[26] Thus, people in uniforms have a great deal of power (ability to influence others), and others tend to obey their commands.

Since most large organizations have a number of uniformed people, they need to consciously consider the impact of the uniform on their customers and on the general public. For example, a department store might want to reduce shoplifting by placing uniformed guards at strategic positions throughout the store. While customers might be deterred from shoplifting, they might perceive the store as an armed camp that is unsafe or unpleasant to shop in. Hence, the store may lose more in sales than it does in shoplifting. Although there are no clear-cut answers to such problems, managers need to be aware that uniforms have a strong psychological impact and plan accordingly.

■ Verbal and Nonverbal Impressions

Every time you speak, you are making yet another important impression. Voice quality, pitch, accent, speed, articulation, and content reveal a great deal about you and are important to the impression-forming process. Verbal behavior, while not impossible to change, is much more difficult to change than dress.

4.5 How Top Executives Described Successful Dress

Clothing consultant and syndicated columnist, John T. Molloy, queried 100 top corporate executives in medium to large organizations to determine their attitudes about appropriate business dress. The following excerpt from *Dress for Success* shows Molloy's research strategy for this study and his results:[27]

I showed the executives five pictures of men, each of them wearing expensive, well-tailored, but high-fashion clothing. I asked if this was a proper look for the junior business executive. Ninety-two of the men said no, eight said yes.

I showed them five pictures of men neatly dressed in obvious lower-middle-class attire and asked if these men were dressed in proper attire for a young executive. Forty-six said yes, fifty-four said no.

I next showed them five pictures of men dressed in conservative upper-middle-class clothing and asked if they were dressed in proper attire for the young executive. All one hundred said yes.

I asked them whether they thought the men in the upper-middle-class garb would succeed better in corporate life than the men in the lower-middle-class uniform. Eighty-eight said yes, twelve said no.

I asked if they would choose one of the men in the lower-middle-class dress as their assistant. Ninety-two said no, eight said yes.

Nonverbal impressions are also crucial for controlling impressions.[28] For example, during your initial contact with another person you may go through the ritual handshake. If your handshake is limp, your face is unsmiling, and your eye contact poor, the other person will probably get a very aloof and unfavorable impression of you. In contrast, if you have a firm, warm handshake, with a smile and good eye contact, the other person will probably feel very favorable toward you. We will discuss nonverbal communication more fully in Chapter 8.

■ Implications of Impression Management

The positive application of the perception process is becoming more important to organizations in a number of ways. Impressions help create halos that may impair or enhance the performance appraisal system. Dress makes a substantial difference in how people are perceived and how people act in response to their perceptions. Impressions are also important when dealing with customers and other contacts outside the organization. Representatives of the organization should make impressions that are appropriate for that organization. Thus skillful impression management can contribute to organizational effectiveness.

Perception and Organizations: Some Conclusions

■ Employees' Perceptions

The most far-reaching impact of perception in organizations is that it affects the way individuals perceive the workplace and their interaction with their work. Since perceptual reality is in the mind of the perceiver, distortions often occur. For example, if people believe they are being paid inequitably, then that perception, rather than the objective reality of the situation, will govern their behavior. They may be disgruntled, alienated, and more likely to leave the organization. In addition, employees may perceive inequities in assignments, promotions, racial or sex treatment, or discipline. Almost all organizational situations offer the potential for perceptual distortion.

To minimize perceptual problems, clear communication about organizational processes helps prevent misunderstandings. For example, a pay system that clearly specifies the level of pay, the relative pay levels between different employees, and the level of pay in relation to the local market, will be more likely to be perceived as equitable. An additional strategy for clarifying perceptions, which will be covered in Chapter 13, is participation in decision making. When people take part in decisions that affect them, then their perceptions will be more accurate, and fewer perceptual problems will arise.

■ Performance Evaluation

Organizations must often rely on subjective performance evaluations because we cannot always measure the objective performance of people. For example, most managers' jobs involve a number of different skills and behaviors (i.e., ability to work with people, problem-solving ability, communication skills) that cannot be measured by direct, objective measures like units produced or items sold. This means that perceptual distortions like stereotyping, the halo effect, the self-fulfilling prophecy, and leniency are inevitable and must be carefully avoided or minimized.

We have already discussed the methods for minimizing such errors in performance evaluation, such as establishing clear performance criteria or increasing rater familiarity.[29]

■ Interviewing

Interviewing is a key method used for selecting new employees, reassigning existing employees, and providing feedback on performance to employees.[30] In addition, many one-on-one communication interactions in organizations might be considered to be interviews. Almost everyone has had or will have some type of interview experience when pursuing a job. Here again, stereotyping and the halo effect are ever present. In addition, there are other problems that are more likely to occur in an interview, such as differences in the frame of reference between the interviewer and interviewee caused by their differing values systems, experiences, and attitudes.[31]

Interviewers and interviewees often have little in common and care must be taken to clarify possible misperceptions. A good strategy is for the interviewer to ask questions like, "How do you mean that?" or "Can you clarify what you mean by that?" Possible misperceptions should be carefully explored rather than merely assuming that both people are talking about the same thing.

■ Organizational Impression Management

Much of our discussion of impression management focused on how individuals manage their impressions through ingratiation, appearance, and nonverbal cues. Another important consideration is that organizations need to be concerned about the impressions they make as well. The way an organization is perceived also depends on the way its employees look and act. Can you imagine a banker in Boston or Chicago dressing in an open-necked shirt with no coat? And what about a computer salesman in Dayton who is dressed in blue jeans and cowboy boots. While both of these examples are extreme, there are often important decisions to be made about what type of impression the organization wants to project.

For example, in a shopping mall in the Pacific Northwest there are two large department stores. Store A allows its employees to wear practically anything to work while Store B has a very strict dress code that calls for everyone to dress in nice, fashionable clothes. Store B has an image of being a high quality store suitable for more affluent customers while Store A is seen as catering to lower-middle-class customers. If these two stores are in fact targeting two different types of customers, then this strategy may be good for both. If they are pursuing the same customers, then one or both of the stores may be using the wrong strategy.

Organizational-level impression management requires careful analysis of the impacts of impressions, and a clear idea of whom the organization is trying to impress.

■ Perception and Motivation

For people to be motivated they must perceive that rewards will be forthcoming if they expend the effort to perform. They must also perceive some need that is unsatisfied so that their behavior is energized. In addition, clear goals are needed so they know where to channel their effort. In the next chapter, we will discuss these issues and more when we study the motivation process.

SUMMARY

Chapter Review

■ A key to understanding the **perception process** is that reality is in the mind of the perceiver. There are a number of **physiological and psychological filters** that distort the process and cause us to **selectively perceive** our environment.

■ Perceptual distortions can occur within the individual (**person factors**) or within the object being perceived. Person-factor distortions are caused by values, attitudes, needs, past experience, and expectations. **Object factors** include size, novelty, contrast, similarity, and proximity.

■ The **self-fulfilling prophecy** results when expectations cause behavior that makes the expectation come true. It seems to be most strongly influenced by nonverbal behavior.

■ A **stereotype** is a generalization about a class or group of people. Stereotypes serve a useful purpose of simplifying the complex environment, but they cause problems in organizations such as fostering prejudice and distorting performance appraisals. Stereotypes may become **self-fulfilling stereotypes** when people who hold stereotypes treat the targets in a way that results in the stereotype coming true.

■ The **halo effect** is operating when a person is rated good or bad in one area, and this is generalized to other areas of their behavior. The halo effect has a particularly strong impact on performance appraisals. Halo effects are controlled by establishing clear performance criteria, increasing rater familiarity, using multiple raters, and improving training for raters.

■ **Impression Management,** controlling the images and perceptions that others form about us, involves ingratiation, appearance, and nonverbal expressions. **Ingratiation** using such strategies as flattery, conforming with others, doing favors, or presenting yourself in a favorable light, are often seen as socially undesirable strategies. Dress is one of the most powerful inputs to an impression. The way you dress has a strong impact on how others perceive you and may have a substantial bearing on your ultimate organizational success. Verbal and nonverbal impressions are also very important elements of the impression process.

■ Perception has far-reaching impacts on organizational systems. The success of motivation strategies, performance appraisals, employee selection, and customer impressions may all rest on the understanding and effective use of the perception process.

For Discussion

1. Pick an example of some event or circumstance that has happened to you lately that resulted in a misperception. What filters seem to best explain why you did not accurately perceive the situation?
2. Describe the factors that cause selective perception.
3. Based on your personal experience relate an example of the self-fulfilling prophecy. What factors seemed to be primarily responsible for it?
4. How can stereotypes affect the success of minorities in organizational situations?
5. Explain the relationship between the halo effect and impression management.
6. What can be done to minimize the impact of stereotypes and the halo effect?
7. What impression do you intend to make when starting a new managerial job or being promoted to a higher position? How will you dress differently? Will your behavior change?
8. How is the concept of perception related to organizational performance and job satisfaction?

Key Concepts and Terms

perception	expectations
sensing systems	self-fulfilling prophecy
psychological filters	person factors
selective perception	object factors

Understanding Organizational Behavior

stereotyping
self-fulfilling stereotypes
halo effect
performance appraisal

managerial myopia
impression management
ingratiation

Suggested Readings

Molloy, J. T. (1975). *Dress for success*. New York: Warner; or (1978). *The woman's dress for success book*. New York: Warner.

Schlenker, B. R. (1980). *Impression management*. Monterey, Ca.: Brooks/Cole.

Schneider, D. J.; Hastorf, A. H.; and Ellsworth; P. C. (1979). *Person perception*. Reading, Mass.: Addison-Wesley.

Snyder, M. (1982). Self-fulfilling stereotypes. *Psychology Today* 16(7):60cf.

Zima, J. P. (1983). *Interviewing: Key to effective management*. Chicago: SRA.

CASES AND INCIDENTS

Sean O'Flaretty

"Bleeding us! Taking what rightfully belongs to us workers. How can Portley have that big fat smile on his face with his right hand stuffed so deep into my wallet? Look at this picture in the paper. Look at him! Proud that he's taking 18% profit out of the company. Bragging about it. Look at my hands. Look at your own hands. That's what makes the pumps—and the money—for this company! Not Portley sitting around on his big fat chair in his big fancy office! Not the stockholders. What have they ever done to turn out one single pump? Little old ladies doing nothing but pampering their dogs are the ones who get all that profit. Doing nothing. And their dogs eat better than I do!"

Sean O'Flaretty, fiery old unreconstructed Trotskyite, was very upset by Mr. Portley's announcement in the company paper that profits were up for the year. Holding forth to the luncheon crowd lounging on the castings pile outside the foundry, as orange peels, egg shells and "baggies" were gathered up and stuffed back into lunch boxes, Sean continued. "I ask you guys, why is it we do all the work around here and Portley and the little old ladies take all the money out of the place? It's not fair, never been fair, and one of these days you guys will quit sitting around doing nothing and demand your rightful share."

Discussion questions

1. What factors are affecting Sean's perceptions?

2. Do you think Sean really believes what he is saying?

3. How might Mr. Portley correct the misperceptions?

Stanley's Overcoat

"It all started out innocently enough, I suppose," reflected Stanley. "I was in New York for a week to go to this 'systems procedures' seminar for all new plant people. One day it was really cold, windy, just miserable weather. The warmest thing I had was this old Army overcoat and headgear, but I figured, What the hell, who cares what you look like for one day? So I walk into the Headquarters building where this seminar is being given and the first thing I know this older guy gives me this fishy look. Then he says, 'Can I help you. Who do you want to see?', so I say, 'It's OK, I work here.' While we're waiting for the elevator you can see him kind of working up to something, and finally he says, '*You* work for The Company?'

"I tell him I do, and then after awhile he says, 'Don't you think it's a little risky to dress that way?'

"Now I'm starting to get the picture. But even if I didn't, as we ride up the elevator he gives it to me in detail. 'People in The Company don't dress that way,' he says, 'and if you ever want to get anywhere son, you'd better think it over and change your ways.'

"I go up to the seminar room and take off my coat. Now I've got on this wool checked shirt, you know the kind. No room for a jacket under the overcoat, and just a shirt and tie isn't warm enough, so I've got this shirt on.

"Things go OK until we break up into work groups. Everybody introduces himself and someone says to me, 'Where do you work, Stan?' So I say, 'The Company, just like you.' The guy says, 'Come on, you're kidding me. *You* work for The Company?'

"Now he's a young guy, but he sounds just like the older guy. So he starts laughing. I mean uncontrollably. Then he says. 'Hey, this guy works for The Company, he really does, can you believe it?'

"Well, this breaks them all up. They all sit there, sort of pointing their fingers at me and saying, '*He* works for *The Company!*'"

Reprinted with permission from *The Ropes to Skip and the Ropes to Know: Studies in Organizational Behavior*, First Edition by R. Richard Ritti and G. Ray Funkhouser. Copyright 1979. Chapter 4, page 33. Grid, Inc., Columbus, Ohio, 1979.

Discussion questions

1. What's wrong with wearing this type of overcoat?
2. Why do you think his colleagues reacted so violently?
3. What do you suspect the appropriate dress was?

REFERENCES

1. For in-depth coverage of perception, *see* Levine, M. W. and Shefner, J. M. (1981), *Fundamentals of sensation and perception* Reading, Mass.: Addison-Wesley; and Schiff, W. (1980), *Perception: An applied approach*, Boston: Houghton Mifflin.

2. Schiff, *Perception*, provides a complete discussion of the sensing systems.

3. *See* Haber, R. N. and Hershenson, M. (1980), *The psychology of visual perception*, 2nd ed., New York: Holt, Rinehart, and Winston.

4. Based on an incident related in Senger, J. (1980), *Individuals, groups, and the organization*, Cambridge, Mass.: Winthrop.

5. Merton, R. K. (1948), The self-fulfilling prophecy, *Antioch Review* 8:193–210. The discussion in this perspective is based largely on Darley, J. M. and Fazio, R. H. (1980), Expectancy confirmation processes arising in the social interaction sequence, *American Psychologist* 35:867–881.

6. *See* Rosenthal, R. and Rubin, D. B. (1978), Interpersonal expectancy effects: The first 345 studies, *Behavioral Brain Science* 1:377–386, for a more complete analysis of research on the self-fulfilling prophecy.

7. Schneider, D. J.; Hastorf, A. H.; and Ellsworth, P. C. (1979), *Person perception*, Reading, Mass.: Addison-Wesley.

8. Dipboye, R. L. (1982), Self-fulfilling prophecies in the selection-recruitment interview, *Academy of Management Review* 7:579–586.

9. McCauley, C.; Stitt, C. L.; and Segal, M. (1980), Stereotyping: From prejudice to prediction, *Psychological Bulletin* 7(1): p. 196.

10. McCauley, et al., Stereotyping.

11. Speech given by Lucy Schlosser in Denver, Colo., 1975.

12. Snyder, M. (1982), Self-fulfilling stereotypes, *Psychology Today* 16(7):60cf. *Also see* Skrypnek, B. J. and Snyder, M. (1982), On the self-perpetuating nature of stereotypes about women and men, *Journal of Experimental Social Psychology* 18:277–291.

13. Snyder, Self-fulfilling stereotypes.

14. Cooper, W. H. (1981), The ubiquitous halo, *Psycological Bulletin* 90:218–244.

15. Cooper, The ubiquitous halo. *Also see* Landy, F. J. and Farr, J. L. (1980), Performance rating, *Psycological Bulletin* 87:72–107.

16. Cooper, The ubiquitous halo. *Also see* Holzbach, R. L. (1978), Rater bias in performance ratings: Superior, self-, and peer ratings, *Journal of Applied Psychology* 63:579–588.

17. Bernardin, H. J. and Buckley, M. R. (1981), Strategies in rater training, *Academy of Management Review* 6:205–212.

18. Larwood, L. and Whittaker, W. (1977), Managerial myopia: Self-serving biases in organizational planning, *Journal of Applied Psychology* 62(2): p. 198.

19. This definition is similar to the one used by Schlenker, B. R. (1980), *Impression management,* Monterey, Ca.: Brooks/Cole, p. 6.

20. *See* Schlenker, *Impression management*, Chapter 6; and Jones, E. E. (1964), *Ingratiation: A social-psychological approach*, New York: Appleton-Century-Crofts.

21. Jones, *Ingratiation*.

22. Adapted from Carnegie, D. (1936), *How to win friends and influence people*. New York: Simon and Schuster. (This is the earliest of numerous editions.)

23. Molloy, J. T. (1975), *Dress for success*, New York: Warner. p. 77.

24. Molloy, J. T. (1978), *The woman's dress for success book*. New York: Warner.

25. *See* Schlenker, Impression management, Chapter 9.

26. Bickman, L. (1974), Clothes make the person, *Psychology Today* 7(11):49–51.

27. Molloy, *Dress for Success*, pp. 35-36.

28. *See* Edinger, J. A. and Patterson, M. L. (1983), Nonverbal involvement and social control, *Psycological Bulletin* 93:30–56; and Buck, R. (1983), *Nonverbal behavior and the communication of affect*, New York: Guilford Press.

29. Landy and Farr, Performance rating.

30. *See* Cederblom, D. (1982), The performance appraisal interview: A review, implications and suggestions, *Academy of Management Review* 7:219–227.

31. Zima, J. P. (1983), *Interviewing: Key to effective management* Chicago: SRA. *Also see* Arvey, R. D. and Campion, J. E. (1982), The employment interview: A summary and review of recent research, *Personnel Psychology* 35:281–322.

Motivating Work Behavior

PREVIEW

- Why is motivation one of the most troublesome problems for managers?

- When is it impossible to motivate work behavior?

- What happens to people whose needs for growth are continually frustrated?

- How can the social environment influence motivation?

- What work outcomes do you value? Find out by filling out a questionnaire.

- Which rewards are more powerful: those from sources within the person or those from the environment?

- Why do we so often engage in the folly of rewarding *A* while hoping for *B*?

- Why is equity a crucial element of the motivation process?

Preview Case: A Tale of Two Cities

An Introduction to Work Motivation
- What do we mean by motivation?
- Motivation and job performance
- *Perspective:* When Is Motivating Work Behavior Impossible?

Energizing Behavior
- Needs—An energizing force
- Maslow's need hierarchy theory
- *Perspective:* Does a Hierarchy of Needs Really Exist?
- Alderfer's ERG theory
- Applying need theory: An Example
- Social influences as energizing forces

Directing Behavior
- Expectancy theory: Making choices
- Using expectancy theory: An example
- Using expectancy theory: Managerial implications
- *Perspective:* What Work Outcomes Are Valued?
- Goal Setting

Sustaining Behavior with Rewards
- Sources of rewards
- *Perspective:* Organizational Hygiene Factors
- Fairness of rewards: Equity theory
- *Perspective:* On the Folly of Rewarding *A*, while Hoping for *B*

Work Motivation: Conclusions for Managers

Summary
- Chapter review
- For discussion
- Key concepts and terms
- Suggested readings

Cases and Incidents
- Motivation Overdose: The Workaholics
- Rollie on the Assembly Line

References

PREVIEW CASE: A TALE OF TWO CITIES

Ferndale

Jim Matsumoto, head of the Public Works Department for Ferndale, was upset. He tossed the Refuse Utility Division study on his desk in disgust. The study concluded that yet another refuse collection crew and truck are needed. This is the second new truck and crew this year and funds are tight. Squeezing another $200,000 out of the city council will be very difficult. But if the garbage is not picked up, everyone gets in an uproar. If only he could motivate the crews to make five more stops a day, then no new crew or truck would be needed.

Going from 110 to 115 stops would not seem to make that much difference. Yet the last time he tried to get the crews to increase their production, it resulted in a wildcat strike (a one-day work stoppage) that almost got him fired. The crews work a forty-hour week and resist overtime, even at double-time rates—they say the work is too tiring to work overtime. Perhaps their current pay of $12.33 per hour is so high that they do not care about money? If only he could find some way to motivate the crews, life would be much simpler and more pleasant.

Martinsville

Things were different in Martinsville. Refuse service is contracted to the Quickpik Company headed by Marlo Bennett. Her crews are paid $8 per hour for the first 100 stops and then $.50 per stop for anything over 100. But in contrast to the Ferndale crews who must be on the job eight hours a day, the Martinsville crews can go home as soon as their stops are completed. It usually takes them about six hours for 200 stops! The Martinsville crews make more money for working less time, and they are highly productive.

Certainly one of the most common managerial problems is how to motivate employees. If you take a poll of workers in almost any organization, most will say they are working at considerably lower than their full potential. On the other hand, the supervisors of these workers may say that they have tried "everything" to get them to be more productive, to use more of their potential.

The key to improving motivation is to obtain greater use of people's capabilities without exploiting them. However, motivating employees is not easy. There are no simple, foolproof methods that can be applied to everyone. What works in Martinsville might not work in Ferndale, depending on the individuals involved and the situation.

Our task in this chapter is to gain an understanding of the basic concepts of motivation. To do that we will use an approach that divides motivation into three general areas: energizing behavior, directing behavior, and substaining behavior. In the next two chapters we will turn to some techniques that are used to motivate people.

An Introduction to Work Motivation

In this introductory section, we will define motivation and look at some fundamental relationships between motivation and performance.

■ What Do We Mean by Motivation?

When we speak of motivation, we are interested in *behavior* as opposed to attitudes. What we are interested in is why people work faster or harder, why they come to work on time, why they produce high quality work, or why they decide to join or to leave our organization? **Motivation** is the process that causes behavior to be energized, directed, and sustained.[1]

Behavior is normally **energized** or aroused by an unfulfilled need or desire. A desire for money, promotion, time off, social contacts, or job challenge can all affect motivation. Once energized, the behavior must be *directed* in some way by making sure the effort is channeled where it is needed or desired. Making it clear how rewards can be obtained by meeting goals or behaving in a certain way is directing behavior. And finally, we need to *sustain* desired behavior through rewards and feedback. We want people to keep on performing over the long run. Figure 5.1 shows a model representing an overview of the motivation process.

■ Motivation and Job Performance

Have you ever been highly motivated to make an *A* in a course only to wind up with a *B* or *C*? Obviously, performance depends upon more than just motivation—they are not the same.[2] People must have the *capacity* to perform. This means they must also have the ability, aptitude, skill, training, tools, and technology to be able to perform. The simple model in Figure 5.2 illustrates this relationship.

To illustrate how performance depends upon capacity as well as motivation, return to the opening example. A refuse collector for Quickpik Company has to lift cans weighing over 100 pounds all day long. Not everyone can do it—some people simply lack size and strength. Training is prob-

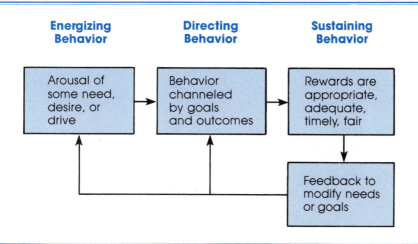

Energizing Behavior   **Directing Behavior**   **Sustaining Behavior**

Arousal of some need, desire, or drive → Behavior channeled by goals and outcomes → Rewards are appropriate, adequate, timely, fair → Feedback to modify needs or goals

Figure 5.1. Model of the motivation process.[3]

Figure 5.2. General model of performance.

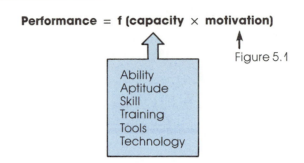

Performance = f (capacity × motivation)

Ability
Aptitude
Skill
Training
Tools
Technology

Figure 5.1

ably less important than ability for refuse collectors because the job is relatively simple and easy to learn. However, tools and technology are crucial. If the collectors were limited to old-fashioned open trucks rather than the modern trucks with hydraulic trash compactors, they could not perform nearly as well. It is doubtful that fifty stops a day could be completed. Thus, one must have the capacity to perform as well as the motivation or inclination.

While our emphasis will be directed primarily at motivation, capacity should always be considered as a possible cause of performance problems.

Energizing Behavior

In this section, we will cover two major approaches to explaining what energizes behavior—needs and social forces.

■ Needs—An Energizing Force

What Are Needs? A **need** is tension created by a deficiency that arouses an individual to behave in the direction of accomplishing some goal.[4] Hunger is a basic *physiological* need for food. If you are hungry, you are motivated to do something that will result in eating—you will drive to the restaurant or you will prepare and cook some food. Once satisfied, hunger is no longer a motivator, or for the moment, a need. The refuse collectors in Ferndale were more motivated by a need for rest after the eight-hour workday than they were by a need for the extra money that overtime work would bring.

Categorizing Needs. There are a number of different classification schemes that attempt to put needs in categories to simplify understanding. Two approaches that are often used by managers are Maslow's Need Hierarchy Theory and Alderfer's E.R.G. Theory. We will discuss both of these theories later in this section. Both these theories limit the number of needs they consider (five for Maslow; three for Alderfer) and combine a number of needs together. A more complete, but still partial, list of needs that seem relevant for organizations is presented in Table 5.1.

Understanding Organizational Behavior

Table 5.1 A partial list of needs that are relevant to organizations.[8]

Need	Description
Achievement	To do one's best; to accomplish something difficult and significant.
Affiliation	The desire for relationships with others; to share and do things with friends; to love; to relate to others on an interpersonal basis.
Autonomy	To seek independence, freedom; to avoid domineering authority; to be unattached; to resist coercion and restriction.
Esteem	Self-respect and respect from others; to have a good reputation; to have prestige and status.
Growth	To develop; to learn; to experience new skills and knowledge; challenge.
Physiological	The basic needs of the body to stay alive: food, water, air, temperature.
Power	To control one's environment; to be dominant; to direct and control others; to supervise others; to be regarded as a leader.
Safety	To seek freedom from the threat or reality of physical or psychological harm; to live in a secure environment.
Self-actualization	The desire for self-fulfillment; to realize one's potential; to become everything that one is capable of becoming; to achieve fulfillment of one's life goals; to realize the potential of one's personality.

Figure 5.3.
Maslow's hierarchy
of needs.

A review of motivation theory and practice concludes that it may not always be possible to motivate behavior, even if we know how. "There are situations and settings that make it exceptionally difficult for a motivational system to work. These circumstances may involve the kinds of jobs or people present, the technology, the union, and so on."[5] If a manager has to answer *yes* to the following four questions, then some other form of behavior-change strategy other than motivation may be appropriate:[6]

1. Is the reward system rigid and flexible? In other words, are people and tasks grouped into large categories for reward purposes?
2. Is an individual's behavior dependent on the actions of others?
3. Are there lots of changes in people, jobs, or expected behavior?
4. Are social pressures the major determinants of what people are doing on the job?

■ Maslow's Need Hierarchy Theory

Maslow's Need Hierarchy Theory[7] is probably the best known and most widely used need theory of motivation. Maslow classifies needs into five sets: *physiological, safety, love* (or affiliation), *esteem,* and *self-actualization* (*see* Table 5.1 for definitions). As shown in Figure 5.3, these needs are arranged in a *hierarchy* that begins with basic physiological needs and ends with self-actualization. While the hierarchy is a general guide, it is not rigid. Many people will show patterns that do not precisely follow the hierarchy and some researchers question whether the hierarchy even exists (*see* the Perspective: Does a Hierarchy of Needs Really Exist?)

Need Satisfaction   The strongest need at the moment, say hunger, will predominate until it is gratified, then the next need in the hierarchy will take over since a gratified need is not a motivator. However, just because another need in the hierarchy becomes predominant does not mean that the previous ones on the hierarchy have been 100 percent satisfied. A more common case would be for all needs to be partially satisfied.

For example, take Jane Hernandez, a new engineer for Solar Electronics Company, who wants to gain the respect of other engineers and establish a good reputation. Jane's need profile at the moment might be something like this: physiological needs, 90 percent satisfied; safety needs, 80 percent satisfied; love needs, 70 percent satisfied; esteem needs, 40 percent satisfied; and self-actualization needs, 10 percent satisfied. Thus, esteem needs may be the predominant need or deficiency at the moment for Jane. However, once her esteem needs have been satisfied, she may be more interested in self-actualization—a need that Maslow says can never be completely satiated.

■ Alderfer's ERG Theory

The ERG theory collapes Maslow's five levels into three—existence (*E*), relatedness (*R*), and growth (*G*)—hence the ERG theory.[9] Physiological and safety needs are combined into existence, and esteem and self-actualization are combined into growth. Other than the differing categorization system, two main differences exist between Alderfer and Maslow.

Frustration-regression of needs   Maslow says that we progress from one need to another in the hierarchy. While Alderfer agrees with this process, he also says that if we are continually frustrated in our attempts to satisfy a need, then we will give up and redirect our efforts toward some lower need. For example, if an electrician's needs for growth are frustrated, he or she will probably give up and regress to the pursuit of social needs. Figure 5.5 illustrates this process.

Multiple Needs Operate Simultaneously   ERG theory says that people may experience several needs simultaneously. For example, a person may be hungry and at the same time need love and affection. Figure 5.6 illustrates this process. You might contrast this approach with Maslow's shown in Figure 5.4.

■ Applying Need Theory: An Example

Jim Matsumoto, Head of Ferndale's Public Works Department, might rethink his refuse collection motivation problem using Maslow's concepts. His first step might be to talk to the informal leader of the refuse collectors, Mac Gorst (An ***informal leader*** is someone who is not officially appointed but who nonetheless serves as the leader of the group.) What follows is the conversation between Jim and Mac.

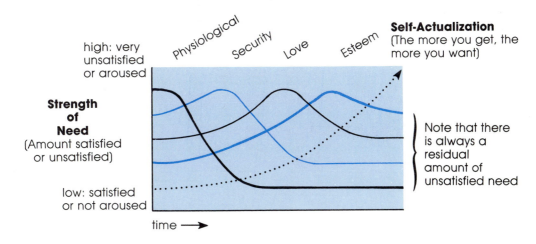

(Hypothetical pattern of need arousal.)

Figure 5.4. Maslow's heirarchy of needs satisfaction process.

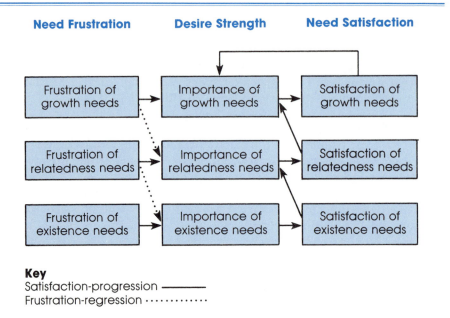

Figure 5.5. Need satisfaction and frustration-regression using ERG theory.

From F. Landy and D. Trumbo, 1980, *Psychology and Work Behavior*, p. 341. Copyright © 1980 by The Dorsey Press, Homewood, Illinois.

Key
Satisfaction-progression ————
Frustration-regression ············

"Mac, why don't you want to work overtime to help me solve our collection problem?"

Mac: "Well, we're really dragging after eight hours of work. All I can do is go home and flake out on the couch. In fact, I don't usually make it through the good TV programs before I fall asleep in my chair. No sir, I've had enough with forty hours! Even though I could use the money, I just can't take any more." (Sounds like Mac's physiological or existence needs are predominant.)

"Then what about establishing a goal of say five or ten more pickups a day for each crew—still working only forty hours?"

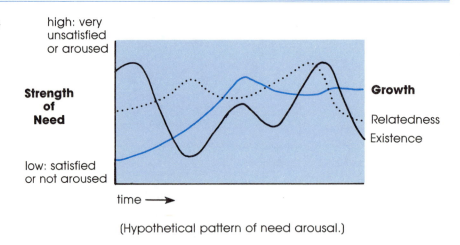

Figure 5.6. The ERG approach to the need satisfaction process.

(Hypothetical pattern of need arousal.)

Understanding Organizational Behavior

5.2 | Does a Hierarchy of Needs Really Exist?

Little evidence exists to support the notion that Maslow's hierarchy of needs exists. An extensive review of the literature[10] found that a hierarchy tended to exist only between deficiency needs (physiological, safety, and social) and growth needs (esteem and self-actualization). Does this mean the theory is invalid? Possibly. It is certainly not as robust as we might desire. But, there are also some other competing explanations:

1. The theory may not be testable using traditional research methods. For example, Maslow developed his theory based on deduc-

tion and clinical insights with a very special group of people—self-actualizers. Thus, it may not be possible to evaluate the theory using research designs that differ greatly from Maslow's design.

2. It is very difficult to develop questionnaires that measure such elusive variables as needs.

From a practical standpoint, his theory is logically appealing, easy-to-remember guide for understanding human need processes in organizations.

"Here in private I can tell you that I could do it. But if the other guys were to know I said that they would really be mad. A lot of men feel that if we agree to do more we will be continually asked to up the goals until we are working so hard we are falling out like flies." (Mac is still concerned about physiological needs, but now it sounds like the affiliation or relatedness needs could be threatened. Do we have several needs arising at once as ERG would predict?)

"Is there some way to get a contest going that might pit crew against crew to determine a winner?"

"That might be fun, but what would the payoff be for us?" (The idea appeals to his esteem or growth needs, but he has reservations)

"Maybe we could develop a goal, say 125 pickups a day, and have each crew try to meet the goal as fast as they could. When the goal is met, they might take off for the rest of the day. Maybe you would have more energy left for the evenings." (Jim is appealing to the esteem [growth] and physiological [existence] needs, and by encouraging team cohesiveness he may be improving satisfaction of affiliation needs.)

"Yeh, that sounds interesting. I'll talk to the rest of the guys and get back to you."

The example makes it sound easier to analyze needs than it really is. Needs are very complex and often difficult to understand. Nevertheless, they do serve as one of the primary ways behavior is energized. In the next section, we will cover another way behavior is energized using social cues.

■ Social Influences as Energizing Forces

So far we have discussed forces or drives within a person that energize behavior. Another important energizing force is the social situation. The **social influence** approach suggests that "people are aroused by the presence of others and the knowledge that other people are evaluating them."[11] Social cues, in the form of expectations, are given off by coworkers, supervisors, or subordinates. These cues then become powerful energizing forces for motivating behavior.

The example we just reviewed with Jim and Mac in Ferndale can be extended to illustrate the social influence approach. When Mac expressed concern about how his fellow workers would react to an increase in the performance goal, he was probably responding to social pressure. Mac knows the expectations of the group, and since he is the informal leader, he is under considerable pressure to support the group. If we were to unilaterally agree to an increase in workload, he would probably be ostracized from the group. Thus, Mac is motivated to maintain behavior at the level sanctioned by the group.

In Chapters 9, 12, and 14, we will learn much more about such social influence processes as group dynamics, power, and leadership. Now that we have considered some forces that energize behavior, we will turn to the forces that direct behavior.

Directing Behavior

Why do you choose to behave in one way rather than some other one? Why do you choose to try to attain one goal while ignoring another? One way of answering these questions is to consider what forces and processes direct or channel behavior. Two theories will help us explain this process: expectancy theory and goal theory.

Expectancy theory is concerned with why we choose certain paths to obtaining an outcome that will result in a satisfied need.[12] The central focus of the theory is on **expectancies**, which are beliefs, based on perception, that a particular behavior will result in an outcome. Expectancies are normally expressed as probabilities (ranging from 0 to 1.0) or chances that a certain outcome will be obtained.

Goal theory[13] comes into action after a path has been chosen—goals concentrate energy on the end result that we are trying to obtain. Our discussion will focus first on expectancy theory and then turn to goal theory.

■ Expectancy Theory: Making Choices

There are three major aspects of expectancy theory: the relationship between effort and performance, the relationship between performance and outcomes, and the valences associated with a given outcome. We will discuss each of these aspects in the following paragraphs.

The Effort-Performance Relationship   Expectancy theory begins with what is called the **effort-performance expectancy** (E→P); that is, if you expend the effort, what are the chances that you can perform? This E→P expectancy ties in directly with the model discussed earlier that performance was a function of capacity (ability, skill, technology) and motivation. If you do not feel you have much chance of performing because of either capacity or motivation, then you will be unlikely to expend the effort.

For example, say you are installing a new computer-based information system for your financial analysts to use to improve their performance.

However, two months after installation, you find that very few of the analysts are using the system. When you ask why, you get a variety of answers that boil down to a lack of understanding about how to use the system. Thus, the analysts have not been expending the effort because they perceive that they would not be able to perform the task without considerable frustration and effort. The new system may be quite easy to learn and use, but if the analysts think it is difficult, then they are much less likely to take the effort to try to get the new system to work.

Performance-Outcome Expectancies

The **performance-outcome expectancy** (P→O) says that if you perform (P), what is the perceived probability that you will get the outcomes (O) that you want? Individuals expect outcomes (rewards or punishments) to be associated with behaviors, and they evaluate their chances of obtaining these outcomes before they decide to behave.

For example, assume you are a market researcher in a large wood products firm. If you do an outstanding job on the market research report, will obtain the *outcomes* you desire, such as praise and promotion (which will satisfy your esteem needs)? Or, do you perceive that no one will care about the report or that you may even get taken to task because management will not like the results (undesirable outcomes)? If praise and promotion are perceived to be more likely, then you will probably direct your energies toward finishing the report. If indifference or punishment seem probable, you may not be motivated to finish the report.

Outcomes can occur at multiple levels. You might consider money to be a first-level outcome because you might use the money to obtain second-level outcomes like a new car or stereo (*see* Fig. 5.7 for examples of outcomes that might be satisfied by money). Outcomes are not always associated with money. There are an almost infinite variety of outcomes including the following: praise, group approval, sense of accomplishment, vacation time, educational opportunities. Eventually outcomes serve to satisfy needs. For example, the outcome of money buys the stereo that helps satisfy a need for growth and relatedness.

Valence of Outcomes

Some outcomes are desirable, like praise and promotion, while others are undesirable, like punishment or being ignored. Thus each outcome (O) always has a valence (V) associated with it. **Valence** is simply how desirable or undesirable a given outcome is perceived to be by a specific individual. Outcomes have different valences for different people—not everyone values the same outcomes. The valences are determined by an individual's needs, values, and perceptions.

Valences can be expressed in numerical terms. The relative size of the valences and their direction (+ or −) is important. We will use the arbitrary range from +10 to −10 to represent the strength of a valence (you might use −1 to +1 or any other convenient number). To illustrate how the process works, assume you hold the market researcher's job referred to in an earlier paragraph in this section. Praise is a very important outcome to you with a valence of +7. Promotion, a very long-term outcome since you are just starting, has a valence of +5. Being ignored has a −3 valence while being punished has a −8 valence.

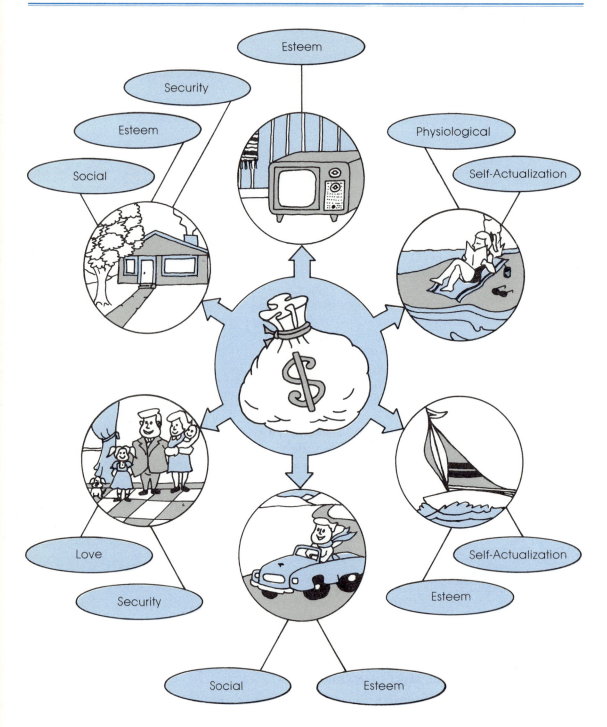

Figure 5.7. One outcome, such as money, can fulfill other outcomes.

Understanding Organizational Behavior

It is now possible to combine all the expectancy theory dimensions into the model illustrated in Figure 5.8.

■ Using Expectancy Theory: An Example

Return to our refuse collection example. If the collectors at Ferndale decide to work overtime to complete the additional pickups, several positive outcomes are obtained as shown in Figure 5.9. But note that the outcome with the highest valence (in this case a negative valence) is "more fatigue," This high negative valence offsets the relatively high positive valence for money, resulting in an overall negative motivation force of − 2.2. The net motivation force for each plan is figured by multiplying the effort-performance expectancy (E→P), in this case 1.0, by the performance-outcome expectancy (P→O), then multiplying it by the valence (V) for each outcome and finally summing for all the outcomes (*see* Fig. 5.8 for the entire formula and reference 14 for detailed computation procedures).

In comparison, the proposal for using competition among crews with the outcome of more time away from the job results in an overall positive motivating force of + 7.3. This motivational force is driven by the very high

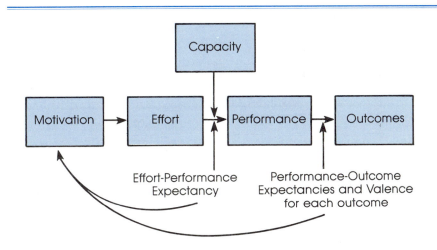

Figure 5.8. Model of the expectancy theory process.

Mathematical Formula for the Model (15)

$$M = (E \rightarrow P) \times \sum (P \rightarrow O)V$$

Where:

M = Motivation
(E→P) = Effort   Performance expectancy
  $\sum$ = Sum of all
(P→O) = Performance leads to an outcome expectancy
V = Valence of a given outcome

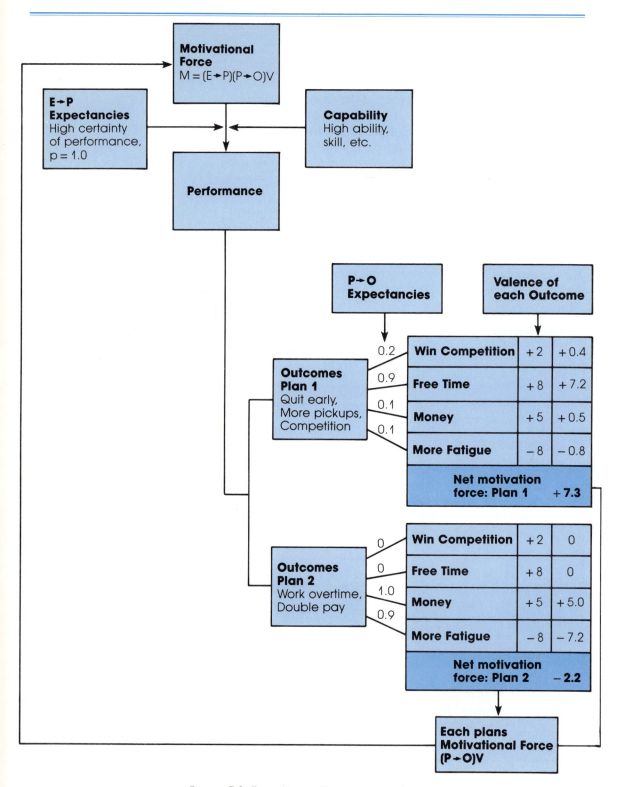

Figure 5.9. Expectancy theory example.

valence associated with the "free-time" outcome. Note that the increased motivation force from winning is not very high. That outcome alone would not be strong enough to motivate the crews to change.

■ Using Expectancy Theory: Managerial Implications

Managers tend to find expectancy theory quite useful for understanding the general nature of the motivation process. In the following paragraphs we will discuss several implications for practice that arise from expectancy theory.[15]

Find Out What Rewards an Employee Values   If you know which outcomes are important to an employee or group of employees and how important each is in relation to the other (the valences), then you may be able to offer outcomes that will be strong enough to motivate. For example, we saw that we could motivate the Ferndale refuse collectors solely by offering time off. That's handy information. Had we not found this out, we might have been tempted to offer them a plan similar to the one in Martinsville—*both* time off *and* more money! So expectancy theory can also teach us to offer only enough to motivate.

There is another related implication. Often, employees will value different outcomes and have considerably different valences for outcomes. When this happens we have a "motivation nightmare" in that what works to motivate one person may not work for another. In this situation, we must design motivation systems that offer flexibility and choice to the employee—an often difficult task that may involve designing a choice of a number of different rewards for performance.[16]

Link Desired Outcomes to Desired Performance   If you find that your employees value promotion and yet promotion is based solely on sen-

| 5.3 | *What Work Outcomes Are Valued?*[17] |

Directions: Rank-order the outcomes you prefer starting with the most preferred outcome as 1 and winding up with the least preferred outcome as 10.

_____ 1. Achievement or sense of accomplishment
_____ 2. Interpersonal relationships or friendships
_____ 3. Job or company status
_____ 4. Job security
_____ 5. Opportunity for growth
_____ 6. Pay or monetary rewards
_____ 7. Provision for family
_____ 8. Recognition from community and friends
_____ 9. Responsibility or control
_____10. Support for hobbies or avocational activities

To compare your rankings with others, turn to the end of the references in the back of this chapter.

Motivating Work Behavior

iority, then you are not effectively using your motivation resources. You need to redesign the promotion system to make sure it is linked to performance. Then, when an employee performs well there will be a high probability (P→O) of promotion and a much stronger force toward motivation. If employees seek responsibility, growth, and achievement, then some form of job enrichment might be in order. (Chapter 7 contains a detailed description of job enrichment.)

Use Social Influence   Group membership and acceptance can be a very potent outcome with a high valence because of the energizing force of social influence. Groups have the power to provide or withhold approval, assistance, friendliness, and inclusion. Thus, if groups can be directed toward organizationally desirable outcomes, then it can be an effective motivation strategy.

The example related earlier involving Jim Matsumoto's discussion with Mac Gorst, the informal group leader in Ferndale, involved the use of group forces to improve motivation. If Mac thinks the group will go for an idea, such as the early quitting idea, then he can exert a great deal of influence that may result in the idea being accepted. On the other hand, Mac is not about to bring an idea, such as the one to establish a goal of five to ten more pickups a day, to the group. He might be severely chastised for even considering such an idea. Of course, Mac knows this and will avoid the idea.

■ Goal Setting

Goal setting is a way of channeling employee's energy and efforts toward an outcome that is desirable for both the employer and employee. **Goal setting** is the process of developing, negotiating, and formalizing targets that an employee is responsible for accomplishing.[18] An outcome, in expectancy-theory terms, and a goal may be the same. In fact, in many cases a goal is a first-level outcome.

If goals and first-level outcomes are pretty much the same, how do they differ? Goals concentrate effort and direction on a single outcome, while expectancy theory predicts that many diverse outcomes will govern behavior. Hence, goal setting seems like it would be a cure for our motivation problems. All we have to do is select the outcome, set the goal, and motivated work behavior results. Too bad it is not this simple. There is one big ringer—the goals must be *accepted* for them to motivate.

If Jim Matsumoto simply tells the refuse crews that there is a new production goal of 110 pickups per day, they will probably not accept the goal. They can cope with the nonacceptance in a number of ways. They might just ignore the goal and say, "sure, boss, we'll try out best," but expend the same amount of effort as previously with no improvement in production. Or they might react by getting angry and calling a wildcat strike, which might result in a public outcry and major problems for Jim. Thus, the key to goal setting is getting goals accepted by those that have to do the work. Goal setting strategies will be discussed more fully in Chapter 7.

Now that we have seen how people channel their energies through the expectancy model and goal setting, we are ready to examine how behavior is maintained.

Sustaining Behavior with Rewards

Equitable and timely rewards are the key to sustaining behavior—people work for the outcomes they value or find rewarding and avoid those outcomes they find punishing. Thus, reward management is a key part of the motivation process. In this section we will discuss sources of rewards and their fairness. In the next chapter on behavior modification, we will discuss timing of rewards.

■ Sources of Rewards

While rewards can come from a number of sources, it is useful to distinguish between those that come from the person or the job itself, called **intrinsic rewards**, and those that come from others such as the boss or co-workers, called **extrinsic rewards**.[19] Intrinsic rewards include such factors as a sense of accomplishment, feelings of creativity, and a positive sense of having performed with excellence. An architect who feels a sense of accomplishment when a building is completed is experiencing an intrinsic reward. These types of rewards are long lasting and often fulfill a need for esteem, self-actualization, and psychological growth.

Extrinsic rewards are given to you by others. They include such factors as pay, recognition from supervisors or the workgroup, fringe benefits, and promotions. People seem to react differently to self-administered, or intrinsic, rewards than they do to other-administered, or extrinsic, rewards.[20] Intrinsic rewards may have longer-lasting effects and be more effective for sustaining motivation than extrinsic rewards.

Another interesting interaction between intrinsic and extrinsic rewards is that extrinsic rewards, such as pay, enhance performance on routine task, but may degrade performance on more interesting, challenging, intrinsically-rewarding tasks.[21] This means that if you have an interesting, enriched task, let intrinsic rewards suffice; but if you have a routine task, use extrinsic rewards for better performance.

■ Fairness of Rewards: Equity Theory

Have you ever done a thorough job of preparing for an exam only to have your roommate, who did not study at all, do better than you did? Were you motivated to continue your thorough preparation for that course? Most likely you were not. If people are not rewarded fairly and equitably for the work they do, then they will be extremely dissatisfied with their rewards, and behavior will not be sustained. Whether equity exists depends upon the perceived relationship between your inputs and the rewards or outcomes you receive when compared to some other person's inputs and rewards.[22] The *equity* relationship can be diagrammed as shown below:

$$\frac{\text{Yours}}{\text{Inputs}} \quad \frac{\text{Rewards or Outcomes}}{\text{Inputs}} \quad = \quad \frac{\text{Comparison Others}}{\text{Inputs}} \quad \frac{\text{Rewards or Outcomes}}{\text{Inputs}}$$

A key element of equity theory is that you are comparing your inputs (education, effort, skill, motivation) and rewards (pay, recognition, achievement, praise) with a "comparison other's" inputs and rewards. A "comparison other" is any person or group of people who you perceive that you should be compared with.[23] For example, college professors often use

5.4 Organizational Hygiene Factors

One of the most controversial motivation theories is Herzberg's Motivation-Hygiene Theory.[24] The theory states that what motivates people is achievement, recognition for a job well done, the work itself, responsibility, and advancement. In addition to these motivating factors there are a number of factors associated with job dissatisfaction, called the hygiene factors. Examples of hygienes are supervision, salary, company policies, co-workers, and working conditions. These types of items are called hygienes because they are necessary for a good working environment, but they do not motivate. Herzberg's motivators may be roughly equated with intrinsic factors and his hygienes with extrinsic factors. The following quote from an interview with Herzberg illustrates the hygiene part of his theory:[25]

The hygiene factors are always short term, like the length of time you're not dissatisfied with your salary. It takes about two weeks for the effects of a raise to wear off . . . The hygiene factors are all subject to the "what have you done for me lately" syndrome. A colonel bucking for general in the Army feels as deprived status-wise as a private bucking

for corporal. A colonel is the zero point. If you get a $4,000 increase in salary and the next year they give you a $2,000 increase in salary, psychologically you have taken a $2,000 cut.

By contrast, the motivators are long term and don't go back to zero. I write a book and I achieve some growth. If I don't write another book, I don't get back to where I was before. When I achieve, that achievement never disappears . . . You see, with the hygiene factors, you've got to have as much as, or more than, you had before to notice any difference, but with the motivators, you do not have to have as much as before to know the difference and feel the growth.

The controversy surrounding Herzberg's theory revolves primarily around methodological issues that show that his two separate factors may not really exist and thus his theory may not be valid.[26] In spite of the problems with the theory, it has been influential in focusing managers' attention on the intrinsic aspects of the job as potential motivators. It was also influential in popularizing job enrichment, the topic of Chapter 7.[27]

---

other college professors as the "comparison others" rather than a business executive. We usually choose people who are similar to us as "comparison others."

Outcomes of Inequity The ideal reward position is perfect equity. Inequity in either direction—overrewards or underrewards—creates discomfort and tension, although the tolerance for overreward is probably higher than for underreward. Inequity can be resolved in a number of ways. Inputs can be distorted so that the person perceives his or her inputs are greater or lesser than they really are. Outputs, or performance may also be increased or decreased to balance the equation.[28]

Past History of Inequity   Another aspect of equity theory is that past inequities may affect future reactions to inequitable situations.[29] An example might be an employee who was denied a day off when he or she believes that others have been granted this time off in the past. This person may react much more violently than would be expected, not because of the denial but because of a history of inequities that have built up to such a degree that the person explodes. These past inequities might have involved a missed promotion, unexpectedly low bonus, and lack of praise for doing a good job. The accumulation of past inequities built up and caused a serious reaction.

Equity, an Example   It would seem like $12.33 an hour for the Ferndale refuse collectors would be a more-than-fair pay. And yet, what if the Leesburg refuse collectors, who also work for the city and who also have 110 pickups a day, were receiving $13.50 per hour. Would the Ferndale collectors be dissatisfied? The answer would depend on whether they considered Leesburg collectors to be a "comparison other." If Leesburg were Ferndale's sister city just across the river, then it is very likely that inequity would be perceived. On the other hand if Leesburg were in another state, 100 miles away, then the wage differential would not be a problem.

But what about Ferndale Municipal Hospital's nurses—they make only $8.25 per hour. If they compare themselves with the refuse collectors, they may perceive that they are grossly underpaid. If they compare their pay with Leesburg nurses, who make $8.00 per hour, they may consider themselves fairly paid. It depends on perception and especially who the "comparison other" is.

Work Motivation: Conclusions for Managers

The discussion in this chapter makes it clear that there is a great deal of complexity in predicting and managing work motivation. There is no single "master theory" that can explain the entire motivation process. Thus, we must turn to a series of theories, each providing a partial and sometimes overlapping explanation of the motivation process. Categorizing the theories into those that focus on energizing, directing, or substaining motivation provides a loose overall framework for understanding their interlocking nature.

Throughout the chapter we have discussed a number of ways that managers can improve motivation. In this final section, we will summarize a number of conclusions about the motivation process:

1. *Motivation must be managed.* Managers need to take an active role in designing and implementing motivation systems and monitor the motivation process on a daily basis.[30]
2. *Recognize individual differences.* Managers must be sensitive to the differing needs that arouse behavior of their subordinates. Rewards should be tailored to the ones that an individual employee values.
3. *Clearly link performance and rewards.* We noted that behavior was most powerfully energized when employees saw clearly that valued out-

5.5 | On the Folly of Rewarding A, While Hoping for B

War *as an Example*

If some oversimplification may be permitted, let it be assumed that the primary goal of the organization (Pentagon, Luftwaffe, or whatever) is to win. Let it be assumed further that the primary goal of most individuals on the front lines is to get home alive. Then there appears to be an important conflict in goals—personally rational behavior by those at the bottom will endanger goal attainment by those at the top.

But not necessarily! It depends on how the reward system is set up. The Vietnam war was indeed a study of disobedience and rebellion, with terms such as "fragging" (killing one's own commanding officer) and "search and evade" becoming part of the military vocabulary. The difference in subordinates' acceptance of authority between World War II and Vietnam is reported to be considerable, and veterans of the Second World War often have been quoted as being outraged at the mutinous actions of many American soldiers in Vietnam.

Consider, however, some critical differences in the reward system in use during the two conflicts. What did the GI in World War II want? To go home. And when did he get to go home? When the war was won! If he disobeyed the orders to clean out the trenches and take the hills, the war would not be won and he would not go home. Furthermore, what were his chances of attaining his goal (getting home alive) if he obeyed the orders compared to his chances if he did not? What is being suggested is that the rational soldier in World War II, *whether patriotic or not*, probably found it expedient to obey.

Consider the reward system in use in Vietnam. What did the man at the bottom want? To go home. And when did he get to go home? When his tour of duty was over! This was the case *whether or not* the war was won. Furthermore, concerning the relative chance of getting home alive by obeying orders compared to the chance if they were disobeyed, it is worth noting that a mutineer in Vietnam was far more likely to be assigned rest and rehabilitation (on the assumption that fatigue was the cause) than he was to suffer any negative consequence.

. . . In light of the reward system used in Vietnam, would it not have been personally irrational for some orders to have been obeyed? Was not the military implementing a system which *rewarded* disobedience, while *hoping* that soldiers (despite the reward system) would obey orders?

From S. Kerr, 1975, On the folly of rewarding A, While hoping for B, *Academy of Management Journal* 18:769–71. Copyright © 1975 by Academy of Management, Mississippi State University. Reprinted with permission of author and publisher.

comes would be realized if they performed. Systematically rewarding superior performers with promotions and pay are ways of clarifying this link.

4. *Improve people's capacity to perform.* Since performance often depends upon ability, aptitude, skill, training, tools, and technology, these determiners of performance should be carefully reviewed for adequacy. Training programs and new tools and technology are potentially powerful ways of improving performance with no change in motivation levels.

5. *Use social influence strategies.* Since the need for social approval is great in most employees, managers can design situations where group

pressures can be used to motivate employees and provide rewards to keep their behavior sustained.

6. *Establish goals to direct behavior.* Clear goals serve to direct behavior toward goals the manager wants accomplished. This relatively simple strategy is quite powerful for clarifying expectancies and insuring accurate rewards for performance.

7. *Reward people equitably.* The best motivation system will fail without fair and equitable rewards because people get very uncomfortable or even alienated when rewards are not fair.

SUMMARY

Chapter Review

■ **Performance** depends on more than just motivation. The **capacity** of the person in terms of ability, skill, training, tools, and technology also are important.

■ There may be times when motivation is impossible because of rigid reward systems, social pressures, changes in the job situation, and when an individual's performance depends upon others.

■ A **need** is a tension created by a deficiency that arouses an individual to behave. A gratified need is not a motivator. Maslow classifies needs into five categories: **physiological, security, affiliation, esteem,** and **self-actualization.** Alderfer, on the other hand, uses only three: **existence, relatedness,** and **growth.**

■ There are several views of how needs operate. Maslow says that needs tend to be arranged in a general **hierarchy** from basic physiological on up to self-actualization. One set of needs should be at least partially satisfied before proceeding to the next. Alderfer says that a number of different needs can be operating simultaneously and that if a need is constantly **frustrated,** the person will **regress** and seek a lower-level need.

■ **Expectancy theory** helps explain how behavior is directed. It is concerned with why we choose certain paths to obtaining an outcome that will satisfy our needs. There are two types of expectancies: the **effort-performance expectancy** (What are the chances you can perform if you expend the effort?); and the **performance-outcome expectancy** (What are the chances that you will get the outcomes you want if you perform?). **Valence** is a measure of how desirable or undesirable an outcome is.

■ **Goal setting** helps channel an employee's energy toward a specific outcome. Goals are a simple and powerful motivational devices, if they are accepted by the employee.

■ **Intrinsic rewards**, such as a sense of accomplishment, seem to have more long-lasting reward properties than do **extrinsic rewards**, such as pay.

■ Fairness of rewards is also very important. **Equity theory** states that the perception of equity will depend on a comparison with another individual in terms of rewards received versus inputs to the task (motivation, skill, education). Perceptions of equity are influenced by past inequity experiences as well as the specific instance at hand.

For Discussion

1. Since performance is a function of capacity and motivation, what can you do to select people who have the potential to perform?
2. Are there instances when motivating behavior is impossible? If you think so, describe such an instance.
3. Which needs (shown in Table 5.1) seem most relevant for energizing your behavior?
4. Compare and contrast Maslow's hierarchy of needs with Alderfer's ERG theory.
5. Using the model of the expectancy theory process shown in Figure 5.9, outline the motivation for directing your behavior to attend college.
6. What are some practical ways that a manager can use expectancy theory.
7. Explain the difference between intrinsic and extrinsic rewards. Which do you prefer? Why?
8. Explain how equity theory works. How is the comparison other determined?
9. Can you think of an example of the "folly of rewarding A, while hoping for B"?
10. What are the most important elements to consider when managing the motivation process?

Key Concepts and Terms

motivation
capacity to perform
need
Maslow's hierarchy of needs
E.R.G. theory
frustration-regression
expectancy theory
expectancies

effort-performance
   expectancies
performance-outcome
   expectancies
valence
goal setting
intrinsic rewards
extrinsic rewards
hygiene factors
equity theory

Suggested Readings

Freedman, S. M., and Montanari, J. R. (1980). An integrative model of managerial reward allocation. *Academy of Management Review* 5:381–390.

Mitchell, T. R. (1982). Motivation: New directions for theory, research, and practice. *Academy of Management Review* 7:80–88.

Nadler, D. A., and Lawler, E. E., III. (1983). Motivation: A diagnostic approach. In *Perspectives on Behavior in Organizations,* 2nd ed., eds. J. R. Hackman, E. E. Lawler, III, and L. W. Porter, pp. 67–78.

Steers, R. M., and Porter, L. W. (1983). *Motivation and work behavior.* 3rd ed. New York: McGraw-Hill.

Sussman, M., and Vecchio, R. P. (1982). A social influence interpretation of worker motivation. *Academy of Management Review* 7:177–186.

Motivation Overdose: The Workaholics

A "workaholic" may work a 100-hour week—and love it—according to Marilyn Machlowitz,[31] who has done research on these unusual people. A workaholic may arrive at 6:00 a.m. and leave at 7:00 p.m. with a brief-case full of work to do at home. There is no such thing as the "thank-goodness-it's-Friday" syndrome for the workaholic. On weekends they get anxious to get back to work and may have brought enough work home to tide them over. Vacations are a real drag. Workaholics would just as soon not take one and, if they have to take one for some reason, they may wind up climbing the walls before it is over. Machlowitz found fifteen characteristics that are common to workaholics:

- an ongoing work style
- an ability to work anywhere
- a broad view of what the job requires
- initiative
- a sense of scarcity of time
- the use of lists and time-saving gadgets
- long work days
- little sleep
- quick meals
- an awareness of what their work effort can accomplish
- overlapping of work and leisure
- an inability to enjoy idleness
- a dread of retirement
- a desire to excel
- and intense energy

Discussion questions

1. Using the motivation theories discussed in the chapter, determine why a person might work so hard.
2. What outcomes do workaholics seem to value?
3. Should we purposely try to find workaholics for organizational positions?

Rollie on the Assemby Line[32]

A fact of life that Rollie discovered at this stage was that while most assembly-line jobs were hard and demanding, a few were soft touches. Installing windshields was one of the soft ones. Workers doing this, however, were cagey when being watched and indulged in extra, unneeded motions to make their task look tougher. Rollie worked on windshields, but only a few days because Parkland [the foreman] moved him back down the line to one of the difficult jobs—scrabbling and twisting around inside car bodies to insert complicated wiring harness. Later still, Rollie handled a "blind operation"—the toughest kind of all, where bolts had to be inserted out of sight, then tightened, also by feel alone.

That was the day Parkland confided to him, "It isn't a fair system. Guys who work best, who a foreman can rely on, get the stinkingest jobs and a lousy deal. The trouble is, I need somebody on those bolts who I know for sure'll fix'em and not goof off."

Discussion questions

1. Why do you think Rollie is motivated to do the tough jobs?
2. What are the rewards or punishments for being a competent, dependable worker?
3. How could the reward system be designed to remedy this problem?
4. What impact would a change in the reward system have on quality control?

REFERENCES

1. This definition is based on Steers, R. M. and Porter, L. W. (1983), *Motivation and work behavior,* 3rd ed., New York: McGraw-Hill. It is also similar to the one used by Mitchell, T. R. (1982), Motivation: New directions for theory, research, and practice, *Academy of Management Review* 7:80–88.

2. Adapted from the ideas of Dunnette, M. D. and Kirchner, W. K. (1965), *Psychology applied to industry*, New York: Appleton-Century-Crofts; and Steers and Porter, *Motivation and work behavior*.

3. Mitchell, Motivation.

4. Mitchell, Motivation, p. 81.

5. Mitchell, Motivation, p. 86.

6. *See* Steers and Porter, *Motivation and work behavior*, for a good overview of need theories.

7. The table is based on a variety of sources including Maslow, A. H. (1943), A theory of human motivation, *Psychological Review* 50:370–396; Alderfer, C. P. (1972), *Existence, relatedness, and growth*, New York: The Free Press; and Senger, J. (1980), *Individuals, groups, and the organization,* Cambridge, Mass.: Winthrop.

8. Maslow, A theory of human motivation; Maslow, A. H. (1970), *Motivation and personality*, rev. ed., New York: Harper and Row.

9. Wahba, M. A. and Bridwell, L. G. (1976), Maslow reconsidered: A review of the research on the need hierarchy theory, *Organizational Behavior and Human Performance* 15:212–240; Salancik, G. R. and Pfeffer, J. (1977), An examination of need-satisfaction models of job attitudes, *Administrative Science Quarterly* 22:427–456; Miner, J. (1980), *Theories of organizational behavior* Hinsdale, Ill: Dryden; and Rauschenberger, J.; Schmitt, N.; and Hunter, J. E. (1980), A test of the need hierarchy concept by a markov model of change in need strength, *Administrative Science Quarterly* 25:654–670.

10. Alderfer, *Existence, relatedness, and growth*.

11. Mitchell, Motivation, p. 84. For more complete information on the social influence approach to motivation, *see* Sussman, M. and Vecchio, R. P. (1982), A social influence interpretation of worker motivation, *Academy of Management Review* 7:177–186; and Salancik, G. R. and Pfeffer, J. (1978), A social information processing approach to job attitudes and task design, *Administrative Science Quarterly* 23:224–253.

12. Vroom, V. H. (1964), *Work and motivation*, New York: Wiley. For reviews of expectancy theory *see* Mitchell, T. (1974), Expectancy models of job satisfaction, occupational preference, and effort: A theoretical, methodological, and empirical appraisal, *Psychological Bulletin* 81:1053–1077; and Mitchell, T. R. (1980), Expectancy-value models on organizational psychology, in *Expectancy, incentive and action*, ed. N. Feather, Hillsdale, N.J.: Erlblaum and Associates.

13. Locke, E. A. (1968), Toward a theory of task motivation and incentives, *Organizational Behavior and Human Performance* 3:157–189. For reviews *see* Steers, R. M. and Porter, L. W. (1974), The role of task-goal attributes in employee performance, *Psychological Bulletin* 81:432–452;

and Locke, E. A. (1978), The ubiquity of the technique of goal setting in theories of and approaches to employee motivation, *Academy of Management Review* 3:594–601.

14. For more information on how to compute these forces, *see* Vroom, *Work and motivation* and Mitchell, Expectancy models of job satisfaction, occupational preference and effort.

15. Some of the ideas in this section were based on those in Nadler, D. A. and Lawler, E. E. III, (1983), Motivation: A diagnostic approach, in *Perspectives on behavior in organizations*, 2nd ed., eds. J. R. Hackman; E. E. Lawler, III; and L. W. Porter, New York: McGraw-Hill.

16. For ways to individualize pay systems, *see* Lawler, E. E., III (1976), New approaches to pay administration, *Personnel* 53:11–23.

17. Adapted from Rand, T. M. (1977), Diagnosing the valued reward orientations of employees, *Personnel Journal* 56(9):451cf.

18. Umstot, D. D.; Bell, C. H.; and Mitchell, T. R. (1976), Effects of job enrichment and task goals on satisfaction and productivity: Implications for job design, *Journal of Applied Psychology* 61:p.381.

19. Deci, E. L. (1972), The effects of contingent and noncontingent rewards and controls on intrinsic motivation, *Organizational Behavior and Human Performance* 8:217–229.

20. Hamner, W. C. (1979), Motivation theories and work applications, in *Organizational behavior*, ed. S. Kerr, pp. 41–58, Columbus, Ohio: Grid.

21. Daniel, T. L. and Esser, J. K. (1980), Intrinsic motivation as influenced by rewards, task, interest and task structure, *Journal of Applied Psychology* 65:566–573.

22. Adams, J. S. (1965), Inequity in social exchange, in *Advances in experimental social psychology,* Vol. 2, ed. L. Berkowitz, New York: Academic Press; and Carrell, M. R. and Dittrich, J. B. (1978), Equity theory: The recent literature, methodological considerations, and new directions, *Academy of Management Review* 3:202–212; and Mowday, R. T. (1983), Equity theory predictions in organizations, in Steers and Porter, *Motivation and work behavior.*

23. For a discussion of "referent others," *See* Goodman, P. S. (1974), An examination of referents used in the evaluation of pay, *Organziational Behavior and Human Performance* 12:170–195.

24. Herzberg, F. (1966), *Work and the nature of man* Cleveland: World. *Also see* his article, (1968) One more time: How do you motivate employees? *Harvard Business Review* 46(1):53–62, for a summary of his theory.

25. Quote from (1971) A conversation with Frederick Herzberg, *Management Review* July, p.41.

26. *See* House, R. and Wigdor, L. (1967), Herzberg's dual-factor theory of job satisfaction and motivation: A review of the empirical evidence and criticism, *Personnel Psychology* 20:369–380; and Kerr, S.; Harlan, A.; and Stogdill, R. (1974), Preference for motivator and hygiene factors in a hypothetical interview situation, *Personnel Psychology* 25:109–124.

27. *See* Chapter 7 for a discussion of job enrichment; also *see* Herzberg, How do you motivate employees?, for his version of applying the motivation hygiene theory to job enrichment.

28. Mowday, in Steers and Porter, *Motivation and work behavior*.

29. Cosier, R. A. and Dalton, D. R. (1983), Equity theory and time: A reformulation, *Academy of Management Review* 8:311–319.

30. The first three are based in part on Steers and Porter, *Motivation and work behavior*, pp. 642–643.

31. Machlowitz, M. M. (1980), *Workaholics*, Reading, Mass.: Addison-Wesley.

32. Hailey, A. (1973), *Wheels*, New York: Bantam, pp. 242–243.

Answers to questions posed in the Perspective: What Work Outcomes Are Valued? *See* reference 18 for source.

Outcome	A*	B*	C*
1. Achievement or sense of accomplishment	2	2	2
2. Interpersonal relationships or friendships	9	8	9
3. Job or company status	7	7	8
4. Job security	10	10	4
5. Opportunity for growth	1	1	1
6. Pay or monetary rewards	5	6	6
7. Provision for family	3	5	3
8. Recognition from community and friends	8	9	10
9. Responsibility or control	4	3	7
10. Support for hobbies or avocational activities	6	4	5

*A = Upper management
B = Middle management
C = Hourly employees

Motivation Using Behavior Modification and Pay

CHAPTER 6

PREVIEW

- Can behavior mod, a technique that has proven successful for changing behavior of rats and pigeons, be applied in organizations?

- Find out how behavior mod is solving a number of organizational problems relating to performance, absenteeism, and safety.

- Do you know the steps to systematically change anyone's behavior? Learn them in this chapter.

- When should punishment be used or avoided?

- Is negative reinforcement the same thing as punishment?

- Will behavior change be more effective if the reward is given every time a behavior occurs or if it is given more randomly?

- How can vicarious reinforcement be used?

- Why don't salaries motivate?

- Why do merit pay and piecework pay systems often fail?

Preview Case: Reliance Development Company

Motivating With Organizational Behavior Modification
- The behavior modification process
- *Perspective:* Examples of Behavior Modification
- Targeting behavior
- Charting target behavior
- Managing the contingencies
- Using contingencies
- Schedules of reinforcement
- *Perspective:* Vicarious Reinforcement at Reno
- How often to reward?
- *Perspective:* Rules for Using Behavior Mod in Organizations
- An example of OB mod
- Summary of behavior and application steps
- Controversies surrounding behavior mod

Motivating with Pay
- Wages and salaries
- Merit pay
- Piece-rate pay
- Commissions
- Conclusions about using pay for motivation
- *Perspective:* The Tricky Business of Giving Rewards

Summary
- Chapter review
- For discussion
- Key concepts and terms
- Suggested readings

Cases and Incidents
- The Sloppy Secretary
- The Rate-Busting Saleswoman

References

Reliance Development Company, referred to as RDC by most of its employees, is a young company that was founded after the sky-high interest rates of the early 1980s made many homes unaffordable for the average buyer. RDC capitalized on this market by building large numbers of low-cost, energy efficient, small homes. The homes were attractively designed and reasonably priced and there were plenty of buyers. The company had succeeded beyond the wildest dreams of the four partners who founded it—it was now a multimillion dollar business with over 400 employees.

The four founders of RDC are meeting this morning to try to solve a problem: The framing costs have been rising and now exceed the estimate by 20 percent. (Framing is the basic skeleton of a house, the studs, floors, rafters. It is done by a special type of carpenter, called a framer.) Since the company is committed to keeping the costs down, something must be done. The key to their success has been cost consciousness. RDC has been able to build a good quality home for less money than their competitors. If costs are allowed to rise, then their competitive edge may be lost.

The directors who are meeting this morning are John Rosenberg, President; Helen Knapp, Vice-President for Finance; Roy Steele, Vice-President for Production; and Ronda Cole, Vice-President for Sales. All are recent graduates of undergraduate or graduate schools of business—they are familiar with motivation theories and concepts.

John: Helen tells me we've exceeded our framing costs by 20 percent on the last block of ten houses. What can we do about it?

Roy: The big problem seems to be quality—that is, too much quality. Several of the new guys we've hired were finish carpenters before. They think that each joint should be perfect; that everything should be perfectly level and square. You know we don't need that level of quality in framing. The house will be just as good, strong and saleable with a much lower level of quality. I've told them several times to try to speed it up; to lower their standards, but to no avail. Worse yet, the old framers seem to have caught the "quality fever." They are also working slower and more carefully. We can't just fire the lot of them because of the shortage of carpenters. They are hard to find. We will incur some terrific interest expenses if we slip behind schedule because of a shortage of carpenters. Plus, it would throw our other crews out of schedule and delay everything. I'm just not sure what we can do about the problem. Maybe we're just going to have to live with it and raise our prices.

Ronda: It looks like we have a classic motivation problem here: how do we motivate the crews to work faster with lower quality? Perhaps we could give a bonus for each house that is done on time or early?

Helen: If we pay a bonus, we're still going to be in a cost bind. Somehow we've got to toe the line on costs. And I don't think we can raise our prices. Our competitors are getting pretty close already.

John: Are they being oversupervised? Perhaps their jobs could be changed so that they would feel the responsibility for costs?

Roy: Well, they sure don't seem to give a damn about costs. If we could just do something to instill a sense of responsibility for costs; but they can't seem to get this quality thing out of their heads. I believe they probably think of their jobs as already pretty enriched. Maybe that's the reason they're so concerned about quality—they're craftsmen and they intend to do a first-class job, whether it's needed or not.

Helen: What about using behavior mod on them? I seem to remember from my org behavior course that if we can develop a schedule or plan for rewards and punishments we can change almost any behavior.

John: Yes, but behavior mod always kind of turned me off. You know, all that manipulation and control stuff. I'm for using a more humanistic motivation technique. What about using goal setting? I've heard that it's been successful in a number of industries.

Roy: Isn't goal setting a rather simplistic approach to a complicated problem? I don't think the framers would go for goals that we imposed on them; and if you ask them to set a goal, they would probably set one even lower so they would have more time to do a real quality job.

Do you have an answer for RDC's behavior problem? If not, perhaps the concepts in this and the next chapter will clarify some issues and help you when you run up against behavioral problems. As you can see from the RDC example, motivation is rather complex with no simple answers. In the next two chapters we will cover four widely used motivation strategies: organizational behavior modification, pay, job design, and goal setting. A basic understanding of these techniques will give you some insights into solving complex motivation problems, such as the one faced by RDC. The key is to use the theoretical knowledge from the last chapter in combination with the practical knowledge presented in this and the next chapter.

Motivating with Organizational Behavior Modification

The most basic goal of motivation is changing behavior. While there are many strategies to accomplish this goal, one of the most powerful is behavior modification (or "behavior mod" as it is often called)—the process of changing behavior by managing the consequences that follow some behavior. While behavior mod has been around for a long time, its use for modifying work behavior is quite recent.[1] Behavior modification applied to organizational situations is often termed **organizational behavior modification** (or "OB mod" for short).

The key to applying OB mod is to decide which behaviors to target for change, what rewards to use, and how often to give rewards. This section will cover each of these topics along with an evaluation of the pros and cons of using OB mod. The chapter begins with an overview of the behavorial change process.

■ The Behavior Modification Process

Before we begin with the strategies for changing behaviors, it will be useful to put behavior mod in a conceptual framework. The **S-O-B-C model** is one useful way of looking at the behavior modification process.[2] It recognizes four parts of the process: *S*, for stimulus; *O*, for the human organism or person; *B*, for behavior; and *C*, for consequences. Figure 6.1 outlines the S-O-B-C process and the next few paragraphs define the terms.

Stimulus   The *S* in the model stands for stimulus, which includes any environmental cue that plays a role in eliciting behavior. Examples might include noise, a coworker's comment, a machine's actions, or a paycheck received. The stimulus is a cue for behavior, not necessarily the direct cause.

Person or Organism   The *O* part of the model stands for the person, including motivational patterns, personality, perception processes. Much of what we discussed in the last chapter about motivating behavior with expectancy theory and need theory applies to this part of the model.

Behavior   The *B* aspect of the model, behavior, means the observable, tangible things a person does. Behavior includes speech, nonverbal cues, movements. In organizations, we are particularly interested in work

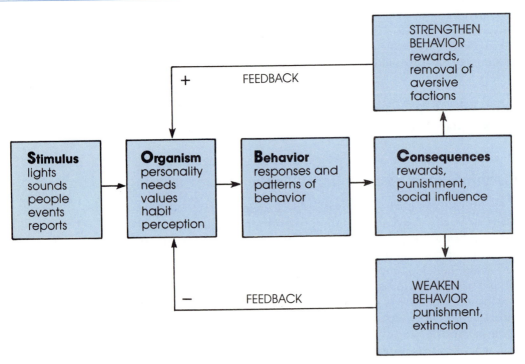

Figure 6.1. The behavior modification process.[3]

6.1 | *Examples of Behavior Modification*

While behavior modification has numerous possible organizational applications, examples of the most common uses are presented below:

To improve system performance. Emery Air Freight saved an estimated $3 million a year by using a behavior mod strategy that involved carefully measuring performance behaviors, charting these behaviors, and positively rewarding improvements. Behavior mod was employed in three main areas: sales and sales training, operations, and containerized shipments. An example of a behavioral change is that on-time deliveries were happening only 30 to 40 percent of the time before OB mod and 90 to 95 percent of the time after behavior mod.[4]

To improve attendance. Analysis of the process of attendance using OB mod shows that people are often rewarded for not coming to work because of sick pay or recreation programs. A large hardware store used a system where those people who had been at work

and on time were eligible to participate in a monthly drawing for a major prize such as a color television. As a result "sick leave payments decreased by 62 percent and absenteeism and tardiness were down by 75 percent."[5]

To reduce accidents. A behavior mod incentive program to reduce accidents among bus drivers resulted in a 25 percent decrease when compared to a control group who did not receive the incentives. Incentives (average value $5) included free gasoline, bus passes, plus the personal congratulations of the director of operations.[6]

For training. Programmed instruction methods are often based on behavior modification techniques. The trainee proceeds from one question to the next with immediate feedback about how accurate the answers (behaviors) are. This type of training has been used by IBM to train computer programmers, by Maytag to teach electronics skills, and by Zenith to teach sales representatives the features of their television sets.[7]

---

behaviors such as production, arriving for work on time, talking between two employees, not coming to work, or quitting the job.

Consequences The *C* part of the model is also environmental since it refers to the consequences that result from behaving such as praise or reprimands. This is a critical part of the model because behavior is very much a function of the rewards, punishments, or other outcomes that follow a given behavior. Some types of consequences strengthen behavior while others weaken behavior. We will discuss this process more fully later in the chapter.

Contingencies of Reinforcement Systematically changing the interrelationships between environmental cues (*S*), person (*O*), task performance or behavior (*B*), and consequences of reinforcements (*C*) is often referred to as managing the **contingencies of reinforcement**.[8] If a reward is contingent upon good performance, then it serves to motivate future performance. If rewards are not contingent upon performance, the they will not motivate behavior. The key parts of the process are knowing what be-

Motivation Using Behavior Modification and Pay

haviors represent good performance and developing a strategy for rewarding desired behaviors so that they will be strengthened. The first step in this management process is to target behaviors we may wish to change and then develop consequences that either strengthen or weaken the targeted behaviors.

■ Targeting Behavior

The first step in applying OB mod is to identify the critical performance-related behaviors, called **target behaviors**. These are behaviors

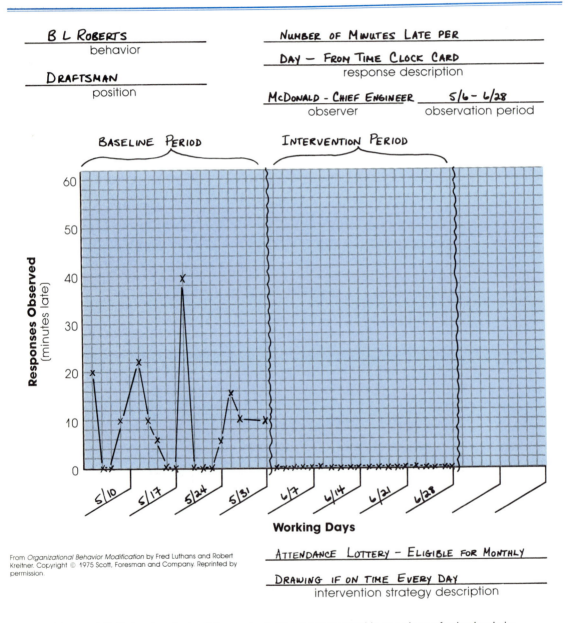

Figure 6.2. Behavioral chart for an individual expressed in number of minutes late.

chosen by the manager for emphasis or focus. If OB mod were to be used to solve RDC's problems in the opening example, the first step would be to pinpoint those behaviors they wished to change. Perhaps the behavior might be the number of hours it takes for two framers to complete one house. It is important to concentrate on actual, specific behaviors—something that can be measured, observed, described, and counted.

Another example of targeting might be the case of Helen Knapp, vice-president of Finance for RDC, who is having trouble with one of her employees. When Helen first described the employee, Marline Godell, she did not do a very good job of identifying specific behaviors. What follows are some comments Helen makes about Marline:

> *I'm fed up with Marline. She is sullen and hostile. Her constant talking annoys me and others. She has a very poor attitude and often talks back. And, she does poor quality work when and if she works at all.*

What are the target behaviors here? It's hard to tell for sure, but the words "sullen," "hostile," "poor attitude," and "annoys me," are not specific enough to begin targeting. Later, when Helen learned to be more specific, she described Marline's behaviors as follows:

> *Marline talks almost constantly. In a one-hour period, I observed her to spend forty eight minutes talking. She constantly frowns; I almost never see her smile. She is absent two or three times per month and late on the average of twice a week. Her error rate of 8 percent is much higher than the other clerk's average of three percent and the standard of five percent.*

Now we have some specific behaviors that might be used for targets for change:

1. Talking frequency
2. Frowns; doesn't smile
3. Absent
4. Late
5. Error rate

■ Charting Target Behaviors

The next step is to precisely measure the current behaviors. We need to know not only what behaviors to target, but how much and how often the behavior is happening. To systematically accomplish this task, we must measure and chart the frequency of behavior on some time dimension. This means we must **chart** how many hours it takes a carpenter to complete a house; or, in the case of Marline's problems, how often she talks, how often she smiles, how many days per month she is absent, how many minutes or times she is late per week, and what percentage error rate she maintains over the past month.

Normally, we would not attempt to change a large number of behaviors at one time because it just gets too complex. We would target a few critical ones for charting and change. Perhaps, we would start with Marline's low quality or her tendency to come in late. Charting is usually done for a single employee who is the target of the change (*see* Fig. 6.2 for an ex-

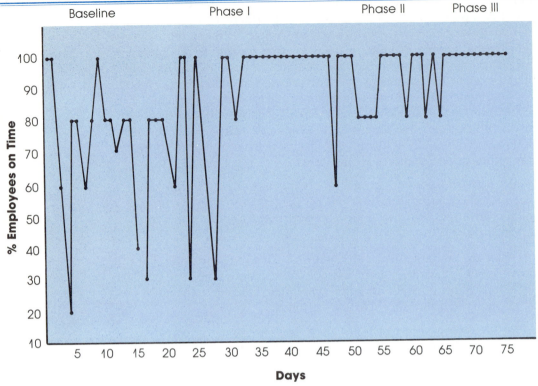

Figure 6.3. Behavioral chart for an organization expressed in percentage of employees on time.

From L. M. Miller, 1978, *Behavior Management: The New Science of Managing People at Work*, p. 299. Copyright © 1978 by John Wiley & Sons, Inc. Reprinted by permission of John Wiley & Sons, Inc.

ample of charting the late behavior of a draftsman). However, charting can also be done for an entire work unit or organization to measure organizational behavior from an overall perspective (*see* Fig. 6.3 for an example).

Charting serves two purposes. First, it provides a way of observing actual behavior to see its scope and dimensions. For example, Helen may perceive that Marline never smiles when in fact Marline smiles often except when Helen is around. Thus, a frequency count might show less of a problem with this behavior than Helen perceived. The second purpose of charting is to provide a **baseline** (a trend over a period of time to serve as the base) for measuring change. The only way we can tell if our change strategy is working is to observe actual changes in behavior over time. Referring to Figure 6.2, note the improvement in the on-time behavior of B. L. Roberts after an attendance lottery was started.

■ Managing the Contingencies

Once we have charted the targeted behavior, we get down to the crux of the problem: developing the contingency relationships between behavior and consequences. The consequences that will increase behavior are positive reinforcement (application of a desirable consequence) or negative reinforcement (removal of an aversive consequence). The strategies for decreasing behavior are extinction (doing nothing) and punishment (applica-

138   *Understanding Organizational Behavior*

tion of an unpleasant, repugnant, or aversive consequence). Each of these consequences is described in the following paragraphs.

Positive Reinforcement   When a desirable or pleasant outcome occurs after some behavior, the tendency is for us to repeat the behavior in the future. In other words **positive reinforcement** strengthens the response. Examples of positive reinforcements might be praise, doing a job particularly well, money, or simply a smile. It is important to note that all reinforcement strategies are specific to a given individual and situation. For example, RDC's framers would consider the completion of high quality work as positively reinforcing. Management, on the other hand, might see a high quantity of work to be positively reinforcing. Another example of individual differences might be the refuse collectors in the last chapter who considered time off to be positively reinforcing. Others might find time off to be punishing.

Punishment   When something bad or undesirable happens to you, the tendency is to avoid the behavior that caused it. **Punishment** is the application of an aversive or unpleasant stimulus that results in a decrease in the behavior. Examples of punishment are reprimands, assignment to unpleasant duties, frowns, fines.[9]

While punishment tends to decrease behavior, there are often undesirable side effects. We have all experienced the stomach-churning effects from punishment. It can arouse very strong emotions that can interfere with performance. There is also the possibility that the person who is punished may try to "get even" through sabotage or a work "slow down." consequently, most experts recommend avoiding punishment except when there is a need to immediately stop some behavior, such as when safety is involved.[10]

HERMAN

"Is the guy in the green jacket the one who complained about the baked potatoes?"

Figure 6.4.
Punishment may have undesirable side effects.

Motivation Using Behavior Modification and Pay

Negative Reinforcement   When someone wishes to escape or avoid some aversive situation or outcome, their behavior will be strengthened if they avoid the unpleasant situation. Another term is often used for this strategy is **negative reinforcement**, which is often confused with punishment even though the two differ rather sharply. Negative reinforcement or **escape conditioning** as it is also called,[11] is the removal of an unpleasant stimulus that results in an increase in behavior. This strategy is often confused with punishment, but the two differ rather sharply. Punishment is the application of an aversive stimulus, which later results in a decrease in behavior. Negative reinforcement involves the existence or presentation of an aversive stimulus before the behavior occurs. It is then stopped or withdrawn when the desired behavior occurs.

An example of negative reinforcement might be a manager who requires all subordinates to attend an early morning staff meeting whenever performance of the organization falls below a certain level. Subordinates would then work very hard to avoid the unpleasant early morning meetings and strive for a high level of performance.

Extinction   When nothing happens, no reinforcement or punishment follows a behavior, the behavior may decrease and eventually stop. Ignoring someone is a conscious strategy of extinction.

For an example of the extinction strategy, say you have a secretary who just loves to spend the first fifteen or twenty minutes of each morning relating various stories about the previous evening. In the past, you have been politely listening, nodding, and smiling; in other words you have been positively reinforcing the behavior. But you would like to stop the behavior and decide on extinction as your strategy. You ignore all conversation after the first two or three minutes unless it pertains to work. After a few minutes without the reinforcement of your listening and responding, the secretary stops the conversation. Of course, there are limits on extinction because others may continue reinforcing the behavior even though you have stopped.

More examples of the contingencies are presented in Table 6.1.

■ Using Contingencies

Sometimes, an even more effective strategy is to use a combination of strategies, like positive reinforcement for desired behaviors and extinction or punishment for undesirable behaviors. The key issue is to decide whether you want to increase or decrease a behavior. Once that decision is made, you must select the appropriate strategy or combination of strategies as illustrated in Figure 6.5 and the specific reward or punishment to accompany the strategy.

Avoid Negative Strategies   Normally, negative strategies should be avoided because of the possibility of undesirable side effects; such as, alienation, dissatisfaction, emotional turmoil, conflict, and even sabotage. Threatening punishment to control behavior is almost like using blackmail—avoid it whenever possible because of the problems it causes. However, there are times when behavior is so disruptive or dangerous that punishment must be used to achieve a rapid stop to the behavior, but even then

Understanding Organizational Behavior

Table 6.1 Examples of types of contingencies.

Type of Contingency	Behavior	Managerial Action	Expected Outcome
Positive Reinforcement	Subordinate completes an accurate and thorough report	Praise the employee and make a note on the employee's performance appraisal	Increased performance
Negative Reinforcement	Angry verbalization by a valued employee about having to punch a time clock	Allow the employee to keep his or her own time record	More positive verbal support for the company
Punishment	Failure of a subordinate to wear safety glasses required by company regulations	Verbally reprimand and fined	Employee will wear glasses in the future, but may be alienated from manager and company
Extinction	Co-worker frequently drops by your desk and interrupts your work	Keep on working with little or no interaction with the interrupting co-worker	Decreased interruptions from the co-worker

it may be a good idea to use a positive reinforcement-punishment combination.

Which Rewards to Use?   There are many rewards to choose from. Table 6.2 provides a list of many common ones. The key is to find the rewards that work, are easy to administer, and are cost effective for the organization. Recognition, praise, and feedback are among the most common rewards. In a behavior modification program at Emery Air Freight (*see* the Perspective: Examples of Behavior Modification), managers were taught to administer 150 kinds of recognition and praise such:[13]

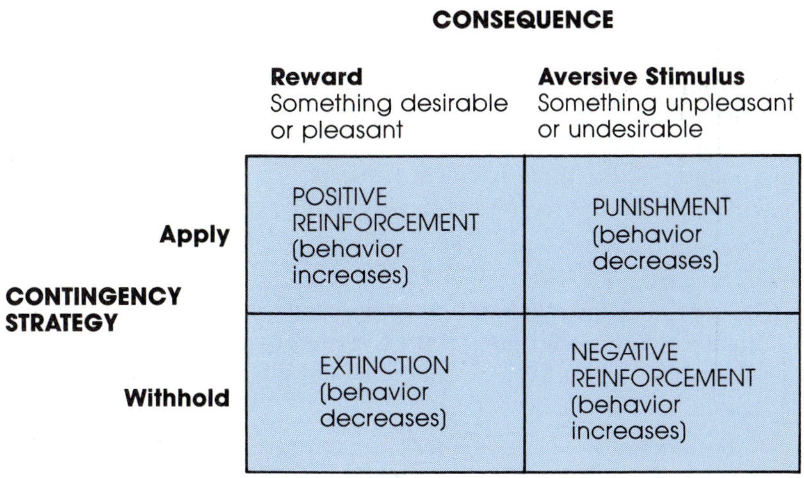

CONSEQUENCE

Figure 6.5. Contingency strategies.[14]

CONTINGENCY STRATEGY	Reward Something desirable or pleasant	Aversive Stimulus Something unpleasant or undesirable
Apply	POSITIVE REINFORCEMENT (behavior increases)	PUNISHMENT (behavior decreases)
Withhold	EXTINCTION (behavior decreases)	NEGATIVE REINFORCEMENT (behavior increases)

Table 6.2. Possible on-the-job rewards for reinforcing behavior.

Negotiables	(exchange for other rewards) Money Stocks and stock options Movie and theater tickets Vacation trips Time off with pay Profit sharing
Job-related	More job responsibility More task variety More feedback on job performance Opportunities to learn and grow Make decisions about work schedule and pace Recognition for achievements
Social	Pat on the back; compliments on work Smile; friendly greetings Verbal or nonverbal recognition or praise Friendly greetings Assignment to a desired work group
Consumables	After work wine and cheese parties Coffee break treats Dinners for two at company expense Beer parties Free lunches
Status	Office size Company car Office furnishings, chairs, desks
Visual and auditory	Office with a window Chance to redecorate work environment Plants

■ Schedules of Reinforcement

There are a number of different ways you can schedule the rewards we discussed in the last section. You can reward every desired behavior (called a *continuous* schedule); or you can reward based on a certain number of desirable responses (called a *ratio* schedule); or you can reward after a specified time period, (called an *interval* schedule). Since rewards, such as the ones shown in Table 6.2, are often expensive and difficult to administer, the ratio or interval methods are most commonly used. In the sections below, we will discuss combinations of these schedules with examples of each.

☐ "Keep up the good work, Murray"
☐ "Great going, Joe"
☐ "I liked the ingenuity you showed just now getting those crates into that container. You're running pretty consistently at 98 percent of standard. And after watching you, I can understand why."
☐ "Let me buy you a cup of coffee."

Fixed Interval   When there is a fixed time period between reinforcements, we have a **fixed interval schedule**. For example, performance appraisals in most organizations are done annually (a fixed interval).

6.2 *Vicarious Reinforcement at Reno*[15]

Casino owners are very much aware of the danger of players (particularly inexperienced ones) not being reinforced quickly enough. They know that continuous reinforcement is the quickest method of establishing desirable behavior (in this case, putting money into the machine). However, to institute a continuous method at the outset would require either that the machine be rigged (which is against the law) or that they lose money. So to approximate as closely as possible the continuous reinforcement schedule, the owners employ a concept known as "vicarious reinforcement," or reinforcement through another person's experiences. Each machine is wired into a central control, so that, when any machine hits the jackpot, sirens wail, lights flash, and bells ring. This lets everyone else in the casino know that reinforcement is possible—for those who continue to insert money!

With this type of reinforcement, behavior seems to increase as we get closer to the known time of reinforcement. For example, a person may perform rather sluggishly throughout much of the year, but when it gets close to performance appraisal time the person becomes a "ball of fire." A weekly or monthly paycheck is another example of a fixed interval schedule, since the pay comes at the same time period throughout the year. With fixed interval strategies, performance tends to improve just prior to reinforcement and fall off after reinforcement. If reinforcement stops, behavior will decrease rather rapidly.

Variable Interval   When a reward is given at variable times (variable around some average time), then we have a **variable interval schedule**. An example of a variable interval schedule might be a boss who makes an inspection of work facilities twice a week, but with no specified times for making the inspections. This schedule keeps behavior, such as cleaning work areas, at higher levels because people do not know when they will be inspected (or reinforced)—thus they are always ready.

Fixed Ratio   In a **fixed-ratio schedule** reinforcement is given after some fixed, or specified, number of responses. For example, fruit pickers on a farm who are paid by the bushel for the fruit they pick are working under a fixed-ratio schedule. In fact almost all **piece-rate** pay systems (where people are paid for each piece produced) are fixed-ratio schedules. Another example might be a firm that gives an extra day of vacation for each 30 days worked without an absence or tardiness. Fixed-ratio schedules are powerful behavior modifiers, but if the rewards are removed behavior will decline very rapidly.

Variable Ratio   Under the **variable-ratio schedule** an employee would perform the desired behavior a variable number of times before being reinforced. The reinforcement will vary around some average number of behaviors. For example, an office computer salesperson knows that on

Motivation Using Behavior Modification and Pay

Table 6.3. Intermittent schedules of reinforcement.

Schedule of reinforcement	Nature of reinforcement	Effects on behavior when applied	Effects on behavior when perceived	Example
Fixed interval	Reward on fixed time basis	Leads to average and irregular performance	Quick extinction of behavior	Weekly paycheck
Fixed ratio	Reward consistently tied to output	Leads quickly to very high and stable performance	Quick extinction of behavior	Piece-rate pay system
Variable interval	Reward given at variable intervals around some average time	Leads to moderately high and stable performance	Slow extinction of behavior	Monthly performance appraisal and reward at random times each month
Variable ratio	Reward given at variable output levels around some average output	Leads to very high performance	Slow extinction of behavior	Sales bonus tied to selling X accounts, but X constantly changes around some mean

From *Introduction to Organizational Behavior* by Richard M. Steers. Copyright © 1981 Scott, Foresman and Company. Reprinted by permission.

PERSPECTIVE

6.3 | *Rules for Using Behavior Mod in Organizations*[16]

Rule 1: Don't reward all people the same. Pay people based on their performance rather than rewarding all people the same. When everyone is paid the same, the behavior of high-performing workers is being extinguished, while low performers are being rewarded.

Rule 2: Failure to respond has reinforcing consequences. Doing nothing shapes behavior, too. Managers need to examine the consequences of doing nothing because it is an extinction strategy.

Rule 3: Be sure to tell a person what must be done to get reinforced. The behaviors that are desired should be clear to the employee. Goals and standards should be specified and the rewards readily apparent.

Rule 4: Be sure to tell people what they are doing wrong. If a manager fails to specify why a person is being punished or why a reward is being witheld, the person may associate the contingency with some past behavior rather than the target behavior.

Rule 5: Don't punish in front of others. Punishing in front of others results in double punishment since the person not only receives the punishment but also must experience a loss of face or embarrassment in front of the group. In addition, the people who witness the punishment may also feel punished vicariously (*see* the Perspective: Vicarious Reinforcement at Reno).

Rule 6: Make the consequences equal to the behavior. Be fair; do not overreward or underreward behavior. (See the discussion of equity theory in Chapter 5.)

Understanding Organizational Behavior

the average two sales will be made for every twenty five calls; however, the salesperson does not know which customers will order. The slot machines in Atlantic City are geared for a variable ratio payoff. Each time you pull the handle there is a chance, say one in ten, that there will be some type of payoff. The payoff may come after inserting one quarter or 100 quarters. Ratio schedules are the most powerful sustainers of behavior; they decline very slowly if the reinforcement is removed.[17]

■ How Often to Reward?

There is one other important consideration when designing OB mod programs: the frequency of reward. Rewards can be administered **continuously**—every desired behavior can be reinforced—or they can be administered on an **intermittent or variable basis**. Normally a behavioral change strategy will begin by reinforcing every desired response. A secretary may be complimented every time an error-free letter is typed. Then, the rewards are gradually tapered off to a variable-ratio or variable-interval schedule. Instead of praising the secretary for every perfect letter, you begin skipping a time or two until you move to a schedule where you reinforce on the average every three perfect letters, but you do the reinforcement on a random basis. The gradual movement from continuous rewards to a more variable reward pattern is called **shaping**.[18]

■ An Example of OB Mod

Rick Gomez, a production foreman in the Rockard Machinery Manufacturing plant, noted that production for the past month was down.[18] He believed that the problem was centered around workers taking unscheduled breaks. Rick had observed people wandering around and going to the bathroom at times other than during the authorized break (10:00 to 10:15 A.M. or 3:00 to 3:15 P.M.). Thus, the target behavior was taking unauthorized breaks. Rick carefully observed the behavior over the period of a week and noted each instance of an unscheduled break. He found that indeed the workers were taking unauthorized breaks, mostly about 9:00 A.M., 11:00 A.M., 2:00 P.M. and 4:00 P.M.; in other words, in the hour between the scheduled breaks. When asked why they were taking an unscheduled break the usual excuse was having to go to the bathroom—"I just couldn't wait."

From a behavior mod standpoint, Rick figured that the workers were being negatively reinforced for their behavior (they were escaping from a dull, boring, hot job) and at the same time they were being positively reinforced for the behavior (they had an extra chance to smoke, to socialize, to rest). Thus there was a powerful force toward maintaining and strengthening the behavior.

What should Rick do? In most organizations where the managers are not familiar with behavior mod, they would attempt to punish the offenders. This would be difficult because it is hard to prevent people from going to the bathroom if they really have to go, and how to do you know if they do or don't? While punishment or the threat of punishment might decrease the undesirable behavior, it might also result in union grievances, production slowdowns, quality problems, or sabotage.

Rick solved the problem by computing the dollar value of the group incentive pay that was lost because of unscheduled breaks. He then fed this information back to the workers while pointing out that staying on the job meant money to them all. In this case Rick was successful—the workers decided that money was a stronger reward than socializing with friends and withdrawing from the job. However, it is possible that the incentive reward would not be strong enough to offset the other behavior. If this had been the case, Rick would have the difficult problem searching for other reinforcers to resolve his problem.

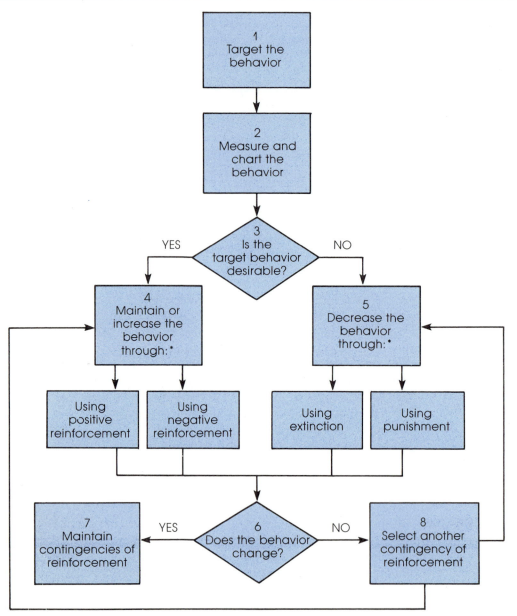

*A schedule of reinforcement (Table 6.3) must also be designed.

Figure 6.6. Behavior modification application.

Understanding Organizational Behavior

■ Summary of Behavior Mod Application Steps

Now that we have covered the major aspects of OB mod, let's summarize how it is applied by referring to Figure 6.6. Behavior is first targeted for change [1] and charted [2] to formulate a baseline for measuring behavioral change. Then, depending upon whether the behavior is desirable or undesirable [3], a change strategy is chosen. For increasing desirable behaviors, we can use either positive or negative reinforcement [4]. For eliminating undesirable behaviors, we use extinction and/or punishment [5]. A schedule of reinforcement (fixed interval, fixed-ratio, variable interval, or variable-ratio) must also be chosen. If the actual behavior we have been charting changes [6], then all we have to do is keep up the same reinforcement contingencies and schedule [7]. But, if the behavior does not change, we must select another contingency of reinforcement, or another schedule of reinforcement or both [8]. The process is continued until the desired behavioral response is obtained.

■ Controversies Surrounding Behavior Mod

Do managers have the ethical right to manipulate and control their employees' behavior? This issue is a central focus of Skinner's book, *Beyond Freedom and Dignity*.[19] It has also been a concern of a number of organizational theorists.[20] It can be argued that behavior mod strategies ignore the individuality of people, restrict freedom of choice, and ignore the fact that people can be motivated by intrinsic rewards.[21] Each of these arguments has some merit, but the position of the critics often misrepresents and distorts the recommendations of behaviorists.[22]

On the positive side the argument runs like this: since a manager's task is to manage the behavior of employees so that they accomplish organization objectives, behavior mod is a natural and inevitable part of the managerial process. Skinner argues that we are constantly affecting others' behavior whether we intend to or not. Every time we smile, frown, criticize, or praise, we are reinforcing or punishing a behavior. We are all conscious or unconscious behavior modifiers. If so, why not recognize and understand what we are doing and make sure we reinforce those behaviors that are desirable?

An important aspect of any management strategy, including OB mod, is to avoid the misuse of behavioral control. In fact, if managers misuse behavior mod, they may find that workers will "no longer allow themselves to be pushed around,"[23] but instead will insist on fair and equitable treatment.

Motivating with Pay

Pay is one of the most widely used, and often misused, rewards applied to motivate work behavior. Pay is simple because it can serve to reinforce so many needs. One person may want money to remodel a house while another may want money to buy a car. Most people find money to be desirable and positively reinforcing. Money can serve to fulfill our basic needs for shelter and food. It can and does serve as a status or esteem-related reward for many people, especially at management levels. But money costs the organization—it directly affects the bottom line. Thus, it may be one of the most costly ways of motivating people unless the increased performance pays for the increased pay.

In this section, we will briefly examine four major pay strategies: wages and salaries, merit pay, piece rates, and commissions.[24]

■ Wages and Salaries

Hourly, weekly, or monthly pay seldom motivates the work behavior except for the decision to join or leave the organization—a very important consideration. The reason salary does not motivate is that wages and salaries are usually not *tied to performance*. For example, a carpenter with RDC receives $10 per hour while an office worker receives $1,800 per month. Each is paid regularly as long as they maintain some minimal level of performance. When there is no monetary incentive to perform, people are likely to perform only at a minimally acceptable level. Of course, people are often motivated by other factors such as the possibility of promotion or recognition; or, in the case of RDC's carpenters, by doing high quality work that resulted in feelings of satisfaction.

For pay to motivate, it must be tied to performance. In the next section, we will look at how merit pay attempts to do this.

■ Merit Pay

To solve the problems posed by wages and salaries, we try to design **incentive systems**—those that will provide an incentive to perform. The first of three we will discuss is **merit pay**, a system used primarily with white-collar workers, that attempts to link pay with merit or performance. People who have performed the best this year will get, say a 20 percent pay raise, while those who are mediocre performers will get no raise. While this scheme sounds easy enough, it does not always work in practice.[25] The central problem is measuring work performance. Performance appraisals are often distorted and biased and thus not related to performance. In Chapter 4, we covered some of the perceptual problems that contribute to this problem.[26]

There are a number of reasons for poor performance appraisals in addition to perceptual errors. For example, supervisors are sometimes more interested in keeping their employees happy than in improving performance. In addition, pay may not be seen as a reward if the person perceives inequities (*see* the discussion in Chapter 5 on equity theory). Even a pay raise may be seen as a threat if it is not as much as expected or lower than the raises of others.[27]

But, in spite of these difficulties, merit pay can be properly designed to motivate, and some organizations have been successful with this approach.[28] The key is to use a fair and accurate performance appraisal system, such as management-by-objectives (to be discussed in the next chapter). When merit pay is clearly tied to performance, it does motivate effective work behavior.

■ Piece-Rate Pay

When someone is paid for the number of pieces or units that are produced, it is called **piece-rate** pay. In theory, a fixed-ratio reinforcement schedule, such as earning $1 for each toaster produced, should be a powerful motivator. It can be, but seldom is.

The problem with piece rates revolves around *standards*. How much time should be allowed to produce one toaster? Say the standard says it should take ten minutes for a skilled employee to make a toaster. If the piece-rate is $1 for each toaster completed, then the skilled employee should make about $6 per hour. Ideally, the company would like to see each employee produce more, say seven to eight an hour. But what if almost everyone produces twelve toasters per hour with what seems to be little effort? And what if the foreman only makes $10 per hour—$2 less than the average employee? Something has to give. What usually happens is that management says, "Woops, we made a mistake. The rate should be $.50 per toaster, not the overly generous dollar." It is pretty easy to predict what will happen. The employees will be disgruntled, they will feel betrayed and punished, they will cease to respond to piecework as a motivation scheme.

Thus, piece-rate pay schemes may not result in improved performance because workers may perceive that performance will not lead to the desired outcomes in the long run.[29] Even when an individual believes that performance will lead to outcomes, group members may exert so much pressure that the individual conforms (more information on these group issues will be covered in Chapter 9).

■ Commissions

Many sales positions are paid on a **commission** or commission-plus-salary basis. The pay is usually based on a percentage of the value of the total sales made by the individual; for example, 5 percent of every sale made by the car salesperson goes to the individual as pay. Some of the same problems discussed under piecework apply to commission pay schemes. It is possible to find an organization's best sales representative making more than the boss. Thus, informal limits to sales commissions are sometimes established and enforced.

Another problem with commissions is that they foster competition between salespeople that can cause problems. For example, in a furniture sales business the salespeople were stealing each others customers, thus causing a great deal of friction and conflict that was alienating customers. In this case there may be a tendency for the short-term goal of commission maximization to overrule the perhaps more important long-term goal of customer satisfaction.

In spite of these problems, commission-pay systems can work quite well, especially when a salesperson works alone. Many sales jobs do not require teamwork, and thus group pressure to conform is often lower than with piecework. Commissions provide immediate and direct link of pay with performance (behavior and contingency are linked), and they may provide a gauge of achievement for a high-achieving individual who often gravitates to sales.

■ Conclusions About Using Pay for Motivation

Most wage and salary systems do not motivate behavior because they are based on a fixed interval schedule with little direct ties with work performance. Merit, incentive, and commission pay all seek to rectify this problem by linking pay with performance. While there are problems with evaluating performance and setting standards that may frustrate our efforts to design these systems, these incentive systems can and often do serve as effective motivators of work behavior. The key is to unambiguously and fairly link pay with the desired work behavior. One effective way to do this is by setting clear goals, the topic covered in the next chapter.

6.4 The Tricky Business of Giving Rewards

When B.F. Skinner taught pigeons to play ping-pong by rewarding them with food pellets, the world sat up and took notice. Clearly his methods of producing and reinforcing behavior were impressive, and if they worked with birds, they might augur well for molding human behavior. Teachers began using more incentives to learning in the classroom. They found that rewards can backfire. A psychologist, Edward L. Deci, at the University of Rochester, learned the same thing about college students. They also lose interest in an activity if researchers reward it to death.

Employers uncovered a nest of other problems as they restudied traditional incentive pay. In his study of piece-rate pay in industry, William F. Whyte found it is tricky to know just how much more pay is necessary to get employees to work faster. And then it looked like praise, not money, might be a cheaper and more successful reinforcer. But management has had difficulty tooling up factories to give compliments. When industry began to institute piece-rate incentives, employees learned to slow down production while the rate was being set. Then they could easily earn bonuses by producing more items than necessary to earn their old salaries. Rewards, Whyte reported, motivate workers only when they fit into the social fabric of the factory or office. Humans are more complicated to manipulate than pigeons.

An old man in a folk tale, however, learned to turn confusion into order, to right the upside-down effects of rewards.

He lived alone on a street where boys played noisily every afternoon. One day the din became too much, and he called the boys into his house. He told them he liked to listen to them play, but his hearing was failing and he could no longer hear their games. He asked them to come around each day and play noisily in front of his house. If they did, he would give them each a quarter. The youngsters raced back the following day, and made a tremendous racket in front of the house. The old man paid them, and asked them to return the next day. Again they made noise, and again the old man paid them for it. But this time he gave each boy only 20 cents, explaining that he was running out of money. On the following day, they got only 15 cents each. Furthermore, the old man told them, he would have to reduce the fee to five cents on the fourth day. The boys became angry, and told the old man they would not be back. It was not worth the effort, they said, to make noise for only five cents a day.

Chapter Review

■ **Behavior modification** or **organizational behavior modification**, the process of changing behavior by managing the consequences that follow some behavior, follows a process known as **S-O-B-C**. An environmental **stimulus** is a cue to the person or **organism** for **behavior**. Then, the **consequences** that follow the behavior will either strengthen or weaken future behavior. Systematically changing the interrelationships between the S-O-B-C variables is known as managing the **contingencies of reinforcement**.

■ Behavior mod has been used for a number of different organizational purposes, including improving system performance, reducing accidents, improving attendance, and for training.

■ The key elements of behavior mod process are: deciding which behaviors to **target**, **charting** the target behaviors, and developing the **contingencies** between behavior and consequences.

■ To increase a desirable behavior, use **positive reinforcement** or **negative reinforcement (escape conditioning)**. To decrease an undesirable behavior, use **extinction** or **punishment**. It is usually desirable to avoid negative strategies because they may have undesired side effects.

■ **Schedules of reinforcement** also have a powerful effect on the strength and duration of contingent behavior. A **fixed interval** schedule, such as a weekly paycheck, tends to elicit performance improvements just prior to the reward. **Variable interval** schedules do a much better job of maintaining behavior because the person does not know when reinforcement will happen. **Fixed ratio schedules**, involving a reward for a fixed number of responses, such as units produced, are powerful behavior modifiers although behavior will decline rapidly if the rewards are removed. **Variable ratio schedules**, such as the reinforcement a salesperson receives for making every tenth sale on the average, are quite powerful and persistent.

■ **Shaping** involves varying the frequency of rewards from **continuous** to **intermittent** so that a person's behavior is shaped in the way a manager desires.

■ **Vicarious reinforcement** is a way of providing positive reinforcement through another person's favorable experiences.

■ There is a great deal of controversy surrounding the organizational use of behavior mod. Critics claim that behavior mod ignores the individuality of people, restricts freedom of choice, and ignores intrinsic rewards. Proponents claim that since behavior modification is a natural and inevitable part of management, why not do it systematically.

■ Pay is a very useful reinforcer. It satisfies a number of needs including esteem, but it can be costly. **Wages** and **salaries** motivate people to join and organization, but they do not motivate work performance because they are not tied to behavior. **Merit pay** can motivate if it is clearly tied to performance, but accurate performance appraisal is often a problem. **Piece-rates** can also motivate because they are tied to performance; however, group dynamics and fear of a change in standards often prevents this system from reaching its' potential. **Commissions**, while also having some drawbacks like fostering competition, seem to work well when people work independently.

For Discussion

1. How does the S-O-B-C process, shown in Figure 6.1, relate to the motivation theories discussed in Chapter 5?
2. What managerial problems seem most susceptible to behavior mod strategies? Why?
3. Identify some behavior you wish to change. Precisely target the behavior and actually record the frequency of behavior on a chart. What problems did you encounter?
4. What is the difference between negative reinforcement and punishment?
5. Weigh the pros and cons of all the contingency strategies.
6. How does a manager determine which reward is appropriate for changing behavior?
7. How often must behavior be reinforced to maintain or increase it? Which reinforcement schedule is the most long-lasting?
8. Why does a manager need to consider the rules of using behavior mod shown in the Perspective: Rules for Using Behavior Mod in Organizations?
9. Do you believe that behavior mod is ethical? Defend your position.
10. Design a pay system for a fast-food restaurant that would be motivating.
11. Under what circumstances is pay not motivating?

Key Concepts and Terms

behavior modification	fixed-interval schedules
S-O-B-C model	variable-ratio schedules
contingencies of reinforcement	variable-interval schedules
	vicarious reinforcement
target behaviors	shaping
positive reinforcement	merit pay
negative reinforcement	incentive pay
punishment	piece-rate pay
extinction	commissions
fixed-ratio schedules	

Suggested Readings

Babb, H. W. and Kopp D. G. (1978). Applications of behavior modification in organizations: A review and critique. *Academy of Management Review* 3:281–92.

Fedor, D. B. and Ferris, G. R. (1981). Integrating OB mod with cognitive approaches to motivation. *Academy of Management Review* 6:115–25.

Hamner, W. C. and Hamner, E. P. (1976). Behavior modification on the bottom line. *Organizational Dynamics* Spring:3–21.

Lawler, E. E. III (1976). New approaches to pay: Innovations that work. *Personnel*, 53.

Wallace, M. J., Jr., and Fay, C. H. (1983). *Compensation theory and practice*. Boston: Kent.

The Sloppy Secretary

Helen Greco has recently been promoted to the position of senior analyst for the Research Directorate for a federal space agency. She has a personal secretary, Gladys Moore, who types research reports and correspondence, and does other normal secretarial duties. Gladys is a career civil servant. She has worked for the agency for over ten years. She is personable and performs most of her secretarial duties quite well.

But Gladys has a serious problem with typing accuracy. She types extremely fast—over 100 words per minute—but she makes many errors. She is not good at proofreading so most of the errors go undetected until Helen reviews the report. With two to three errors per page, Helen finds she is quite frustrated trying to find and correct them. Then, upon retyping, she has to carefully read again because new errors crop up. Helen has talked to Gladys and urged her to be more careful, but her performance has not changed. It is almost impossible to fire a career civil servant like Gladys, and a transfer is out of the question.

Discussion questions
1. How could behavior modification be used to improve Gladys' error rate?
2. Design a behavior mod program to correct the problem. Specify the steps that would be taken.

The Ratebusting Saleswoman[30]

Of the six people in the boy's department of a large department store, one stood out as a ratebuster: Mrs. Brown. She was small physically and very active. She had worked for the store for eight years. The other people in the department were quite cool towards Mrs. Brown since they thought she was a "*saleshog*." In other words, she would do her best to get every sale she could even at the expense of the other clerks.

The pay system was based on an hourly rate plus commission. The amount of commission was based on a quota for the current year based on the past year's performance. Clerks were paid only the hourly rate until the quota had been reached and then they were paid a commission of 5 percent of total sales for every sale they made above the quota. Commissions were paid monthly.

Mrs. Brown's sales were consistently almost twice as much as the other people in the department. Her high sales were attributable to several tactics:

- She learned when special sales were scheduled and called her customers about possible layaways.
- She acted as if she had an exclusive right to any customer that she had ever served before.
- She would skip lunch and breaks so she could be on the lookout for affluent new customers.
- She would lay claim to as many customers as possible. If she was serving one person and a likely customer came through the door, she would lay their merchandise aside and greet the new customer even though other salespersons were not busy.

Discussion questions
1. Did this pay system motivate? Why?
2. Is the system appropriate for this type of organization?
3. What dysfunctional consequences from Mrs. Brown's behavior do you predict?
4. Could the system be redesigned to be more effective?

Motivation Using Behavior Modification and Pay

REFERENCES

1. For reviews of the application of behavior mod to organizations, *see* Schneider, C. E. (1974), Behavior modification in management: A review and critique, *Academy of Management Journal* 17:528–48; Hamner, W. C. and Hamner, E. P. (1976), Behavior modification on the bottom line, *Organizational Dynamics* Spring:3–21; and Babb, H. W. and Kopp, D. G. (1978), Applications of behavior modification in organizations: A review and critique, *Academy of Management Review* 3:281–292.

2. Davis, T. R. V. and Luthans, F. (1980), A social learning approach to organizational behavior, *Academy of Management Review* 5:281–290.

3. Adapted from the S-O-B-C model developed by Davis and Luthans, A social learning approach to organizational behavior.

4. *See* 1973, At Emery Air Freight: Positive reinforcement boosts performance, *Organizational Dynamics* 1:41–50.

5. Babb, H. W. and Kopp, D. G. (1978), Applications of behavior modification in organizations: A review and critique, *Academy of Management Review* 3:281–292.

6. Hayes, R. S.; Pine, R. C.; and Fitch, H. G. 1982, Reducing accident rates with organizational behavior modification, *Academy of Management Journal* 25:407–416.

7. Babb and Kopp, Applications of behavior modification in organizations, p. 285.

8. Hamner and Hamner, Behavior modification on the bottom line.

9. A more detailed discussion of punishment in organizations can be found in Arvey, R. D. and Ivancevich, J. M. (1980), Punishment in organizations: A review, propositions, and research suggestions, *Academy of Management Review* 5:123–132; and Sims, H. P., Jr. (1980), Further thoughts on punishment in organizations, *Academy of Management Review* 5:133–138.

10. Wheeler, H. N. (1976), Punishment theory and industrial discipline, *Industrial Relations* 15:235–43.

11. This term is used by Hamner and Hamner, Behavior modification on the bottom line.

12. Adapted from Luthans, F. (1981), *Organizational behavior*, 3rd ed., New York: McGraw-Hill, p. 251.

13. Examples from At Emery Air Freight: Positive reinforcement boosts productivity.

14. From Gray, J. L. and Starke, F. A. (1980), *Organizational behavior concepts and applications*, 2nd ed., Columbus, Ohio: Charles E. Merrill, p. 86. For another perspective on this topic *see* Manz, C. C. and Sims, H. P., Jr. (1981), Vicarious learning: The influence of modeling on organizational behavior, *Academy of Management Review* 6:105–113.

15. Based on Hamner, W. C. (1983), Using reinforcement theory in organizational settings, in *Organizational behavior and management*, ed. H. L. Tosi and W. C. Hamner, pp. 534–541.

16. Hamner, W. C. (1982), Reinforcement theory, in *Organizational behavior and management: A contingency approach*, 3rd ed., eds. H. L.

Tosi and W. C. Hamner, New York: Wiley; and Jablonsky, S. and Devries, D. (1972), Operant conditioning principles extrapolated to the theory of management, *Organizational Behavior and Human Performance* 7:340–358.

17. Skinner, B. F. (1969), *Contingencies of reinforcement*, New York: Appleton-Century-Crofts.

18. Based on an example originally presented in Luthans, *Organizational behavior.* For additional information about implementing behavior mod programs, *see* Luthans and Kreitner, Organizational behavior modification; and Miller, L. M. (1978), *Behavior management: The new science of managing people at work,* New York: Wiley.

19. Skinner, B. F. (1971), *Beyond freedom and dignity*, New York: Knopf.

20. *See* Fry, F. L. (1974), Operant conditioning in organizational settings: Of mice or men?, *Personnel* 51(4):17–24; and a whole series of articles in the *Academy of Management Review* beginning with Locke, E. A. (1977), The myths of behavior mod in organizations, 2:543–553; and ending with Parmerlee, M. and Schwenk, C. (1979), Radical behaviorism in organizations: Misconceptions in the Locke-Gray debate, 4:601–607. For an interesting debate on organizational behavior mod *see* the Luthans-Smith debate in Karmel, B., ed. (1980), *Point and counterpoint in organizational behavior*, Hinsdale: Dryden, pp. 47–93.

21. For a review *see* W. C. Hamner, (1983), Using reinforcement theory in organizational settings, in *Organizational behavior and management*, ed. H. L. Tosi and W. C. Hamner.

22. Hamner, Using reinforcement theory in organizational settings.

23. Hamner, Using reinforcement theory in organizational settings, p. 541.

24. For thorough coverage of pay issues *see* Wallace, M. J., Jr. and Fay, C. H. (1983) *Compensation theory and practice*, Boston: Kent; and Lawler, E. E., III (1981), *Pay and organizational development* Reading, Mass.: Addison-Wesley.

25. *See* Hamner, W. C. (1975), How to ruin motivation with pay, *Compensation Review*, third quarter; and Golberg, M. H. (1977), Another look at merit pay programs, *Compensation Review*, third quarter:20–28.

26. Latham, G. P. and Wexley, K. N. (1981), *Increasing productivity through performance appraisal*, Reading, Mass.: Addison-Wesley.

27. *See* Lawler, E. E., III (1971), *Pay and organizational effectiveness: A psychological view*, New York: McGraw-Hill for a complete discussion of pay issues including equity.

28. Hamner, How to ruin motivation with pay; and Golberg, Another look at merit pay programs, have some suggestions for making merit pay systems work.

29. *See* Wallace and Fay, *Compensation theory and practice.* For classic studies showing the effects of piece work, *see* Whyte, W. (1955), *Money and motivation* New York: Harper and Row; and Hickson, D. (1961), Motives of people who restrict their output, *Occupational Psychology* 35:479–503.

30. Adapted from an example given by Dalton, M. (1974), The rate-buster: The case of the salewoman, in *Varieties of work experience: The social control of occupational groups and roles*, ed. P. L. Steward and M. G. Cantor, pp. 206–214 New York: Schenkman.

Job Design and Goal Setting

PREVIEW

- What makes one job so good that we really like it and another one so bad we cannot stand it?

- How can flexible working hours help enrich almost any job?

- Why is the statement "job enrichment usually increases effort and productivity" false?

- How can a manager actually conduct a job enrichment effort? Learn the steps with the aid of a self-help guide.

- Did you know that the mere presence of goals can result in increase performance?

- Can you write a clear, specific goal? Learn how.

- Is management by objectives a concept whose "time is past"?

- Which motivation strategy should you use?

- Which motivation strategy is the most powerful: goals, job enrichment, or money?

Preview Case: The Word Processing Center

Job Design
- ■ What is job design?
- ■ Job enrichment concepts
- ■ Applying the job characteristics model
- ■ How to enrich jobs
- ■ *Perspective*: Flexitime
- ■ Benefits of job enrichment
- ■ *Perspective*: A Manager's Self-Help Guide to Job Enrichment
- ■ The sociotechnical approach: Enriching jobs at Volvo

Goal Setting
- ■ Goal-setting theory
- ■ Goal setting with loggers: An example
- ■ Management by objectives (MBO)
- ■ *Perspective*: Is MBO Effective?
- ■ Goal setting: A technique that works

Choosing a Motivation Strategy
- ■ The job itself and the motivation strategy
- ■ Organizational climate and motivation strategy
- ■ *Perspective*: Motivation Techniques: Which Work Best?

Summary
- ■ Chapter review
- ■ For discussion
- ■ Key concepts and terms
- ■ Suggested readings

Cases and Incidents
- ■ Keypunch Operation
- ■ The Reluctant Entrepreneurs

References

PREVIEW CASE: THE WORD PROCESSING CENTER

Wendy Maki thought to herself that she had worked hard to get here. And she was pleased. Just think, only six years ago she had been a typist (for another firm)—now she was the new Director of Administration for Sun Island Corporation. It had been a lot of work to finish college on a part-time basis, but she had done it and now she was beginning to reap the rewards.

During her interviews Wendy had learned that the past director left because he could not get the Word Processing Center (one of several divisions under her) performance up to the level expected by top management. It seems that all the operators are disgruntled and dissatisfied. They leave the first chance they get. So far it has been relatively easy to find replacements, but each new person must be trained and some just don't work out.

Sun Island seems to be losing money and effectiveness because of the problem. There has even been discussion that the word processing center is nothing but a typing pool and should thus be disbanded and all the operators returned to separate directors. (Perhaps the word processing center *is* the modern-day equivalent of a typing pool using sophisticated technology, including computers.)

Wendy figures that her knowledge of working-level people combined with her academic preparation will yield the key to motivating these people.

Managers are sometimes confronted with complex problems that simultaneously involve poor performance and job dissatisfaction. Sometimes these problems are centered around the very structure of the job itself—its design. In this chapter, we will discuss two major strategies for dealing with structural problems: job enrichment and goal setting. We may also see some possible solutions to Wendy's problem and for the problem that Reliance Development Company was experiencing in Chapter 6—that of framers who were motivated to produce high quality but low quantity.

Job Design

Every time a manager assigns work, gives instructions, or checks to make sure something is done, job redesign is taking place.[1] Consciously or unconsciously, managers are constantly changing the jobs of their subordinates. Since this type of change is inevitable, it makes sense to plan the structure of jobs deliberately so that they are as motivating as possible. That is what this section is about—systematically redesigning jobs as part of the basic managerial task.

■ What Is Job Design?

Job design is the deliberate, purposeful planning of the job including all its structural and social aspects and their effects on the employee. It is a broad concept that can refer to any part or combination of parts of the job. Figure 7.1 provides an overview of the dimensions of job design that high-

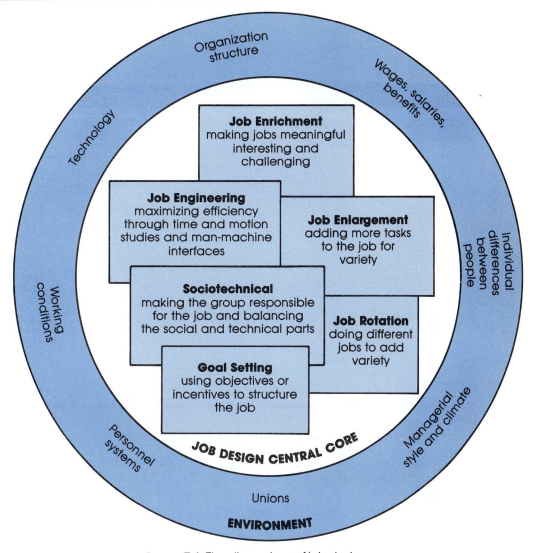

Figure 7.1. The dimensions of job design.

From D. Umstot, 1979, Job design, in *Organizational behavior*, 2nd ed., ed. D. Hellriegel and J. W. Slocum. Copyright © 1979 by West Publishing Company, St. Paul, Minn. Used with permission.

lights their interconnecting, overlapping nature. It also indicates that the *environment*—unions, bosses, technology, working conditions, personnel policies, wages, structure—all affect job design.

In this section, we will concentrate most heavily on one aspect of job design—job enrichment; a strategy that is particularly aimed at improving employee motivation and work satisfaction.[2] We will also briefly cover the sociotechnical approach to job design that is being used by Volvo and many other companies.

■ Job Enrichment Concepts

Job Characteristics   While there are several valid approaches to job enrichment,[3] the **job characteristics model**, developed by Hackman

Figure 7.2. Job characteristics model.

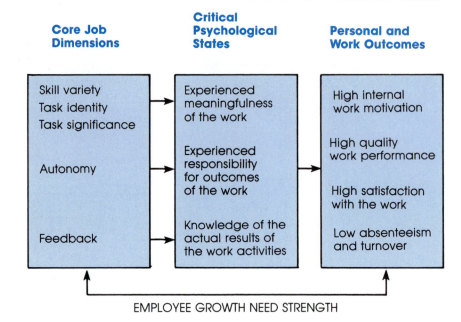

Core Job Dimensions

Skill variety
Task identity
Task significance

Autonomy

Feedback

Critical Psychological States

Experienced meaningfulness of the work

Experienced responsibility for outcomes of the work

Knowledge of the actual results of the work activities

Personal and Work Outcomes

High internal work motivation

High quality work performance

High satisfaction with the work

Low absenteeism and turnover

EMPLOYEE GROWTH NEED STRENGTH

From J. R. Hackman and G. R. Oldham, 1975, Development of the diagnostic survey, *Journal of Applied Psychology* 60:161. Copyright 1975 by the American Psychological Association. Reprinted/adapted by permission of the authors and publisher.

and Oldham[4] and shown in Figure 7.2, has been selected because it clearly specifies the characteristics that are needed to create an enriching job. Thus, we will define **job enrichment** as the process of making jobs more interesting, meaningful, and challenging by using the proper blend of the following job dimensions or characteristics:

☐ *Skill variety*—doing different things; using valued skills, abilities, and talents.

☐ *Task identity*—doing a job from beginning to end; the whole job rather than bits and pieces.

☐ *Task significance*—the degree that the job has a meaningful impact on others in the organization; the importance of the job.

☐ *Autonomy*—freedom to do the work; discretion in scheduling, decision making, and means for accomplishing the job.

☐ *Feedback*—clear and direct information from the job itself about job outcomes and performances.

Psychological States   If the first three job characteristics—skill variety, task identity, and task significance—are sufficiently present, then the job will probably have *meaning* for the individual. If the fourth characteristic, autonomy, is sufficiently present, then the individual will experience a sense of *responsibility*. If the fifth characteristic, feedback from the job, is present, the individual will experience the *knowledge of results* of work performance, thus providing feedback for correction and satisfaction for achievement. If any one of the three psychological states is missing, the job will be unenriched even if the others are present.

Understanding Organizational Behavior

Growth Need Strength   As we saw in Chapter 5, **growth needs** are the need to develop, to learn, to experience new skills, and to have a challenge. Growth need strength moderates the relationship between the job characteristics and the predicted outcomes. People with high growth need strength respond more favorably to job enrichment than do those with low growth need strength.[5] Apparently, a low growth need strength inhibits the formation of the critical psychological states, and thus, for that person, the job may be unenriched in spite of a generous amount of all the job characteristics.

An Enriched Job: The Surgeon   A job that is high on all the core job dimensions is the surgeon. There is a constant opportunity for using highly varied skills, abilities, and talents in diagnosing and treating illnesses. There is plenty of task identity since the same surgeon normally does the diagnosis, performs the operation, and monitors the convalescence. Task significance is also high, since much of the surgeon's work is life or death to the patient. Autonomy is quite high since the physician is the final authority on the procedures and techniques of the job (perhaps malpractice suits are causing a lower sense of autonomy than surgeons once had). Finally, the feedback from the job is excellent because the surgeon can tell almost immediately if the operation was successful. And, of course, a fully recovered patient is powerful feedback.

■ Applying the Job Characteristics Model

There are a number of different ways to find out or diagnose job enrichment problems, including observations, interviews, work-flow analysis and questionnaires.[6] Perhaps the simplest way is to just observe what is going on with a critical eye. For example, go back to the problem faced by Wendy Maki in the introductory case. On a tour of the various functions that report to her, Wendy visits the Word Processing Center.

Ken Asato, the supervisor of the center, says, "The operators just don't seem to be motivated toward anything except avoiding work. Turnover and absence rates are much higher than for other administrative jobs in the company. I've tried everything I can think of including piped-in music, carpeted floors, special pay, and special attention. Nothing seems to work. I'm really at my wits end. Maybe the best thing for me to do is find another job."

Wendy replies, "Hang in there, Ken. Maybe I can help you solve this problem."

Having recently completed a course in organizational behavior, Wendy is particularly attuned to the possibility of using job enrichment. After Wendy spent some time analyzing the job, she came up with a number of observations about the word processing jobs. They are listed below using job characteristics terminology:

☐ *Skill variety*—Moderately low. Once the machines are mastered, the job is basically just different forms of a single skill—typing. Thus there is little skill variety or challenge.

☐ *Task identity*—Virtually nonexistent. Jobs are assigned to keep a continuous workload rather than to provide whole, identifiable jobs.

☐ *Task significance*—Low, because the employees do not see the importance of the seemingly endless flow of paperwork.

☐ *Autonomy*—None. Employees punch in and out on time clocks and breaks are rigidly controlled. The supervisors arrange and direct the daily tasks. Quality control and proofreading are done by another section.

☐ *Feedback*—Very low. Once the product is sent back to the using department, there is no contact with the typist concerning the quality or acceptability of the product. If retyping or corrections are needed, they are given to the first available typist rather than the person who originally typed the product.

Wendy observes that this is a very unenriched job with particular problems in the areas of task identity, autonomy, and feedback. She figures that if she can do something to enrich the job, she can probably cure some of the problems with dissatisfaction and turnover.

■ How to Enrich Jobs

Although the techniques used for enriching jobs are often specific to the job being redesigned, there are several common **implementing concepts** that are applicable to a wide variety of jobs.[7]

Client Relationships

One of the most important approaches is to get the worker in touch with the user of the output. Too often employees wind up working for the boss rather than the customer or client. In the word processing example, Wendy suggested that certain operators be assigned to specific clients or groups of clients, such as sales or engineering, so that when problems arise or peculiarities are present the operator can work directly with the client.

Schedule Own Work

Most employees are fully capable of scheduling their own work. Deadlines or goals may be set by the supervisor. Within that broad guidance, the individual worker can be allowed to set the pace for meeting the deadline.

Another form of scheduling that is becoming very common is **flexitime**,[8] which allows the employee, within certain limits, to vary arrival and departure times to suit individual needs and desires. Flexitime facilitates self-work scheduling, since the supervisor cannot always be there to breathe down the employee's neck. Wendy knows flexitime is particularly applicable to the jobs in word processing because the operators do their work independently—they are alone in front of their machine. Thus it will not make any difference if an operator works from 6:00 A.M. to 3:00 P.M. or from 9:00 A.M. to 6:00 P.M.

Ownership of the Whole Product

An employee who builds an entire television set, assembles an entire washing machine, or types a whole report feels more identification with the finished product. Allowing employees to perform a whole or complete task cycle helps create a sense of pride and achievement. Another version of this concept is to assign drivers their own vehicle so they can take pride in its upkeep and repair. Ownership can also be created by assigning people total responsibility for a certain geographical area. The Indiana Bell Company found substantial improvements in performance and satisfaction when telephone directory compilers were

7.1 Flexitime

Flexitime is an import from Germany where it has become extremely popular.[9] The simplist form of flexitime is shown in the example below. Here we find that Connie Young is an early riser. She starts work at 6:30 A.M., works eight hours with one-half hour for lunch, and gets off work at 3 P.M. On the other hand Joe Knapp likes to sleep late so he arrives at work at 9:30 A.M. and works until 6:00 P.M. Their fellow employees arrive at the time of their choice so long as it is before core hours begin at 9:30 A.M.

The idea behind flexitime is that employees can choose from day to day what their work schedules will be without having prior permission from the boss. Even though Connie usually come in early, she may wish to come in late one morning because of some late-night event the evening before. Often, restrictions are used by management to make sure that certain vital functions are covered during specified times. This can be done without adversly impacting flexitime if the employees themselves are given the responsibility for making sure a function is covered.

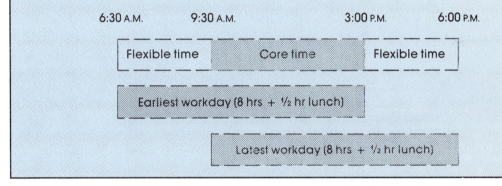

assigned a city or part of a city of their very own.[10] In Wendy's case, she made sure that each operator performed the complete task, including all aspects of the work being produced.

Direct Feedback Structures   Most feedback is filtered through the boss, and it often has a negative connotation. This job design strategy focuses attention on getting feedback directly back to the worker without management filtering. It may be a simple matter of routing reports or computer outputs directly to the employees instead of to their manager. An often-used technique is to let people check their own work so they catch their own errors.

Direct communication with others may be another way of opening feedback channels. If people in different divisions or companies are allowed to communicate directly by phone and letter, distortions and delays in feedback may be eliminated. In the word processing case, direct contact between the typist and the author was authorized in order to allow both positive and negative feedback to directly occur between the two.

7.2 | *A Manager's Self-Help Guide to Job Enrichment*[11]

Learn all you can about job enrichment. Read all the references cited in this article. Become an expert in the concepts.

Is job design a problem? Look carefully at the jobs. Are they enriched already? Ask people how they feel about the job itself—perhaps they like it the way it is. Do not rock the boat unnecessarily.

Is there some other problem besides job enrichment? Perhaps supervision, communication, or lack of planning are the real problems.

Ask the employees if they want job enrichment. If it looks like job enrichment is appropriate, then teach them what job enrichment is, what it can do for them and you, and see if they are interested in pursuing it. If not, do not begin an effort until they are ready. One aid to overcoming initial resistance is to make the job enrichment program an "experiment" done on a trial basis.

Establish the goals that you want job enrichment to accomplish. Be sure they are specific and that the end results desired are measurable and time-phased.

Hold a concept workshop with key supervisors and workers away from your office. Get a room in a local hotel or motel so that you will not be interrupted during the workshop. Be sure that everyone understands job enrichment theory and the implementing concepts.

Brainstorm job enrichment ideas during the workshop. Allow one hour for brainstorming ideas. The purpose of brainstorming is only to generate ideas, not to evaluate. The rule against any form of evaluation or criticism of any idea should be strictly enforced. Another key rule is to avoid "war stories"—you are looking for ideas, large numbers of ideas. During a one-hour brainstorming session, you should have between 100 and 200 ideas. (*see* Chapter 13 for details on brainstorming) Try to use two recorders, preferably people who are not part of the group, to write the ideas on flipcharts and post the completed pages on the wall.

Pick out the top ten ideas. Have each participant pick his top ten ideas and put them on 3 x 5 cards so that a preliminary cut of the important ideas has been made. (Number all the ideas on the flipcharts to make the process easier.)

Sort and categorize the ideas into some meaningful sets for discussion and analysis.

Analyze the ideas. If they have merit, study and implement them. If not, discard them. (Be sure to provide feedback to the participants of the session about the ideas that were discarded or disapproved.)

Implement the ideas.

Evaluate the job enrichment effort. Did the jobs change? Were your goals met? What improvements resulted?

From D. D. Umstot and W. E. Rosenbach, From theory to action: Implementing job enrichment in the Air Force, *Air University Review*, Vol. XXXI no. 3, March–April 1980.

■ Benefits of Job Enrichment

Job enrichment can lead to improvements in both job performance and job satisfaction.

Performance Improvements Job enrichment does not usually result in increased effort or individual productivity gains.[12] Motivation changes are often directed more toward improved quality or service. However, this does not mean that major performance benefits do not accrue. For example, one common theme of job enrichment is to get rid of inspectors and checkers so than feedback and autonomy can be improved. This action frees up the former inspectors for direct production. Also, the emphasis on quality can result in fewer rejects, lower parts consumption, less waste, and improved customer satisfaction.

Satisfaction Impact   Job enrichment consistently results in improved attitudes and quality of working life.[13] These outcomes are not only socially desirable, but have bottom-line benefits to the organization.[14] People who are satisfied are more likely to come to work (absenteeism declines), and they are more likely to stay in the job (turnover rates are lower). Both of these outcomes have major impact on organizational costs. There are also many less tangible benefits, such as employee goodwill, family support and happiness, and even improved employee health.

■ The Sociotechnical Approach: Enriching Jobs at Volvo

Volvo has been an innovator in another form of job design, **sociotechnical systems**.[15] This approach attempts to design jobs to optimize the relationship between the technical system (such as the auto assembly line) and the social system (the people who work on the assembly line). The sociotechnical approach often centers around the use of **self-managing work groups** (teams who are given autonomy over many aspects of the job) for tasks that were formerly done on an assembly line.[16]

The president of Volvo, Pehr Gyllenhammar, decided on a risky course to improve the quality of working life at Volvo—he built an entirely new plant at Kalmar that was designed around sociotechnical concepts.[17] To accomplish the job redesign, the conventional auto assembly line that moved through a warehouse had to be changed so that the work remained relatively stationary and the materials were brought to the work station. To accomplish this task, a special car carrier had to be built that could transport and position an entire car (*see* Fig. 7.3).

The basis of sociotechnical approaches is not only technology, such as new carriers and plant layouts, but also work groups organized so as to optimize the social aspects of the system. The Kalmar plant uses twenty-percent groups organized to perform all work on certain subsystems, such as electrical systems, instrumentation, steering and controls, and interiors. Each team has its own area of the shop floor and its own rest area. Each team organizes itself. Responsibilities and work procedures are not dictated by management. Teams may elect to organize so that each member specializes in an individual job, they may organize into subteams to do parts of the job, or they may devise rotation schemes.

The opportunities for self-control are substantial. Teams contract with management to deliver a certain number of items such as finished brake systems or interiors per day. The pace of work and break times are determined by the groups. Teams conduct their own inspections, and a special computer-based quality control system flashes the results back to the work stations on TV.

The results indicate that while productivity is about the same as the other Volvo plants, turnover and absenteeism are about 5 percent lower, and 80 percent of the employees think that the sociotechnical approach is a good way of organizing the workplace.

a

b

Figure 7.3. Application of the sociotechnical approach. *a.* A traditional assembly line at Volvo. *b.* Volvo's new patented car carrier.

Pehr Gyllenhammar, *People At Work*, © 1977, Addison-Wesley, Reading, Massachusetts, pp. 57, 97. Reprinted with permission.

Goal Setting

Goal setting is one of the most widely used techniques for improving motivation.[18] It is particularly important because many managers tend to focus on *activities* of their subordinates rather than *end results*. Goal setting is a way of focusing attention where it is needed—on performance. **Goal setting** is the process of developing, negotiating, and formalizing targets that an employee is responsible for accomplishing.

Even the most casual observation will reveal that people with indefinite goals often work slowly, perform poorly, lack interest, and accomplish little. On the other hand, people with clearly defined goals appear to be more energetic and more productive—they get things done within a specified time period and move on to other activities (and goals). Goals may be implicit or explicit, vague or clearly defined, self-imposed or externally imposed; but whatever their form, they serve to structure time and activities for people.

■ Goal-Setting Theory

A basis for much of the recent goal-setting research and practice has been Locke's theory of goal setting, which states that clear, moderately difficult goals, if accepted, will result in higher performance.[19] Three factors particularly important in the theory—goal clarity, goal difficulty, and goal acceptance—will be discussed in the following paragraphs.

Goal Clarity   Goals must be clear and specific to be effective directors of motivation. A goal such as "do your best to improve production" is not nearly as effective as a specific goal such as, "You are to increase production of motors by 5 percent by the end of March of this year." A goal should specify *what* is to be done (increase production of motors), *who* is to do it (you are), and *when* it is to be accomplished (by the end of March of this year). The goal should also be *measurable*—how will you know when it is done? With motor production, all we have to do is count completed motors. But what about a goal involving customer satisfaction? That is more difficult to measure (perhaps the number of complaints or a questionnaire might be used). Figure 7.4 provides a guide for writing a clear goal.

	Fill in the Blanks		Completed Example
To	(action verb)	**To**	increase
	(end result desired)		sales of tractors
by	(how much)	**by**	25 percent
within	(time)	**within**	3 months (by December 31, 1985)
	(name of person responsible)		Deryl Hardwich, sales manager

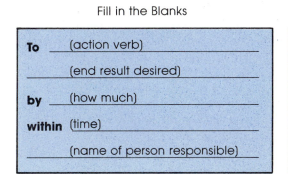
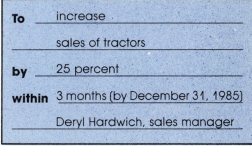

Figure 7.4. Guide for writing a clear goal.

Goal Difficulty   Setting the level of goal difficulty is an art. You want *moderately difficult* goals that will be challenging and stretching, but not too difficult. If goals are too easy, an employee may procrastinate or attack the goal lackadaisically. If the goals are too difficult, the employee may not accept the goal or attempt to meet it. In addition, a goal that is set unrealistically high may cause frustration and dissatisfaction if the goal is not attained. There can be no sense of achievement if the goal is never reached.

Goal Acceptance   If goals are not accepted, then they do not direct behavior or effort and are therefore worthless. Acceptance is a complicated issue that seems to be related to goal difficulty, whether or not the employee participated in setting the goal (to be discussed in Chapter 13), and the organizational climate (to be discussed in Chapter 17). Goals must be fair and reasonable, *and* employees must trust management.

Remember when we were discussing piecework pay in the last chapter? We noted that standards or goals seemed to be the key for designing an effective piecework system. If employees think that management is using goals as a way of squeezing out more work or exploiting them, they will be unlikely to accept the goals. A manager who uses goals as a way of clarifying what is expected rather than as a threat is more likely to be successful in obtaining goal commitment.[20]

■ Goal Setting with Loggers: An Example

There was an immediate problem confronting a large logging company located in the western United States.[21] Their truck drivers, who were unionized and paid by the hour, were underloading their trucks—they averaged only 60 percent of the truck's capacity. This cost the company dearly—extra trips, extra pay, extra trucks. The problem seemed to revolve around state laws that limited the maximum weight for each truck. If the Highway Department found a truck to be overweight, the driver would be fined and might eventually be fired.

The company negotiated with the union to set a goal. The strategy was to set a difficult, but attainable goal of loading a truck to 94 percent of its legal net weight. No monetary rewards or fringe benefits other than verbal praise were provided, and no one was to be reprimanded or criticized for not making the goal. The union felt the idea was too incredible to be taken seriously, so they said OK.

The very first month, performance increased to 80 percent of capacity, but in the second month performance declined to 70 percent capacity, apparently as a test of management's statements that no punitive steps would be taken. Fortunately, none were. By the third month performance had increased to 90 percent of capacity and remained at this level for the next seven years.

One reason this goal-setting effort worked and the goals were accepted was that informal competition developed between drivers to see who could do the best job of loading their truck to maximum capacity. They began to brag about their accomplishments. They viewed goal setting as a challenging game. They said, "It was great to beat the other guy."

■ Management by Objectives (MBO)

MBO is a widely used technique that employs goal setting as its central thrust. But MBO is a broader concept that may be closer to a philosophy of management than a specific motivation concept. **MBO** can be defined as a managerial process where superiors and subordinates jointly identify common goals needed to support the organization's purposes, define the specific areas of responsibility in terms of results expected, measure progress toward goals, and assess performance in terms of goal accomplishment.[22]

MBO differs from ordinary goal-setting programs in that it is usually company wide, it usually involves boss-subordinate dialogue about goals, and it is normally an intregral part of the organization's appraisal system, perhaps even its incentive pay system. While MBO is usually employed only at managerial levels, goal setting is often employed at lower levels as well as at managerial levels. MBO often involves complex systems of control that sometimes become its downfall if the MBO system becomes too bureaucratic and losses its original meaning.

Implementing MBO Programs

Because MBO is usually organization wide, it requires a great deal of planning and knowledge to implement effectively.[23] Figure 7.5 outlines the basic MBO process. It starts at top management level—the corporate president and board of directors. These people will often meet at some retreat site and, with the aid of a consultant, develop the long-range objectives and plans for the firm; for example, to increase our market share by reducing our prices and costs.

Next, the specific overall organizational objectives will be devised; for example, to reduce energy costs by 10 percent during the next year. Then, the objectives "waterfall" down the organizational hierarchy. Each department establishes objectives and individuals are asked to develop objectives that dovetail with corporate objectives. Once objectives are agreed upon,

PERSPECTIVE

7.3 | *Is MBO Effective?*

There seems to be a great deal of controversy about how well MBO works. One author even titled his article "MBO: An Idea Whose Time Has Gone?"[24] Apparently, the success of MBO depends a great deal on how it is installed and administered. Perhaps it is only another "gimick" that is more for show than for action?

A recent review of the literature would lead to a different conclusion.[25] Many of the 185 studies showed positive results for MBO. In fact, in 141 case studies, the ratio of positive to not-positive results was 12 to 1. More sophisticated experimental research designs were 3 to 1 in favor of MBO.

There seems to be tendencies for MBO to be more effective in the short term, say less than two years. Apparently, the initial effort generates a lot of interest, but it declines over time. Also, MBO was found to be more effective in the private sector than in the public sector and more effective in organizations that do not have direct customer contact.

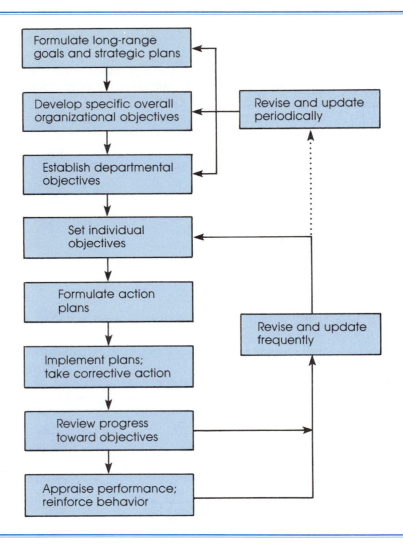

Figure 7.5. The MBO process.[26]

individuals make action plans and are allowed to pursue their objectives with some degree of freedom and discretion. Periodic progress reviews keep control without getting too overbearing.

Goals are revised frequently. For example, if our goal to reduce energy costs by 10 percent is frustrated by a 50 percent rise in electric rates, then the goal needs to be modified. Finally, the time frame for completing the objective arrives, and the person is evaluated. Was the goal met? If not, why? Is a revised goal needed? There is a continuing cycle of examination, review, and revision. It occurs more frequently at operating levels than at strategic levels.

■ Goal Setting: A Technique That Works

Goal setting is an effective strategy for changing behavior and improving performance. A review of research found that 90 percent of the studies setting specific challenging goals led to higher performance.[27] Goals clarify what is expected and provide a framework for action; and they are relative-

Understanding Organizational Behavior

ly simple to implement on an individual basis. Goals also mobilize effort, increase persistence, and direct attention.

On the other hand, MBO is considerably more difficult to put into action because it requires many changes in organizational subsystems. There is some evidence that it is an effective strategy, but given the number of research studies completed, its impact has not been as consistent as the results of simple goal-setting efforts (*see* the Perspective: Is MBO Effective?).

In the concluding section, we will examine several criteria for selecting a motivation strategy.

Choosing a Motivation Strategy

In the past chapters we have covered four basic applied motivation techniques: behavior modification, pay, job design, and goal setting. The question is, which technique to use? The answer is not simple as it will depend on the circumstances or the situation. The information presented in Figure 7.6 should aid in diagnosing motivation problems. Although the table is an oversimplification and does not cover all the possibilities, it does provide some guidance for addressing complex motivation problems in work settings.

Before proceeding with an explanation of the table, recall that the Reliance Development Company (or RDC, the opening case for Chapter 6) was having trouble motivating its framers to complete their jobs on time because the framers were so concerned about doing high quality work that it took them longer than projected to finish a job. We will use this example to illustrate how to choose and apply motivation techniques.

■ The Job Itself and the Motivation Strategy

The first step job is to ask if the job itself is boring, unenriched, and uninteresting to the people who are doing it. If the answer is "yes," then the next question is, can you do anything about it? If the answer is "yes," then

	Job itself a problem		Job itself not a problem	
	changeable	not changeable	good organizational climate	poor organizational climate
Behavior modification		X	X	X
Pay			X	
Job redesign	X			
Goal setting	X	X	X	

Figure 7.6. Application of motivation techniques.

job redesign seems to be appropriate. In addition, it would be useful to combine job redesign with goal setting to obtain maximum motivational effects.

If the job cannot be changed, and many cannot because of technology or system design, then the best way to motivate may be to combine behavior modification and goal setting. Often, the goals will provide some amount of interest to an otherwise unenriched job, and behavior mod will develop reinforcement strategies to keep the behavior sustained.

In the RDC example with the framers, we note that they already have an enriched job. They have a great deal of autonomy and feedback. They use many skills and see the whole task of building a house enfold in front of them. Thus, the job itself is not a problem.

■ Organizational Climate and Motivation Strategy

If there is nothing wrong with the job's design, then the next consideration is the organizational climate (the degree of trust, open communication, or fairness—to be covered in Chapter 17). If the climate is good, where trust and mutual respect prevail, then goal setting is appropriate, augmented by behavior modification and perhaps an incentive pay scheme (*see* the Perspective: Motivation Techniques). If the climate is poor, then goal setting will be ineffective, and we are left with behavior modification as the only strategy for dealing with the problem.

The framers at RDC work in a good organizational climate. Management has a good reputation with them, and there is mutual trust and respect—they do not feel like management is out to exploit them. Thus, goal setting may be the most effective technique. The framers could be given a goal of so many days to complete a job. The goal could be posted and compared with other framing teams. Positive reinforcement should be used for

PERSPECTIVE

7.4 | *Motivation Techniques: Which Work Best?*[28]

What does research say about which motivation technique works best? A review by Locke and his associates involved an analysis of all the field experimental studies that related motivational strategy with "hard" performance criteria for employees. The researchers did not consider such important additional measures as job satisfaction, absenteeism, or even costs. Thus the results cover only one aspect of total performance.

Four motivational strategies were examined: incentive pay (ten studies), goal setting (seventeen studies), job enrichment (thirteen studies), and employee participation (sixteen studies—*see* Chapter 13 for information on this strategy). Two studies in behavior modification were included within the goal-setting figures.

They found that money (incentives) resulted in the highest increase in performance: 30 percent. Goal setting resulted in improvements of 16 percent, and job enrichment resulted in about 9 percent. Participation resulted in little or no change. When goals and incentives were combined, improvements of over 40 percent resulted.

The authors concluded that money has much more potency as a motivator than other strategies of motivation.

Understanding Organizational Behavior

those teams that complete their jobs on time or early. Pay might be used as an incentive, but in a thin-profit-margin business, such as low-cost housing, it is probably better to try other reinforcements first.

SUMMARY

Chapter Review

■ **Job design**, the deliberate, purposeful planning of the job including all its structural and social aspects, encompasses a number of approaches. Two of the major ones are **job enrichment**, aimed at making the job more interesting, meaningful, and challenging; and **socio-technical systems**, aimed at optimizing the interrelationship between technology and people.

■ The core **job characteristics** include: **skill variety, task identity, task significance, autonomy**, and **feedback**. If the job contains a sufficient amount of these characteristics, the resultant psychological states of experienced **meaningfulness** of work activities, **responsibility** for work outcomes, and **knowledge of the results** of work activities, will result in a state of job enrichment.

■ Not all people respond positively to job enrichment. People with low **growth need strength** may prefer unenriched jobs.

■ Jobs can be enriched by using **implementing concepts** that include: building **client relationships**, allowing workers to **schedule** their own work, developing a sense of **ownership** of the whole product, and establishing direct **feedback** channels.

■ **Flexitime** is a way of allowing people to schedule their own workday within limits. It involves specifying certain times as **flexible time** and others as **core time** (when everyone has to be there).

■ Job enrichment can lead to gains in both performance and job satisfaction, although people seldom seem to increase their efforts to produce more as a result of job enrichment.

■ Volvo's efforts to design enriching jobs for auto assembly-plant workers has been relatively successful. They established twenty-person, self-managing work teams to build major subsystems of the car using a specialized car carrier and plant design.

■ Three factors are crucial for effective goal setting: **clear and specific** goals, **moderately difficult** goals, and goals that are **accepted** by the people who have to accomplish them. **Goal acceptance** seems to depend on how difficult the goal is, whether or not the employee participated in setting the goal, and on a trusting organizational climate.

■ **Management by objectives**, or **MBO**, is a broad concept of management that includes goal setting as its central theme. In addition to setting goals, MBO usually involves boss-subordinate dialogue and is often part of the performance appraisal and incentive system. MBO usually starts with top management, who formulate strategic and long-range goals, and "waterfalls" down the organizational hierarchy, with each department and finally each manager establishing goals that support the overall organizational goals. The rest of the MBO process includes formulating action plans, taking action, reviewing progress, appraising performance, and revising and updating objectives as needed.

■ While goal setting and MBO have been shown to be effective, adding monetary incentives to a goal-setting or MBO program may make it even more powerful.

■ The decision to use a given motivation strategy depends on the situation. One way of analyzing the applicability of various techniques is to break the situation down in terms of the job itself and the **organizational climate**. Various combinations of these factors will point the way to effective motivational mixes.

For Discussion

1. What are the major approaches to job design? What do you think would be an advantage and a disadvantage of each?
2. How do the five job characteristics relate to job satisfaction? To job performance?
3. Based upon your own work experience, describe either an enriched or an unenriched job using the job characteristics model.
4. Describe the major strategies for enriching jobs. How are these strategies related to the five job characteristics (skill variety, task identity).
5. Explain how flexitime works.
6. How does the sociotechnical approach to job design differ from job enrichment?
7. What are the three key elements of Locke's theory of goal setting? Which element do you see as most important and least important? Why?
8. Explain why MBO often runs into problems. How could you design an MBO program that would avoid these problems?
9. Using Figure 7.6 as the model, try to think up an example of where each of the strategies that are X'd would apply.
10. Are you surprised at the research results presented in the Perspective: Motivation Techniques about the effectiveness of various motivation strategies? How can you explain the differences between the strategies.

Key Concepts and Terms

job design
job enrichment
job characteristics model
skill variety
task identity
task significance
autonomy
feedback
psychological states
growth need strength

implementing concepts
flexitime
sociotechnical systems
self-managing work groups
goal clarity
goal difficulty
goal acceptance
MBO
organizational climate

Suggested Readings

Griffin, R.W. (1982). *Task design*. Glenview, Ill.: Scott, Foresman.

Hackman, J.R.; Oldham, G.R.; Janson, R.; and Purdy, K. (1975). A new strategy for job enrichment. *California Management Review* 17: 51–57.

Handy, C. (1980). The changing shape of work. *Organizational Dynamics* Autumn: 26–34.

Latham, G.P.; Cummings, L.L.; and Mitchell, T.R. (1981). Behavioral strategies to improve productivity. *Organizational Dynamics* Winter: 4–23.

Passmore, W.A. (1982). Overcoming the roadblocks to work restructuring efforts. *Organizational Dynamics* Spring: 54–67.

CASES AND INCIDENTS

Keypunch Operation

The function of the keypunch division is to transfer written or typed insurance documents on to computer cards. The division consists of ninety-eight keypunch operators and verifiers (both have the same job classification), seven assignment clerks, and seven supervisors. There are two keypunch supervisors (each with about twenty-five keypunch operators), two verification supervisors (again with about twenty-five verifiers each), and an assignment supervisor (with all seven assignment clerks). All the supervisors report to an assistant manager who then reports to the keypunch division manager.

The size of the jobs vary from just a few cards to as many as 2,500 cards. Some jobs are prescheduled while others come in with due dates—often in the form of crash projects that need to be done "right now." All jobs are received by the assignment branch where they are checked for obvious errors, omissions, and legibility. Any problems found are reported to the supervisor who contacts the user department to resolve the problem. If the departmental input is satisfactory, the assignment clerk divides up the work into batches that will take about one hour to complete so that each operator will have an equal workload. These batches are sent to the keypunching branches with the instructions to "Punch only what you see. Don't correct errors, no matter how obvious they look." Operators have no freedom to arrange their schedules or tasks. They also have little knowledge concerning the meaning and use of the data they are punching.

Because of the high cost of computer time, all keypunching is 100 percent verified. The verification process is done by having another operator completely repunch the data to see if the two inputs match. Thus, it takes just as long to verify as it does to punch the data in the first place. After verification, the cards are sent to the supervisor. If errors are detected, they are sent to the first available operator for correction. Next, the cards are sent to the computer division where they are checked for accuracy using a computer program. The cards and the computer output are sent directly to the originating department, which checks the cards and output and returns the cards to the supervisor if any errors are found.

Many motivational problems exist. There are numerous grievances from the operators. Employees frequently display apathy or outright hostility toward their jobs. Rates of work output are low and schedules are frequently missed. Absenteeism is much higher than average, especially on Mondays and Fridays. Supervisors spend most of their time controlling the work and resolving crisis situations. In short, the performance of the keypunch division is marginal at best.

Adapted by D. Umstot from J.R. Hackman, et al., (1975). A new strategy for job enrichment, as published in *Organizational behavior*, 3rd ed., ed. D. Hellriegel; J.W. Slocum, Jr.; and R.W. Woodman. Copyright © 1983 by West Publishing Company, St. Paul, Minn. Used with permission.

Discussion questions
1. What is the most appropriate motivational strategy in this case? Why?
2. Analyze this case in terms of the job characteristics model.
3. How would you enrich the jobs in the keypunch division?

The Reluctant Entrepreneurs

In the southern United States, the large multimillion dollar pulpwood processing plants are dependent on independent loggers.[29] These entrepreneurs own their own trucks and hire their own crews. But since these loggers do not work for any single company and, in fact work only for themselves, they set their own schedules. One week they might work two days (the fishing is good), the next week they might work four days, and the third week they might work five, one-half days. The production and reliability of these workers is poor at best, but huge investments in equipment would be needed to develop in-house capability. Even then there might still be the same motivation problem.

Discussion questions
1. What is the most appropriate motivational strategy in this case? Why?
2. Develop a plan to motivate the loggers so that production will be at 95 percent, five, full-days a week.

REFERENCES

1. Parts of this chapter are abridged and adapted from Umstot, Job design, in *Organizational behavior*, 3rd ed., D. Hellriegel; J.W. Slocum, Jr.; and R.W. Woodman, St. Paul, Minn.: West, pp. 280–307. Used with permission.

2. For more thorough coverage of job design issues *see* Hackman, J.R. and Oldham, G.R. (1980), *Work redesign*, Reading, Mass.: Addison-Wesley; Cummings, T.G. and Srivastva, S. (1977), *Management of work: A socio-technical systems approach*, Kent, Ill.: Kent State University; Aldag, R.J. and Brief, A.P. (1979), *Task design and employee motivation*, Glenview, Ill.: Scott, Foresman; and Griffin, R.W. (1982), *Task design* Glenview, Ill.: Scott, Foresman. *Also see* the classic readings in Davis, L.E. and Taylor, J.C., eds. (1979), *Design of jobs*, 2nd ed., Santa Monica, Ca.: Goodyear.

3. *See* Herzberg, F. (1966), *Work and the nature of man*, Cleveland: World; and (1976), *The managerial choice*, Homewood, Ill.: Dow Jones-Irwin.

Understanding Organizational Behavior

4. Hackman, J.R. and Oldham, G.R. (1976), Motivation through the design of work: Test of a theory, *Organizational Behavior and Human Performance* 16: pp. 250–279. For a review of this model, *see* Roberts, K.H. and Glick, W. (1981), The job characteristics approach to task design: A critical review, *Journal of Applied Psychology* 66: 193–217.

5. Hackman and Oldham, Motivation through the design of work. There has been limited research support for the growth need strength moderator; *see* Roberts and Glick, The job characteristics approach to task design; Griffin, R.W.; Welsh, A.; and Moorhead, G. (1981), Perceived task characteristics and employee performance: A literature review, *Academy of Management Review* 6: 655–664.

6. For more detailed information on implementing job enrichment, *see* Walters, R.W. (1975), *Job enrichment for results: Strategies for successful implementation*, Reading, Mass.: Addison-Wesley.

7. For more information on implementing concepts, *see* Walters, *Job enrichment for results*; Hackman, J.R.; Oldham, G. R., Janson R., Purdy, K.; (1975), A new strategy for job enrichment, *California Management Review* 17: 51–57; and Herzberg, F. (1974), The wise old Turk, *Harvard Business Review* 52: 70–80.

8. For more information about flexitime, *see* Cohen, A.R. and Gadon, H. (1978), *Alternative work schedules: Integrating individual and organizational needs*. Reading, Mass.: Addison-Wesley; and Ronen, S. (1981), *Flexible working hours*, New York: McGraw-Hill. For a review of the effects of flexitime, *see* Narayanan, V.K. and Nath, R.A. (1982), A field test of some attitudinal and behavioral consequences of flexitime, *Journal of Applied Psychology* 67: 214–218.

9. Ronen, *Flexible working hours*.

10. Ford, R.N. (1973), Job enrichment lessons from AT&T, *Harvard Business Review* 51: 96–106.

11. Adapted from Umstot, D.D. and Rosenbach, W.E. (1980), From theory to action: Implementing job enrichment in the Air Force, *Air University Review* 31(3): 74–81. Used with permission.

12. Griffin, et al., Perceived task characteristics and employee performance.

13. Pierce, J.L. and Dunham, R.B. (1976), Task design: A literature review, *Academy of Management Review* 1(4): 83–97.

14. Passmore, W.A. (1982), Overcoming the roadblocks to work restructuring efforts, *Organizational Dynamics* Spring: 54–67.

15. Cummings and Srivastva, *Management of work*.

16. *See* Cummings, T. (1978), Self-regulating work groups: A sociotechnical synthesis, *Academy of Management Review* 3: 625–634.

17. Based on Gyllenhammar, P.G. (1977), *People at work*, Reading, Mass.: Addison-Wesley.

18. Locke, E.A. (1978), The ubiquity of the technique of goal setting in theories and approaches to motivation, *Academy of Management Review* 3: 594–601.

19. Locke, E.A. (1968), Toward a theory of task motivation and incentives, *Organizational Behavior and Human Performance* 3: 157–189.

20. *See* Latham, G.P. and Locke, E.A. (1979), Goal setting—A motivational technique that works, *Organizational Dynamics* Autumn: 68–80.

21. Adapted from Latham and Locke, Goal setting pp. 72–73.

22. Based on the definitions of Odiorne, G.S. (1979), *M.B.O. II*, Belmont, Calif.: Fearon; and McConkie, M.L. (1979), A clarification of the goal setting and appraisal processes in MBO, *Academy of Management Review* 4: 29–40.

23. There are a number of good books on MBO that provide implementing guidance including Odiorne, *M.B.O. II*; Morrisey, G.L. (1977), *Management by objectives and results for business and industry*, Reading, Mass.: Addison-Wesley; and Raia, A.P. (1974), *Managing by objectives*, Glenview, Ill.: Scott, Foresman.

24. Ford, C.H. (1979), MBO: An idea whose time has gone?, *Business Horizons* 22(12): 48–56.

25. For a review *see* Kondrasuk, J.N. (1981), Studies in MBO effectiveness, *Academy of Management Review* 6: 419–430.

26. Adapted from Raia, *Managing by objectives*, p. 16.

27. Locke, E.A.; Shaw, K. N., Saari, L. M., Latham, G. P. (1981), Goal setting and task performance: 1969–1980, *Psychological Bulletin* 90: 125–152.

28. Locke, E.A.; Feren, D. B., McCaleb, V. M., Shaw, K. N., and Denny, A. T., (1981), The relative effectiveness of four methods of motivating employee performance, in *Changes in working life: Proceedings of the NATO international conference*, eds. K.D. Duncan, et al., London: Wiley.

29. Adapted from Latham and Locke, Goal setting.

The Interaction Between People

Communication: The Link Between Individuals

PREVIEW

■ How do you behave when confronted by an angry boss or coworker? Learn an effective way.

■ Why is it that when you tell someone they should do something they often react unfavorably, even if it is to their benefit?

■ What is the organizational grapevine?

■ How can transactional analysis be used to improve organizational communication?

■ Are you a good listener or do you daydream? Find out how to improve your listening skills.

■ What does it mean when a boss looks you steadily in the eye? Find out about this and other nonverbal signals.

■ Why do managers in Japanese-owned plants sometimes not have an office?

Preview Case: The Managerial Treadmill

The Communication Process
- The source: Encoding messages
- The message: Transmitting meaning
- *Perspective:* The Grapevine
- The receiver: Decoding the message
- Feedback

Interpersonal Communication Dynamics
- Transactional analysis
- Ego states
- Analyzing transactions between two people
- Using transactional analysis
- *Perspective:* Transactional Analysis Applications in Organizations

Listening Behavior
- Interpersonal listening
- The problem-ownership model
- Informational listening
- *Perspective:* Keys to Effective Informational Listening

Nonverbal Communication
- The nature of nonverbal communication
- Vocal cues
- Facial expressions
- Body position
- Physical environment
- *Perspective:* Open Communication in Japanese-Owned Companies

Managerial Use of Communication

Summary
- Chapter review
- For discussion
- Key concepts and terms
- Suggested readings

Cases and Incidents
- Lafayette Aerodynamics
- What Is Happening Here?
- Joe's Benders

References

PREVIEW CASE: THE MANAGERIAL TREADMILL

Barbara Lopez is a middle-level manager in charge of the electronics systems for a new series of naval vessels. We are going to see what Barbara does on Tuesday morning between nine and ten.

9:00 A.M.—She meets with Ray Morse, one of her subordinates who was late this morning for the third time this month. She tells Ray that the late behavior is causing delays in the coordination of important subsystems and could result in a delay in the entire project. Ray is obviously upset; his face shows anxiety and he is nervous and fidgety. She asks him what is causing the late behavior. A discussion ensues revolving around some serious health problems with Ray's wife. Barbara listens attentively and with empathy. At the end of the discussion, Ray resolves to get to work on time in spite of his difficulties at home.

9:12 A.M.—She begins scanning a report that summarizes the progress on the ship. The report highlights any delays or problems with the electronics of a ship.

9:14 A.M.—A telephone call from Louise McIntosh in procurement; there will be a two-week delay in delivery of the cable needed for the radar harnesses.

9:16 A.M.—Barbara calls her chief engineer, Vern Smith, and informs him of the delay. Vern gets quite angry and asks if he can come up and talk to her. Yes, she says.

9:18 A.M.—She continues scanning the report. She jots a short note to one of the project engineers about a possible change in specifications of another electronics subsystem.

9:22 A.M.—Vern bursts into the office. His fists are balled up and his face shows anger. He says, "Why didn't you let me know sooner that we might be having this delay. I'm the chief engineer here, but it seems that I'm always the last to know." Barbara explains to Vern in a level-headed manner that she did not have any idea that the delay was in the wind and that it was news to her too. This cools Vern down, and they discuss how they might solve the problem.

9:30 A.M.—Her secretary buzzes on the intercom and says that Leslie Thompson is here for her performance appraisal interview. Barbara almost forgot this rather important appointment in the light of the cable problem. She tells her secretary to delay the appointment for a few minutes so she can get rid of Vern and collect her thoughts.

9:36 A.M.—Leslie enters Barbara's office. Telling someone who is performing at less than expected level is always difficult. Leslie becomes emotionally upset and begins to sob. Barbara handles the emotion as if it were entirely natural. Leslie spends several minutes venting her frustrations and discussing the reasons for her low performance. Barbara gradually develops a set of objectives for Leslie. If they are completed, Leslie's performance will improve. Although still somewhat upset, Leslie departs with positive feeling that she can improve.

9:52 A.M.—Barbara returns the calls of two people who called while she was in conference with Leslie.

9:57 A.M.—Captain York, the project director, calls and asks her what is happening on the cable delay problem. He's worried that it will delay the whole project. She tells him that she is on top of the problem and will let him know as soon as they have an impact statement. The Captain's call puts a lot more pressure on them than she would like.

9:59 A.M.—Her secretary buzzes to remind her of the 10:00 a.m. meeting with other system directors. She grabs the progress report and heads for the conference room.

Barbara Lopez spends most of her time communicating. She must deal with several types of communication including interpersonal contacts with subordinates, peers, and superiors; the impersonal inputs from computer-generated reports; written memos and reports; and formal oral presentations. While all these aspects of communication are important, the primary focus of this chapter is on the interpersonal aspects of organizational communication.

Barbara's workday is not unusual for most managers spend a large portion of their time verbally communicating. A study of managerial activities found that managers spend 78 percent of their time in oral communication.[1] Thus, communication is one of the most important skills for a manager to have.

In this chapter, we will cover the basic communication process and then turn to transactional analysis as a way of understanding interpersonal communication. Then we will turn to improving listening skills, including a strategy for solving various types of communication problems. Finally, we will cover nonverbal communication, a critical and often overlooked aspect of communication.

The Communication Process

A model of the communication process such as the one presented in Figure 8.1 helps us understand what happens when one person communicates with another.[2] It also shows where the process can break down. Basically, there are four major parts to the communication process: source, message or media, receiver, and feedback. Person *A*, the **source**, encodes the message into words and nonverbal signals. These **messages** are transmitted in oral, written, nonverbal, or other **media** to Person *B*, the **receiver** who **decodes** the message and gives it meaning. Person *B* may transmit **feedback** to Person *A* so that receipt of the message is confirmed.

■ The Source: Encoding Messages

When you originate a communication, you are the source. Based on your **field of experience**, which is developed from your past experiences, your personality, and your self-concept (the topics discussed in Chapters 2, 3, and 4), you use certain words, gestures, facial expressions, posture, and voice to encode your message. You need to be aware of your own field of experience and the receiver's field of experience so you can properly en-

Figure 8.1. The communication process.

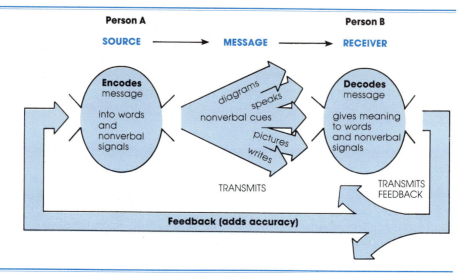

code the message. College professors often have problems encoding so that their students understand and receive the message; and many students have experienced the results of such a mismatch.

This same problem is common in all organizations. For example, managers often have a different frame of reference than do hourly employees; engineers have a different one from managers; and marketing people differ from production. Everyone has a somewhat different set of experiences and perceptions that colors their ability to decode the other's messages. If you are dealing with managers from another country and culture, there may be

Figure 8.2. Fields of experience.

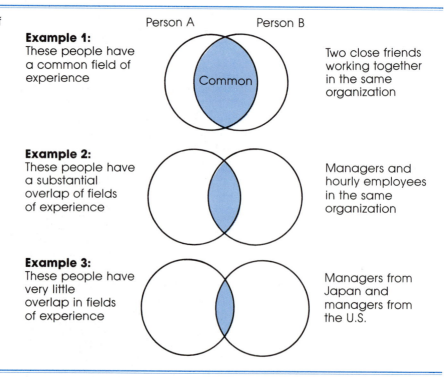

Example 1:
These people have a common field of experience

Two close friends working together in the same organization

Example 2:
These people have a substantial overlap of fields of experience

Managers and hourly employees in the same organization

Example 3:
These people have very little overlap in fields of experience

Managers from Japan and managers from the U.S.

Understanding Organizational Behavior

very little common field of experience (*see* Figure 8.2). To effectively communicate, you must use the proper words and **nonverbal signals** (smiles, nods, voice, eye contact) to match the frame of reference of your receiver.

■ The Message: Transmitting Meaning

Messages can be transmitted in many ways, mediums, or **channels**. They may be written, spoken over the telephone, delivered face-to-face, or transmitted nonverbally, as with a wink.[3] People may react differently to various channels. For example, people may respond much more favorably to a face-to-face request for information than they would to a written memo.[4] People may also react adversely to impersonal, computer-generated messages.[5]

8.1 | *The Grapevine*

The company "grapevine," a term which refers to all informal communication in organizations, is a central part of the informal organization. Ordinarily, communication and authority travel along organizational lines, from supervisor to subordinate or viceversa. However, the grapevine follows the informal organization. It skips levels; it moves laterally; and it moves fast. For example, the wife of the plant supervisor had a baby at 11 P.M. on Tuesday. By 2 P.M. on Wednesday, 46 percent of the management personnel knew of the birth through the grapevine. The following chart depicts grapevine communication patterns.[6]

From K. Davis, 1981, *Human behavior at work: Organizational behavior*, 6th ed., p. 336. Copyright © 1981 by McGraw-Hill, New York. Used with permission.

An event is known to managers in positions **A** and **B** in a manufacturing company

Another problem with the message is that people often send conflicting messages. For example, a salesperson who is doing an excellent job of presenting the product on a verbal level may be sending a nonverbal signal of apprehension and nervousness that results in conflicting signals.

■ The Receiver: Decoding the Message

From the study of perception in Chapter 4, we know that we selectively pick up messages from the environment. Communication works the same way—we **selectively receive** messages based on our field of experience, our emotional mood, our reaction to the sender, and the form of the communication. If someone criticizes us or talks down to us, we may cut off the communication and simply "not hear" what is being said. Or, we may react with anger and lash back at the sender (certainly a strong form of feedback for the sender).

To be good receivers we must be good listeners and be able to decode the verbal and nonverbal signals of the sender. Then we must, of course, respond in a way that facilitates communication. The application of these topics will be covered in greater detail later in the chapter.

■ Feedback

One central part of the communication process is **feedback**, or the information that returns to the sender from the receiver.[7] Feedback is a natural part of most communication transactions although some types of communication, such as face-to-face, offer more opportunities for feedback than others. Feedback may also be a formal process, such as the performance appraisal interview that Barbara was conducting with Leslie in our opening case. Examples of the types of organizational feedback that might be encountered are provided in Table 8.1.

One-way communication, such as a lecture without interaction or a business letter, does not allow corrective feedback from the receiver. If the message is misunderstood, there is no way to verify it. **Two-way communication**, on the other hand, allows the sender to test the receiver's understanding of the message. A humorous example of the types of distortions that happen when one-way communication prevents feedback is Operation Halley's Comment related below:

A COLONEL ISSUED THE FOLLOWING DIRECTIVE TO HIS EXECUTIVE OFFICERS:
"Tomorrow evening at approximately 2000 hours Halley's Comet will be visible in this area, an event which occurs only once every 75 years. Have the men fall out in the battalion area in fatigues, and I will explain this rare phenomenon to them. In case of rain, we will not be able to see anything, so assemble the men in the theater and I will show them films of it."
EXECUTIVE OFFICER TO COMPANY COMMANDER:
"By order of the Colonel, tomorrow at 2000 hours, Halley's Comet will appear above the battalion area. If it rains, fall the men out in fatigues, then march to the theater where this rare phenomenon will take place, something which occurs only once every 75 years.
COMPANY COMMANDER TO LIEUTENANT:
"By order of the Colonel be in fatigues at 2000 hours tomorrow

Table 8.1. Examples of organizational feedback.

Positive feedback from the organization	You receive a formal report of good performance.
	Your supervisor tells you that you are doing a good job.
	You are promoted to a more responsible job.
	You get a raise.
Negative feedback from the organization	The supervisor really lets you have it.
	Coworkers tell you that you did something wrong.
	The supervisor makes back-handed comments (like "Have a hard night?")
	You are demoted to a less responsible job.
Internal feedback from the job	You find better ways of doing the job.
	Everything goes smoothly.
	You are able to finish all the work.
	You have good feelings about how well you did the job.

Adapted from D. M. Herold and M. M. Greller, 1977, Feedback: Definition of a construct, *Academy of Management Journal* 20:144–45. Copyright 1977 by Academy of Management Review. Used with permission.

evening, the phenomenal Halley's Comet will appear in the theater. In case of rain, in the battalion area, the Colonel will give another order, something which occurs once every 75 years."
LIEUTENANT TO SERGEANT:
"Tomorrow at 2000 hours, the Colonel will appear in the theater with Halley's Comet, something which happens every 75 years. If it rains, the Colonel will order the comet into the battalion area."
SERGEANT TO SQUAD:
"When it rains tomorrow at 2000 hours, the phenomenal 75-year-old General Halley, accompanied by the Colonel, will drive his comet through the battalion area theater in fatigues."

A speech by Dan Bellus of Bellus & Associates, Santa Monica, California in *DS Letter* 1(1971):3. Copyright © 1971 by Didactic Systems, Cranford, N.J. Used with permission.

One final concept to keep in mind is that communication is *continuous*; it is a series of transactions between the sender and the receiver with feedback and reinforcement constantly occurring. Transactions tend to overlap; as one person talks the other may laugh, smile, frown, nod, or interrupt.

Interpersonal Communication Dynamics

While it is certainly very important that managers be able to write clearly and to speak well in formal, oral presentations, the majority of all managerial communication is between two people—it is at the interpersonal level. For this reason, we will concentrate our attention on interpersonal communication dynamics.

In the opening case, Barbara had to deal on an interpersonal level with Vern, the angry project engineer; Leslie, the distraught low performer; and Captain York, the worried supervisor. All these interpersonal communications might have caused problems if they had not been understood and resolved. One way of understanding and dealing with interpersonal communication is through transactional analysis, the subject of this section.

■ Transactional Analysis

One of the best ways to understand and sort out interpersonal communication is by using transactional analysis theory.[8] In Chapter 2, we discussed how the self-concept could be understood by using transactional analysis (I'm OK, You're OK). The study of psychological positions in relation to personality is only one part of the theory. Another important part, which is particularly applicable to communication, is the structural analysis of ego states and transactions—the focus of our study in this section. We will define these aspects of **transactional analysis** (TA) as a system for understanding human communication by analyzing transactions and chains of transactions and their associated ego states.[9]

Eric Berne, a psychiatrist, invented TA as a way of getting his patients involved in their own treatment. Thus, he used terms that were understandable and vivid. For some time TA was used only in psychotherapy, but in the past ten or fifteen years managers began to realize that TA could help them understand and solve organizational problems.[10]

■ Ego States

An **ego state** is a consistent pattern of feeling, thinking, and experiencing that is related to a corresponding consistent pattern of behavior.[11] Ego states are a reflection of our past experience. They are a natural way of recording and experiencing life. In fact, a common analogy is to say that ego states are videotapes of our past feelings and memories. When a given ego state is aroused, the tape can be replayed and the event may even be re-experienced.

There are three ego states: Parent, Adult, and Child (when these words are capitalized, they refer to ego states rather than actual parents, adults, or children). The ego states have no relation to the age or family status of the person. Young children can have an active Parent ego state (*see* cartoon in Fig. 8.3), just as older people can have an active Child ego state; however, some people will tend to favor one ego state over the others. There is no one single ego state that is more desirable than the others—all are important.

The Parent Ego State   This ego state is developed by observing our parents and other authority figures and by developing a set of behaviors that seem to be appropriate. The Parent contains "shoulds" and "oughts" or standards of behavior; it contains prejudices and critical behaviors; and it also contains nurturing behaviors and feelings. An impatient, scowling, angry airline passenger who says: "You should not allow this type of foul-up, I'll certainly not fly with this airline again!", is behaving in the Parent ego state. An angry boss who shouts at an employee, "Can't you ever get your reports in on time!", is also acting in the Parent ego state.

The Parent ego state is not always controlling and critical because it also contains our nurturing, encouraging, and supportive behaviors. It is also a Parent behavior when the boss warmly pats you on the back and says, "You're doing fine. Keep up the good work." Certainly, these behaviors are important in organizations. Some of us did not learn them well as children and are not very skillful with this type of Parent behavior.

The Adult Ego State   The Adult, which is not related to a person's age, has to do with that part of a person that seeks knowledge, gathers facts, analyzes data, organizes, and tests reality. This part of the ego is computer-like and objective. It deals with problem solving. An example of Adult behavior is when the ticket counter employee says to the irate customer, "I'll check my computer for a connection on another airline." The majority of organizational communication probably takes place in the Adult ego state. This ego state seldom gets us into communication difficulties and may even be used to get ourselves out of a communication predicament such as the one faced by the ticket counter person.

"Don't try to tell *me* what's right! I've lived a lot longer than you, young man!"

Figure 8.3. The Parent ego state develops at an early age.

A Ted Key cartoon from K. S. Keyes, 1950, *How to Develop Your Thinking Ability*, p. 231. Copyright © 1950 by McGraw-Hill, New York. Used with permission.

Communication: The Link Between Individuals

The Child Ego State   This ego state, also unrelated to age, contains all the impulses and feelings that come naturally to a child. Impulsive and uninhibited release of emotions such as anger, joy, excitement, and fun are part of the Child. The Child is creative and intuitive, and it may also be manipulative. An example of a Child behavior might be a suggestion from a co-worker that "Let's go out after work and play tennis. Wow! Wouldn't that be fun on a beautiful day like today?" Another example might be a response to the boss' critical remark about the late report mentioned earlier: "(Head

Table 8.2 Ego state identifiers.

Ego State Behaviors			Ego State Indicators		
	Nurtures Criticizes		BODY LANGUAGE	EXPRESSIONS	VOCAL TONE
WHAT THE PARENT DOES 	Restricts Judges Blames Encourages	PARENT INDICATORS	Looking down over rim of glasses. Pointing an accusing finger. Hands on hip.	"You should . . . you ought . . . you must" "Be cool" "Don't tell me . . ." "You disappoint me" "Poor thing" "I'll protect you"	Harsh Judgmental Soothing Indignant Commanding Comforting

WHAT THE
ADULT DOES
 	
	Processes
	  information
	Takes objective
	  action
	Organizes
	Plans
	Solves problems
	Estimates risks
		ADULT
		INDICATORS
			A straight,
			  relaxed
			  stance.
			Slightly tilted
			  head.
			Appearance of
			  active
			  listening.
			Regular eye
			  contact.
			Confident
			  appearance.
				"Aha, I see"
				"I see your
				  point"
				"I
				  recognize..."
				"How do you
				  feel
				  about . . ."
					Relaxed
					Assertive
					Somewhat
					  deliberative
					Self-assertive

WHAT THE
CHILD DOES
 	
	Invents
	Expresses
	  curiosity
	
	Acts on impulse
	Acts selfishly
	Loves
	Imagines
	  brainstorms
	Acts
	  belligerently
	Complains
		CHILD
		INDICATORS
			Forlorn
			  appearance.
			Drooping
			  shoulders.
			Withdrawal.
			Pursed lips.
			Scowling.
			Skipping.
			Hugging.
			Twinkle in eyes.
				"I want" "I wish"
				"Wow" "I
				  should" "Did I
				  do okay?"
				"One of these
				  days" "It's not
				  fair" "It's not
				  my fault" "Oh
				  boy!"
					Appealing
					Complaining
					Nagging
					Indignant
					Cheerful
					Protesting
					Grumbling

From C. Albano, 1974, *Transactional analysis on the job,* pp. 7–8. Copyright © 1974 by AMACOM, a division of American Management Associations, New York, N.Y. Used with permission.

Understanding Organizational Behavior

and eyes down.) I'm sorry boss, I'll try not to do it again. I just can't understand why I can't get done on time. (Wipes tears from eyes.)"

■ Analyzing Transactions Between Two People

A **transaction** occurs when one person recognizes another with a verbal or nonverbal transmission, and the other person responds. Each transaction originates in one of the three ego states—Parent, Adult, or Child—and the response also comes from one of the three ego states. There are three types of transactions: complementary, crossed, and ulterior.

A **complementary transaction** occurs when a message that is sent to a specific ego state gets the predicted or expected response. The transaction may involve the same or different ego states. The set of examples illustrated in Figure 8.4 explain and clarify the nature of complementary transactions. While we can infer that these examples may be actually complementary transactions, we must make several assumptions to do so. We must assume that the transaction actually originates in the specified ego state and that verbal and nonverbal cues are congruent.

Crossed transactions cause many interpersonal communication failures. In a crossed transaction, people receive a message or behavior that disconfirms their own position, their view of the other person, or both. In other words, an inappropriate ego state is aroused, and the lines of communication between ego states are crossed—an unexpected outcome of the transaction.

However, some crossed transactions do not present problems for communication. An Adult ego state transaction that crosses another may serve to arouse the adult in the other person and change the direction of the transaction from an emotional, angry exchange to a rational, problem-solving one. In fact, intentionally responding to a transaction with an Adult crossing transaction is a major strategy for smoothing conflict and solving communication difficulties. This is the strategy Barbara used in the opening example to cool Vern's anger.

Figure 8.4. Examples of complementary transactions.

M. James, *The OK Boss*, pp. 92–93, copyright 1975 by Addison-Westly, reprinted with permission.

Communication: The Link Between Individuals

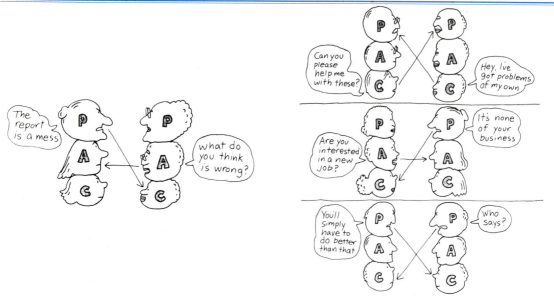

Figure 8.5. Examples of crossed transactions.

M. James, *The OK Boss*, pp. 94–95, copyright 1975 by Addison-Westly, reprinted with permission.

The examples of crossed transactions in Figure 8.4 illustrate this concept. Note that the last example is a desirable use of the crossed transaction.

Ulterior transactions always involve more than two ego states. There is always a hidden message that is often disguised in some socially acceptable form. For example, when the boss says, "The Morrison case may be a little too tough for you," the real transaction expressed privately as an ulterior one is, "You're too stupid to do a challenging case like that." Ulterior transactions are also not necessarily bad in themselves. For example, ulterior transactions are almost always involved in courtship behavior. Figure 8.6 presents examples of ulterior transactions.

■ Using Transactional Analysis

Now that you understand the ego states and how transactions work, you can apply the theory to organizational situations. The key is skillful use of the adult ego state.

Use an Adult Bossing Style   People often evaluate a comment as good or bad, forming a corresponding opinion about the sender. For example, when a boss tells a subordinate to do something using the critical-Parent ego state, then the subordinate often gets defensive and reacts like an angry, rebellious child. A good way to avoid this is to use the Adult ego state when giving assignments or interacting with subordinates—use an Adult bossing style.[12] Along this same line, a manager who uses a participative style of leadership is probably one that concentrates on using the Adult ego state. On the other hand, an authoritative leader may be likely to use the Parent.[13]

Figure 8.6.
Examples of
ulterior
transactions.

Communication: The Link Between Individuals

Transactional Analysis Applications in Organizations

Transactional analysis has been used by a number of firms. Bank of America has used it to train "disadvantaged" people to be more effective and efficient employees.[14] AT&T used it to improve communication between employees.[15] IBM found it was effective for training sales personnel.[16] In addition, the U.S. Civil Service found it effective for training women for upwardly mobile careers.[17]

One of the most effective uses of TA is in emotional, high-pressure jobs, such as those who work for the airlines. One example of how TA helps in these positions is the case of a stewardess working for American Airlines who had been trained in TA:[18]

I remember one flight between Toronto and Chicago that took three hours be- *cause of a snow storm at Chicago. The passengers were mostly business men with connections to make and meetings to attend. My first inclination was to grumble along with them as to how awful the situation was, but then I thought: "Is this the way to make a fun trip?" So, I smiled, and smiled, and smiled. I made it a point to chat with each passenger, feeding their Child with the attention it needed and answering their Adult questions. Pretty soon everyone in the first-class cabin was chatting with each other. By trying to be happy myself, it brushed off on others who, in turn, infected the whole cabin: A ballooning "I'm OK— You're OK" feeling.*

Use the Adult to Cross Undesirable Transactions One of the most effective ways of using TA is to defuse undesirable situations but using the Adult to cross the transaction. While this type of cross does tend to stop communication, there is a strong inclination for the other person to respond in the Adult. Since the Adult is problem-solving oriented and non-emotional, it is difficult to remain angry when facing a series of Adult transactions. The key here is to counter each transaction from the critical parent with an Adult transaction.

An example using airline ticket counter employees is appropriate. When an angry customer berates the person because a flight was cancelled or plane delayed, the best response is to go into an Adult, problem-solving mode. Examine various alternatives, check the computer, check for local hotel availability. A continuous chain of Adult transactions is hard to resist. People are often reinforced for angry behavior when they get the response they want. They want to let off steam at your expense.

Listening Behavior

What aspect of communication do you spend the most time doing— speaking, writing, reading, or listening? If you answered *listening* you were right. Approximately 45 percent of all time spent communicating involves listening; next comes speaking with 30 percent, reading with 16 percent, and writing with 9 percent.[19]

The listening process concentrates on the *receiver* part of our communication model. There are four stages of listening:

Understanding Organizational Behavior

1. **Sensing** the message through verbal or nonverbal channels.
2. **Interpreting**, clarifying, and understanding the message.
3. **Evaluating** and appraising it.
4. **Responding** or doing something about the message.

We will discuss two general types of listening: **interpersonal**, which involves interaction between the speaker and the listener, and **informational**, which involves primarily the transmission of information between a speaker and a listener. Both are important in organizations. Interpersonal listening is the most common type and is illustrated by counseling sessions, informal discussions, and telephone conversations. Informational listening may involve such activities as staff meetings, lectures, and videotape playbacks. The key difference between the two types is the opportunity for interaction. Interpersonal listening involves extensive interaction while informational listening involves little or no interaction.

■ Interpersonal Listening

Listener Ego States   An important aspect of interpersonal listening is your ego state during the listening. Are you listening with an evaluative tone? Are you conveying approval, disapproval, or opinions? Are you giving advice? These very common organizational behaviors indicate that the Parent ego state is being used. When the Parent ego state is used by the boss, a subordinate may respond in the Child. For example, the subordinate may seem impatient and squirm in the chair and may even withdraw, pout, or giggle. The Adult listening mode is evidenced by a more rational approach to listening. It involves evaluating the situation and then behaving in a manner that is considered to be most effective to solve the problem at hand. Table 8.3 provides examples of nonverbal indicators of various listening ego states.

Table 8.3.   Nonverbal indicators of listening ego states.[20]

Ego State	Nonverbal Indicators
Parent	Scowl on a tilted head with any amount of side-to-side head rotation indicates parental disciplining or "no!"
	Head motions, normally evidenced by approving or disapproving nods of the head and often accompanied by tone and words that indicate "It is for your own good" or "the truth is perfectly obvious."
Adult	Level-headed, balanced, straightforward posture with the head slightly turned toward the speaker.
	Gives the appearance of concentration on what the speaker is saying.
Child	Defiant with head tipped up and to one side, often flat or "stony-faced" with jaw jutting forward.
	Restless and impatient behavior such as turning toward and then away from the speaker with gross body movements.
	Pouting and defiantly compliant with face tilted down and gaze averted.

We will concentrate on the Adult approach to listening because most organizational situations can be handled best with this approach.

■ The Problem-Ownership Model

One way of understanding how to approach various interpersonal listening situations is the **problem-ownership model**.[21] You analyze the situation by asking: "Is there a problem?" If there is no problem, then the appropriate ego state can be used to receive the information being transmitted. For example, a foreman may simply listen to a report of one of the workers about a defective machine, noting the fact in memory so it can be reported at the next staff meeting.

However, if there is a problem, ask the question, "Who owns this problem, the speaker or me?" If the speaker owns the problem, such as an unhappy marital situation at home, then the listener should use *active listening*. If you own the problem—for example, an employee who is not performing up to par—then another approach, called the *I-message*, is appropriate. Figure 8.7 diagrams the problem-ownership model.

Active Listening   Whenever the speaker (subordinate) owns the problem and the behaviors of the speaker are acceptable to the listener (boss), then active listening is necessary. **Active listening** means that you concentrate on listening to other person; on helping him or her to work through the problem. You do it with *empathy* and often using restatements and reflections as a way of checking understanding and showing the speaker that you hear what is being said. You pay particular attention to the emotional tone of the message and respond to it rather than referring only to the verbal content. Active listening takes time, so it should not be attempted unless a substantial amount of time is available to work on the problem.

Examples of Active Listening   Here are some statements by employees that seem to call for an active listening response:

Figure 8.7.
Problem-
ownership
model.[22]

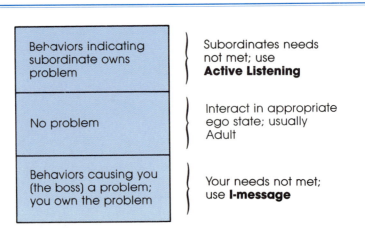

Understanding Organizational Behavior

☐ Sender: "I'm worried that I might not get promoted on time."
☐ Listener: "You're concerned about your chances of promotion."
☐ Sender: "The big layoffs are really frightening. I don't know what will happen if I lose my job."
☐ Listener: "Sounds like you're worried about being laid off."
☐ Sender: "I just can't seem to get anything done anymore with all the damn noise from the grinding machine."
☐ Listener: "You're upset because your performance isn't what it used to be."
☐ Sender: "My supervisor is always criticising me. She never has anything positive to say about me."
☐ Listener: "You're pretty upset with your boss."
☐ Sender: "This company just doesn't seem to be a good place to work nowadays."
☐ Listener: "It seems you're disappointed with the company."

Confronting Unacceptable Behavior with I-messages   Communication cannot always be nondirective. Sometimes, especially in organizational situations, you have to change behavior even when the other person does not see the need for change. The best way to do this is with an **I-message**, composed of a statement with three major elements: behavior, effects, and feelings.

An I-message to an employee who is late might go like this: "I am afraid that the director will come around at eight o'clock and see that everyone isn't here." In this case the behavior is implied since the employee was missing at eight o'clock this morning. The effects on you, the boss, are that you might get into a lot of trouble with the director if everyone is not here on time. The feelings reflect your fear that you will be harmed, perhaps reprimanded or passed over for promotion. Other ways you might respond to this same situation might be:

☐ "I am concerned that others in the office may start coming in late too."
☐ "I am really discouraged when I think of all the work we have to do today and I can't get the crew started until you get here."
☐ "When you come in late, I figure that you don't care about your job and that makes me angry."

■ Informational Listening

There are a number of important techniques and skills that can improve informational listening.[23] Listening skills can help improve your retention and understanding of information that is presented in briefings, staff meetings, or training films. Improving your informational listening skills can also have payoffs in the college classroom.

There are four strategies for effective listening: clarifying the purpose, concentrating on the speaker, listening for the main ideas, and avoiding premature evaluation. These are discussed in the following paragraphs.

What Is the Purpose?   Perhaps the most important question to ask in an informational listening situation, such as a briefing on a new product

8.3 *Keys to Effective Informational Listening[24]*

Listening Technique	Ineffective Behavior	Effective Behavior
Concentrate on the message.	Faking attention; easily distracted; avoids difficult material.	Actively displays energy and attention; does not become distracted; works hard to understand difficult material.
Listen for ideas.	Tries to remember all the facts.	Searches for ideas or central themes that facts support.
Judge content, not delivery or appearance.	Does not listen if delivery is poor or appearance is unsuitable.	Looks for the content of the message; ignores delivery and appearance problems.
Develop motivation to listen.	Dismisses subject as uninteresting.	Does not prematurely judge interest; searches for reasons to listen.
Avoid premature evaluation.	Tends to think of arguments opposed to speaker's ideas.	Listens with an open mind; does not prematurely decide upon the merits of the arguments.

or the introduction of a new computer system, is: "Why am I here?" In other words you should have a purpose for listening. Listen for what you can use.

Work Hard at Listening   Do not tune out the speaker just because the delivery is boring or inept. Work hard to get the meaning. Avoid daydreaming, for once you go off on a tangent it is hard to get back in the track. In addition, do not give up just because the material is difficult. Not everything is easy. Many important things in life take discipline and persistence to learn.

Listen for Main Ideas   Listen for the speaker's main points or themes. The worst thing you could do is to take lots of notes about the facts and miss the real meaning of the message. Along this line it is important to take notes, but not necessarily to outline the speaker's presentation. One proven way to take notes is to draw a line down the middle of the page and on one side list facts; on the other principles or themes.

Avoid Premature Evaluation   Try to avoid making judgments about the presentation or the speaker until the presentation is over. Often, people tend to make up their mind that the speaker is "all wet" because of some early statement or an emotional word that colors their perception.

Nonverbal Communication

Nonverbal communication is so important that it deserves a special section for emphasis. All of us use nonverbal communication, but often we do it unconsciously. We are quite unaware of the signals we are sending. For example, a manager may be trying to communicate the directions for accomplishing a task in a straightforward, Adult way. However, the manager's nonverbal behavior may send different signals. The manager may be sitting behind the desk, arms crossed, and a slight frown on the face. A subordinate may read the nonverbal behavior as a desire for dominance and power, originating from the Parent ego state.[25] The employee may leave the session feeling criticized, attacked, and defensive.

■ The Nature of Nonverbal Communication

Nonverbal communication involves vocal cues, facial expressions, posture, hand movements, touch, dress, and spatial relationships. In the previous section, we covered a number of nonverbal behaviors that are associated with listening skills (*see* Table 8.3). In Chapter 4 we discussed impression management, the systematic management of nonverbal behavior to create a favorable image. In this section we will review the major concepts so you will have an awareness of nonverbal communication.

One researcher found that the overall impact of a message depends more on nonverbal behavior than on verbal behavior.[26] Only 7 percent of a message's impact was due to the actual verbal content (the words and grammar). The rest was due to the nonverbal impact—38 percent for the vocal content, and 55 percent for facial content. While not every message would have this same proportion, it is apparent that nonverbal communication is a substantial part of the total message.

When verbal and nonverbal information conflict, nonverbal almost always wins out. For example, "If someone calls you 'honey' in a nasty tone of voice, you are likely to feel disliked; it is also possible to say 'I hate you' in a way that conveys exactly the opposite feeling."[27]

In the following paragraphs, we will cover four elements of nonverbal communication: vocal cues, body position, facial expressions, and physical settings.

■ Vocal Cues

The vocal part of a message, sometimes referred to as **paralinguistics**, pertains to how the message is transmitted in terms of range, resonance, rate, control, intensity, pitch, and inflection. Figure 8.8 illustrates the differences in vocal cues that add meaning to our verbal messages.

■ Facial Expressions

The face and head are perhaps the most important source of nonverbal signals. By just looking at people we can tell roughly how old they are, whether they are awake and alert, or if they are listening. We may also be able to tell an individual's sex, race, ethnic origin, status, or occupation. Our cues might include baldness, gray hair, wrinkles, pigmentation of the skin, eye and hair color, and makeup of the person's features. Facial hair (beard or mustache), eyebrows, cleanliness, and makeup are superficial

Figure 8.8. Vocal cues.

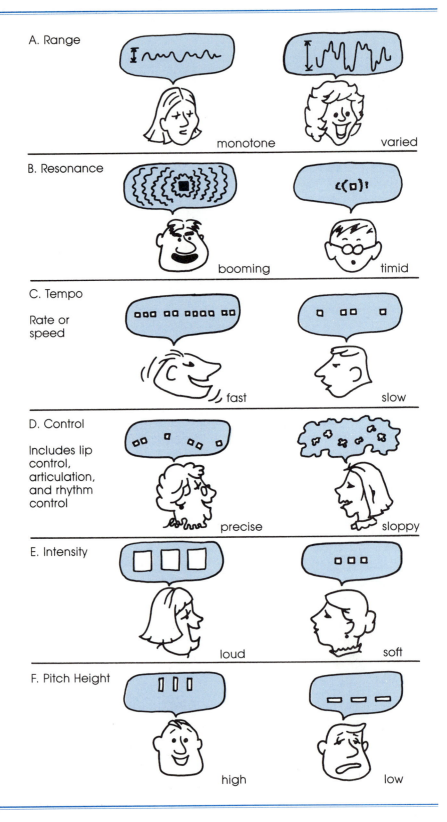

A. Range

monotone   varied

B. Resonance

booming   timid

C. Tempo

Rate or speed

fast   slow

D. Control

Includes lip control, articulation, and rhythm control

precise   sloppy

E. Intensity

loud   soft

F. Pitch Height

high   low

Randall P. Harrison, *Beyond Words: An Introduction to Nonverbal Communication,* © 1974, pp. 106–107. Adapted by permission of Prentice-Hall, Inc., Englewood Cliffs, N.J.

Understanding Organizational Behavior

ways of judging how people feel about themselves and how they want to be perceived by others.

■ Emotional Displays

People's faces show happiness, sadness, surprise, anger, joy, distress, fear, disgust, and interest. Figure 8.8 shows the exaggerations of the eyes, mouth, forehead, eyebrows, and nose that result in these basic emotional displays. Test your ability to recognize emotional displays by taking the quiz in Figure 8.9.

Emotional display rules are often established by the culture or subculture, even at the organizational level. In organizations it is important to know which facial behaviors are OK or not OK for display. For example, some organizational cultures would call for "businesslike" unemotional behavior, while others would value the display of authentic emotions.

Eye behavior is particularly powerful. When you want to be recognized at a staff meeting, you "catch the eye" of the leader. On the other hand, students who do not want to be recognized in class often avoid the eye of the instructor. One of the principle rules of public speaking is to have good eye contact with your audience. In a one-on-one situation, averting another's eyes or a downward gaze indicates lower status. A steady gaze is a **visual dominance** technique. If you want to be treated as an equal, when someone looks at you, look back, maintain eye contact. Loss of eye contact during a conversation may mean that a touchy subject has been encountered.

Smiling is another behavior that may have several meanings. It may simply mean that you are happy. But, it also may mean that you are uncomfortable and are displaying nervous grinning. Phony smiling puts you in a lower-status position.

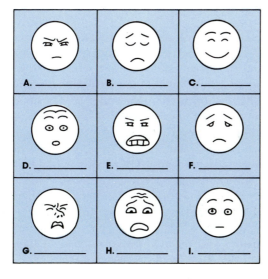

Can you match the above sketches with the correct affects? (1) happy, (2) sad, (3) surprise, (4) fear, (5) anger, (6) disgust.

Answers: A–5, B–2, C–1, D–3, E–5, F–2, G–6, H–4, I–3.

Figure 8.9.
Emotional display quiz.[28]

Randall P. Harrison, *Beyond Words: An Introduction to Nonverbal Communication*, © 1974, pp 106–107. Reprinted by permission of Prentice-Hall, Inc., Englewood Cliffs, N.J.

Even high-ranking managers in Japanese companies may not have private offices. "In one Japanese-owned TV plant on the West Coast, the top manager's office is next to the receptionist—open and visible to everybody who walks into the building, whether employee, supplier, or customer."[30] Privacy for meetings and conferences is afforded by several small conference rooms and meeting areas. The Japanese encourage this type of office arrangement so face-to-face communication will be easier.

In Japanese companies, the plant manager may also spend at least two hours per day out on the shop floor talking to employees and supervisors. This presence gives a strong non-verbal signal that the manager cares and is interested in everyone's problems.

Foremen (the lowest-level supervisors in the plant) may not have an office at all. They are expected to work with the employees on the shop floor. Thus, there is good communication and less feeling of isolation between supervisors and workers.

An American personnel manager in a Japanese motorcycle plant spends two to four hours per day on the shop floor discussing personnel problems. His conclusion about the arrangement is: "We have an open-door policy—but it's their door, not management's (that's open)."[31]

Head position and tilt are another important key. A head tilted too far up gives an air of superiority, while a head tilted downward shows passiveness and submission. A level head is more indicative of a confident, neutral style. Head nods are also important; a nod, up and down, no matter how slight, is seen as agreement. Whereas, a head shake, from side to side, indicates disagreement.

Body Position

Just like eye contact indicates higher status, a relaxed body position also indicates high status. When people of unequal status interact, the higher-status person takes a more relaxed position while the lower-status person takes the more "at attention" position.[32] Extreme relaxation is a common behavior with disliked, nonthreatening addressees.[33] In addition, posture gives an indication of how much a speaker likes another. Leaning towards another indicates liking and away, dislike.

If you are making a presentation to the Corporate Vice-President for Finance for a new system you want to buy, you might adjust your presentation based on the body language you observe. If the Vice-President is slightly relaxed, friendly, and greets you with a straight gaze, then you may have a receptive person. If, on the other hand, the VP is leaning back in the chair with folded arms and a wrinkled brow, you may need to be particularly persuasive. If the posture and facial expression change, then you can tailor your presentation to the nonverbal signals.

Physical Environment

A typical chief executive's office is large, carpeted, and well protected by secretaries and assistants. This type of office says: "I'm important. Don't bother me with anything unless it is also important."[34] This nonverbal communication tends to purposely inhibit the flow of information to and from the chief. While executive isolation is typical for American top managers, the Japanese use a more open structure (*see* the Perspective: Open Communication in Japanese-Owned Companies).

Managerial Use of Communication

Understanding the communication process (source, message, receiver, and feedback) is vital for managers because a great deal of the managerial task involves communicating effectively. Much of interpersonal communication can be understood by using transactional analysis. The key here is to use the Adult ego state for most management communication.

Listening is also an important managerial skill, whether it be interpersonal listening or informational listening. Interpersonal listening is used to open communication channels and solve problems that are of concern to either the employee or the manager. It helps us learn how to confront problems. Informational listening helps in assimilating and storing information more effectively. Each of these types of listening require different skills and techniques.

Nonverbal communication permeates everything that we do and is very influential in determining the overall impact of a message. Managers need to be attuned to theirs and other's nonverbal signals to fully manage the communication process.

SUMMARY

Chapter Review

■ Communication is a most important skill because managers spend 78 percent of their time communicating. The communication process is continuous and has four parts: **source, message, receiver**, and **feedback**.

■ **Transactional analysis**, a system for understanding human behavior based upon transactions and chains of transactions and their ego states, is useful for understanding interpersonal communication. TA identifies three **ego states: Parent, Adult**, and **Child**, that are used to explain transactions. The ego states have nothing to do with age or maturity but reflect patterns of feeling, thinking, and behaving. Healthy individuals use all three ego states.

■ A **complementary** transaction occurs when a message that is sent gets the expected response. If an unexpected response occurs, the transaction is **crossed** and communication becomes more difficult. **Ulterior** transactions always involve some hidden message.

■ The most effective way to use TA is to make skillful use of the Adult ego state for interacting with subordinates and defusing emotional confrontations. Companies have found TA useful for training women for nontraditional careers, improving sales, training disadvantaged workers, and dealing with angry and hostile customers.

- **Listening** concentrates on the receiver part of the communication model and involves four stages: **sensing, interpreting, evaluating**, and **responding**. We can listen to solve interpersonal problems or we can listen for information. Interpersonal listening concentrates on using the **problem-ownership model** to determine where to focus the efforts. If the subordinate owns the problem, use **active listening**; if the boss owns the problem, use an **I-messages. Informational listening** is used for more formal, one-way situations.
- **Nonverbal communication** involves coding and decoding vocal cues, facial expressions, posture, hand movements, touch and space to more effectively understand the message. The physical environment also sends nonverbal signals that may enhance or inhibit the free flow of communication.

For Discussion

1. Pick an example of a communication that you have participated in in the past day or two, and analyze it using the model shown in Figure 8.1. Was the communication accurate? If distortion were observed, what part of the process do you believe caused it?
2. Is the grapevine something to be discouraged or encouraged? Why?
3. How might a manager design communication systems to stimulate two-way communication rather than one-way?
4. Explain why the ego states are not related to the degree of maturity of the individual.
5. Based upon your own recent experience, give an example of a transaction that originated in each of the three ego states. What was the reaction to each transaction?
6. What is the best way to deal with transactions that are seen as undesirable by the manager, such as one originating from the Child ego state at an inappropriate time?
7. Explain how the problem-ownership model works.
8. Give an organizational example of the use of I-messages and active listening.
9. Observe the nonverbal communication behavior of people for fifteen minutes. What nonverbal behaviors did you observe? Did people respond more powerfully to nonverbal or verbal comments?
10. Do you think the open communication used by many Japanese companies (described in the Perspective: Open Communication in Japanese-Owned Companies) is appropriate for American companies? Why or why not?

Key Concepts and Terms

communication process
fields of experience
grapevine
one-way communication
two-way communication
transactional analysis

ulterior transactions
interpersonal listening
informational listening
problem-ownership model
active listening
I-messages

ego states   nonverbal communication
crossed transactions   paralinguistics
complementary transactions

Suggested Readings

Villere, M.F. (1981). *Transactional analysis at work*. Englewood Cliffs, N.J.: Prentice-Hall.

D'Aprix, R. (1982). *Communicating for productivity*. New York: Harper and Row.

Gordon, T. (1977). *Leader effectiveness training L.E.T.* New York: Wyden.

Harrison, R.P. (1974). *Beyond words: An introduction to nonverbal communication*. Englewood Cliffs, N.J.: Prentice-Hall.

Nichols, R.G., and Stevens, L.A. (1957). *Are you listening?* New York: McGraw-Hill. (A classic in the field.)

CASES AND INCIDENTS

LaFayette Aerodynamics

Mark Brodstreet is a manager of technical budgets and expenses for LaFayette Aerodynamics. Technical cost analyst Leonardo Schultz reports to him. Communication between these two people is deplorable.

Part of the problem is that Leonardo was originally trained as an engineer and learned his cost accounting in night school. Brodstreet is a CPA with no technical training. He is forever holding forth in Leonardo's presence that engineers are an inferior breed with no conception of cost or profit.

For his part, Leonardo believes in the notion of "the whole man," and he feels that anyone who is monitoring costs should have a basic understanding of design and of the impact of cost cuts on the final product.

Recently, Leonardo supported a group of design engineers who protested Brodstreet's edict that 20 percent of the material cost had to be pruned from a new braking system for jet aircraft. In the middle of a group discussion, Brodstreet lost his temper, abruptly ended the

meeting, and stated that he was going to carry the whole matter to the vice-president of engineering.

Privately, he read the riot act to Leonardo and accused him of being "a frustrated engineer who couldn't make a living at it." He finished the confrontation by questioning Leonardo's "two-bit night-school accounting degree" and reminding him that his first loyalty was to Brodstreet and not to a bunch of spendthrift engineers. They haven't spoken to each other for two weeks now, except to carry on the most essential and rudimentary communication.

From R. D'Aprix, 1972, Why they tune you out. *Machine Design*, December 28. Copyright 1972 by Penton Industrial Publishing Co., Inc., Cleveland, Ohio. Used with permission.

Discussion questions

1. Describe the transactions between Mark and Leonardo using TA.
2. How might this communication problem be handled more effectively using the problem-ownership model?

What Is Happening Here?

Discussion questions

1. Read the nonverbal behavior. What do you see happening here?
2. Describe the specific parts of the nonverbal behavior—face, posture, head position—that caused you to make your conclusions.

Reprinted with permission of Hilton Hotel Corporation, Beverly Hills, California.

Joe's Benders

A foreman found that one of his men, Joe, was punching in late almost every Monday morning. He talked with Joe about this and Joe readily admitted that he was having trouble getting up on Mondays because of too much celebrating on weekends.

The next Monday, Joe rang in late again and, when the foreman saw him, Joe just grinned. Again, the foreman talked to Joe and asked him to cooperate by getting to work on time. Joe promised that he would try.

However, the following Monday, Joe was late again. This time, the foreman called Joe in and gave him a written reprimand. He also told him that if he was late again, it would mean time off without pay. Joe realized that the foreman meant business and promised that it would not happen again.

For three Mondays in a row, Joe was on time. The foreman began to think that he had solved the problem. But, on the fourth Monday, Joe did not appear. The later it got, the angrier the foreman got.

When Joe finally walked in, the foreman met him at the door. "All right," he said angrily, "you've asked for it. That will cost you time off without pay."

When Joe tried to talk, the foreman shut him off by saying, "I don't want to hear any alibis. You can't talk me into changing my mind."[35]

Discussion questions

1. Was the foreman's action appropriate? Why or why not?

Additional Information:

During the remainder of that day and the next, the foreman noticed that the other men were acting cold and resentful toward him. He couldn't figure it out until another foreman told him that the man he had suspended was late, not because he had been on a bender the night before, but because he had wrecked his car on the way to work to keep from hitting a boy on a bike who had swerved in front of him. Joe had even refused to go to a doctor to check for possible injury to himself because he wanted to get to work as soon as possible.

2. Now, what should the foreman do?

3. How would the problem-ownership model apply here?

REFERENCES

1. Mintzberg, H. (1975), The manager's job: Folklore and fact, *Harvard Business Review* 53. (4): 49–61.

2. For more information on communication theory and processes, *see* Fischer, D. (1981), *Communication in organizations*, St. Paul, Minn.: West; Rosenblatt, S.B.; Cheatham, T.R.; and Watt, J.T. (1982), *Communication in business*, 2nd ed., Englewood Cliffs, N.J.: Prentice-Hall; and Porter, L.W. and Roberts, K.H. (1976), Communication in organizations, in *Handbook of industrial and organizational psychology*, ed. M.D. Dunnette, pp. 1553–89 Chicago: Rand-McNally.

3. Daft, R.L. and Wiginton, J.S. (1979), Language and organization, *Academy of Management Review* 4: 179–91.

4. D'Aprix, R. (1982), The oldest (and best) way to communicate with employees, *Harvard Business Review* Sep.–Oct.: 30–32.

5. Zuboff, S. (1982), New worlds of computer-mediated work, *Harvard Business Review* Sep.–Oct.: 142–53.

6. For more information about the grapevine, *see* Davis, K. (1973), The care and cultivation of the corporate grapevine, *Dun's Review* July: 44–77; and Rowan, R. (1979), Where did that rumor come from?, *Fortune* August: 130–37. This example is adapted from Davis, K. (1953), Management communication and the grapevine, *Harvard Business Review* Sep.–Oct.: 44.

7. *See* Herold, D.M. and Greller, M.M. (1977), Feedback: Definition of a construct, *Academy of Management Journal* 20: 142–47.

8. Berne, E. (1972), *What do you say after you say hello?*, New York: Grove Press.

9. Berne, *What do you say after you say hello?*

10. For more coverage of TA, *see* Villere, M.F., (1981), *Transactional analysis at work*. Englewood Cliffs, N.J.: Prentice-Hall; James, M. and Jongeward, D. (1971), *Born to Win: Transactional analysis with gestalt experiments*, Reading, Mass.: Addison-Wesley; and Jongeward, D., ed. (1976), *Everybody wins: Transactional analysis applied to organizations*, rev. ed., Reading, Mass.: Addison-Wesley.

11. Berne, *What do you say after you say hello?*

12. James, M. (1975), *The OK boss*, Reading, Mass.: Addison-Wesley.

13. Bowen, D.D. and Nath, R. (1975), Transactions in management, *California Management Review* 18(2): 73–85.

14. Harper, M.B. (1976), Banking on people and TA, in *Everybody wins*, ed. D. Jongeward, pp. 189–96.

15. Tiano, K.O. (1976), Transactional analysis applied to Mountain Bell, in *Everybody wins*, ed. D. Jongeward, pp. 197–218.

16. Musselwhite, E. (1976), TA in selling, in *Everybody wins*, ed. D. Jongeward, pp. 219–29.

17. Scott, D. (1976), Using transactional analysis in seminars for career women, in *Everybody wins*, ed. D. Jongeward, pp. 151–88.

18. Quote from Randall, L.K. (1976), Red, white, and blue TA at 600 MPH, in *Everybody wins*, ed. D. Jongeward, p. 133.

19. Barker, L.L. (1971), *Listening behavior*. Englewood Cliffs, N.J.: Prentice-Hall; and Steil, L.K. (undated), Your listening profile. Sperry Corporation.

20. Adapted from Ernst, F.H., Jr. (1968), *Who's listening?*, Vallejo, Ca.: Addressoset.

21. Based on the works of Gordon, T. (1977), *Leader effectiveness training L.E.T.*, New York: Wyden.

22. Adapted from Gordon, *Leader effectiveness training L.E.T.*

23. Nichols, R.G. and Stevens, L.A. (1957), *Are you listening?*. New York: McGraw-Hill; Weaver, C.H. (1972), *Human listening: Processes and behavior*, Indianapolis, Ind.: Bobbs-Merrill. Langs, R. (1978), *The listening process*, New York: Aronson, E. and Devine, T.G. (1978), Listening: What do we know after fifty years of research and theorizing, *Journal of Reading* January.

24. Adapted from Nichols and Stevens, *Are you listening?*

25. Edinger, J.A. and Patterson, M.L. (1983), Nonverbal involvement and social control, *Psychological Bulletin* 93: 30–56.

26. Mehrabian, A. (1968), Communication without words, *Psychology Today* 1: 53–55. *Also see* Mehrabian, A. (1971), *Silent Messages*, Belmont, Calif.: Wadsworth.

27. Mehrabian, Communication without words.

28. For more complete coverage of facial expressions, *see* Ekman, P. and Friesen, W.V. (1975), *Unmasking the face: A guide to recognizing emotions from facial cues*, Englewood Cliffs, N.J.: Prentice-Hall.

29. Hatvany, N. and Pucik, V. 1981, Japanese management practices and productivity, *Organizational Dynamics* Spring: 4–21.

30. Hatvany and Pucik, Japanese management practices and productivity, p. 16.

31. Hatvany and Pucik, Japanese management practices and productivity, p. 16.

32. LaFrance, M. and Mayo, C. (1978), *Moving bodies: Nonverbal communication in social relationships*, Monterey, Ca.: Brooks/Cole.

33. Mehrabin, Communication without words.

34. *See* Goldhaber, G.M. (1983), *Organizational communication*, 3rd ed., Dubuque, Ia.: Wm C. Brown.

35. Abridged from Hall, W.S. (1974), Lessons from a communication blunder, in *Transactional analysis on the job & communicating with subordinates*, rev. ed., ed. C. Albano and T. Rendero, pp. 163–64, New York: AMACOM.

Group Dynamics: Individuals Working Together

PREVIEW

- Why are some groups very effective while others can go so far as to be destructive?

- How can task, maintenance, and blocking roles affect the performance of groups?

- Will people always work harder if they get paid a lot more for their effort?

- How can you earn idiosyncratic credits?

- When should you avoid a big office with carpets?

- When should you avoid a cohesive group?

- What is "schmoozing" and "social loafing"?

- How do you prevent "reality shock" for new employees?

- When is teamwork needed and how can you get it?

PREVIEW CASE: THE EXIT INTERVIEW

Karen Lopez is a personnel specialist who conducts exit interviews of employees who are leaving to find out why they are quitting with the ultimate goal of lowering quit rates. There has been a continuing problem with the Machine Department. New people just don't seem to last more than a few months. Karen is interviewing the latest quitter, Roy Zukowski, to see if she can get to the heart of the problem.

Karen: Roy, why are you quitting?

Roy: I just didn't seem to fit in. The group made it rough on me. They all seemed to be mad at me for some reason.

Karen: What did you do that made them mad?

Roy: Well, I'm not really sure, but I believe it all started my first day of work when I came in fifteen minutes early to get my tools ready so I'd be all set to start at 7:30. One of the guys came over to me and said: "We don't do any work at all before 7:30, so don't get here early. First thing you know the foreman will want all of us to get here fifteen minutes early." I took his advice and didn't start before 7:30 any more.

Karen: Was that the only thing?

Roy: Oh, no, there were plenty of other incidents. It wasn't long before I was cornered in the washroom and told that I was working too hard. If I didn't watch out I would machine over twenty-five units a day, which is more than the twenty units most others produce. Since I was working pretty easily to produce that many and I wanted to earn the maximum bonus for extra production, I kept making more in spite of what the others said. Besides the foreman, Joe Taylor, told me I was really doing a great job when I made twenty-five or even thirty units a day.

Karen: Sounds like you were doing a good job.

Roy: Yea, but the others started making life miserable for me. They started insulting me and making fun of me whenever they could. I tried to ignore it, but after a while it gets under your skin.

Also, I started to get more than my share of the dirty work. We are supposed to rotate the undesirable jobs, like cleaning the tool dip solution, but somehow I seem to be getting saddled with too many of these "skut" jobs. When I complained, it just seemed to make things worse. The foreman called me in and said how disappointed he was that I was getting the reputation as a "troublemaker" and complainer and that I should just do what I'm told. Then I got chewed out because someone in the shop had filed a grievance against me for doing a job they were assigned—it doesn't pay to have initiative around here!

Karen: Do you have any idea why you weren't accepted by the others?

Roy: Maybe it's because I like to dress nice. I always come to work with a clean and neatly pressed set of work clothes. The others are pretty sloppy and dirty. They wear the same pair of jeans all week long.

Another thing might be that I just don't seem to be interested in the same things they are. If you don't like football or baseball, and

Understanding Organizational Behavior

I don't, then you can't really join in the conversations. So I always felt left out.

I guess the main reason for leaving is that I just couldn't work with the people down there. The company is good, the pay is high, the benefits are terrific, but when you hate to come to work every day because of your co-workers, it's time to change.

Almost everyone in an organization is a member of one or more groups. A typical manager belongs to many groups; for example, a primary workgroup, the strategic planning committee, the social committee, the engineering-change task force, a lunch-time jogging group, the department's bowling league. Groups are often useful for getting the job done, but they can cause problems as indicated in the exit interview just described. This chapter is about an extremely important aspect of managing organizations—understanding group dynamics and making effective use of groups to get the job done.

Group dynamics includes a number of concepts that help explain how groups function. We will cover several of these concepts in this chapter including: the nature of groups, group roles, norms, status, cohesiveness, and socialization. In addition, we will briefly look at managing work groups into effective teams.

The Nature of Groups

Since group behavior is a central concern of organizational behavior, we will begin the chapter with a discussion of some basic definitional issues. Then we will cover why people join groups and problems that happen when people are excluded from groups.

■ What Is a Group?

A **group** is a collection of individuals who have interactions with one another toward some common goal or purpose.[1] Groups are different from a collection of individuals in several ways.[2] Group members interact with one another and share a set of goals, roles, and norms that give direction to their activities. We will discuss these issues later in the chapter. They also have some common bonds that tend to develop from common likes, dislikes, and interests. Not all interacting sets of people are groups. The engineering department at Boeing Aircraft Corporation is too large to be a group. So is the junior class at most universities. In larger conglomerations of people, there will be a number of groups coexisting together, each with its own thread of commonality. People can also be excluded from groups even when they wish they were members, as was Roy in our opening example.

■ Why Do People Join Groups?

For thousands of years people have formed groups to get a job done more effectively whether it be hunting, erecting a home, defending a village, or building a boat. Since groups are generally more effective at solving complex problems than are individuals, organizations are constantly form-

Table 9.1. Positive impact of groups on organizational and individual effectiveness.

The impact of groups on organizational effectiveness	The impact of groups on individual employee effectiveness
Accomplishing tasks that could not be done by individual employees	Aiding in learning about the organization and its environment
Bringing a number of skills and talents to bear on complex, difficult tasks	Aiding in learning about one's self
Providing a vehicle for decision making that permits multiple and conflicting views to be aired and considered	Providing help in gaining new skills
Providing an efficient means for organizational control of employee behavior	Obtaining valued rewards that are not accessible by one's self
Increasing organizational stability by transmitting shared beliefs and values to new employees	Satisfying important personal needs, especially needs for social acceptance and affiliation

Adapted from David A. Nadler, J. Richard Hackman, and Edward E. Lawler, III, *Managing Organizational Behavior*, p. 102. Copyright © 1979 by David A. Nadler, J. Richard Hackman, and Edward E. Lawler, III. Used by permission of the publisher, Little, Brown and Company.

ing task forces and committees to cope with organizational problems. (We will talk more about using groups for decision making in later chapters.)

Social Interaction and Commitment   Groups provide opportunities for social interaction; they facilitate friendships, companionship, and satisfaction of our social needs. Groups help develop commitment and loyalty. One of the first things the armed forces do with new recruits is form them into groups. These groups often develop a tremendous esprit de corps during basic training. They serve as a support system, a training vehicle, and a source of obtaining commitment to the goals of the service.

Interpersonal Attraction   If a person finds a group or a person in a group particularly attractive, then that will be a strong motivator to join that group. Research has shown that there are several factors that influence attractiveness.[3] The first, close proximity, means that we are usually attracted to those that are near us. It is much more likely that we will join an attractive group in our own office rather than in sales, which is located across the street. In addition, people who have to spend a lot of time interacting are also more likely to form groups. Physical and emotional attractiveness are powerful magnets between people. Finally, we tend to see people as more attractive if they are like us in terms of sex, race, interests, or background.

■ Problems When People Are Excluded from Groups

While the tendency to include or exclude people from a group based on attractiveness seems normal, it can cause a number of organizational problems, especially for minorities. A recent study of five organizations[4] found that friendship groups for people working in the organizations tended to exclude women and nonwhites. Work group inclusion, on the other

Understanding Organizational Behavior

9.1 | *Perspective, Group Size: Bigger is NOT Better*[5]

A group should be big enough to get the job done, but not too big. Adding people to a group beyond the minimum number required will tend to decrease productivity because of group process losses. Process losses mean the inevitable inefficiencies that result from people working, interacting, and communicating together. Students working in groups on a class project is a good example—isn't there always someone who is unmotivated or someone who can never come to meetings or fails to get the word? Also, the marginal contribution of adding one more person gets lower as the size of the group gets larger. Adding a person to a two-member group might add significant new resources. But adding one more person to a ten-member group will generally add little if any new resources. The three hypothetical graphs below illustrate this point.[6]

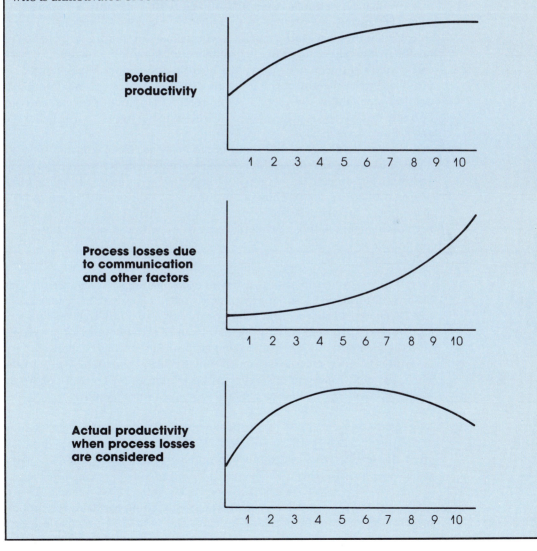

hand, seemed to be more influenced by authority position (such as being a director or vice-president) and the education of the group member.

A widely recognized problem of women in managerial positions is the natural exclusion of women from many of the informal groups to which males belong.[7] In addition, there are often sexual overtones to including women in male friendship groups. Sometimes a woman is *too* attractive for the male group member's comfort.

Role Behavior: Doing What's Expected

Just as an actor learns how to play a role, organizational participants learn how to play their roles as manager, subordinate, machine operator, popular person, or politician. A **role** is a set of expectations believed by the individual or group to be associated with a person who occupies a given position in the group or organization.[8] Roles are learned in many complex ways.[9] Business schools attempt to develop students into a "managerial role." Organizations attempt to socialize "newcomers" into their proper role. Group members indoctrinate new members in the proper role behavior for that group. One of Roy's problems in the opening incident was the role conflict between what he saw as his role (to produce a high number of units) and what the group saw as his role (to conform to the maximum production specified by the group). While role-development processes are important, we will focus primarily on the relationship between role behaviors and group effectiveness.

It takes a number of different roles to make an effective group. The primary ones are **task roles,** which are concerned with getting the job done, and **maintenance roles,** which are concerned with maintaining the interpersonal relationships within the group.[10] In addition, some group roles may oppose the group's goals. These dysfunctional roles are called **blocking roles.** Figure 9.1 visually depicts the roles people play in groups.

■ Task Roles

While a group can have a variety of tasks or things it is trying to accomplish, a common one is solving problems so that a goal may be reached. The role behaviors in this section relate primarily to groups engaged in some type of group problem-solving activity. In an effectively functioning group, both the members and the leader will play a variety of roles. As you read the descriptions of the roles ask yourself which roles you may play in a group. Then, the next time you observe a group in action, try to pick out which roles lead to more effective group behavior. Task roles include:

Initiator-Contributor   Proposing new ideas, starting the discussion, or proposing a task, goal, or solution are all initiating activities. While it is often the leader who is the most frequent initiator, any member of the group can play this role.

Information Seeker   Seeking facts, searching for data, researching sources, asking experts, or asking for clarifications are all information-seeking activities. This is a particularly important role, since many groups tend to act without full information.

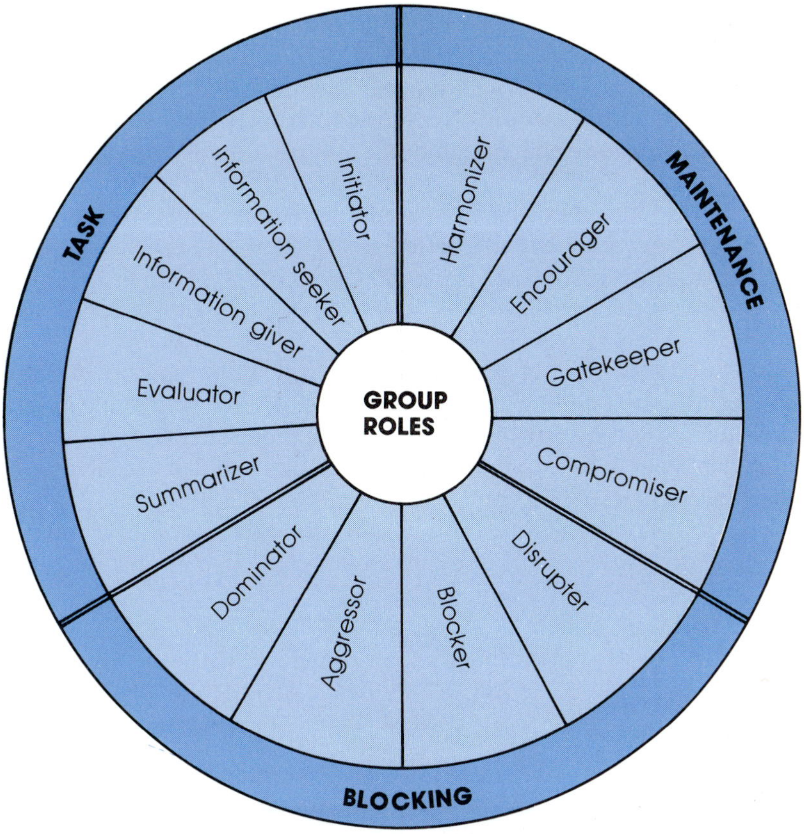

Figure 9.1. Roles in groups.[11]

Information Giver   Offering authoritative facts or relevant experiences provides the group with more data for their decision. Providing examples to elaborate a suggestion or issue might also be part of this role. Interpreting ideas, defining terms, and clarifying the issues before the group all help the group understand the issues.

Evaluator   Questioning the practicality, logic, or procedures may be a help or hindrance to the group. If the group sees the evaluation as critical and threatening, members may get defensive and interaction may decline or stop. This is especially likely to happen if the leader criticizes the idea. If the evaluation is seen as reality testing, then the reaction may be more positive.

Summarizer   Pulling together all the related issues, restating positions, and sometimes checking to see if the group is ready to make a decision by proposing alternatives are all parts of the summarizer role.

■ Maintenance Roles

Role behavior that contributes to building and maintaining the interpersonal relationships of the group is referred to as **maintenance.** If people do not feel good about the group, they may leave it (as Roy did in the opening incident) or be ineffective members. Maintenance roles are considered to be group-centered because they tend to build or keep the group at a given level of energy. Maintenance roles include:

Harmonizer   This role involves reconciling differences between other members, getting people to explore differences, and minimizing conflicts and reducing tension through humor or other diversionary tactics.

Encourager   Praising and providing reinforcement to other group members encourages them to participate and contribute. Being friendly, warm, and accepting is part of this role. Obviously, Roy did not encounter an encourager in the machine shop.

Gatekeeper   This very important role involves controlling the communication by opening and closing the "gate" in a way that gets everyone involved. It means getting people to share their ideas with the group by encouraging quiet people to talk (we haven't heard from Sue yet) or suggesting procedures that let everyone contribute, such as going "round robin" to everyone. Regulating the flow of communication (why not limit the length of our presentations so everyone will have a chance to contribute?) is also part of the gatekeeping role.

Compromiser   Offering to meet someone "half way" or providing a face-saving way out of a conflict is evidence that the compromiser role is being used.

■ Blocking Roles

Not all group roles are helpful. Often people try to meet their own needs without regard for the group. This results in a block for the group in accomplishing its goals. Sometimes the group leader is the blocker without realizing it, although just as with task and maintenance roles, anyone can play a blocking role. When blocking roles arise, it is important the group members be trained to recognize them and deal with them with the effective use of task and maintenance roles. The following are examples of blocking roles:

Dominator   This is a role that is easy for the leader to play. The dominator trys to control the group by asserting authority or by appearing superior. In addition, a dominator may try to interrupt or otherwise control the contributions of others. The dominator is best dealt with by another member playing a gatekeeping role, although this may prove difficult if the leader is the problem.

Blocker   Stubbornly opposing the group beyond reason, often for personally oriented reasons is the main thrust of the blocker's role. Other forms of blocking behavior may involve the use of hidden agendas or attempting to bring back an issue that the group has previously rejected.

Aggressor   The aggressor uses a number of tactics to express disapproval of another's suggestion including attacking the person, group, or problem; joking in a sarcastic or barbed way; or trying to take credit for contributions of others. This behavior is especially destructive and difficult to handle. If the behavior cannot be brought under control, it is often better to remove such people from the group.

Disrupter   This person does not share the group's goals and is not really involved. Cynicism, nonchalance, withdrawal and irrelevant humor or horseplay are examples of disruptive behavior.

Norms: Governors of Group Behavior

Groups have powerful ways to control group behavior. One of the strongest and most pervasive ways that groups control behavior is through **norms,** which are rules of behavior and expected ways of acting, that have been accepted as legitimate by members of the group.[12] Groups expect their members to behave in certain ways, such as not coming to work until the exact starting time of 7:30 or not producing over twenty units per day. Members are expected to conform. If they do not, they are considered to be deviants and pressure is applied to make them conform. Norms and roles are related. Whereas a norm is an expectation applying to all group members, a role is an expectation about behavior that applies to a specific position, such as group leader. A leader who quits leading would encounter much the same kind of pressure to conform as a group member who was producing too much.

■ The Importance of Norms

Norms can be positive, neutral, or negative in their effect on organizations. A norm that is negative from the organization's perspective may be

Figure 9.2. Norms influence work behavior

"Delehanty, we've been getting reports that you're always cheery on the job. What's your game?"

quite positive from the employee's perspective. In the following paragraphs, we take an organizational perspective, but the example at the end of the next paragraph shows a different point of view

Negative Norms

Norms often make the difference between a high-performing, effective organization and a marginal one. The behavior of management, especially if Theory X values are predominant, may cause negative norms. For example, if the work groups are alienated so that norms develop around production restriction, poor quality, avoiding communications with management, and minimizing the amount of time spent working, then the organization has big problems. The following excerpt is a classic example of how an experienced worker, Starkey, indoctrinates a new guy, Tennessee, into the norms that apply to dealings with the industrial engineer who does the time and motion studies for their job.[13]

> *"If you expect to get any kind of a price, you got to outwit that son-of-a-bitch! You got to use your noodle while you're working, and think your work out ahead as you go along! You got to add in movements you know you ain't going to make when you're running the job! Remember, if you don't screw them, they're going to screw you! . . . Every movement counts!"*
>
> *"Another thing," said Starkey, "You were running that job too damn fast before they timed you on it! I was watching you yesterday. If you don't run a job slow before you get timed, you won't get a good price. They'll look at the record of what you do before they come around and compare it with the timing speed. Those time-study men are sharp!"*
>
> *"I wasn't going very fast yesterday," exclaimed Tennessee. "Hell, I was going as slow as I could without wearing myself out slowing down."*
>
> *"Well, maybe it just looked fast, because you were going so steady at it," said Starkey.*
>
> *"I don't see how I could of run it any slower," said Tennessee, "I stood there like I was practically paralyzed!"*
>
> *"Remember those bastards are paid to screw you," said Starkey. "And that's all they got to think about. They'll stay up half the night figuring out how to beat you out of a dime. They figure you're going to try to fool them, so they make allowances for that. They set the prices low enough to allow for what you do."*
>
> *"Well, then, what the hell chance have I got?" asked Tennessee.*
>
> *"It's up to you to figure out how to fool them more than they allow for," said Starkey.*
>
> *"The trouble with me is I get nervous with that guy standing in back of me, and I can't think," said Tennessee.*
>
> *"You just haven't had enough experience yet," said Starkey. "Wait until you have been here a couple of years and you'll do your best thinking when those guys are standing behind you."*

From page 15 of *Money and Motivation: An Analysis of Incentives* by William Foote Whyte. Copyright © 1955, by Harper & Row, Publishers, Inc. Reprinted by permission of the publisher.

Positive Norms

Positive norms contribute to organizational effectiveness. For example, a norm of cost consciousness or positive customer

Table 9.2. Example of positive and negative organizational norms.

| | Examples | |
Categories	Positive Norms	Negative Norms
Organizational and personal pride	Members speak up for the company when it is criticized unfairly	Members don't care about company problems
Performance/Excellence	Members try to improve, even if they are doing well.	Members are satisfied with the minimum level of performance necessary.
Leadership/Supervision	Members ask for help when they need it	Members hide their problems and avoid their superiors
Customer/Consumer relations	Members show concern about serving the customers	Members are indifferent and, when possible, hostile to customers
Innovation and change	Members are usually looking for better ways of doing their job	Members stick to the old ways of doing their jobs

Abridged from P. F. Allen and S. Pilnick, 1973, Confronting the shadow organization: How to detect and defeat negative norms, *Organizational Dynamics* 1:3–18. Copyright © 1973 by AMACOM, a division of American Management Associations, New York, N.Y. Used with permission.

relations can have strong payoffs for the organization. Examples of positive and negative norms are shown in Table 9.2.

■ How Groups Control Deviance from the Norm[14]

Even though group members generally conform with the norms, groups must deal with the deviate. The first thing a group does when someone steps out of line is apply some type of pressure. Often this is a warning accompanied by a frown or anguished face—in other words, a mild form of punishment. This may be enough to correct the behavior, especially if the group member is new and wants to be a part of the group. If the deviant behavior continues, the group will constantly apply pressure until such time as the group physically or psychologically rejects the deviant. The amount of effort a group will expend trying to correct a deviant depends on who is deviating. If a long-time, highly valued group member is deviating, this person may be able to get away with more and will be pressured for a much longer time before rejection.

In our opening example, Roy was a new person on the floor and, when he deviated from the norms by producing too much, the pressure did not last long before he was rejected from the group. In Roy's case, he seemed to value the extra money more than membership in the group—at least at first. If the group had more powerful rewards and punishments at its disposal, then the chances of bringing Roy into compliance with the norms would have been much better.

In contrast to Roy, an old-timer like Starkey in the time study incident could deviate from group norms and get away with it. Deviations by "old-timers" are tolerated because these people have accumulated "idiosyncratic credits" (*see* the Perspective: Idiosyncratic Credits).

Over a period of time a group member can accrue **idiosyncratic credits** by being a good member of the group, by conforming to group norms and expectations, and by developing a history of working to accomplish group goals. By being a good "group citizen" a positive balance is built up and may be called upon to excuse some deviant behaviors. For example, an executive who has built up idiosyncratic credits might use them to deviate from a norm calling for conservative business attire and wear sports attire to a sales meeting.

■ Developing and Changing Norms

Evolutionary Norm Development

Norms may be developed in an evolutionary manner—often almost accidently. For example, one day a highly valued group member may say, "I don't think managers are to be trusted. Look what they did to me." Other group members may say, "Yea, he's right, we just can't trust managers." Thus, a norm is born. The incident that caused the norm may be long forgotten. Even the people may change, but the norm is still there.

Systematically Analyzing and Changing Norms

Another way norms may be developed is for a group to consciously discuss and decide what its norms should be. Newly formed groups sometimes use this method to develop norms. This strategy is also the key for changing norms. Existing norms can be clearly defined and analyzed and, if needed, changed. Let's say an analysis shows that a norm for customer service is indifference—customers are tolerated but we do not go out of our way to help them. Once this norm has surfaced, we can discuss it as a group and perhaps decide that it is contrary to our group goal of organizational effectiveness. Then we must set a new norm to replace the old one and put emphasis on reinforcing behavior that conforms to the new norm. However, some norms may be very difficult to change regardless of the amount of analysis and effort expended in the change attempt.

Norm Profiles

Another strategy for changing norms is for the group to determine which categories of norms are important for maintaining the group and accomplishing the group's task. These might include such items as teamwork, colleagual relationships, personal pride in the work, or customer relations. Each norm might then be evaluated in a graphic profile like the one in Table 9.3. Then strong and weak areas could be analyzed and changes implemented where desired. The profile in Table 9.3 shows several areas that may need improvement including pride in work, customer relations, and leadership.

Table 9.3. Norm profile.[16]

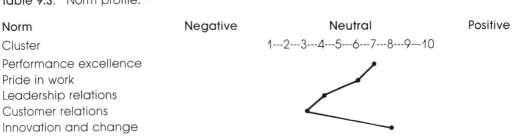

Norm Cluster	Negative	Neutral 1---2---3---4---5---6---7---8---9---10	Positive
Performance excellence			
Pride in work			
Leadership relations			
Customer relations			
Innovation and change			

Status: A System of Ranking

■ What Is Status?

Within a group, an individual has a rank or worth that is their **status** in that group. Status is determined by the group using the behaviors, attributes, characteristics, and possessions that are valued by that group. Status sometimes comes with the position, such as union steward or finance director. Status in the group is also related to status in society. A handsome medical doctor from a well-known family, who drives a new Mercedes and heads the local civic club, may have a great deal of status in a group such as the local school board. Most groups are influenced by the overall person; one's overall status in society is just one important input.

■ Status and Behavior

Status determines what behaviors are appropriate for group members. A common group norm is for low-status people to defer to high-status people. In Japan, for example, where status is largely determined by age, one always defers to and bows to an elder. In our culture, a high-status person will initiate more conversations with low-status people. Also, when a high-status person talks, group members pay attention. The high-status person has power and influence and of course more idiosyncratic credits. Usually, the group leader is a high-status person, especially if the person has become leader because of personal attributes, effective judgement, and long service to the group.

■ Status Incongruence

When a person is high on some valued characteristic, like education, but low on others such as experience, or when talents seem inappropriate for the position, then **status incongruence** exists.[17] One common example is the new college graduate who is placed in charge of a number of experienced production workers. This is often an uncomfortable position for both sets of people. The production group may reconcile their discomfort by finding sufficient reasons to accept the status of their new boss. Or, they may resist by covertly trying to sabotage the boss or letting him blunder into mistakes. Lt. Fuzz, in the comic strip "Beatle Bailey," was always getting into some kind of trouble because of status incongruence.

An important part of maintaining and displaying status is the use of possessions, clothes, office, or voice to show our status. These are called **status symbols,** since they are visual, physical, or audible indicators of our relative status. Here is an example of how one manager got into trouble because of the misuse of status symbols that resulted in status incongruence:

An "up-and-coming" young middle-manager had a relatively responsible job with his own office and a private secretary. The trouble was that the manager's office looked drab—small painted desk, common low-backed chair, tiled floor. He decided to fix up the office at his own expense. He built a large walnut top to go over the desk, then bought a piece of carpet, a high-backed executive chair, and some paintings and plants. The office was beautiful! Unfortunately, his supervisors were not thrilled. Every time one of them would come in the office, a sarcastic remark or nonverbal cue would be uttered about his "fancy office." The manager did not take the hints; and, when his performance evaluation was due, it turned out lower than he had expected. While we cannot be certain of the reason for the lower rating, it is possible that the status incongruence made his supervisor so uncomfortable that it affected the performance rating.

Cohesiveness: How Tight the Group?

When a group has a very strong hold on its members because of the attractiveness of the group, it is a **cohesive** group.[18] Strong loyalty to the group and a desire to remain a group member are indicators of cohesiveness, especially when everyone in the group shares these feelings. Cohesive groups tend to feel good about themselves and evaluate themselves quite favorably. In fact, cohesion often results in distorted perceptions of both group members and the outsiders.

■ What Makes a Group Cohesive?

Cohesiveness is related to attractiveness.[19] If a group is attractive to its members, it is more likely to be cohesive. Groups whose members share backgrounds, attitudes and interests also develop more cohesion than groups that do not. Agreement with the group's goals, leadership, and at-

Table 9.4. Examples of high-status items.

Furniture	Large wood desk, couch, high-backed chair.
Interior decorations	Rugs, paintings, plants, draperies.
Location of office	Top floor, corner, good view.
Facilities	Large-sized office, computer terminal, private bathroom, desk water bottle.
Quality of equipment	New Cadillac for company car.
Type of clothes worn	Expensive suits, silk ties.
Privileges given	Club membership, company jet, and car.
Job titles	Director, vice-president, chief.
Employees assigned	Private secretary, executive assistant.

Adapted from K. Davis, 1981, *Human behavior at work*, 6th ed., p. 37. Copyright © 1981 by McGraw-Hill. Reprinted by permission of the publisher.

mosphere also have an impact on the group's desirability. High entrance requirements are often used for entry into certain groups, like a fraternity or an elite military unit. The initiation rites into these groups create a common bond of accomplishment that results in cohesion. A final, powerful factor that makes groups cohesive is success; groups that succeed are more desirable.

■ Is Cohesiveness Desirable?

The effectiveness of highly cohesive groups depends on the direction of their effort and their norms. If they have norms of high performance that agree with organizational goals, then the group probably will be effective. If, on the other hand, their efforts are directed toward restricting production because of negative norms, the group can be a powerful negative force. Research results seem to support this view. One review of thirty-four research studies found twelve positive relationships between cohesion and productivity, eleven negative relationships, and eleven insignificant relationships.[20] Group drive (motivation, enthusiasm, esprit) was a more powerful predictor of performance than cohesion. The key to using cohesive groups is to harness their energy toward positive norms. You must also be

9.3 "Schmoozing" or "Social Loafing"?

Two recent approaches to understanding group performance offer contrasting approaches to using group dynamics.

Schmoozing[21]

Groups should be designed so they can schmooze; So they can get together in groups of four or five and talk, fool around, or use the telephone. "There is no reason why workers cannot complete their tasks while schmoozing. Anyone who is familiar with factory life knows that workers find informal ways of doing this anyway, by having their 'buddies' cover for them. Why not recognize this basic human need to socialize, and build it into the work structure. Given the same level of freedom, a community of workers could organize this informal buddy system to make their work life more humane, and still complete the amount of work expected of them, as they presently do."

Social Loafing[22]

The researchers who coined the term *social loafing* believe that groups produce less than individuals because individual group members feel less pressure to perform when they are working with others. This may be because when they are carrying part of the load, no one can tell who is loafing. In addition to avoiding the consequences of slacking off, individuals also may be "lost in the crowd" and not receive credit for working hard. The researchers cite a number of experiments including a rope-pulling task where individuals are blindfolded and believe they are pulling as part of a group when they are really pulling alone. When they believe they are acting with one other person, they pulled at 90 percent of what they did when alone. When they believed two people were pulling, they pulled only 85 percent. The researchers conclude that social loafing is "a kind of social disease, with negative consequences for individuals, institutions, and societies."

careful about decisions made by cohesive groups since they tend to distort inputs. More will be said about this tendency in the chapter on decision making.

Socialization: Learning the Ropes

So far in this chapter we have covered the dynamics that govern group behavior. In this section, we discuss how individuals are integrated into the group through **socialization**—the process of learning the norms, values, and behavior patterns of the group and the organization.[23] New members have to learn the goals, the preferred means for reaching the goals, the behaviors that are expected for their role, and the norms of the group. When a newcomer has high motivation to be a member of the group and has correctly anticipated the norms of the group, then socialization is easy. Under these circumstances a new person will work hard and adapt easily. However, a complete match in expectations is seldom achieved as Table 9.5 would indicate.

■ Unrealistic Expectations

Reality Shock   When the new group is not what a person expects, he or she may be surprised in either a positive or negative way.[24] If the surprise is positive, then the decision to join the group is positively reinforced, and the person feels good about the decision. If the surprise is negative, reality shock develops. Expectations are either unmet or are very different than anticipated. Perhaps this is what happened to Roy in the opening incident. He had expectations about how much he could produce and how

Table 9.5. Expectation and reality for managerial jobs.

Expectations	Reality
Thoughtful decision making	Most of the workday is devoted to interaction with other people; getting and exchanging information, persuading and negotiating.
Clearly scheduled and logically planned workday.	Impromptu, sporadic, and unplanned contacts; jumping from issue to issue and among different people.
Efforts devoted to "leading" subordinates, who defer to higher status.	Most of the time with outsiders; even subordinates challenge frequently the manager's authority.
Decisions made by rational judgment of individual in correct position to evaluate all the factors.	Decisions are the product of a complex brokerage and negotiation process, extending over time and involving large numbers of interested parties.
Objectives and goals clear and consistent.	Multiplicity of goals identified with different groups and interests that are conflicting and even contradictory; often-changing priorities.

Reprinted from L. R. Sayles, 1979, *Leadership: What effective managers really do . . . and how they do it*, p. 12. Copyright © 1979 by McGraw-Hill, New York. Used with permission of the publisher and approval of the author.

Understanding Organizational Behavior

much money he could make. He also expected management to value his efforts. Reality was that both the group and the organization valued adherence to the group's norms, which differed radically from Roy's. The result of reality shock is often disillusionment and exit from the organization.

Overcoming Reality Shock   One of the ways for dealing with unrealistic expectations is to give potential employees a more realistic and accurate picture of what it is like in the organization. Anyone who has ever been associated with the military knows that the recruiter's picture of what life is like in the service is considerably different from reality. The same thing happens with other organizations. Desirable candidates are given a very rosy picture of the organization. When they are actually hired, they find out that everything is not quite as they expected. To overcome this problem, a strategy is being used called **realistic job previews** (*see* the Perspective: Traditional and Realistic Job Previews and reference 25.) The idea is to give job applicants a preview of the job's positive *and* negative aspects so that expectations are more accurate. This method results in lower quit rates and higher job satisfaction.

■ Realistic Job Previews

Realistic previews are most useful when there are relatively large numbers of people seeking entry level jobs.[25] For example, when recruiting secretarial help, a traditional recruiting videotape might show exciting, challenging work, where everyone seems to be smiling and happy. A more realistic view might be that the job is routine and lacking in challenge and that there is close supervision with little opportunity to socialize with coworkers. Here is an example of a realistic preview used in a classified advertisement:[26]

WORKAHOLIC WANTED

As personal aide to tyrannical president and demanding general manager. Will be responsible for representing company in absence of above. Claims, administration, typing, general secretarial work, and coffee-making. Work load from panic to boredom. Applicant should have transportation background. Starting $14,000 PA. Applicants MUST write two-page letter explaining why they qualify including resume.

Realistic techniques can also be used by interviewers and in recruiting brochures. Realistic previews have been used in many varied situations, including college recruiting, insurance, and the armed forces.[27]

Workgroups: Managing Effective Teams

Using the concepts of group dynamics, it is now possible to design high-performing workgroups. In this section, we examine teambuilding as an approach to developing effective work teams. We also cover one example of the use of self-managing work teams. Since there are many different types of groups and numerous approaches to developing them, this section provides only a very basic introduction.

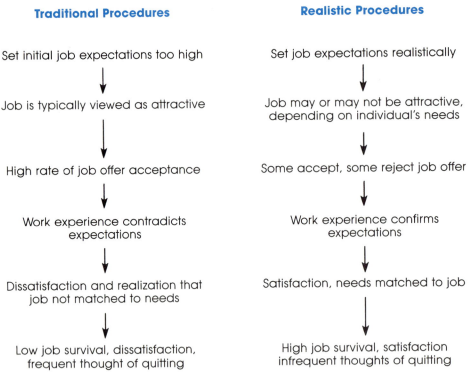

Traditional Procedures	Realistic Procedures
Set initial job expectations too high	Set job expectations realistically
↓	↓
Job is typically viewed as attractive	Job may or may not be attractive, depending on individual's needs
↓	↓
High rate of job offer acceptance	Some accept, some reject job offer
↓	↓
Work experience contradicts expectations	Work experience confirms expectations
↓	↓
Dissatisfaction and realization that job not matched to needs	Satisfaction, needs matched to job
↓	↓
Low job survival, dissatisfaction, frequent thought of quitting	High job survival, satisfaction infrequent thoughts of quitting

Figure 9.3. Traditional and realistic job previews.

From J. P. Wanous, 1975, Tell it like it is at realistic job previews, *Personnel* July-Aug.:54. Copyright © 1975 by AMACOM, a division of American Management Associations, New York, N.Y. Used with permission.

■ Teamwork Is Important

A **team** is a group who must work together in a collaborative way if individual and group goals are to be achieved.[28] While there are many different types of groups and teams, work teams are particularly important to organizations because many organizational tasks and goals are accomplished through teamwork. Attention to teamwork is an important managerial task. One way to think of teamwork is to use a sports analogy; to compare one type of work team, the management team, with a football team.

> It is obvious that to score touchdowns (and prevent the opponent from scoring) a football team has to play together. It should be just as obvious that a work unit or a management group must also work together to insure success. A football team practices over and over again how it will execute its plays. The team has "skull" practice— they talk over plans and strategies. They review films of past games, identify mistakes, set up goals for next week. Unfortunately, management groups [seldom] engage in similar types of activities. They do not review their past actions and they do not really plan new strategies. They do not come together to learn from their mistakes, nor do they practice or get coaching in new methods, set new goals, or build up their team "spirit."[29]

Understanding Organizational Behavior

■ Using Teambuilding

Developing teams so they work together more effectively, called **teambuilding**, requires some mechanism to review past actions, identify problems, and then develop strategies and skills for coping with the problems. This process is far from simple and often requires an outside consultant to help develop new norms centered around these behaviors.[30] Teambuilding involves trying to find out what problems are keeping the group from being as effective as it might be by collecting data through interviews or questionnaires. The results are fed back to the team, and they work on the problems they believe are most crucial. In the process, they learn skills of communicating and group decision making. The group develops action plans and monitors its progress toward the goals. If the teambuilding effort is a success, and it usually is, the group will more closely approach the ideal one described in the Perspective: Ideal Characteristics of an Effective Work Team.

■ Self-Managing Work Groups

Recently, there has been a great deal of interest in designing jobs around **self-managing work groups**.[31] These groups are given considerable freedom to design their own jobs, set their own goals, control and reward group members, and sometimes even hire their own members. Self-managing work groups can only be designed when people must **interact** to get the job done—when they need others to completely reach their goal. An example of an interacting group is the air crew of a large commercial airliner. The pilot depends on the engineer and other flight crew members to do their jobs.

Coacting workgroups, in contrast, consist of people who work together, share the same norms, work for the same boss, and interact socially. But, the task of each group member is independent of the other group members. For example, the classified ad clerks in a large newspaper are all members of one work group, but since they may complete their tasks independently of one another, they are members of a coacting group.

PERSPECTIVE

9.4 | Ideal Characteristics of an Effective Work Team[32]

■ The group atmosphere is informal, comfortable, and relaxed. When there is criticism, it is constructive and comfortable; there are no personal attacks.

■ There is lots of discussion and almost everyone participates. People listen to one another; every position is given a hearing.

■ The goals, tasks, and objectives are clearly understood and accepted by group members.

■ Decisions are based on consensus (it is clear that there is general agreement and everyone is willing to go along), but there is certainly discussion of disagreements; there is very little majority voting.

■ When action is taken, clear assignments are made and accepted.

■ The leader does not dominate the team or unduly defer to it.

Designing self-managing work groups is complex. You have to design not only the task itself, but the group composition, size, goals, norms, and skills. In addition, there may be problems with discipline, conflict resolution, and leadership. The following example shows how self-managing work groups were used at Butler Manufacturing.

> *A few years ago the management of Butler Manufacturing Company opened a new plant in Story City, Iowa, for the assembly of two-story-high grain driers that sell for about $25,000 each. Assembly of the grain driers is a fairly complicated operation, involving as many as 3000 different parts. Butler management decided that it would set up the work so that teams of workers would have autonomous responsibility for constructing the driers, rather than use a traditional production line.*
>
> *Members of the Butler work teams can work together pretty much as they wish in getting the driers assembled. Employees change their particular job assignments frequently within the teams, both as part of a formal rotational program and informally with the approval of other work-team members. Typically, operators in their first 18 months on the job master three of five basic tasks: assembly, fabricating, machining, painting, and shipping. In addition, they gain some experience with the other two types of work. At the end of 18 months, most employees are able to build an entire grain drier by themselves.*
>
> *There are no quality inspectors at Butler, only two engineers, and very few foremen. As a result, there is a substantial team involvement in supervisory functions, including hiring and promotion. Peers help select new team members, and two supervisors were picked by other staff from among the employees.*
>
> *One supervisor described how his functions are different than those of traditional first-line managers: "It's not the traditional scheduling, pushing people, and taking names. My job is heavily counseling people and behavior modification, and that's more interesting. Meanwhile, every night the conference room is filled with people having their team meetings during working hours and carrying on joint supervision."*
>
> *There are many kinds of meetings. Probably the most important are the weekly team meetings, in which production, quality, tooling, maintenance, and behavioral problems are considered. Leadership of the meetings rotates weekly. A monthly plant-wide meeting is held to discuss financial results and economic trends (productivity data are provided daily to each team).* [33]
>
> Reprinted from the *World of Work Report*, November 1977 by permission of the publisher. © 1977 Work in America Institute.

Self-managing work groups succeeded at Butler Manufacturing Company for a number of reasons. First, positive group norms encouraged members to reinforce the self-managing behavior. In addition, the supervisor's role was perceived to be that of a counselor and behavior modifier (perhaps more emphasis on maintenance roles). Group members seemed to experience a sense of freedom that may have resulted in a more enriched job with a heightened sense of responsibility. Another factor that helped foster success was the weekly and monthly meetings to iron out problems and discuss results.

Using self-managing work groups is only one way of making effective use of groups in organizational situations. Managers who consistently use the concepts of group dynamics explained in this chapter will find they are more effective in dealing with a wide range of group-related management issues.

SUMMARY

Chapter Review

- **Groups** are collections of individuals who have interactions with each other toward some common goal and share a set of roles and norms that give direction to their activities.
- People **join** groups because they get the job done more effectively, because they like the social interaction, or because they are attracted to the group or a member of the group.
- Three major types of roles are exhibited in problem-solving groups: **task, maintenance, and blocking.** Understanding and using appropriate roles can increase group effectiveness.
- **Norms** are the governors of group behavior. They establish the rules of behavior that are acceptable to the group. Establishing positive norms and eliminating negative norms, while difficult to do, is particularly critical for organizational effectiveness.
- **Status**, a person's rank or worth to a group, influences individual behavior within the group. When **status incongruence** occurs it creates tension and discomfort.
- A **cohesive group** has a very strong hold on its members because of the attractiveness of the group to the members. When cohesive groups are directed toward positive norms, they can be very beneficial to the organization.
- **Socialization** is the process of learning the ropes in an organization or group. Unrealistic expectations about a group may lead to poor socialization, dissatisfaction, and leaving the organization.
- **Teambuilding** is one way of improving group functioning; it is important for those groups that need to collaborate to get the job done, such as management teams.

For Discussion

1. Based on your own experience, give an example of an interacting set of people who are and are not members of a group.
2. What are some of the positive and negative impacts of groups on organizational effectiveness?
3. Give separate examples of when task roles *and* maintenance roles should be used by the group leader.
4. How do you deal with someone who is exhibiting a blocking role?

5. Describe an example of how norms can influence organizational effectiveness in a positive and a negative way.
6. How can norms be changed?
7. When is a highly cohesive group desirable or undesirable?
8. Do you agree with the Perspective: "Schmoozing" or "Social Loafing" that groups should be allowed to schmooze, or do you believe that social loafing may be the result?
9. Contrast a realistic job preview for work at a fast-food restaurant with a traditional job preview.
10. Give examples of three jobs where self-managing work groups would be appropriate. Do these jobs all involve interacting rather than coacting work groups?

Key Concepts and Terms

group	status symbols
task roles	cohesiveness
maintenance roles	schmoozing
blocking roles	social loafing
norms	socialization
idiosyncratic credits	realistic job previews
interacting work groups	teambuilding
status	self-managing work groups
status incongruence	coacting work groups

Suggested Readings

Allen, P. F., and Pilnick, S. (1973). Confronting the shadow organization: How to detect and defeat negative norms. *Organizational Dynamics,* 1:3–18.

Davis, K. (1980). Low productivity? Try improving the social environment. *Business Horizons,* June:27–29.

Hackman, J. R., and Oldham, G. R. (1980). *Work redesign.* Reading, Mass.: Addison-Wesley. (Especially Chapters 7 and 8.)

Jewell, L. N., and Reitz, H. J. (1981). *Group effectiveness in organizations.* Glenview, Ill.: Scott, Foresman.

Wanous, J. P. (1980). *Organizational entry: Recruitment, selection, and socialization of newcomers.* Reading, Mass.: Addison-Wesley.

CASES AND INCIDENTS

Dennis Calhoun

"What's wrong with me?", Dennis Calhoun thought to himself on his way home after eight hours at the bank. This was only his second week at work, but he was already disillusioned about his job and was seriously considering quitting once he could find a position that paid at least as much and offered a fairly secure future.

Since the first day on the job, he had experienced nothing but trouble. The trouble was not with the job itself but with the other people working there. Although he thought he got along well with some of the older employees, there was a group of young male employees that seemed to have something against him. He had tried to be friendly and listen to their instructions as they taught him the various jobs, but they seemed to exclude him from their social activities—such as going to lunch, having a beer after work, and idle chit-chat. Although he didn't know everyone very well, it appeared that this group consisted mostly of the male, part-time college students that worked at the bank during their free time. They didn't seem to be very committed to their job although their work was generally satisfactory as far as Dennis could tell. Most of their conversation was about activities at college, such as football games, fraternity parties, and school work.

In a way, Dennis kind of envied them. After finishing high school he had decided not to go on to college since his high school grades were not that good and his family could not take the financial burden of a college education. After working two years at a local supermarket, then taking a brief fling at selling insurance, he was particularly pleased at being offered a job as a management trainee with the bank. The bank planned to put him on a program which would allow him to rotate through the various departments over a five-year period, after which time he would be in a better position to decide in which area he wished to make his career. He thought this to be an excellent opportunity and was determined to make a good impression on the bank management.

In thinking now about his job, he recalled how unpleasant the last two weeks had been. Not long after he started to work, someone loosened the casters on his chair so that when he sat down, the chair collapsed on to the floor. Later, while on an errand to another bank after banking hours, one of the fellows was supposed to telephone the other bank to inform them that Dennis was on his way; when Dennis arrived, the front door was locked and no one was around, forcing him to pound on the front door until someone inside heard him. When he came back to the bank, the rear entrance was locked and he had to find a pay telephone to call inside for someone to let him in. And today was the crowning blow. In the middle of trying to balance a deposit containing over two hundred checks, he left briefly to go to the restroom. When he returned and finished the task, his total didn't balance with the deposit slip. When he rechecked his figures, he discovered that someone had added in a few numbers on the calculator while he was out.

From J. L. Gray and F. A. Starke, 1980, *Organizational behavior concepts and applications*, 2nd ed., p. 227. Copyright © 1980 by Charles E. Merrill, Columbus, Ohio.

Discussion questions
1. Why is Dennis having trouble?
2. How do the goals of the group differ from Dennis' goals?
3. What could he do to minimize this uncomfortable situation short of quitting?

The New Foreman

John Adams, a recent college graduate in engineering, had accepted as his first full time job the position of foreman at a local auto parts manufacturing division of a national manufacturing corporation. After a brief two-week training program, he was assigned as a foreman trainee to a production department. This department included about forty-five production employees. Adams soon noted that the department was fairly efficient with the exception of one small group of younger male employees. This group was made up of six employees and had an indirect influence over a fringe group of about six more. The main problem causing the inefficiency was the amount of time the employees in this group spent off the job in nonwork related activities.

Correcting this problem would be difficult due to the Union-Management Labor Contract. In effect, it read that the employees would not be held responsible for a specified number of units per day, but were expected to remain on the job except for reasonable personal delays. No specific times for rest breaks, rest room, etc., were spelled out. It was up to each employee to fairly set his own break time. Adams decided to attack the problem in the following manner. He picked out the worst offender in the group and noted his time off the job for a twelve-hour period. The time off the job amounted to not quite four hours. Armed with this data and the fact that the employee had been verbally warned twice before, Adams issued a written reprimand to the employee. The employee requested and received aid from the union steward. As a result, a written grievance was filed charging Adams with discrimination against the employee because he was singled out from the others. The next day, at the start of the shift, the remainder of this employee's peer group, plus the afore-

mentioned fringe group, all requested aid from the union steward. They numbered about ten employees in all.

For three more days, these ten employees and the union steward subjected Adams to mental pressure and harassment in an effort to have him remove the reprimand from the employee's work record. The reprimand was not removed. Oddly, however, though the production output of the eleven employees directly involved fell drastically, the remainder of the employees in the department continued at about average rate of output. Also, on several occasions, Adams received verbal support and encouragement from these employees.

From J. V. Murray and T. J. von der Embse, *Organizational behavior: Critical incidents and analysis*, p. 117. Copyright © 1973 by Charles E. Merrill, Columbus, Ohio.

Discussion questions

1. How can group dynamics explain what is happening here? Use as many concepts as you can.

2. Did John Adams use the best approach to the problem? Explain.

3. What should be done about the labor relations aspects of this case?

REFERENCES

1. Cartwright, D. and Zander, A., eds. (1968), *Group dynamics: Research and theory*, 3rd ed., New York: Harper and Row, p. 46; and Hare, A. P. (1976), *Handbook of small group research*, 2nd ed., New York: The Free Press, p. 5.

2. Hare, *Handbook of small group research*.

3. For a summary of the research on group attractiveness *see* Shaw, M. E. (1976), *Group dynamics: The pscyhology of small group behavior,* New York: McGraw-Hill; and An overview of small group behavior, in *Contemporary topics in Psychology*, pp. 335-368, Morristown, N.J.: Silver Burdett Company, General Learning Press.

4. Lincoln, J. R. and Miller, J. (1979), Work and friendship ties in organizations: A Comparative analysis of relational networks, *Administrative Science Quarterly,* 24:181–199.

5. *See* Hackman, J. R. and Oldham, G. R. (1980), *Work redesign,* Reading, Mass.: Addison-Wesley; and Hare, A. P., (1981), Group size, *American Behavioral Scientist* 24:695–708.

6. Steiner, I. D. (1972), *Group processes and productivity,* New York: Academic Press, p. 96.

7. Epstein, C. F. (1975), Institutional barriers: What keeps women out of the executive suite?, in *Bringing women into management,* eds. F. E. Gordon and M. H. Strober, pp. 7–21, New York: McGraw-Hill.

8. Hare, *Handbook of small group research*, p. 131.

9. For a discussion of role-making processes see Graen, G. (1976), Role-making processes within complex organizations, in *Handbook of industrial and organizational psychology,* ed. M. D. Dunnette, pp. 1201–1245, Chicago: Rand-McNally.

10. Based on Benne and Sheats, Functional roles of group members.

11. The discussion in this section is based on the concepts of Benne, K. D. and Sheats, P. (1948), Functional roles of group members, *Journal of Social Issues* 4:41–49.

12. Hare, *Handbook of small group research,* p. 19.

13. Donald Roy as quoted from page 15 of *Money and Motivation: An Analysis of Incentives* by W.F. Whyte. Copyright 1955, by Harper & Row Publishers, Inc.

14. Hackman, J. R., (1976), Group influences on individuals, in *Handbook of industrial and organizational psychology,* ed. M. D. Dunnette, pp. 1455–1525, Chicago: Rand-McNally.

15. Hollander, E. P. (1958), Conformity, status, and idiosyncracy credits, *Psychological Review* 65:117–27; and (1964), *Leaders, groups and influence,* New York: Oxford University Press.

16. Adapted from Andre de la Porte, P. C. (1974), Group norms: Key to building a winning team, *Personnel* Sept.-Oct.

17. Mitchell, T. R. (1982), *People in organizations*, 2nd ed., New York: McGraw-Hill, p. 277.

18. Jewell, L. N. and Reitz, H. J. (1981), *Group effectiveness in organizations,*Glenview, Ill.: Scott, Foresman.

19. This section draws heavily from Jewell and Reitz, Group effectiveness in organizations; and Cartwright, D. (1968), The nature of group cohesiveness, in *Group dynamics: Research and theory,* 3rd ed., ed. D. Cartwright and A. Zander, pp. 91–109, New York: Harper & Row.

20. Stogdill, R. M. (1972), Group productivity, drive, and cohesiveness, *Organizational Behavior and Human Performance* 8:26–43. *Also see* Tziner, A. and Vardi, Y., (1982), Effects of command style and group cohesiveness on performance effectiveness of self-selected tank crews, *Journal of Applied Psychology* 67:769–775.

21. From Schrank, R. (1978), How to relieve worker boredom, *Psychology Today* 12 (2):79–80. *Also see* Davis, K. (1980), Low productivity? Try improving the social environment, *Business Horizons* June:27–29.

22. From Latane, B.; Williams, K.; and Harkins, S. (1979), Social loafing, *Psychology Today* 13(4):104cf.

23. Schein, E. F. (1968), Organizational socialization and the profession of management, *Industrial Management Review* 9:1–6; VanMaanen, J. and Schein, E. F. (1979), Toward a theory of organizational socialization, in *Research in organizational behavior,* vol. 1, ed. B. M. Staw, pp. 209–264, Greenwich, Conn.: JAI Press. For more in-depth coverage of organizational socialization, *see* Wanous, J. P. (1977), Organizational entry: Newcomers

moving from outside to inside, *Psychological Bulletin* 84:601–618; and 1980, *Organizational entry: Recruitment, selection, and socialization of newcomers,* Reading, Mass.: Addison-Wesley.

24. For a much more extensive discussion, *see* Louis, M. B. (1980), Surprise and sensemaking: What newcomers experience in entering unfamiliar organizational settings, *Administrative Science Quarterly* 25:226–251.

25. Wanous, *Organizational entry.*

26. Seattle *Post-Intelligencer,* 1 May 1983.

27. For reviews *see* Reilly, R. R. ; Brown, B.; Blood, M. R.; and Malatesta, C. Z. (1981), The effects of realistic previews: A study and discussion of the literature, *Personnel Psychology* 34:823–834; and Popovich, P. and Wanous, J. P. (1982), The realistic job preview as a persuasive communication, *Academy of Management Reveiw* 7:570–578.

28. Dyer, W. G. (1977), *Teambuilding: Issues and alternatives,* Reading, Mass.: Addison-Wesley.

29. Dyer, *Teambuilding,* p. 4.

30. *See* Dyer, *Teambuilding,* for a complete discussion of teambuilding techniques.

31. This section is based on Hackman and Oldham, *Work redesign. Also see* Cummings, T. G. (1978), Self-regulating work groups: A socio-technical synthesis, *Academy of Management Review* 3:625–634.

32. Adapted and abridged from McGregor, D. (1960), *The human side of enterprise,* New York: McGraw-Hill, pp. 232–235.

33. Adapted by Hackman and Oldham, Work redesign, pp. 165–167.

Conflict, Competition, and Cooperation

CHAPTER 10

- Why do seemingly minor events trigger major conflicts?

- When is conflict desirable? When do we want to encourage it?

- Which conflict resolution technique works best? When should a particular resolution strategy be used or avoided?

- Have you ever tried be a mediator of a conflict between two subordinates or friends? This chapter will help you be more effective.

- Would it be good to organize a company like a football team?

- When can a competitive, win-lose situation deteriorate into a lose-lose situation?

- How can competition be effectively used in organizations?

Preview Case: Warfare at Advanced Proaucts

Understanding Conflict
- What is conflict?
- How conflict works
- Sources of conflict
- *Perspective:* The First-Line Supervisor: Role Conflict in Action
- Is conflict good or bad?

Managing Conflict
- Raising conflict levels
- Lowering conflict levels
- *Perspective:* The Language of Conflict
- Using third parties for conflict resolution
- *Perspective:* How to Be an Effective Third Party

Competition and Cooperation
- Competition, conflict, and cooperation
- The win-lose model: Outcomes of competition and cooperation
- Effects of win-lose competition
- When to use competition
- *Perspective:* Competition Versus Cooperation: Research Results
- Managing competition

Conflict and Competition in Organizations

Summary
- Chapter review
- For discussion
- Key concepts and terms
- Suggested readings

Cases and Incidents
- James Farris
- Inflated Performance Appraisals

References

PREVIEW CASE: WARFARE AT ADVANCED PRODUCTS

Advanced Products, Inc., is a small office machine manufacturing company with about 400 employees. Herb Thorpe, a long-time employee who came up through the ranks, heads up the production department. Liz Rosenberg, who was very successful in the marketing department of the Xerox Corp., was hired as the sales manager about two years ago. Both Herb and Liz are on the same organizational level—they report to the president and owner, Mr. Asato.

For the past few months Herb and Liz just do not seem to be getting along. It seems like they butt heads almost all the time; it is almost open warfare between the two. The most recent problem involves a promise that Liz made to one of Advanced's largest customers, Allied Insurance, for early delivery on a shipment of sorting machines. When Liz told Herb about her promise to Allied, he blew his stack. He told her there was no way he could modify his production schedules without costing the firm plenty and making his subordinates mad. His face turned red, the veins in his neck stood out, and he said, "This is a bunch of bull. It's impossible. We can't do it. We'll see who wins this one. Let's go see Mr. Asato."

(*What are Herb's and Liz's private thoughts about this confrontation?*)

Herb: She's done it to me again! After I spent all last week figuring out the most efficient use of our equipment, she comes up with this hairbrain promise that I can't possibly fulfill without screwing up everything. And besides, if we don't stay on the production schedule, we won't make our goals and won't get our bonus. Boy, would everyone be mad if that happened! That's money out of our pocket. That woman's a menace to this company. I've had it! I can't take any more of her.

Liz: These old-timers like Herb are just too inflexible. How can I get my job done with people like him around? If we can't produce the sorters early, then Allied will probably go to another supplier. We could even lose them permanently. Doesn't that old bastard know he's screwing up the company, not to mention our sales record and commissions. If they're going to keep Herb then maybe I better start looking around for another company where I can work with the people.

Later: Liz and Herb enter the president's office later that day to get a decision. Herb is obviously still agitated and angry. He tells Mr. Asato: "It's either her or me! One of us has got to go!" Liz turns to Mr. Asato and says: "I agree. It's time for obsolete old-timers like Herb to retire! Tomorrow wouldn't be too soon as far as I'm concerned!"

Conflict such as that experienced by Herb and Liz, while not an every-day occurrence, does happen. Almost everyone who manages faces conflict situations on a regular basis, either by being directly involved in the conflict or as a mediator. In fact, research indicates that managers spend about 20 percent of their time dealing with conflict.[1]

Understanding Organizational Behavior

In this chapter, we will try to understand how conflict works and how to manage it. We will also see how competition relates to conflict, what its effects are, and when it is desirable. Conflict can also cause stress, the subject of the next chapter.

Understanding Conflict

In this section of the chapter, we will learn about the nature of the conflict process—how it works, its sources, and its desirability.

■ What Is Conflict?

When two coworkers are having a heated discussion about the nature of the new incentive program, they may or may not be in conflict. If one of the workers perceives that the other is frustrating, or about to frustrate, something that is of concern to him or her, then **conflict** exists.[2] For example, if one worker is proposing a change in the rules that will result in less bonus for the other, conflict probably exists. On the other hand, when there is no perceived frustration of an important concern, then there is simply a disagreement, not a conflict. For example, the coworkers may be arguing over the interpretation of the bonus plan that has little or no long-lasting concern for either.

However, it is sometimes difficult to separate conflict and disagreement unless you know how people perceive the situation. While conflict usually involves disagreements over substantive issues, such as the difference in policies, pay systems, or working hours, it may also arise over seemingly trivial issues such as placement of a desk in a different location. In the opening example, it is obvious that Herb and Liz have built up a great deal of resentment and antagonism between each other because each sees the other as frustrating his or her vital concerns. They are in conflict and not merely having a disagreement.

Levels of Conflict   Conflict can occur at a number of levels. **Intrapersonal conflict** happens entirely within the individual. This often results from feeling of obligation in several competing directions. Later we will discuss role conflict, an important source of intrapersonal conflict. Another type of conflict, illustrated by the opening case, is **interpersonal conflict** or conflict between two people. There can also be a number of ways of looking at conflict within groups, such as **intragroup conflict** (conflict within the group of an interpersonal nature) and **intergroup conflict** (when two or more groups are involved).

Types of Conflict   There are two general types of conflict issues, substantive and emotional.[3] **Substantive issues** include disagreements over policies and practices, competition for scarce resources, and conflict over roles and responsibilities. **Emotional issues** involve negative feelings between the people, such as fear, rejection, resentment, anger, and distrust. Conflicts in values, discussed in Chapter 3, are also important emotional issues. Substantive and emotional issues are often mixed, as they were in our opening example where the substantive issue of scheduling the early delivery of goods was combined with the emotional issues of distrust, scorn, and resentment. Emotional issues tend to be more destructive and more difficult to resolve than substantive issues.

■ How Conflict Works

A Cyclical Process   Conflict in organizations usually builds through a series of conflict episodes, although it is certainly possible for one powerful incident to provoke extreme conflict. A **conflict episode** occurs when some event, such as the Allied Insurance sale, triggers conflict behaviors. The triggering event causes the conflict to surface, to be felt—you get mad and do something (behave) to get it off your chest (an angry outburst, leaving the room, or even quitting). The outcome or consequences of this conflict episode will strongly influence what happens in the future. If the conflict is fully resolved so that the hostility is removed, then there may be no future conflict. If, on the other hand, the conflict is suppressed, then the next time a triggering event occurs there may be an even bigger blowup.

■ Sources of Conflict[4]

Recognizing the sources of conflicts helps us to understand why conflict arises from some situations naturally. Conflict can be stimulated or reduced by changing or eliminating the source. While there are many sources of conflict, including value issues, personality differences, and communication (discussed earlier in the book), several additional ones are noted in the following paragraphs.

Conflict over Resources   Competition for scarce resources is a very common basis for conflict. Say the equipment budget is being cut by 10 percent, but the research department needs a 20 percent increase. There is a conflict between research, finance, and the other departments over the allocation of these funds. Another type of conflict of interest was illustrated

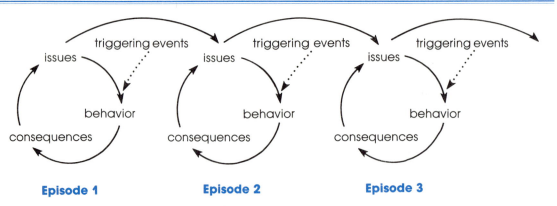

Figure 10.1. The conflict process.

Richard E. Walton, *Interpersonal Peacemaking: Confrontations and Third Party Consultation,* © 1969. Addison-Wesley, Reading, Massachusetts. Pp. 72. Reprinted with permission.

in our opening incident. If the Allied sale were to fall through Liz would lose the commission. If the production schedule was accelerated, Herb would lose his bonus for meeting his production goals.

Ambiguous Jurisdictions   When responsibilities and roles are clear, people know who must make decisions, and conflicts seldom arise. However, in a large, complex organization responsibilities are often unclear; turf is often unspecified and conflicts occur when two groups go after the same responsibilities or try to avoid the responsibility. For example, operations management experts may feel that they should select the type of desk computer to be used for solving problems. Purchasing may disagree. They may believe that their task is to find the lowest cost item that will do the job. Hence there may be a conflict between operations management and purchasing.[5]

Role Conflicts   A role is a set of expectations that are believed to be associated with a given position in a group or organization. Role conflict occurs when various people, including the person playing the role, have differing expectations about how the role should be acted. The resulting pressure causes psychological conflict, and, as we will see in Chapter 11, stress. The Perspective: The First-Line Supervisor: Role Conflict in Action gives an example of how role conflict affects the first-line supervisor.

Communication Barriers   People or groups who do not communicate are more likely to encounter conflict. Sometimes the barriers are physical, such as the difference between the day shift and the night shift, and sometimes they are psychological, such as the differences between Liz and Herb's experiences. When people do not communicate, there is more chance for misunderstanding and mistrust, major causes of emotional conflict. The lack of communication serves to perpetuate future conflict cycles.

PERSPECTIVE

10.1 *The First-Line Supervisor: Role Conflict in Action*[6]

A classic example of role conflict is the first-line supervisor, the foreman, the section chief, who is at the lowest level of supervision. Upper managers expect foreman to behave like a manager, to set goals, maintain discipline, maintain schedules, and enforce compliance with company rules. On the other hand, foreman are usually promoted from the shop floor. Subordinates, who were once close friends, expect the role of a friend—to be understanding, lenient, and forgiving. This situation puts the foreman in a bind and creates conflict.

Excessive role conflict results in frustration and strain that affects tension, dissatisfaction, and even health. Often withdrawal from one group or the other by either quitting the job of foreman or isolating oneself from the shop-floor employees, is the only way to resolve the tension. It is no wonder that turnover rates are high for first-line supervisors.

Dependence of One Party   When one must rely upon another to get the job done, there will be more conflict. For example, some organizational designs call for functional experts (engineers) to be permanently assigned to the engineering department, but on call for the various project managers (the J-81 engine manager). Thus the engine manager is dependent upon the engineers who are under the control of someone else.

Domination[7]   When one or more persons or groups are trying to control the behavior of others, they are trying to dominate. This produces conflict because most people do not want to be controlled by others. A boss who overly controls employees creates conflict. A committee chair who tries to control and direct the meeting too tightly may generate conflict.

■ Is Conflict Good or Bad?

A moderate level of conflict is usually constructive. If there is no conflict, the organization may be complacent and stagnant; it may lose much of the energizing force and tension that conflict creates. Change and innovation, two ingredients of healthy organizations, normally mean conflict. As illustrated in Figure 10.2, conflict can be thought of as a continuum of intensities ranging from no conflict to extreme conflict.[8] A manager can plot the "conflict temperature" to see if the level is about where it should be and then take action to either reduce or stimulate conflict.

The Nature of the Conflict   An important consideration when determining if conflict is desirable is the nature of the conflict itself. Conflicts that serve to raise important organizational issues, such as customer deliveries, or to focus on equitable division of scarce resources between two parts of the organization, such as domestic and international operations, are usually desirable types of conflict. On the other hand, conflicts that do not help resolve organizational problems but only create hard feelings and tension, such as the confrontation between Herb and Liz, are usually undesirable. Most emotional conflicts over values, personality issues, or communication are dysfunctional.

An example of when conflict is desirable or good might be when production and sales disagree over how fast an item can be delivered to a cus-

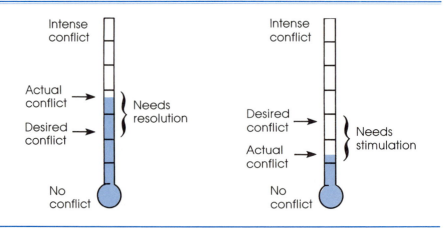

Figure 10.2.
Conflict intensity scales.[9]

tomer as was illustrated in our opening example. If such conflicts do not arise, then important sales may be lost. Let's say that there was no conflict between sales and production. If production says they cannot deliver when the customer wants the product, then the customer is simply told to "take it or leave it." Do you think a customer, such as Allied Insurance, would go elsewhere? Most probably. Of course the emotionally draining type of conflict illustrated in our opening example between Herb and Liz was not a desirable form of conflict. The key here is to recognize that some conflicts can be beneficial while others need to be eliminated. We must develop strategies for dealing with or managing conflict, the topic of our next section.

Managing Conflict

If there is some optimal level of conflict as we have just implied, then conflict must be managed so we can reach it. This means increasing or decreasing the conflict level.

■ Raising Conflict Levels

Conflict can be raised by structuring the organization so that relationships are ambiguous and people are competing for scarce resources (discussed under sources of conflict). Another way to heighten conflict is to structure the organization so that there are opposing interest groups; for example, a department that is concerned with the success of its product, toothpaste, and another department that is responsible for making sure that costs are kept as low as possible, production. Competition, discussed later in this chapter, is another way to heighten conflict.

■ Lowering Conflict Levels

Most of the literature on conflict management deals with reducing conflict levels.[10] In this section, we will cover several methods for dealing with undesirable conflict. The first decision is whether to confront or avoid the conflict. There are times when conflict arises that you will want to put off acting upon it even though it is a problem.

Avoidance and Defusion   Any strategy that avoids a major confrontation or conflict is called **avoidance**. For example, say the Research and Development Manager knows that a major conflict exists over funds allocation for new product development. However, the manager does not want to confront the conflict at this time because there are some important market research studies that have not been completed. The manager takes great care to avoid issues that might trigger the conflict. While avoidance is sometimes useful as a delaying tactic, it can also cause problems. If Mr. Asato had avoided the conflict between Liz and Herb, it might have been disastrous for Advanced Products. Table 10.1 shows situations where chief executives think avoidance or other resolution techniques are appropriate.

Forcing   Using power, coercion, or force to resolve conflict results in an imposed or forced solution. **Forcing** may involve the use of institutional authority and power, rewards and punishments, bribery, or even physical force. In an emergency or under other circumstances shown in Ta-

Table 10.1. CEO recommendations for conflict resolution. A group of twenty-eight chief executives stated their preferences for use of the various conflict-resolution techniques.[12]

Avoiding
1. When an issue is trivial, or more important issues are pressing.
2. When you perceive no chance of satisfying your concerns.
3. When potential disruption outweighs the benefits of resolution.
4. To let people cool down and gain perspective.
5. When gathering information supercedes immediate decision.

Forcing
1. When quick, decisive action is vital—e.g., emergencies.
2. On important issues where unpopular actions need implementing—e.g., cost cutting, enforcing unpopular rules, discipline.
3. On issues vital to company welfare when you know you're right.
4. Against people who take advantage of noncompetitive behavior.

Compromising
1. When goals are important, but not worth the effort or potential disruption of more assertive modes.
2. When opponents with equal power are committed to mutually exclusive goals.
3. To achieve temporary settlements to complex issues.
4. To arrive at expedient solutions under time pressure.
5. As a backup when collaboration or competition is unsuccessful.

Problem solving
1. To find an integrative solution when both sets of concerns are too important to be compromised.
2. When your objective is to learn.
3. To merge insights from people with different perspectives.
4. To gain commitment by incorporating concerns into a concensus.
5. To work through feelings which have interfered with a relationship.

From K. W. Thomas, 1977, Toward multidimensional values in teaching: The example of conflict behavior, *Academy of Management Review* 2:487. Reprinted with permission of the publisher and author. Copyright © 1977 by Academy of Management.

ble 10.1, forcing may be the appropriate resolution method. In our opening case, forcing could be used by the president to resolve the conflict. Depending upon the nature of the forced solution, a number of outcomes are possible. If the president were to make a decision in favor of either Liz or Herb, then problems would be likely to arise. The solution would most probably be only a temporary fix for the problem. Liz and Herb still have lingering resentment and hostility. Another problem with this approach is that the loser, say Herb (if the decision was made in favor of Liz), may get angry and quit or at the very least be demotivated and dissatisfied. Forcing does not seem to be the best solution for our case.

Compromising   A **compromise** solution involves give and take, bargaining, and negotiations. This is the standard method of resolving labor relations conflicts. Compromise is used when there is a relatively equal balance of power between the parties. They negotiate a sharing of limited resources. Bargaining is commonly used when there is some fixed amount of resources to divide, such as new authorizations for personnel or travel funds. During negotiations each party is trying to control and distort information in their favor. There is little concern for the overall good of the organization. The focus is achieving a beneficial solution or minimizing losses.[11] Compromising does not seem to be a good approach for the solution of Herb and Liz's conflict.

Understanding Organizational Behavior

Problem Solving   This is a **collaborative** or problem-solving approach where all parties work together to find a mutually acceptable solution to their conflict. The idea here is to work together so that the conflict is resolved permanently and there is shared commitment to the solution. There are a number of problem-solving techniques that work.[12] One useful and simple approach involves the following steps:

1. *Define and clarify the problem.* What are the tangible issues in the conflict? Where does each party stand? It is helpful to write this information on newsprint.
2. *Search for solutions.* Generate a range of solutions without being judgemental. One way to do this is to use brainstorming (*see* Chapter 13 for details).
3. *Evaluate the solutions.* The parties work to achieve a consensus decision (a solution to which both can generally agree) on the best solution for both parties.
4. *Implement the decision.*
5. *Follow up,* if appropriate, to make sure everything is working out as planned.

The conflict experienced by Liz and Herb might best be resolved through problem solving. In fact, this is the strategy Mr. Asato used to resolve the conflict. He began by asking both Liz and Herb to separately state

| 10.2 | *The Language of Conflict*[13] |

Certain words and phrases serve to intensify or defuse conflict. Careful use or avoidance of this language can help resolve or prevent conflict. Some examples are given below:

Words that intensify conflict	*Words that help resolve conflict*
You . . .	I . . .
You performed poorly.	Performance was 10 percent lower compared to last month.
The way you talk makes me angry.	When you interrupted me just now, you seemed uninterested in what I was saying.
I am right and you are wrong.	How can we find a solution that will satisfy both of us?
You make me mad.	I get angry when you belittle me in front of others.
You said. . .	What I heard you say was. . .

their concerns that resulted in the conflict. From these two statements, it was apparent that a problem existed—how to satisfy Allied Insurance without disrupting the production schedule. Mr. Asata led a discussion of ways that the problem might be resolved. They wrote all the potential solutions on the blackboard in the conference room. Next, the three of them sat back and evaluated the possible solutions (by this time Liz and Herb had cooled off and were actually cooperating). Jointly, they decided that it would be possible to delay a shipment to another company whose needs were not so pressing and still keep their delivery schedule with Allied. In this case, the conflict was resolved, and Herb and Liz were at least communicating more freely than before.

■ Using Third Parties for Conflict Resolution

Third parties are often used to help resolve conflict. A third party can be a coworker, boss, or a conflict-resolution specialist. Almost everyone acts as a third party at one time or another. The major reason for using a third party is to make concessions easier without the loss of face, thus promoting easier and quicker conflict resolution.[15] The third party may absorb some of the responsibility for the concession.

Examples of third parties abound. As related above, Mr. Asato acted as the third party to resolve Herb and Liz's conflict. Mediators or arbitrators are often used to resolve labor contract disputes. Counselors are used to resolve interpersonal disputes between employees or between family members.

Figure 10.3.
Conflict resolution:
What works?

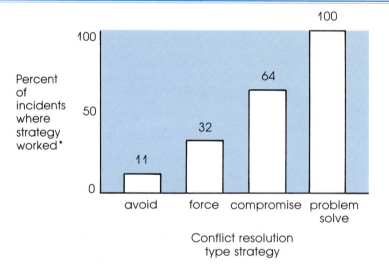

*Based on research results from two different studies comparing four conflict-resolution techniques over 153 incidents.[15] The resolution technique is categorized as "not working" if the respondents felt particularly bad about the way the conflict was handled. In reality, the results of the research do not tell us if the strategy worked, but only how the respondents felt about the outcome of the technique.

Understanding Organizational Behavior

10.3 How to Be an Effective Third Party[16]

Since almost everyone is a third party at one time or another, we need to review some techniques that will make that job easier and more effective. The following list contains some useful and practical hints for improving your conflict-resolution skills.

■ Talk to each conflicting person or group alone and find out where they are coming from. While you are doing this try to establish norms of openness and confrontation.

■ Find an appropriate neutral setting. Go to a location that is neutral, such as a conference room. Stay away from offices. They are perceived as other's turf and inhibit the process.

■ Unless the conflict is minor, be sure to establish a large, open-ended block of time to resolve the conflict. One way to do this is by having the session begin at 3:00P.M. with the understanding that it will continue until it is resolved, even if it takes until midnight.

■ Avoid getting the parties defensive. Avoid crossed transaction, except from the Adult ego state (see Chapter 8). Avoid the critical Parent ego state. Use the right language for problem solving (see the Perspective: The Language of Conflict).

■ Focus on behavior and the tangible effects of the behavior. It is often useful to have each party separately write out the conflict's cause and the tangible effects on them, then share their results. Use I-messages (see Chapter 8).

■ Listen carefully. Use active-listening techniques (Chapter 8).

■ The third party may restate the issues and concerns of each party.

■ Be prepared with a problem-solving procedure such as the one we discussed earlier in this chapter. Suggest its use at an appropriate time if the use seems warranted by the type of conflict.

■ Try to avoid proposing or imposing solutions.

There are a number of skills and techniques that are important for an effective third party. The Perspective: How to Be an Effective Third Party, provides an overview on how to conduct third-party conflict resolution.

Competition and Cooperation

In this section, we will look at the use of competition and cooperation in organizations, including such issues as win-lose dynamics and preventing harmful competition.

■ Competition, Conflict, and Cooperation

Competition   When two or more people or groups are seeking to gain the same thing that the others are seeking, then **competition** exists. Competition is certainly a cornerstone of United States culture. People are taught to be competitive at an early age. Sports and organizational policies often encourage competition. Obviously, competition can be an energizing force, but it can also be quite destructive for organizations that need teamwork to get the job done.

Competition and Conflict

How does competition differ from conflict? The main difference is whether one party is trying to frustrate or block another. If this blocking is present, then competition and conflict co-exist. For example, if all departments are competing with one another for the lowest absentee rate, then competition exists, but not conflict. If all departments are competing for a limited amount of office improvement funds and each is doing their best to win at the expense of the others, then conflict exists.

It is also possible to have conflict without competition when the parties are not seeking to gain over each other. For example, a manager who presents a proposal to the staff to find loopholes, inconsistencies, and problems, is encouraging conflict, but there is no competition.

Cooperation

Cooperation is working together toward mutual goals.[17] One group can cooperate within itself to pursue competitive goals. In fact, a competitive situation often encourages the members of the group to be more cohesive and cooperative. Cooperation is not the opposite of conflict. They exist separately from one another. The opposite of cooperation is no cooperation, while the opposite of conflict is no conflict. Cooperation, in the form of problem solving, is often used as a strategy to reduce conflict, but people can be too cooperative and fall below the desired level of tension.

■ The Win-Lose Model: Outcomes of Competition and Cooperation

When people are striving to attain the same thing, three outcomes are possible: one can win and the other can lose (**win-lose**), they both can lose (**lose-lose**), or they both can win (**win-win**). This way of looking at outcomes, called the **win-lose model**,[18] is a great help in interpreting what happens in competitive situations.

Win-Lose

Our opening example was a good one for win-lose, since either way the decision went—with Liz or with Herb—the other perceived a loss. In this case, the loss was not only psychological but financial, since the system was designed to reward sales differently from production. Sales was rewarded by commissions for sales made. Production was rewarded for making the production schedule on time. If a client, such as Allied Insurance, wanted early delivery, then the system would force a win-lose confrontation.

Lose-Lose

Win-lose can often deteriorate into lose-lose because of the effects of the conflict on the organization. Let's say that the Advanced Products' president had decided in favor of Herb and that Liz quit and Allied Insurance went to another supplier. In this case the organization would have lost. Even. Herb might have lost in the long run if the effects of the loss of the largest client caused production layoffs.

Win-Win

The key strategy of a win-win approach is to seek a way of satisfying the needs of both parties so that both get rewarded and win. A win-win strategy attempts to make the pie (total reward pool) bigger rather than simply slicing up a pie (giving a fixed pool of rewards to the parties).

Understanding Organizational Behavior

This is usually done by problem solving or collaborative approaches. When Mr. Asato used a problem-solving approach to resolve the conflict between Liz and Herb, it resulted in a solution that was good for everyone concerned. It was a win-win situation.

■ Effects of Win-Lose Competition

Suppose the president of your firm decided to use the same techniques that professional sport teams use to improve organizational productivity. Each major department (marketing, production, personnel) will make up a team. These teams would compete against each other to see who can be the most productive. The team that wins will get a major bonus, while the losers get nothing.

There is a strong possibility that this win-lose strategy will create problems. Production and marketing will be looking out for their own interests rather than those of the firm. They may even withhold information from each other so the other will look bad and have a greater chance of losing. After a while they may not even be communicating. Such a competitive climate may result in incidents like our opening one where marketing commits the firm to an impossible delivery schedule. When the delivery fails, both sides may lose if the customer is lost. If marketing perceives itself to be the loser, it will be looking for ways to make those "dunderheads" in production look bad. Instead of a spirit of working together that may have once existed, every department will be out for itself.

Then, is competition always bad? Win-lose situations almost always create conflict since the loser's goals are frustrated. As we discussed earlier, there may be times when such conflict and competition are desirable. The next section addresses this issue.

■ When to Use Competition

The preceding example may give the impression that competition is bad. This is not necessarily so. We all know of situations where people or groups have achieved and performed at very high levels because of competition—in the Olympics, for example. Competition in itself is not necessarily bad. If cooperation is not needed and if tasks are independent, then competition can work well. An organizational example illustrating when competition might work is a situation where a company is organized into autonomous product divisions (such as soap, shampoo, toothpaste). In this case, competition between divisions could be an energizing force that makes the overall organization more productive. However, if the competing groups must cooperate to accomplish the organization's mission, then establishing intergroup competition is undesirable.

The key rule for using competition is to avoid it when individuals or groups are interdependent and must cooperate to reach the organization's goals. Use it if they are independent and cooperation is not needed to reach the goals. The following conditions are favorable for the use of competition.[19]

☐ *When the competitors are from different organizations that do not need to cooperate to get the job done.* An example might be top salesperson at the South branch versus top salesperson at the North branch.

☐ *When each party has a relatively equal chance to win.* No one wants to compete if they are destined to lose; if they have no chance. If absentee rates are the basis for competition and the research department has always had a much lower rate, then production will not be motivated to compete.

☐ *When later cooperation between the parties is not needed.* Since the loser is unlikely to help the winner, people better be independent of one another.

☐ *Winning must be a rewarding experience.* If a pieceworker wins a production competition only to be isolated from the group, then competition will be ineffective.

■ Managing Competition

Since research has shown competition to be generally less effective than cooperation in most organizational situations (*see* the Perspective: Competition Versus Cooperation: Research Results), here are some ways of reducing and managing competition.[20]

Establish Superordinate Goals   By establishing a **superordinate** or overall goal that everyone in all groups can work towards, competition will be directed toward goal accomplishment rather than against other groups. For example, if marketing and production were assigned the superordinate goal of developing a new product, then there would be pressures toward cooperation rather than competition.

Concentrate on Total Organizational Effectiveness   This is another way of implementing superordinate goals. Everyone should be measured and rewarded based on their contribution to the total effort rather than their individual effectiveness.

Increase Communication Between Competitors   Ways can be structured so that people have to get together and communicate. Frequent meetings, joint task forces, geographical relocation, and teambuilding workshops are all ways to get people talking to each other.

PERSPECTIVE

10.4 | *Competition Versus Cooperation: Research Results*

A research review and analysis of 122 studies resulted in the following conclusions:[21]

■ Cooperation is superior to competition in promoting achievement and productivity.

■ When people cooperate together, they perform and achieve at higher levels than if they work as individuals without concern for the goals of others.

■ Cooperation without intergroup competition promotes higher achievement and productivity than cooperation with intergroup competition.

Understanding Organizational Behavior

Avoid Win-Lose Situations   Design organizational systems on a win-win basis. For example, a bonus for reduced costs should be allocated equally between all people in the company rather than just to a few. In fact, many bonus plans are designed in a win-win fashion.[22]

Rotate People Between Departments   When people rotate to other parts of the company, they get a different perspective; they gain empathy.

Conflict and Competition in Organizations

Our discussions have shown that some level of conflict may be useful for energizing or developing "creative tension" in organizations. The key is the basic nature of the conflict. If it centers around resolving important organizational problems and issues, then it is probably "good" conflict. If it only serves to stir up interpersonal animosity, it is probably a "bad" form of conflict.

Competition in organizations also needs careful attention. Managers often create win-lose situations when win-win is just as easily developed. Cooperation helps people work together as a team and prevents the divisions that result from win-lose situations.

SUMMARY

■ **Conflict** exists when one party perceives that another is trying to frustrate some important or vital concern. Conflict can occur on an **intrapersonal, interpersonal, intragroup,** or **intergroup** level. It can also involve **substantive issues** or **emotional issues** or both.

■ Conflict is a cyclical process that builds when some event triggers a **conflict episode.** The outcome of the conflict strongly influences what will happen in the future.

■ Conflict can arise from a number of sources, including division of scarce resources, ambiguous jurisdictions or roles, communication barriers, dependence of one party and domination.

■ Managing conflict involves adjusting the intensity of conflict to the desired level, up or down. A moderate level of conflict is useful to provide force, energy, and tension for organizations. Conflict can be raised by competition, polarizing people around some issue, or intensifying any of the other sources of conflict. Conflict can be lowered in four ways: **avoidance**, **forcing** a resolution, **compromising** or bargaining, or **problem solving**. While each approach is useful, the most universally successful one is problem solving.

■ **Third parties** are useful as arbitrators, mediators, or facilitators. They make concessions easier and help save face for the parties.

■ **Competition** exists when two or more parties are seeking the same thing that others are seeking. Competition can be useful if the competitors are from different organizations, have a relatively equal chance to win, find winning rewarding, and where future cooperation is not needed.

■ **Cooperation**, working together toward mutual goals, is not the opposite of conflict, but is an entirely separate concept. Research has shown that cooperation is generally superior to competition in organizational situations.

■ Where competition results in a undesirable **win-lose** or **lose-lose** situation, it can be reduced by establishing superordinate goals, concentrating on overall organizational effectiveness, increasing communication, avoiding win-lose structures, and rotating people between departments.

For Discussion

1. How does conflict differ from disagreement? From competition?
2. Give an example of each of the four levels of conflict.
3. Based on your experience, explain how a conflict episode might occur.
4. Explain the difference between substantive and emotional conflict.
5. The job of the first-level supervisor is described in the Perspective: The First-Line Supervisor: Role Conflict in Action. What are the sources of conflict for a person in this position?
6. What factors make conflict "good" or "bad"?
7. Discuss the pros and cons of each conflict resolution technique.
8. When should competition be encouraged or discouraged in organizations?
9. Why do win-lose situations often result in lose-lose outcomes?
10. Compare and contrast the methods for managing conflict with those for managing competition. How do they differ? How are they similar?

Suggested Readings

Aram, J. D., and Salipante, P. F. Jr. (1981). An evaluation of organizational due process in the resolution of employee/employer conflict. *Academy of Management Review* 6:197–204.

Brown, D. L. (1983). *Managing conflict at organizational interfaces*. Reading, Mass.: Addison-Wesley.

Filley, A. C. (1975). *Interpersonal conflict resolution*. Glenview, Ill.: Scott, Foresman.

Phillips, E. and Cheston, R. (1979). Conflict resolution: What works? *California Management Review* 21(4)76–83.

Welds, K. (1976). Conflict management in the work place and how to manage it. *Personnel Journal* 58(6): 380–383.

Key Concepts and Terms

conflict	**compromising**
interpersonal conflict	**problem solving**
intrapersonal conflict	**third parties**

intergroup conflict
intragroup conflict
role conflict
avoidance
forcing

competition
cooperation
win-lose model
superordinate goals

CASES AND INCIDENTS

James Farris

James Farris was a college student who, during the summer, worked in Denver plant of Western Gypsum Company, a manufacturer of drywall material, various ready-mix patching compounds, and other assorted home-improvement products. The plant was a small one and employed only twenty-five people. Farris worked on the second floor and mixed raw materials (diatomaceous earth, dolomite, limestone, sand, etc.) together in specified proportions to make the ready-mix compounds. Consumers needed only to add water in the right amount to use the product. Because of this, quality control was a key function in the production process.

Farris hated his job but felt it was necessary to pay his way through college. On several occasions he had argued with his foreman about the level of work demanded, but to no avail. One hot afternoon the foreman approached Farris and the following discussion took place:

Foreman: Farris, you've got to be more careful when mixing the compound. Walters (the quality control inspector) tells me that six of the last eight batches you mixed were no good. All that stuff has to be remixed and that's going to cost the company a lot of money. We're paying you to mix those batches right! And another thing, you're not mixing the required seventeen batches a day. What's the problem?

Farris: I'm making mistakes because you're too demanding. I'm doing only fourteen

batches a day instead of seventeen because I physically can't do seventeen. I'm not about to kill myself running around up here in this heat just so I can mix seventeen batches a day. Look, I'm the fifth guy to have this job in the last seven months, right?

Foreman: Right.

Farris: Doesn't that tell you something?

Foreman: Yeah, it tells me that most people today don't want to do an honest day's work!

Farris: Don't give me that! To do this job right, I can only do eleven batches a day. Besides, I'm not so sure those batches were actually bad. I've heard that Walters is very picky when checking batches because it gives him a sense of power over the other workers. Besides, he's just trying to get me because he thinks I scraped his new car in the parking lot the other day.

Foreman: You college guys are all alike! I used to do this job and I never had any trouble. You're just too lazy. And stop blaming Walters; he's been here for twenty-three years and knows a lot more about ready-mix compounds than you'll ever know! Now get back to work and start pulling your weight around here.

One week later, the foreman was told by the personnel manager that Farris had quit.

From J.L. Gray and F.A. Starke, *Organizational Behavior Concepts and Applications*, 2nd ed., pp. 322–23. Copyright © 1982 by Charles E. Merrill, Columbus, Ohio.

Discussion questions
1. What are the sources of this conflict?
2. What strategies would you use to resolve it?

Inflated Performance Appraisals

The General in charge of Air Force Personnel was worried. Officer effectiveness report (an annual performance appraisal) ratings were getting so inflated that almost all officers were rated "outstanding." He decided to cure the problem by implementing a forced-distribution performance appraisal system. From now on only 22 percent of the officers could be "1's" or outstanding, 28 percent could be "2's" or excellent, and the remaining half of the officers would be "3's" or typically effective. All the senior staff endorsed this new system as a solution to the inflated ratings problem.

The new system worked as planned. Tight controls insured that the distribution was maintained. However, some alarming side effects arose. It seems that many people who had considered themselves to be outstanding, were now getting "3's," which indicated that they were in the lower half of all officers rated; they felt like they had lost and would never be promoted with such ratings. As a result, many of these people were either leaving the service or losing their motivation.

Worse yet was the lack of cooperation and teamwork among the officers. If there were ten captains in an office, then only two could get 1's, three 2's, and the rest 3's. Teamwork began to disappear. Why should you help someone else look good; they might get the 1! Unit effectiveness suffered. Friendships dissolved. Backbiting and political tactics arose.

After several years of denying the problems, it became clear to the General that he had made a mistake. The forced distribution system was replaced with one much like the earlier one. Morale improved and turnover declined.

Discussion questions

1. Explain what happened using the win-lose model. Explain how win-win, win-lose, and lose-lose apply.
2. Was competition appropriate in this case? Why or why not?

REFERENCES

1. Thomas, K.W. and Schmidt, W.H. (1976), A survey of managerial interests with respect to conflict, *Academy of Management Journal* 19:315–318.

2. Thomas, K. (1976), Conflict and conflict management, in *Handbook of industrial and organizational psychology*, ed. M.D. Dunnette, p. 891, Chicago: Rand-McNally. *Also see* Likert, R. and Likert, J.G. (1976), *New ways of managing conflict*, New York: McGraw-Hill; and Blake, R.R.; Shepard, H.A.; and Mouton, J.S. (1964), *Managing intergroup conflict in industry*, Houston: Gulf.

3. Walton, R.E. (1969), *Interpersonal peacemaking: Confrontations and third-party consultation*, Reading, Mass.: Addison-Wesley.

4. Based on Filley, A.C. (1975), *Interpersonal conflict resolution*, Glenview, Ill.: Scott, Foresman, pp. 9–12.

5. For an in depth look at this issue *see* Pearce, J.L. (1981), Bringing some clarity to role ambiguity research, *Academy of Management Review* 6: 665–674.

6. Kahn, R.L.; Wolfe, D. M.; Quinn, R. P.; and Snoek, J. D.; (1964), *Organizational stress: Studies in role conflict and ambiguity*, New York: Wiley.

7. Nye, R.D. (1973), *Conflict among humans*, New York: Springer, pp. 82–84.

8. Robbins, S.P. (1974), *Managing organizational conflict: A non-traditional approach*, Englewood Cliffs, N.J.: Prentice-Hall.

9. Adapted from Robbins, *Managing organizational conflict*, pp. 96–97.

10. Conflict resolution techniques are covered more fully in Filley, *Interpersonal conflict resolution*; and Deer, C.B. (1978), Managing organizational conflict: Collaboration, bargaining and power approaches, *California Management Review* 21(2): 76–81. *Also see* Aram, J.D. and Salipante, P.F. Jr. (1981), An evaluation of organizational due process in the resolution of employee/employer conflict, *Academy of Management Review* 6:197–204.

11. For more thorough coverage of this topic *see* Walton, R.E. and McKersie, R.B. (1965), *A behavioral theory of labor negotiations: An analysis of a social interaction system*, New York: McGraw-Hill.

12. Filley, Interpersonal conflict resolution; Blake, et al., *Managing intergroup conflict in industry*; and Brown, D.L. (1983), *Managing conflict at organizational interfaces*, Reading, Mass.: Addison-Wesley; have detailed presentations or problem solving as it applies to conflict resolution.

13. Filley, *Interpersonal conflict resolution*, Chapter 3.

14. This discussion is based on Ruben, J.Z. (1980), Experimental research on third-party intervention in conflict: Toward some generalizations, *Psychological Bulletin* 87: 379–391.

15. Based on the combined results of Burke, R.J. (1970), Methods of resolving superior-subordinate conflict: The constructive use of subordinate differences and disagreements, *Organizational Behavior and Human Performance* 5, p. 403 and Phillips, E. and Cheston, R. (1979), Conflict resolution: What works? *California Management Review* 21(4), p. 79.

16. *See* Walton, *Interpersonal peacemaking*; Filley, *Interpersonal conflict resolution*; and Gordon, T. (1977), *Leader effectiveness training L.E.T.*, New York: Wyden.

17. Robbins, *Managing organizational conflict*, p. 27.

18. For more information on win-lose dynamics *see* Schein, E.H. (1980), *Organizational psychology*, 3rd ed., Englewood Cliffs, N.J.: Prentice-Hall; and Blake, et al., *Managing intergroup conflict in industry*. For another view of how conflict relates to competition, *see* Cosier, R.A. and Ruble, T.L. (1981), Research on conflict-handling behavior: An experimental approach, *Academy of Management Journal* 24: 816–831.

19. Based on Gray, J.L. and Starke, F.A. (1980), *Organizational behavior concepts and applications* 2nd ed., Columbus, Ohio: Charles E. Merrill.

20. Schein, *Organizational psychology*.

21. Johnson, D.W.; Maruyama, G.; Johnson, R.; Nelson, D.; and Skon, L.; (1981), Effects of cooperative, competitive, and individualistic goal structures on achievement: A meta-analysis, *Psychological Bulletin* 89: 56–57.

22. For an example of a win-win bonus plan, *see* Geare, A.J. (1976), Productivity from Scanlon-type plans, *Academy of Management Review* 1: 99–108.

Management of Stress

PREVIEW

- What are the impacts of stress on physical and mental health?

- How does the fight-or-flight response work?

- What is job burnout and how do you prevent it?

- How much stress is enough? Too much? Too little?

- Are you an aggressive, hard-charging achiever? Then you may be a Type A person.

- Does stress affect women differently than men?

- What are the major causes of stress, and what can you do about them?

- How is shift work like jet lag? What causes the reaction?

- How can meditation and the relaxation response reduce stress?

Preview Case: People Uptight!

The Nature of Stress
- How does stress develop
- Types of stress and the impact on health
- Stress and organizational performance
- *Perspective*: When Managers Burnout
- Individual differences and stress
- *Perspective*: Stress and Women Managers

Sources of Stress
- Personal interfaces with the organization
- Job characteristics
- *Perspective*: Stress and the Air Traffic Controller
- Role characteristics
- Organizational characteristics and processes
- *Perspective*: Shift Work and Stress

Managing Stress
- Individual methods of coping with stress
- Organizational methods of coping with stress
- *Perspective*: Participation in Decision Making to Reduce Stress
- Some conclusions about stress management

Summary
- Chapter review
- For discussion
- Key concepts and terms
- Suggested readings

Cases and Incidents
- The Finance Professor
- Top Executives Thrive on Stress

References

Liz Rosenberg

Liz thought to herself, "My job here at Advanced Products hasn't worked out as well as I planned and it's all Herb Thorpe's fault. If it wasn't for him, I could get my job done easily. But every direction I turn Herb seems to be butting heads with me."

"In fact, I've been really uptight for about a month. I can't sleep at night; I'm not interested in food; and I feel my neck muscles tense up, then I have a whale of a headache. I'm jittery and anxious and it seems that I am constantly annoyed. I wonder if I need to see a psychologist. Am I having a nervous breakdown?"

Herb Thorpe

Herb's feelings were not unlike those of Liz: "I'm fed up with that woman! [Liz Rosenberg] Ever since she arrived I've felt like there's a big heavy chain around my neck. It seems she does everything she can to screw me up."

"But I need to forget Liz for the moment and make an appointment with the doctor because something's wrong with me. My heart beats rapidly, I have constant indigestion, and my hands aren't steady anymore. Maybe I have heart disease or something? I feel so bad it's hard to get up the motivation to come to work, much less put in the kind of effort this job takes. Maybe I should be thinking of an early retirement."

Liz and Herb are experiencing a number of symptoms of stress that may have resulted from their long-standing conflict (see the Preview Case for Chapter 10). While some stress is beneficial for energizing the organization, too much stress can have a powerful negative impact on people and on organizational effectiveness. In this chapter, we will try to understand the nature of stress, its sources, and how to manage it.

The Nature of Stress

Stress is a natural way of coping with changes in our environment. In this section, we will examine the nature of the stress process, the impact of stress on health and organizational performance, and the individual differences that people experience in their response to stress.

■ How Does Stress Develop?

Stress is some type of response, physical or psychological, to an external event or situation that places special physical or psychologcal demands on a person and causes a deviation from their normal functioning.[1] A **stressor** is a stimulus condition that results in the response of stress. For example, a stressor (stimulus) in the environment, such as Herb's hostility, results in stress (a response) within Liz, such as increased heart rate with a jolt of adrenalin, that prepares her to cope with the threat.[2] Figure 11.1 presents a simplified model of the stress process. Notice that people react to stress

Figure 11.1. The stress process.

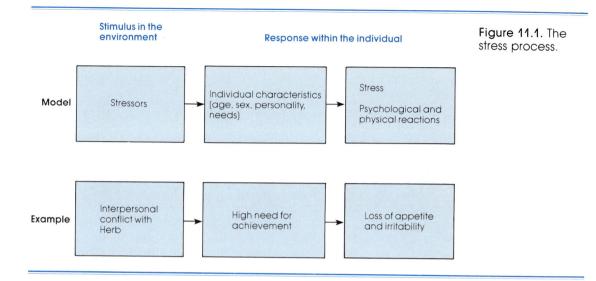

differently depending on individual characteristics. In Liz's case, the problem with Herb (stressor) coupled with her high need for achievement resulted in a loss of appetite and irritability.

Fight-or-flight Response   Our reactions to stress are a product of evolution. Our cave-dwelling ancestors needed to react to threats in the environment, such as an attacking hairy mammoth, by either fighting or fleeing. When such an attack occurred, the body prepared itself by pumping adrenalin, increasing heart and respiration rates, higher blood pressure, and sharpened senses. These physiological reactions, called the **fight-or-flight** response, helped the cave dweller to cope with the emergency.

Although mammoths are gone, we still react as if they were here. When Liz told Herb of her deal with Allied Insurance for early delivery of machines, Herb felt under attack, and his body reacted as if Liz were a modern-day mammoth. But Herb cannot fight Liz, at least not physically; and he cannot flee from the situation. The problem is that the physiological response to a threat is not as appropriate in work situations in the 1980s as it was in prehistoric times, and stress results.[3] Some of the common symptoms of stress can be seen in Table 11.1.

■ Types of Stress and The Impact on Health

Some amount of stress is useful for coping with emergencies and everyday management problems, but stress effects seem to build upon one an-

Table 11.1.   Some symptoms of job stress.

1. Rapid pulse or pounding heart.
2. Increased perspiration from hands, underarms, and forehead.
3. Tightening of the forehead and jaw.
4. Inability to sit still or keep your feet still while you are sitting.
5. Tensing of shoulder and neck muscles.

other in a cumulative fashion.[5] The duration and number of stress experiences is important for determining the long-term effects of stress.[6] Single or isolated stress situations probably have little effect on health. However, when a stress situation results in a relatively constant state of agitation, such as the conflict between Liz and Herb, there may be a negative impact on health.

Stress situations can be divided into short-term or low-level, moderate, and severe categories.[7] Short-term situations involve a brief event, such as being caught in traffic or being bawled out by your boss. As long as these situations do not become too frequent, they usually pose no threat to your health.

Moderate stress situations may last a few hours or several days. Examples might be an unresolved disagreement with the boss, new job responsibilities, or making a presentation to a large group. The disagreement between Liz and Herb probably falls in the upper range of this category. Individuals who have predispositions to certain diseases, such as heart problems, may experience health difficulties at this stage.

Severe stress involves chronic situations that may last weeks, months, or years. Prolonged financial difficulties, extremely heavy job demands, or the death of a loved one are examples of such stress. Table 11.2 shows the relative importance of selected stressful events. The death of a spouse with a score of 100 represents twice as much stress as marriage with a score of 50. Even pleasant events such as vacations or graduation from college cause stress.

While the evidence is only preliminary, there seems to be a relationship between stress and physical illnesses, such as hypertension, ulcers, diabetes, headaches, coronary heart disease, and perhaps even cancer.[8]

■ Stress and Organizational Performance

Moderate to severe levels of stress can cause a number of problems for organizations.[9] If employees become physically ill, their attendance and performance will suffer. People under severe stress often seem to care less

Table 11.2. Relative impact of stressful events.

Life event	Scale value
Death of spouse	100
Divorce	73
Marriage	50
Fired from work	47
Retirement	45
Change to a different line of work	36
Change in responsibilities at work	29
Outstanding personal achievement	28
Begin or end school	26
Trouble with boss	23
Change in work hours or conditions	20
Vacation	13
Christmas	12

Understanding Organizational Behavior

11.1 | When Managers Burn Out[10]

There are a number of factors that result in burnout, a state of mental, emotional, and physical exhaustion that results from working with people and complex organizations over an extended period of time in emotionally draining situations.

For example, a high-performing vice-president was transferred from a subsidiary to the corporate headquarters. While he had been recruited to revamp the control system, he was immediately sucked into a major corporate reorganization because he was a newcomer who could be trusted. Here is what happened:

. . . His task was arduous. Not only did the long hours and unremitting pressure of walking a tightrope among conflicting interests exhaust him, but also they made it impossible for him to get control of problems that needed attention. Furthermore, because his family could not move for six months until the school year was over, he commuted on weekends to his previous home 800 miles away. As he tried to perform the unwanted job that had been thrust on him and support the CEO who was counting heavily on his competence,

he felt lonely, harassed, and burdened. Now that his task was coming to an end he was in no psychological shape to take on his formal duties. In short, he had "burned out." [11]

This state of exhaustion, called **burnout** is a special form of stress outcome that often results in withdrawal, low performance, or psychological disorders. Prevention is the best cure for burnout. Here are some steps that may be used to prevent burnout.[12]

1. Recognize burnout situations and rotate people out of potentially exhausting positions.
2. Put time constraints on the job. Do not allow people to work twelve to sixteen hours a day over an extended period.
3. Avoid using the same people as "rescuers" or "trouble-shooters" in problem situations time after time.
4. Take an entire work group on a nominal business trip to a recreational site.
5. Make sure the organization has a systematic, dependable way to recognize people, to provide feedback, to show them how important they are.

about their jobs and their organization. Their commitment is low and the possibility of quitting is quite high. The ultimate result of stress may be "burn out," a condition of exhaustion that results from high levels of energy being expended with little visible result (*see* the Perspective: When Managers Burn Out). If the conflict between Liz and Herb continues, we may predict that the stress will become severe and will affect organizational performance.

While there are many undesirable side effects from severe stress, some stress can be quite beneficial for energizing behavior. While there are a number of examples we might use, two strategies for raising stress are goal setting and job design processes. Setting goals and performance standards raises stress but also results in higher performance. However, if goals are set too high, people may become overstressed and performance may suffer. Another way to increase stress is through job design. When a job is enriched, there is an attempt to instill more responsibility in the job *and* responsibility is quite stressful. If we increase it too much, we may exceed the optimum level of stress and performance may decline. The key is to balance stress so

Table 11.3. The relationship between performance and stress.

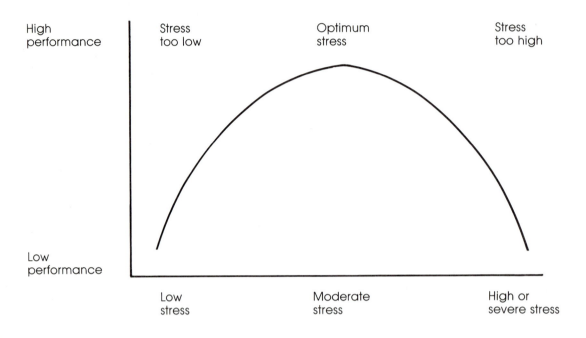

Table 11.4. Type A behavior quiz.[13]

To find out which type you are, circle the number on the scale below that best characterizes your behavior for each trait.

1. Casual about appointments	1 2 3 4 5	Never late, sense of time urgency
2. Not competitive	1 2 3 4 5	Very competitive
3. Never feel rushed even under pressure	1 2 3 4 5	Always pressured for time
4. Take things one at a time	1 2 3 4 5	Try to do many things at once, think about what I am going to do next.
5. Slow doing things	1 2 3 4 5	Fast (eating, walking, ect.)
6. Easy-going reaction to frustrations	1 2 3 4 5	React to frustration with hostility
7. Do not perform at full capacity	1 2 3 4 5	Push myself to capacity

   Scoring: Add your score for each question; then convert it to Type A or Type B behavior using the table below:

Number of Points	Type of Behavior
20 or Less	B
21-24	A
25 or More	A+

that an optimum level is reached. Table 11.3 illustrates the relationship between stress and performance.[14]

■ Individual Differences and Stress

Reactions to stress are also a function of the individual. There are numerous individual differences that may help explain why people react differently to similar levels of stress. These include age, education, occupation, needs, values, abilities, sex, and personality.[15] While space limits our coverage of these differences, one aspect of personality that is often researched is the relationship between Type A behavior, stress, and health. Before we discuss Type A and Type B behavior, you can gain insight into your own behavior pattern by completing the quiz in Table 11.4.

As you may guess from the quiz, the **Type A** pattern applies to people who are involved in a chronic, incessant struggle to achieve more and more in less and less time. In addition, Type A people exhibit patterns of aggressiveness, easily aroused hostility and anger a sense of time urgency, and an achievement orientation.[16] A **Type B** behavior pattern applies when none of the Type A behaviors are present. People who exhibit a Type A behavior pattern are more susceptible to coronary heart disease.[17] The exact relationship between Type A behavior and stress is unclear, although it seems that Type A behaviors may, in the long-run, create stress. In any event it is probably desirable for people who are high on the Type A scale to move more down the continuum toward Type B. This may be done by reestablishing priorities, by allowing more time for activities, and by reducing the total number of activities.[18]

Sources of Stress

Practically any event or situation in an organization that puts abnormal physical or psychological demands on people is a potential source of stress. We will cover four major aspects of stress: personal interfaces with the organization, job characteristics, role characteristics, and organizational characteristics and processes.[19] Figure 11.2 provides a summary of the major sources of job stress.

| 11.2 | *Stress and Women Managers*[20] |

A recent study of 135 top female executives in the United Kingdom found that managerial women face the same stressors as men *plus* some additional ones that make the overall stress level even higher than for men. The strongest reason for stress seemed to be lack of control over the work environment and extreme pressure of the work environment. Women experienced migraine headaches, high blood pressure, tiredness, irritation, anxiety, and other symptoms of stress. The authors of the study conclude that higher stress levels may deter women from entering or remaining in managerial positions, stop women from seeking advancement, enhance Type A behavior patterns in women, and have adverse effects on the physical and mental health of women.

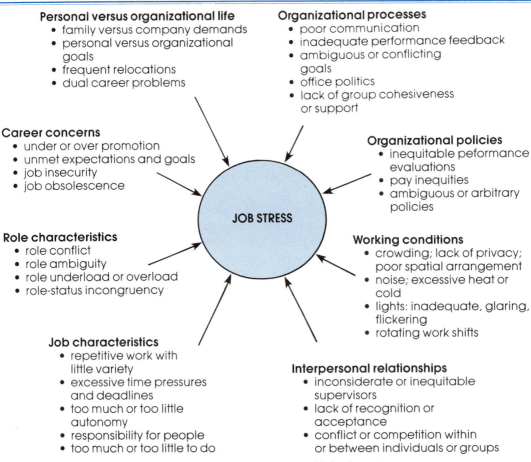

Personal versus organizational life
- family versus company demands
- personal versus organizational goals
- frequent relocations
- dual career problems

Organizational processes
- poor communication
- inadequate performance feedback
- ambiguous or conflicting goals
- office politics
- lack of group cohesiveness or support

Career concerns
- under or over promotion
- unmet expectations and goals
- job insecurity
- job obsolescence

Organizational policies
- inequitable peformance evaluations
- pay inequities
- ambiguous or arbitrary policies

Role characteristics
- role conflict
- role ambiguity
- role underload or overload
- role-status incongruency

JOB STRESS

Working conditions
- crowding; lack of privacy; poor spatial arrangement
- noise; excessive heat or cold
- lights: inadequate, glaring, flickering
- rotating work shifts

Job characteristics
- repetitive work with little variety
- excessive time pressures and deadlines
- too much or too little autonomy
- responsibility for people
- too much or too little to do

Interpersonal relationships
- inconsiderate or inequitable supervisors
- lack of recognition or acceptance
- conflict or competition within or between individuals or groups

Figure 11.2. Major sources of job stress.[21]

■ Personal Interfaces with the Organization

Personal Versus Organizational Life   There are numerous opportunities for conflict between family and personal desires and organizational demands. An example is Brian, a college professor, who is married to a middle manager in a large corporation. His wife, Ellen, has been offered a promotion to vice-president if she will agree to move to the corporate headquarters in San Francisco. Her boss implies that if she does not move she should not expect another chance at a major promotion. Brian is a full professor with tenure and perceives that it will be difficult, if not impossible, to find a faculty position in San Francisco. This decision is causing a great deal of stress in their relationship.

Career Concerns   Unfulfilled career expectations are a major source of stress. If a person's advancement in the organization keeps up with their expectations, then they are likely to be more satisfied and stress free. On the other hand, a person who feels prematurely plateaued or 'topped out" on the advancement ladder may encounter severe stress.

11.3 Stress and the Air Traffic Controller

The following is an excerpt from an article describing air traffic controllers at Chicago's O'Hare Airport.[22]

"HELP WANTED: World's busiest airport seeks radar jockeys for unusually stimulating, high-intensity environment. Must be able to direct at least twelve aircraft at one time and make instant decisions affecting the safety of thousands. No degree required, but prior experience as traffic cop, seeing-eye dog, or God helpful. Severe stress will jeopardize sanity and result in early termination from job, but employer will absorb cost of medical and psychiatric care."

The ad above never appeared, but it could have. The pressures air traffic controllers feel in the control tower have been likened to what pilots experience in combat. Nowhere is that stress more acute than at Chicago's O'Hare Airport, better known to controllers as the ulcer factory.

The herculean task of coping with 1,900 flights a day rests squarely on the O'Hare controllers' shoulders. For some, it is a burden they can't endure. In the last year, at least seven men have been carried out of the O'Hare control tower on stretchers, victims of acute hypertension. Most controllers there have already succumbed to one or more by-products of prolonged stress: ulcers, high blood pressure, arthritis, colitis, skin disorders, headaches, allergies, and upset stomachs. Other controllers struggle with more severe problems, such as alcoholism, depression, horrifying nightmares and acute anxiety.

This journalistic introduction gives a little feel for the type of stress experienced by air traffic controllers. Studies of stress among controllers have reached conflicting conclusions. One review of the literature conducted by the FAA itself found that the demands of the controller's job do not appear to place unusual stress on the controllers.[23] Another more recent study[24] found that the job involved what is termed **acute episodic stress**, or stress caused by intense, relative infrequent events with relatively brief physiological effects but long-lasting psychological effects. The differences in finding may be due to the two types of stress being measured. The controller's job may indeed be of rather moderate stress in terms of the day-to-day task. Their **chronic stress** (stress associated with the normal workload and pressure) level is moderate. But, over a period of years the acute stress episodes may accumulate and cause burnout.

Part of the analysis of the study was to find out which controllers were high on a burnout scale and then try to determine what factors seem to account for the burnout. They found that the burnout sample averaged 41.3 years of age with 19.1 years of service, whereas the sample as a whole averaged 34.4 years of age and had 13.6 years of service. In addition, burnouts accounted for only 21 percent of those who were 41.0 or older, but 69 percent of those with 19.0 or more years of service. They conclude that burnout seems to be more a function of length of service than any other factor. They also speculate that the acute episodic stress events accumulate to cause the eventual burnout.

One case involved a highly successful executive named Bob Lyons.[25] Bob appeared to be a Type A person; he worked hard and drove himself relentlessly. After about ten years with the company, he perceived that his career was plateauing. He was being assigned to jobs where little action was required. Bob began to lose his motivation and become embroiled in conflicts with other executives. Bob's bosses were afraid he was having some type of mental breakdown, so they agreed with the doctor when he said all Bob needed was some time off. When Bob decided that he was ready to come back to work, the president again suggested that he take another week of vacation. A few days later, Bob Lyons committed suicide. While there were a number of complex factors at work here, one important one—Bob's perceived lack of further career opportunities—resulted in severe stress. Bob was not ready to sit back and be a dreamer; he was a doer.

■ Job Characteristics

The Demands of the Job Itself

There are a variety of stressors that fall in this category. Job design, discussed in Chapter 7, can foster or inhibit stress in several ways. If the work is repetitive with little variety, it may be too boring and stressful for some people. If the job contains too little or too much autonomy it may also be stressful. Certainly too many tight deadlines and high standards can cause job stress. In addition to these structural aspects of the job, another important issue is degree that the job entails responsibility for people. Managers must balance conflict and hostility between subordinates, such as the situation of Liz and Herb. They must make hard, disagreeable decisions about their subordinates and appraise their performance. Many of these tasks can be emotionally draining. Over long periods of time it may result in stress and burnout.

■ Role Characteristics

Role conflicts, ambiguity, and overload can be stressors.[26] In the last chapter, we saw that **role conflicts** occur when people disagree about how a role should be performed. The first-line supervisor was singled out as someone who experiences a great deal of role conflict that results in stress. Another example might be a salesperson who is directed to sell something that the customer does not want or need just to meet the company's quota. Table 11.5 shows examples of how this concept is measured.

Role ambiguity occurs when job responsibilities and duties are ambiguous and unclear. A therapist in a hospital may be unclear about the role to be played. What is expected? To treat and cure patients? To keep accurate records? To supervise other newer therapists? In short, the therapist does not know what is expected and thus experiences frustration and stress. In Table 11.5, some items that are used to tap role ambiguity are shown.

Role overload is expecting someone to perform too many jobs or roles at one time. Even though the roles may be compatible, there is just too much to do. **Role and status incongruency**, described in Chapter 9, results when someone is performing a role that is at a lower or higher status level than they are comfortable with. An example might be a new assistant professor who is asked to chair the university's curriculum committee.

Table 11.5. Role conflict and role ambiguity items.[27]

Role Conflict Items	I receive incompatible requests from two or more people. I work on unnecessary things. I work with two or more groups who operate quite differently. I have to buck a rule or policy in order to carry out an assignment.
Role Ambiguity Items	I know that I have divided my time properly. I know exactly what is expected of me. I feel certain about how much authority I have on this job. I have clear, planned goals and objectives for my job.

Adapted from J.R. Rizzo, R.J. House, and S.I. Lirtzman, 1970, Role conflict and role ambiguity measures, *Administrative Science Quarterly* 15: 150-63. Copyright © 1970 by Administrative Science Quarterly, Ithaca, New York. Used with permission.

■ Organizational Characteristics and Processes

Interpersonal Relations   As our opening case involving Liz and Herb illustrates, conflicts over interpersonal relationships can cause severe stress. This type of stress often takes the form of problems between supervisor and subordinate. A supervisor who does not listen or seem to care, or who treats subordinates inequitably, can cause a great deal of stress in the subordinate. An example of this stressor happened in a large hospital. The chief of nursing was professionally competent, but did not know how to manage people. Whenever a subordinate did anything that offended her (and one never quite knew what the offense was), she would completely cut off communication with that subordinate for days or even weeks. This behavior resulted in a great deal of stress, low job satisfaction, and a high turnover rate for nurses under her supervision.

Organizational Processes   Almost all organizational processes—motivation, communication, goal setting, group dynamics, conflict or competition, politics, performance appraisal, controlling—can cause stress. Throughout the book, we discuss problems and issues surrounding various processes. An important point to remember is that most problems cause stress as well as other outcomes.

Organizational Policies   Perhaps the central stressor that results from organizational policies is when rules or systems are perceived to be inequitable or unfair. A policy that the best performance ratings will go only to the production division populated solely by men will cause considerable stress among those who are not assigned to production or who are women. Another example is two managers doing exactly the same job but one is paid more than the other because of being hired more recently at a higher starting salary level.

Working Conditions   While most stressors seem to occur in the psychological environment,[28] there are a number of stressors in the physical environment, particularly for blue-collar jobs.[29] Loud and distracting noise, poor or flickering lighting, crowded conditions, and temperatures that are too hot or too cold have been experienced by most of us. Another impor-

Management of Stress

11.4	*Shift Work and Stress*[30]

Anyone that has ever crossed a number of time zones has experienced "jet lag" because of the in- the interruption of the body's cyclical rhythm. Shift work can also cause the same type of phys- iological reaction. In either the case of jet lag or shift work, it takes several days for the body to adjust. These adjustments are necessary because of the twenty-four hour rhythm of the body called **circadian rhythm**. Body temperatures, urine flow, heartrate, metabolism, sleep cycles, and other changes keep pace with this regular schedule. Shift work, like jet lag, interrupts this rhythm. In addition, those people who work night shift (11 P.M.–7 A.M.) are cut off from the ac- tivities of the daytime-oriented society. The im- pact of shiftwork on the family and other social relationships may be so strong that severe stress results.

important aspect of working conditions is shift work. The Perspective: Shift Work and Stress shows how shift work can affect people and cause stress.

Managing Stress

The goal of stress management is not to eliminate stress but to keep it at optimum levels so that performance is high and that the dysfunctional symptoms of stress are minimized. In practice, the most common problem is that stress levels are too high rather than too low. The thrust of this sec- tion is on reducing stress. We will highlight several individual and organiza- tional strategies for dealing with stress.

■ Individual Methods for Coping With Stress

Start with an example of how stress affects a young attorney:[31]

Jim Gardner, an aggressive and successful attorney, was feeling frightened and angry as he drove home through the heavy rush hour traffic. The doctor's report that afternoon had scared Jim: either he slowed down, stopped smoking, lost weight, drank less, got more exer- cise and—above all—stopped driving himself so hard, or the chest pain would turn into a heart attack before he was forty.

The traffic light turned green, and Jim's car charged into the inter- section, narrowly missing a blue sedan. "Idiot!" Jim exploded at the driver. "How can I slow down? I've got four new cases coming to trial next month. Relax! How can I relax when I'm responsible for those briefs? What am I supposed to do, retire at age thirty six?"

Soberly Jim recalled the doctor's final words: "Jim, right now you have a choice. But if you keep pushing yourself and neglecting your health, you won't live to see your kids grow up."

"Damn it all!" The light changed. "Hey, you!" Jim yelled at the driv- er of the car ahead. "Get moving! I don't have time to waste!"

Jim who appears to be a Type A individual, needs help to cope with a severe stress problem. He might turn first to one of the most effective individual approaches to stress reduction: meditation or the **relaxation response**.[32] The relaxation response is the opposite of the fight-or-flight response discussed earlier. The body's metabolism and heartrate slow down, and the rate of breathing declines. The relaxation response has four elements: a quiet environment, a mental device (a single syllable sound or word), a passive attitude, and a comfortable position. The most popular relaxation technique is transcendental meditation.[33]

How might Jim use **meditation** to reduce his stress? He should set aside about twenty minutes once or twice a day to meditate. He should find a quiet environment, sit in a comfortable position (shoes off, clothing loosened), close his eyes, breath deeply, and relax all muscles. Each time he breathes out through the nose, he should say his mental device or word, such as "one." He should maintain a passive attitude and push distracting thoughts from his mind. For the next twenty minutes he repeats: breathe in . . . breathe out, . . .'one' . . . breathe in . . . breath out . . . 'one'.[34]

There are two other alternatives Jim might consider: exercise and biofeedback.[35] Exercise seems to reduce tension and stress and to strengthen the cardiovascular system. Jim might gradually begin a jogging or other exercise program after checking with his doctor to get advice about how to proceed. A second strategy is to use **biofeedback** devices to monitor bodily processes like pulse, breathing rate, and blood pressure. Various relaxation techniques are then tried with accurate feedback about their effectiveness. Biofeedback is not as commonly used in organizations because complex and expensive equipment is often necessary.

■ Organizational Methods of Coping with Stress

There are a host of organizational methods for dealing with stress, including those we studied in earlier chapters: job enrichment, goal setting, and positive reinforcement. Another strategy, changing the organizational climate or culture, will be discussed in a later chapter. In this section, we will discuss reducing job stress by using role clarification and analysis techniques.[36]

Recognizing Stress   It is not always easy to recognize someone who is experiencing excessive stress. Careful observation of behavior may reveal a number of behavior patterns that indicate stress overload:[37]

1. Working late more than usual or the opposite; increased tardiness or absenteeism.
2. Difficulty in making decisions.
3. Increases in the number of careless mistakes.
4. Missing deadlines or forgetting appointments.
5. Problems interacting and getting along with others.
6. Focusing on mistakes and personal failures.

Role Clarification   Many organizational stressors relate to how an employee perceives the job. The role an employee plays provides the focus of the job and a potential source of stress if it is unclear or if two or more roles conflict. Roles get mixed up with expectations, responsibilities, and reporting relationships. In our opening case regarding Liz and Herb, there

$\boxed{11.5}$ *Participation in Decision Making to Reduce Stress*[38]

Research in a hospital outpatient setting evaluated the effects of participation in decision making on role conflict, role ambiguity, and stress. Over the short-run (three months) there was little effect, but over a more extended period (six months), significant differ- ences were found. People who participated in decisions experienced less role conflict and ambiguity and had greater perceived influence over decisions. These outcomes were in turn related to lower stress levels and higher job satisfaction levels.

was a role conflict brought about when each had differing expectations about what role behaviors would foster organizational effectiveness.

The most common strategy for clarifying roles is **role analysis.** The technique involves open discussion of role expectations by addressing such questions as:[39]

1. What do you think is expected of you?
2. What do you expect of me (your boss)?
3. What information do you need to do your job well?
4. What areas, if any, trouble you about the nature and scope of your job?

In addition it may be useful to ask a question such as, "If (name of focal person) were operating in an optimally effective way, what would he or she be doing?" The answer to this question can be recorded on a blackboard or on newsprint. Then the person who answered the question discusses the response with the focal person. This process helps clarify roles and reduce role-related stress.

■ Some Conclusions about Stress Management

Almost all organizational processes cause stress for someone, manager or subordinate. Since stress cannot and should not be entirely eliminated, it should be kept at moderate levels where performance and satisfaction are high. Particular care should be exercised by managers to observe stress levels of individual subordinates and, when they are too high, to attempt to lower the stress using some of the strategies that have been discussed.

SUMMARY

Chapter Review

- ■ Stress is a natural way to cope with the environment; however, when the **fight-or-flight** response prepares the body physically to meet some threat and it cannot resolve the threat, stress results.
- ■ Stress situations can be divided into three categories: short-term, moderate, and severe. Prolonged severe stress can cause physical and psychological illness, which can reduce performance.
- ■ **Burn out**, a special form of stress that results from working with people and complex organizational problems in emotionally draining situations, can cause exhaustion and withdrawal from the job.

- ■ The key to managing stress is to design organizational systems with a moderate level of stress to energize behavior.
- ■ **Type A** behavior patterns may result in increased stress and risk of coronary heart disease.
- ■ There are many sources of stress. Almost anything that puts abnormal physical or psychological demands on a person is a **stressor**.
- ■ The air traffic controller's job illustrates how **acute episodic stress** can cause burnout in spite of the lack of excessive stress in the day-to-day job.
- ■ **Role conflict, ambiguity, and overload** are very common sources of stress that can be managed relatively easily using role analysis techniques and participation in decision making.
- ■ Problems regarding fair and equitable treatment in pay, promotions, or discipline seem to be particularly powerful sources of stress.
- ■ Meditation or the **relaxation response** is an effective strategy for countering stress because it acts just the opposite from the fight-or-flight response.

For Discussion

1. Explain how the fight-or-flight process works. Give an example from your personal experience.
2. How can a manager recognize that a subordinate is experiencing too much stress?
3. What types of jobs seem most subject to burnout? Why?
4. If the research reported in the Perspective: Stress and Women Managers is correct in finding that women executives experience even more stress than men, what are the personal and organizational implications?
5. Figure 11.2 indicates eight major sources of stress. Based on your own experience, provide one example of each of these sources.
6. What is the difference between acute episodic stress and chronic stress? Explain the implications of these two types of stress for organizations.
7. Give an example of how role ambiguity, role conflict, and role overload can cause stress.
8. Weigh the advantages and disadvantages of the various methods for coping with stress.

Key Concepts and Terms

stress	**role conflict**
stressor	**role ambiguity**
fight-or-flight response	**role overload**
burnout	**circadian rhythm**
Type A behavior	**relaxation response**
Type B behavior	**biofeedback**
acute episodic stress	**role clarification**
chronic stress	

Suggested Readings

Benson, H. and Allen, R. L. (1980). How much stress is too much? *Harvard Business Review* Sept.–Oct.: 86–92.

Levinson, H. (1981). When executives burn out. *Harvard Business Review* May–June:73–81.

Moss, L. (1981). *Management stress*. Reading, Mass.: Addison-Wesley.

Stostak, A. B. (1980). *Blue-collar stress*. Reading, Mass.: Addison-Wesley.

Wallis, C. (1983). Stress: Can we cope? *Time* June 6:48–54.

CASES AND INCIDENTS

The Finance Professor

Dr. Olivia Shipla, professor of finance, looked up angrily from the budget report she was trying to read before the committee meeting just twenty minutes away. "Come in!" she said, and Ms. Anne Stevens, the department secretary, edged nervously into the room. "Excuse me, Dr. Shipla," she began. Her voice was interrupted by the phone's jangling. Dr. Shipla grabbed it. "No, Mr. Carlson, I have not graded your capital budgeting paper yet. Check back on Monday." She replaced the phone receiver and raised an eyebrow at the waiting secretary. "What is it?"

"Dr. Shipla, perhaps I had trouble reading the note you left with this book on my desk." Ms. Stevens held a thick, faded green book in her hand. "Did you want fifteen copies of one of the chapters by tomorrow morning?"

"Ms. Stevens, can't you read?" Dr. Shipla inquired sarcastically. "I quite clearly asked for fifteen copies of the book. The whole book!"

Anne Steven's jaw jutted forward almost imperceptibly. "I'm sorry, Dr. Shipla, but that's not possible. As you know, the new cost cutting directives, which I *did* read, require that a job of this size have at least five days' notice so

that we can send it through the Central Printing Service. It's cheaper. I'm afraid I have to obey those rules."

Ms. Stevens opened the office door, then turned before closing the door deliberately to say, "I will send it out this afternoon, but I'm afraid it will be at least a week."

Back in her own office, Anne Stevens set the book on her desk and took several deep breaths to calm her anger, then sat down to resume her typing chores. Seeing that Olivia Shipla's "rush job" manuscript was on the top of her stack of typing, she paused a moment, then slid it under the stack and smiled as she began typing a letter.

From Arthur P. Brief, Randall S. Schuler, and Mary Van Sell, *Managing Job Stress*, pp. 64–65. Copyright © 1981 by Arthur P. Brief, Randall S. Schuler, and Mary Van Sell. Reprinted by permission of the publisher, Little, Brown and Company.

Discussion questions
1. What are the sources of stress for Dr. Shipla? For Anne Stevens?
2. What are the effects of stress on performance in this case?
3. How would you recommend that this stress situation be managed?

Top Executives Thrive on Stress

Some stress experts claim that many high-powered executives thrive on stress; that they are adrenalin freaks. For supporting this position they cite a report by Metropolitan Life Insurance Company that found that top executives in the Fortune 500 firms had 40 percent fewer fatal heart attacks than middle

managers in the same companies. The study concluded that stress ranked only tenth out of fourteen factors predicting coronary risk.

Interviews with top managers also supports the notion that many top executives can take stress in stride:

John H. Vogel, chairman of the National Bank of North America, for example, starts his business day at 6 a.m. and does not stop until after a dinner engagement. 'The hours are tough on a typical person,'' he says, but quickly adds, 'I don't think you can get to the top unless you can handle stress.'' Roy A. Anderson, chairman of Lockheed Corp., says he does 'not particularly enjoy stress,'' but he adds: 'Some degree of stress is a motivator. If the job's too soft, you lose your mental acuity.'' And John H. Zimmerman, vice-president of employee relations for Firestone Tire &

Rubber Co., who faces an Apr. 21 contract deadline with the United Rubber Workers, declares: 'Stress is what you make of it, and that can be the difference between coping and collapsing.''[40]

Discussion questions
1. How do you account for the ability of top executives to cope with stress?
2. Would you predict a difference in stress levels between top, middle, and lower level management? How would they differ? Why?
3. Do you think these top executives display Type A behavior patterns?

REFERENCES

1. Beehr, T. A. and J. E. Newman (1978), Job stress, employee health, and organizational effectiveness: A facet analysis, model, and literature review, *Personnel Psychology* 31:665–699; and J. M. Ivancevich and M. T. Matteson (1980), *Stress and work: A managerial perspective*, Glenview, Ill.: Scott-Foresman; and Schuler, R. S. (1980), Definition and conceptualization of stress in organizations, *Organizational Behavior and Human Performance* 25:184–215.

2. Seyle, H. (1976), *The stress of life*, 2nd ed., New York: McGraw-Hill.

3. For more on the fight-or-flight process *see* Seyle, *The stress of life* and Benson, H. (1974), Your innate asset for combating stress, *Harvard Business Review* 52(4):49–60.

4. Ivancevich and Matteson, *Stress and work*, p. 207. For a more thorough review of symptoms, *see* Schuler, Definition and conceptualization of stress in organizations.

5. Schuler, Definition and conceptualization of stress in organizations.

6. Ivancevich and Matteson, *Stress at work*, Chapter 4.

7. Ivancevich and Matteson, *Stress at work*, pp. 78–79.

8. Jenkins, C. D. (1976), Recent evidence supporting psychological and social risk factors in coronary heart disease, *New England Journal of Medicine*, 294:1033–1038; and Ivancevich, J. M.; Matteson, M. T.; and Preston, C. (1982), Occupational stress, Type A behavior, and physical well being, *Academy of Management Journal* 25:373–391; and Ivancevich and Matteson, *Stress at work*, pp. 90–92.

9. *See* Schuler, Definition and conceptualization of stress in organizations; and Allen, R. D.; Hitt, M. A.; and Greer, C. R. (1982), Occupational stress and perceived organizational effectiveness in formal groups: an examination of stress level and stress type, *Personnel Psychology* 35(2):359–370.

10. Levinson, H. (1981), When executives burn out, *Harvard Business Review* May–June:73–81; and Perlman, B. and Hartman, E. A. (1982), Burnout: Summary and future research, *Human Relations* 35:283–305; and (1980) The personal and business cost of job burnout, *Wall Street Journal* 11 Nov, pp. 31, 34.

11. Levinson, When executives burn out, pp. 73–74.

12. Levinson, When executives burn out.

13. Adapted from Bortner, R. W. (1966), A short rating scale as a potential measure of Type A behavior, *Journal of Chronic Diseases* 22:87–91; and Friedman, M. and Rosenman, R. H. (1974), *Type A behavior and your heart*, New York: Knopf.

14. For a discussion of these issues *see* McGrath, J. E. (1976), Stress and behavior in organizations, in *Handbook of industrial and organizational psychology*, ed. M. D. Dunnette, pp. 1351–1395, Chicago: Rand-McNally.

15. *See* Schuler, Definition and conceptualization of stress in organizations; and Ivancevich and Matteson, *Stress at work* for reviews.

16. Friedman and Rosenman, *Type A behavior and your heart*. For a review *see* Matthews, K. A. (1982), Psychological perspectives on Type A behavior pattern, *Psychological Bulletin* 91:293–323. For the role of anger and hostility in Type A behavior, *see* Diamond, E. L. (1982), The role of anger and hostility in essential hypertension and coronary heart disease, *Psychological Bulletin* 92:410–433.

17. Matthews, Psychological perspectives on Type A behavior pattern.

18. Pittner, M. S. and Houston, B. K. (1980), Response to stress, cognitive coping strategies, and Type A behavior pattern, *Journal of Personality of Social Psychology* 39:147–157.

19. For a more complete discussion of the sources of stress, *see* Ivancevich and Matteson, *Stress at work*; Parasuraman, S. and Alutto, J. A. (1981), An examination of the organizational antecedents of stressors at work, *Academy of Management Journal* 24:48–67; Parks, K. R. (1982), Occupational stress among student nurses: A natural experiment, *Journal of Applied Psychology* 67:784–796; and Braum, A.; Singer, J. E.; and Baum, C. S. (1981), Stress and the environment, *Journal of Social Issues* 37:4–35.

20. Cooper, C. L. and Davidson, M. J. (1982), The high cost of stress on women managers, *Organizational Dynamics* Spring:44–53. For more information about women and stress, *see* Brief, A. P.; Schuler, R. S.; and Van Sell, M. (1981), *Managing job stress* Boston: Little, Brown, Chapter 7.

21. Developed in part from the categories proposed by Brief, et al., *Managing Job Stress*; and Cooper C. L. and Marshall, J. (1975), The management of stress, *Personnel Review* 4(4).

22. Martindale, D. (1977), Sweaty palms in the control tower, *Psychology Today* 10(9).

23. Smith, R. (1980), *Stress, anxiety, and the air traffic control specialist: Some conclusions from a decade of research*, FAA Civil Aeromedical Institute, 1980.

24. Bowers, D. B. (1983), What would make 11,500 people quit their jobs?, *Organizational Dynamics* Winter:5–19.

25. Levinson, H. (1981), What killed Bob Lyons?, *Harvard Business Review* Mar.–Apr.:144–162.

26. A classic study in this area is Kahn, R. L. Wolfe, D. M.; Quinn, R. P.; Snoek, J. D.; and Rosenthal, R. A.; (1964), *Organizational stress: Studies in role conflict and ambiguity*, New York: Wiley.

27. For a validation of the scale, *see* Schuler, R. S.; Aldag, R. J.; and Brief, A. P. (1977), Role conflict and ambiguity: A scale analysis, *Organizational Behavior and Human Performance* 20:111–129.

28. Ivancevich and Matteson, *Stress at work*, p. 105.

29. Stostak, A. B. (1980), *Blue-collar stress*, Reading, Mass.: Addison-Wesley.

30. Ivancevich and Matteson, *Stress at work*, pp. 136–138.

31. Brief, et al., *Managing job stress*, p. 64.

32. Benson, Your innate asset for combating stress; and Peters, R. K. and Benson, H. (1978), Time out from tension, *Harvard Business Review*, 56(1):120–124; and Goleman, D. (1976), Meditation helps break the stress spiral, *Psychology Today* 9(9):82cf.

33. Schwartz, G. E. (1974), TM relaxes some people and makes them feel better, *Psychology Today* 7(11):39cf.

34. *See* Benson, Your innate asset for combating stress, for details.

35. Ivancevich and Matteson, *Stress at work*.

36. For details *see* French, W. L. and Bell, C. H. Jr. (1978), *Organization development* 2nd ed., New York: Prentice-Hall, pp. 124–127; and Ivancevich and Matteson, *Stress at work*, pp. 210–211.

37. Ivancevich and Matteson, *Stress at work*, p. 208.

38. Jackson, S. E. (1983), Participation in decision making as a strategy for reducing job-related strain, *Journal of Applied Psychology* 68:3–19.

39. Ivancevich and Matteson, *Stress at work*, p. 210.

40. (1979) Executive stress may not be all bad, *Business Week* April 20:p. 96.

Power and Politics in Organizations

- How appropriate is it for managers to use power or political tactics?

- How can you use expert power to further your career?

- Did you know that the boss' secretary often has more power than many managers?

- Why are organizational IOU's so important for getting things done?

- What kinds of power tactics are used in large corporations?

- Did you know that putting your arm around someone's shoulder may be a sign of superior power?

- How do you know when people are playing organizational politics?

- Is organizational politics always unethical?

PREVIEW CASE: THE POWERLESS ONES

Karen Jennings, Frank Eason, and Stan Sullivan are unhappy executives.[1] All three began new jobs recently, but things aren't working out to expectations, and each is afraid of being fired.

The problem isn't that Karen, Frank, and Stan are incapable of doing their jobs. The big complaint of all three is identical: each feels powerless to do the work he or she was hired to do, and all three feel frustrated at not being able to accomplish the objectives of their basic assignments.

Karen is the first woman to attain a vice-presidency in her company, an architectural firm. Discriminated against, underpaid, and underutilized for years, she was finally promoted to a responsible position six months ago, thanks to affirmative-action legislation. Success in the job is important not only to Karen but also to other women in her highly competitive and male-dominated field. But so far she has been blocked by her male colleagues in every attempt at creativity. Her efforts to be "nice" lead only to being shunted aside again; when she tries being firm and outspoken, she becomes the target of more hostility and derision. She feels helpless and angry, and her work is deteriorating.

Frank was hired to install a new accounting and computer procedure to control the worldwide shipping activities of an international company. The company has needed up-to-date control procedures for some time, and the firm's president hired Frank virtually on the spot after hearing him speak at a computer-systems convention. Unfortunately, the president's enthusiasm for Frank is not shared by other company officers who perceive him as uninformed about the shipping industry, an invader of their territories, and thus a threat to their jobs. They do nothing to help Frank and, in fact, do everything possible to impede him. When Frank reported these problems to the president, he was told that one mark of a successful executive is the ability to handle people.

Stan, who was instrumental in developing a new product line for his company, has been assigned to direct test-marketing of the product in one section of the country. The budget for the project was added to the budget of the division manager, but the manager wants nothing to do with the endeavor, much less with someone assigned by the home office. As a result, Stan receives no cooperation on the new product work and has felt extreme pressure to do other assignments. In addition to battling frustration at not being able to proceed with his assignment. Stan worries because the hostile manager will evaluate him and report on his performance to headquarters.

From W. Reichman and M. Levy, Personal power enhancement: A way to executive success, *Management Review* 66(3):28–29. Copyright© 1977 by American Management Association.

Karen, Frank, and Stan are all having trouble getting their jobs done—they feel powerless in light of the obstacles they face. This chapter is about power and politics. Everyone who manages needs to understand how power and politics work and, to be effective, managers must be able to use the strategies and tactics of power.

Understanding Organizational Behavior

In this chapter we will define the concepts of power and politics, examine the sources of power, and discuss the tactics and strategies of power and politics. We will also look at some ethical issues since these concepts make many people uncomfortable. Many managers might say: "Who me? Use power or political tactics? Not on your life. I'm not that kind of person!" What kind of person are you? Would you use power and politics to get your job done?

Power, Authority, and Influence: Getting Things Done

Before we can learn how to use power to get things done, we need to understand the meanings and interrelationship of power, authority, and influence.

■ What Is Power?

While there a number of ways one might define **power**, we will use it to mean the ability to bring about outcomes that are desired by using influence.[2] Often, this involves getting people to do something they might not otherwise do. It also means the ability to resist others who are trying to get you to do something you do not want to do. You don't have power in a vacuum, but only in relation to other people or groups. For example, you may have power over your secretary, but the controller may have power over you. In addition, your power over another is seldom absolute. The secretary also has power over you; especially if you need something done in a hurry.

■ Power and Influence

Another term that is used in conjunction with power is influence. These two terms are so closely related that they are often used interchangeably. We will use **influence** to mean the process of producing intended effects in individuals, groups, and organizations.[3] Power differs from influence in that power is the capacity or potential for influence.[4] Your capacity to influence your secretary is great because you have power. However, when you·try to get your secretary to work overtime on Saturday you will use influence tactics to obtain the desired behavior.

■ Power and Authority

Authority is the right to order or ask others to do what you want them to do. It is usually associated with some legal or institutional sanction; it is legitimized power. One might think of authority as downward influence.[5] Some of the power you have over your secretary is based on authority. You may have the right to assign tasks, set goals, or rate performance. On the other hand, you may not have the authority to order Saturday work. If you want your secretary to work on Saturday, you may need to use a different source of power. It is possible to have authority without power. In the opening case for this chapter, Karen, Frank, and Stan have authority, but not enough power to get their job done—an extremely frustrating and stressful situation.

Sources of Power

There are a large number of bases or sources of power.[6] Anything that enhances your ability to get others to do what you want them to do is a source of power and influence. The following section covers several important sources.

■ Dependence: The Underlying Basis for Power

When you control what others want, they are dependent upon you and you have power over them. It happens the other way around too. When you are dependent on others, such as people from another department, then they have power over you. Dependence is a normal and natural part of the manager's job. Two factors make this dependence inherent: limited resources and the division of labor.[7] There are never enough scarce resources (funds, people, materials, space, time) to go around. In addition, tasks are divided into specialized subtasks. Bob Goldberg, controller at Ace Freight Company, has accountants, financial analysts, payroll, and benefits people all reporting to him. These people rely upon Bob for career advice and performance appraisals.

The more others are dependent upon you, the greater your power. The more you are dependent upon others, the less your power. In the opening case Karen, Frank, and Stan are dependent upon others in the organization with few people who are dependent upon them.

Another example of how dependence works in managerial situations is the story of John Correa who is Manager of Environmental Engineering Planning for a large corporation. Correa is dependent on his boss and some ten other top managers for information and rewards. Except for his boss, most of the other managers are not dependent on him. Correa is dependent on his subordinates and even his subordinate's subordinates since the work is technical and they would be difficult to replace. In addition, he is dependent on two other department managers in his division—he simply could not do his job without them. The situation is not mutual since they do not need Correa's department. The dependencies go on and on. There is a union of engineers that can shut down his department, and there is a sole outside

PERSPECTIVE

12.1 *Creating Resource Dependence—The 10 Percent Rule*[8]

When you have discretionary control over an organization's resources, you have power. "A relatively small amount of resources, if utilized in a strategically appropriate fashion," can create resource dependence. This is referred to as the **10 percent rule**, which states that "organizations can be taken over by dis- cretionary control over not more than (and frequently less than) 10 percent of the organization's total budget." This is possible because such a large portion of an organization's funds are nondiscretionary and fixed (salaries, interest, leases).

Understanding Organizational Behavior

supplier who does not really care about his department because the size of the orders are so small. Since Correa's department has so little natural power because of dependence on so many others, he has to carefully develop and nurture the power he does have.

■ Reward Power

One important form of dependence is control over rewards, a very scarce and important resource. Anytime you are in a position to reward people with money, recognition, promotion, status and similar outcomes, you have **reward power**.[9] When you offer someone extra pay to do some task, you are using this power. If you can offer the secretaries double-time pay for working Saturday, you may be able to influence their decision favorably in spite of your lack of authority. However, managers are often limited in their reward power. They may not have the authority to offer such financial rewards. Of course, rewards do not have to cost money, A smile, a good performance rating, or a few hours off may be even more effective rewards than money.

■ Coercive Power

When you are able to order someone to do something and back up the order with force or punishments, then **coercive power** exists. When someone has legitimate authority over another then coercive power is often, but not always, present. Coercion power can, of course exist without

PERSPECTIVE

12.2 Power Is Also a Great Motivator

David McClelland has spent several decades working on the power motive. One of his more recent studies concludes that power is the strongest motivator for managers.[10]

In examining the motive scores for over fifty managers of both high and low morale units in all sections of the same large company, we found that most of the managers—over 70 percent—were high in power motivation compared with men in general. This finding confirms the fact that power motivation is important for management. (Remember that as we use the term "power motivation," it refers not to dictatorial behavior, but to a desire to have impact, to be strong and influential.) The better managers, as judged by the morale of those working for them, tended to score even higher in power motivation.

But the most important determining factor of high morale turned out not to be how their power motivation compared to their need to achieve but whether it was higher than their need to be liked. This relationship existed for 80 percent of the better sales managers as compared with only 10 percent of the poorer managers. And the same held true for other managers in nearly all parts of the company.

[In summary,] the better managers we studied are high in power motivation, low in affiliation motivation, and high in [self-control]. They care about institutional power and use it to stimulate their employees to be more productive.

authority. An armed robber has coercive power when he points a gun at you and tells you to lie down. When your boss tells you to fly to Chicago to see a client (even though you had other plans and did not want to go), it is also coercion. The difference between the two types of coercion is that your boss has the legitimate right to order you to do things you might not wish to do (with the threat of losing your job), while the robber is using brute force.

■ Expert Power

When you build a reputation as an expert, people become dependent upon you for advice within your area of expertise; you have **expert power**. You tend to be able to control the information in some specialized area. This type of power is normally developed through achievement and performance. You have to establish a "track record" and a "professional reputation." An example of the use of expert power is Betty Roll, a statistical clerk in a large public-sector organization. While her job was only rated a GS-7 (relatively low ranking), she exerted more power than most GS-12's in the organization because she was an expert in data collection and retrieval. If you wanted an answer to any question, you knew you could turn to Betty and she would find it. Thus, many high-ranking managers became dependent upon Betty to answer their queries. Betty had power. She could pretty much call the shots on anything she wanted.

A variant of expert power is making yourself irreplaceable. In a French tobacco plant,[11] maintenance workers were quite successful in keeping all maintenance procedures and techniques secret. They were able to get rid of all manuals, blueprints, and directions. New people were trained by word of mouth during long apprenticeships. Neither production workers nor managers understood anything about maintaining the complex production equipment. Thus, the maintenance workers, through their monopoly of knowledge, had tremendous power to control the operation of the plant.

Using Power and Influence

While we have been discussing the sources of power, you have probably thought of a few ways to acquire and use power, such as making yourself an expert. In this section, we turn to a more specific discussion of power and influence strategies and tactics—how to use power effectively.

■ Assessing Power Relationships

Perhaps the first step in dealing with any power situation is to analyze what power you have and what powers the other people in the organization have. This may be as simple as just sitting back and thinking about the power situation or as complex as doing a detailed power analysis of your entire organization.[12] If Karen, Frank, and Stan, in our opening incident, had assessed their power, they would have found that they had more power than they thought. Karen has the power of equal opportunity under law in back of her, plus the increased emphasis on opportunity for women in organizations. Frank's power lies in his expertise in a complex, new area and his relationship with the president. Stan's task is directly related to the future of the company. Each needs to assess his or her own power and the power of the people with whom they work. Then, strategies can be devised to improve a low-power position.

■ Creating a Sense of Obligation

A good way to create IOU's is to do favors for people to create a sense of reciprocity. The theory here is that when you help others, they will come to your aid when you need them. This is especially powerful if you do the favor for someone who is in a position to help you later. An example of how this tactic might be used is the case of Barney:[13]

> Barney worked as dispatcher in a national moving and storage company. After spending most of his life in Minneapolis, Barney and his wife longed for the chance to live in a southern climate. One day a unique opportunity presented itself, and Barney had enough foresight to recognize its value. An executive in Barney's company wanted a friend's personal belongings shipped in a hurry. A telephone call to Barney (whom the executive knew only slightly) was all the executive needed to make the necessary arrangements for his friend. Thanking Barney for his quick action, the executive stated, "Let me know if I can ever help you out of a jam."
>
> Six months later Barney telephoned the executive with a request. "Mr. Higgins, do you remember me? I'm Barney Wetherbee, the dispatcher in charge of routing the moving vans. My wife and I have a little problem that requires your help. Her arteries are beginning to harden a little, making cold weather in Minneapolis unsufferable to her. We're wondering if I could be given favorable consideration for a transfer to our Miami or Tampa office. We both would be grateful to you for the rest of our lives if the transfer did come through."
>
> The executive replied, "I'll see what I can do." Within one year Barney, who had extended himself for the executive (slightly bending company regulations in the process), was transferred to a comparable level position in Tampa. His IOU had been reimbursed.

■ Identifying with Powerful People

While knowing the right (powerful) people is important, it is even more important to be known. One of the most effective ways to the executive suite is through a powerful sponsor or **mentor**.[14] Having a mentor who is powerful puts you in a powerful position. This person is often someone who was your boss at one time in your career, but now has rapidly advanced to a high-level position. Getting a mentor is sometimes a matter of luck, although shrewd, upward-bound junior managers will usually make an effort to link up with upwardly mobile senior managers. They accomplish this by joining task forces headed by the mentor or by getting themselves transferred into the mentor's department. Once they are connected with the mentor, they use a combination of high performance and favorable impression management (discussed in Chapter 4) to establish their reputations. Several of the power games related in the Perspective: Power Games in a Large Corporation involve this tactic.

Association with powerful people may increase your power. A classic example of power through association is the secretary to the Chief Executive Officer (CEO) in a large organization. The secretary may not have much formal authority, but there are numerous other ways to gain power because of the position. The secretary knows all the secrets; knows all the people; controls information flow to the CEO; and many other crucial tasks that result in the possession of high power.

■ Controlling Scarce Resources

When you control something that is valued by others, you have power. A controller who approves the budget and allocates funds has power. A pesonnel director who approves requests for manpower has power. Other scarce resources include control of information, control over supplies, and control over the interpretation of rules and regulations.

Controlling Information   Without timely and accurate information, it is impossible for a manager to perform effectively.[15] Thus, anyone who is in a position to control the flow of information is in a powerful position. This may be an expert, like Betty Roll mentioned earlier, or it may be someone who controls access to a top manager, such as an executive secretary.

PERSPECTIVE

| 12.3 | *Power Games in a Large Corporation*[16]

A study of men and women in a large corporation called INDSCO (not its real name) found the following power tactics were used:

■ *Extraordinary job performance.* Performance that is extraordinary, visible, and relevant—and is identified with a solution to a pressing organizational problem—resulted in increased power.

■ *Reorganization to increase power.* "Empire building," as it is sometimes termed, by creating new and seemingly more influential organizations is a way to increase power. A side benefit is that your own "chosen" people can come in to fill the new positions.

■ *Risk taking.* Few people dare to take extraordinary risks, but those who pulled them off became very powerful, for both social and organizational reasons. Organizationally, they have proved they can perform in most difficult circumstances. Socially,

they have developed a charisma in the eyes of those who are less willing to take risks.

■ *Power positions.* Jobs on the boundaries between organizational units or between the company and the outside world often have good visibility and become power positions because of it.

■ *Social connections and sponsors.* Long-term, stable social connections outside your own work group with powerful peers, superiors, and subordinates was a source of power. Sponsors, called "godfathers" at INDSCO, were in a position to fight for protégés, to stand up for them in meetings, and to promote them into promising positions. The sponsor helped distinguish the person from the crowd.

■ *Peer alliances.* Powerful people built a strong network of peer alliances. They had team spirit. They helped others.

Understanding Organizational Behavior

An unusual example of how control of information is used to gain power is the case of Shirley Olsen, who is the personnel director for a medium-sized industrial firm. Shirley suggested to the president that more information was needed about the effectiveness of human resource management. Shirley proposed a quarterly questionnaire of the employees. The president agreed, and before long the survey results became a very important part of the evaluation of manager effectiveness. While Shirley did not create or "doctor" the data, she was in a position to determine what questions would be asked and how the data would be collected and presented. Thus, she could make managers look good or bad by the way she designed the data collection and feedback system. Shirley became a very powerful person in the firm as a result of this information-gathering task.

Controlling Supplies   While a supply supervisor's job does not sound glamorous, there is often a great deal of power associated with it. If people are forced to order all their supplies through a central source, then the supply person is in a good position to control this resource by doing special rush orders, by releasing back orders to certain people first, and by assuring a higher-quality item is ordered than is normally authorized. These are only a few of the ways a supply person can garner power.

Interpreting Rules   While staff lawyers are an obvious example of this type of power, there are often other people in the organization whose task is to interpret rules and thus make powerful decisions. Corporate auditors make many decisions that affect managers and are thus quite powerful. Some organizations have a procedures department whose job it is to write, revise, and control procedures. These people have power because they can affect a manager's discretion about how to do the job.

■ Establishing Power Relationships

There are many opportunities for you to improve your odds of finding or developing a situation where you can become powerful. The most cru-

DOONESBURY   **by Garry Trudeau**

Figure 12.1. The power of information.

Power and Politics in Organizations   287

Table 12.1. Factors that contribute to power or powerlessness.

Organizational factors contribute to whether you have power or do not have power. The following list indicates factors that result in high or low power.

Factors	Generates power when factor is:	Generates powerlessness when factor is:
Rules inherent in the job	few	many
Predecessors in the job	few	many
Rewards for performance	many	few
Flexibility in using people	high	low
Approvals needed for decisions	few	many
Physical location	central	distant
Publicity about job activities	high	low
Interpersonal contact on job	high	low
Contact with senior officials	high	low
Participation in conferences	high	low

cial factor is to seek jobs that are associated with a powerful people, tasks, or departments (*see* Table 12.1 for ideas about the kinds of content such a job should have). If you want to be a senior executive of General Motors, you do not want to start in personnel or marketing because that is not where the power lies. Seven of the last eight chairmen of GM have finance backgrounds;[17] two also had engineering, and one had operations. An obvious choice in that organization is finance. Other organizations will differ. You have to analyze every organization and every job and promotion opportunity to see what effect the situation would have on your power.

■ Making Power Work

Even when you have power and have decided on a good approach for applying the power, your power moves may not work. Three additional factors need to be considered: the zone of acceptance, the power balancing, and possible undesirable side effects.

Zone of Acceptance

People do not always accept your decision even if it is based on formal authority.[18] For every possible use of power there is a **zone of acceptance** where the power move will be successful. Power users must assess this zone before they take action. Even a direct order may fall outside the zone of acceptance. For example, a manager may use legitimate power to order a speed up in an assembly line only to have the union call a "wildcat" (unauthorized) strike resulting in trouble with the president and costing the firm dearly. There are also more subtle ways to avoid an order like working strictly to the rules, which causes a slow down rather than a speed up.

Power Balancing

Every use of power tends to be offset by a counter use of power. Power is normally in a balanced state of equilibrium. When someone uses power, this state becomes unbalanced and the natural tendency is to seek balance again. Skill in exercising power is important here. A blatant use of power, such as an appeal to the president to reorganize

Understanding Organizational Behavior

in such a way as to give you more power, is likely to be offset by a counter-power move, such as an appeal using personal contacts and influence to discredit the proposed reorganization.

Reactions to Power   People may react to some types of power, such as coercion and control, much as they would to punishment. They will comply because they have to, but they will try to get even later through sab-

PERSPECTIVE

12.4 *Nonverbal Signals of Power*[19]

- **Shoulder hold.** A corporation president can put his or her arm around the shoulder of a lower-ranking employee, but the reverse is unthinkable. [The] one-way shoulder hold is also found between teachers and students, coaches and athletes, and parents and children.
- **Interruption license.** One excellent sign of power is the "interruption license." In almost any conversation, interruptions usually involve a more powerful person interrupting a less powerful person. This part of the power script [may be] largely unconscious, but it appears to be extremely consistent. In an organization, the interruption license seems to follow the organizational hierarchy. Presidents do not hesitate to interrupt vice-presidents, vice-presidents interrupt assistant vice-presidents, and so on down the hierarchy.
- **Spatial signs.** There are also spatial signs of power. People tend to stand farther from people who are high in rank or status. For example, on the night John F. Kennedy was elected President, his friends and advisers were watching the election returns, and they suddenly realized that their friend had just become the President of the United States. At that moment, according to one adviser, their spatial interaction with Kennedy changed dramatically—the advisers moved back a "respectful" distance and formed a

sort of circle around Kennedy. This formal distance was in response to the tremendous power Kennedy had just acquired. Another spatial aspect of the power script involves seating position. At a rectangular table, the most powerful person is almost always seated at one end of the table, while less powerful people are seated along the sides of the table.

- **Visual attention.** Powerful people may listen to other people without looking at them. By contrast, less powerful people usually pay close "visual attention" when listening to a powerful person. Visual attention seems to be a gesture of respect in our culture, and powerful people may feel free to make this gesture or not.
- **Eyebrows.** Elevated eyebrows indicate deference, while lowered eyebrows reflect power. . . . A face with the raised eyebrows looks meek or submissive in comparison to the more aggressive, determined, or "powerful" expression conveyed by the lowered eyebrows.

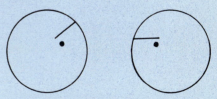

Adapted from *How to Expand Your S.I.Q. (Social Intelligence Quotient)* by Dane Archer. Copyright © 1980 by Dane Archer. Reprinted by permission of the publisher, M. Evans and Co, New York, New York, 10017.

Power and Politics in Organizations

otage or finding a way of getting even. They may also get angry and leave the organization. Coercive power must be used cautiously.

■ Power of Lower-Level Participants

Most of the study of power concerns uses by managers, but lower-level organizational participants (rank and file workers, lower-level clerks and foremen, technicians) are also powerful.[20]

A summary of the methods of upward-oriented power tactics that are used by lower-level participants is provided in Table 12.2. While several of these tactics have already been discussed, some new ones appear, including the most often used one—logically presenting ideas. The second highest ranking, using persistence and repetition or "wearing the boss down," is surprising. Another unexpected result is the power of going over the boss' head. One would think that would be a dangerous strategy indeed.

Political Strategies and Tactics

Have you heard people talk about "playing politics" in some organization? Most people have because it is certainly a widespread and important influence strategy in most organizations. But few people understand what organizational politics is and how it works. This section may help provide some illumination by defining organizational politics and reviewing some of the strategies and tactics of politics. We will also discuss the ethics of organizational politics.

■ What Is Organizational Politics?

Politics is also a concept that is illusive to define.[21] As far as we are concerned **organizational politics** involves seeking selfish ends to enhance or protect the self-interest of individuals or groups.[22] The key words here are *selfish ends* and *self-interest*. For example, power does not have to be directed toward self-interest, although often self-interest motivates one to use power. An example of a nonpolitical use of power is a supervisor who uses power to get competent subordinates promoted even though the promotion will mean a transfer and will be against his or her self-interest. On the other hand, this very same act might be political if the supervisor merely

Table 12.2. The most-often used methods of upward influence from the subordinate's perspective.

Method	Total events	Success ratio*
Logically presenting ideas	143	52%
Using repetition, persistence	51	41
Trading job-related benefits	39	59
Using organizational rules	33	48
Going over supervisor's head	29	62
Using group or peer support	18	67
Threatening to resign	18	17

*The success ratio is the successful events divided by total events (successful plus unsuccessful).

Adapted from W.K. Schilit and E.A. Locke, 1982, A study of upward influence in organizations, *Administrative Science Quarterly* 27:310. Copyright © 1982 by Administrative Science Quarterly, Ithaca, New York. Used with permission.

Table 12.3. How political are business functions?

Test your prediction of how much politics exists in various business functions with the results of a research study reported at the end of this chapter.[23] Rank order the amount of organizational politics that you estimate exists in each area beginning with 1 as the most political and 9 as the least political.

Functional area	Rank for level of politics
Sales	_____
Personnel	_____
Marketing staff	_____
Purchasing	_____
Production	_____
Research and development	_____
Accounting and finance	_____
Board of directors	_____
Manufacturing staff	_____

wanted a "crony " in a position to collect advance information about funding in order to have an advantage over other managers. However, it is not always easy to determine if people are pursuing selfish ends.

To test your knowledge of the amount of organizational politics involved in various business functions, you may wish to take the quiz shown in Table 12.3. Then, check your answers with the research results reported at the end of the chapter. Are you surprised by the results? Why do you think the top-ranked functions are so political?

There is a great deal more politics involved in some organizational processes than in others. Table 12.4 shows that managers perceive much more politics in promotion decisions than in hiring decisions.

■ Political Tactics

To understand organizational politics, we must also understand political tactics. In this section we will cover five tactics: blaming or attacking others, use of information, creating a favorable image, and forming coalitions and coopting opponents.[24]

Table 12.4. Politics in organizational processes.[25]

Process	Percent coded always or frequently
Interdepartmental coordination	68
Promotions and transfers	60
Delegation of authority	59
Facilities, equipment allocation	49
Performance appraisals	42
Budget allocation	38
Pay	33
Grievances and complaints	32
Hiring	23
Disciplinary penalties	21

Blaming or Attacking Others

People who use this tactic try to avoid association with something that has gone wrong. They do not want to be associated with failure. "Scapegoating" is trying to find someone else to blame for a negative outcome; trying to find a scapegoat so you can "get off the hook." Another version of this tactic is to make your rivals look bad by asserting or implying that they made a mistake, have poor judgement, are only lucky or are behaving in a self-serving way.

Use of Information

Information can be withheld, distorted, or used to inundate your opponent with the "facts," or to make a situation so complex that only you can interpret it. You may also use the "your opinion versus my facts" approach,[26] especially when you are in control of the information sources. Say you are faced with a disagreement during a staff meeting that would make you look bad. When your rival provides information contrary to your position, you simply state: "Thank you for your opinion. Now I have the facts here that show a different position." Your opponent is in no position to question your facts and loses that round.

Another, more subtle, use of information is selective use of objective criteria. When you use criteria that are favorable to your position and omit unfavorable criteria, a decision is more likely to be made in your favor. An example of this tactic is a district sales manager who has made sure that the primary criteria for division of this year's budget is the geographical dispersion of customers. This was done because the sales manager knows it will result in a larger travel budget than is actually needed; thus, there will be enough "slack" for some really good trips.

Creating and Maintaining a Favorable Image

Is impression management (discussed in Chapter 4) a political tactic? Yes, when it is directed toward self-interest. People who manage their image to create the impression of success, prestige, or belonging to a certain group may be engaging in political behavior. For example, people who carefully cultivate and develop their reputations and images so that they will be candidates for promotion may be exhibiting political behavior.

Taking credit for another's accomplishments is a form of image-making that is particularly harmful. Most of us have encountered the person or even a boss who says, "I really worked hard to accomplish this task and I'm proud of what I've done," when, in fact, the task was done by someone else in part or completely. For example, Kim Chuong, a production worker in the Advanced Products Plant, developed a process that makes circuit boards much more reliable and will result in saving the company lots of money. But Kim's boss takes credit for the idea and has been promoted because of the favorable attention generated by the improved process. How do you think this political act would affect Kim's motivation? It seems quite likely to decline.

Coalitions

A **coalition** is an alliance or union between two or more people or groups.[27] Because organizations are interdependent—tasks are divided and specialized—coalitions form to further cooperation and get things done. They also form to defeat opponents by outvoting them or to protect the self-interest of the people in the coalition. For example, engi-

Understanding Organizational Behavior

neers and maintanance technicians might form a coalition to lobby against the purchase of new equipment that is desired by production because the new equipment takes less maintenance and engineering work creating a threat to their jobs. The corporate coup d'état, related in the Perspective: Corporate Coup d'État, shows a powerful use of coalitions.

Building External Constituencies   Coalitions are not limited to within the organization. Allies can be recruited from outside sources: government, other organizations, consultants, customers, or clients. A good example of this is accounting groups in business schools. They often get more resources and higher faculty salaries due at least in part to their strong connections with the professional accounting community. Many accounting departments have become so powerful that they have split from the business school and formed their own school of accounting.

PERSPECTIVE

12.5 Corporate Coup d'État

An unsuspecting Marion Harper, Jr., presided over what was to be his last board of directors meeting in a nineteen-year career as chairman and chief executive officer of the Interpublic Group, the world's largest advertising business. Harper was interrupted by one of his six hand-picked directors before he could even bring the first item on his prepared agenda before the board. It was moved that the first order of business be the replacement of the chief executive officer. The motion was immediately seconded, and carried with six "ayes" and one abstention.

An organizational coup can be defined as the infiltration of a small but critical segment of the organization's structure (board of directors) to displace the CEO from control of the organization by an unexpected succession. The plotters are usually some combination of inside and outside directors, often including members of the CEO's palace guard. The term "infiltration" is used to underline the fact that the group's action must be secret if it is to succeed. And, although goals involving change of policy may be significant, the primary goal is succession: a new man at the top.

The corporate coup contrasts in a number of ways with more routine successions to power—replacements resulting from mandatory retirement policies or sudden successions following the serious illness or death of the CEO. When the succession is expected, the process of choosing a new CEO is conducted with considerable awareness on the part of other employees and relevant stockholders and directors. When the CEO dies, the succession is unexpected, but once the initial shock of death wears off, replacement activities follow regular institutionalized procedures.

Corporate coups, on the other hand, are unexpected, and deviate sharply from routinized replacement procedures. They are engineered in secrecy, without the knowledge of the public or most other employees and, most important, without the knowledge of the CEO who is the coup's target. "Going public" before the coup is a *fait accompli* is almost invariably fatal (to the dissidents) since it allows the CEO time to muster his own considerable resources to put down the coup attempt.

Excerpted from "Corporate Coup d'État," by Mayer N. Zald and Michael Berger, *The Wharton Magazine*, Summer 1978. Copyright © 1978 by the Trustees of the University of Pennsylvania. Reprinted by permission.

Cooptation   Another form of building support and creating alliances is **cooptation**. This is done by making people whose support is desired, members of the group with the expectation that they will adopt the group's norms and values and support the group's goals. The most common form of cooptation in organizations is the board of directors. People are selected because they can support the firm in some way. For example, bankers are popular boardmembers. They can provide financial advice and perhaps financial support.

However, cooptation is not reserved only for the boardroom. Whenever you have a task to do that requires broad organizational support, a typical way to do it is to form a task force or committee. The membership of the task force is designed to include those people who are needed to get the idea approved, even though they may be opposed to the idea. The theory here is that when people become part of a problem-solving group, they will be much more easily persuaded to go along with the goals of the group.

The Ethics of Power and Politics

Earlier in the chapter you were asked whether you would be willing to engage in the power of political tactics? What is your answer now? Can you avoid it even if you want to? When then, is it ethical? In this section, we will take a brief look at some of the ethical issues and their managerial implications.

■ Tests for Ethical Behavior

To provide some guidelines for testing ethical political and power tactics, we will pose four tests or questions.[28] For behavior to be ethical, it must meet *all four* tests.

Does the Behavior Support Organizational and Societal Goals?
Behaviors that are self-serving and result in ends that are unfavorable or dysfunctional for the organization are unethical. A person who tries to discredit the boss so that he or she can get the boss' job is behaving in an unethical manner. An act may also be unethical if its aims are in conflict with societal goals (such as blaming another firm for dumping chemicals into a stream when it is really your firm that is dumping them).

Does the Behavior Result in Optimizing the Results?   If the outcome of a political behavior results in the greatest good for the greatest number of people, then it is ethical. For example, if you have figured out a way to distort information to force your opponent to withdraw from a contract that is unfavorable to your firm and its stockholders, then the behavior might meet this test for ethics. But remember that this is not simply a restatement of "the end justifies the means," for this is only one of four tests

the behavior must meet. Certainly, the behavior must support organizational and societal goals as well as resulting in the greatest good. Thus, to violate a contract because it will be more beneficial to the stockholders may be unethical because of societal goals supporting respect for law and order.

Does the Behavior Violate the Rights of the Parties?

There are a number of basic human rights, including the right to privacy, freedom of conscience (you do not have to do something you consider immoral), due process (fair and impartial hearings), free consent (right to be treated only as you knowingly consent to be), and freedom of speech.[29] The notion here is that if any of these basic rights are violated, then the behavior is unethical. An example of unethical behavior is the case of "Lee, 61, who has been Director of Engineering for American Semiconductor for fourteen years. He is very bright and a fine supervisor but has not kept abreast of new developments in technology."[30]

> American Semiconductor's manufacturing process creates substantial quantities of toxic materials. Lee's rather casual attitude toward the disposal of these chemicals has resulted in a number of environmental citations. The firm is now tied up in court on two cases and will probably be forced to pay a considerable amount in damages. Yet, Lee still does not perceive the disposal problem as urgent. For three years, Charlie, the executive vice-president, has tried to persuade Lee to make this a priority issue but has failed. Charlie has reluctantly concluded that Lee must be taken out of his positon as Director of Engineering.
>
> Charlie recognizes that it would demoralize the other managers if he were to fire Lee outright. So, Charlie decides that he will begin to tell selected individuals that he is dissatisfied with Lee's work. When there is open support for Lee, Charlie quietly sides with Lee's opposition. He casually lets Lee's peers know that he thinks Lee may have outlived his usefulness to the firm. He even exaggerates Lee's deficiencies and failures when speaking to Lee's coworkers. Discouraged by the waning support from his colleagues, Lee decides to take an early retirement.

In this case Lee's rights were violated. Charlie's attempt to discredit him behind his back violated his right of consent—his right to be treated honestly and forthrightly.

Does the Behavior Violate the Rules of Justice?

The rules of justice say that people must not be treated arbitrarily but that differences in treatment should be fairly distributed. Individuals who are similar should be treated similarly and those who are different should also be treated accordingly. For example, a job evaluation system that assigns points for various job skills and responsibilities, and is then tied to pay, differentiates accurately and fairly between individuals and is thus fair and ethical. If the system were based more on knowing the right people, then it would be unethical. Another aspect of the rules of justice is that the rules should be clearly stated, well published, and consistently enforced. When Al gets a

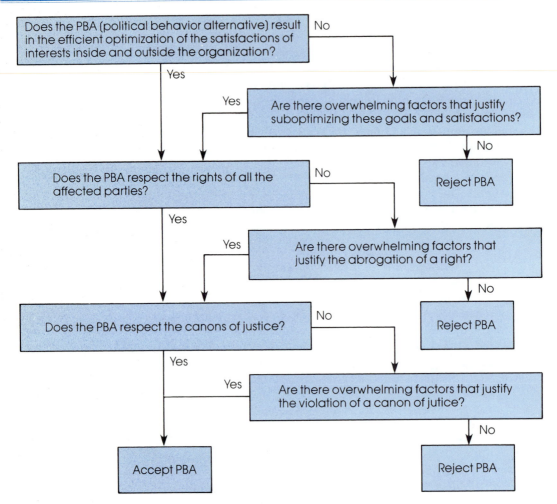

Figure 12.2. Decision-tree approach to resolving ethics decisions.

verbal warning for violating the same rule that Bob was suspended for, then the justice is not consistent and impartial.

■ Power, Politics, and Management

There are no simple answers to the ethics of power and politics. The decision-tree method provided in Figure 12.2 can only be a rough guide. Each manager must personally struggle with ethical questions. In spite of the ethical problems, power and politics are an ever-present part of organizational life. They represent the leverage that allows managers to get their job done. Without power it would be difficult, if not impossible, to lead, motivate, or control organizational behavior.

Understanding Organizational Behavior

Chapter Review

■ When you have **power** you can often bring about the outcomes you wish through **influence** processes or **authority**.

■ Scarcity of resources make dependence a natural part of a manager's job. This **dependence** is a foundation for power.

■ Sources of power include control over rewards, expert knowledge, authority, and coercion.

■ Power is normally thought of as social because it involves two or more people. However, motivation toward personal power is also an important topic for managers since most effective managers are high in power motivation.

■ **Power tactics** include creating a sense of obligation, identifying with powerful people, and controlling scarce resources.

■ Even when you have power, it does not always work. You must be aware of the **zone of acceptance, power balance**, and possible undesirable side effects.

■ Lower-level organizational participants also have power. They tend to use somewhat different tactics like logical presentation of ideas, wearing the boss down, and going over the boss' head.

■ There are a number of **nonverbal signals of power** including body use of the shoulders, interruption license, visual attention, eyebrows, and various spatial arrangements.

■ Organizational **political tactics** include use of information, creating and maintaining a favorable image, developing coalitions, and cooptation.

■ Power and political behavior can be **ethical** if it meets a number of criteria relating to the outcomes, the rights of the players, and whether the application is just.

For Discussion

1. How does power differ from influence? From politics?
2. Give an example of how you might create power through dependence. Would your example be ethical?
3. When the tactic of "identifying with powerful people" is used, what sources of power (reward, coercive, expert) are involved?
4. How do the power games described in the Perspective: Power Games in a Large Corporation relate to power tactics?
5. Explain why the use of coercive power may cause problems for the manager.
6. Table 12.2 gives a number of methods used for upward influence by subordinates. Which of these methods do you recommend using or avoiding? Why?
7. Analyze the reasons for the degree of political activity in various business functions indicated by the answers to the quiz in Table 12.3.
8. Using the four tests for ethical behavior, make an ethical determination for each of the political tactics (for example, blaming or attacking others, use of information).

Power and Politics in Organizations

9. How does the use of power apply to other topics in organizational behavior, such as motivation, decision making, and leadership?

Key Concepts and Terms

power	zone of acceptance
influence	power balancing
authority	nonverbal signals of power
dependence	organizational politics
reward power	political tactics
coercive power	coalitions
expert power	cooptation
tactics for using power	ethics of organizational politics

Suggested Readings

Bacharach, S. B., and Lawler, E. E. (1980). *Power and politics in organizations*. San Francisco: Jossey-Bass.

Farrell, D., and Petersen, J. C. (1982). Patterns of political behavior in organizations. *Academy of Management Review*, 7:403–12.

Kanter, R. M. (1979). Power failure in management circuits. *Harvard Business Review*, July–Aug.

Pfeffer, J. (1981). *Power in organizations*. Boston: Pitman.

Reichman, W., and Levy, M. (1977). Personal power enhancement: A way to executive success. *Management Review* 66(3):28–34.

CASES AND INCIDENTS

Blue Collars in the Board Room

When Douglas Fraser, president of the United Auto Workers Union, was appointed to the board of Chrysler Corporation, there was little enthusiasm among auto industry executives. It was the first time a major union had joined the board of a major U.S. company. *Time* quoted the General Motors Chairman as saying, "It makes as much sense as having a member of GM's management sitting on the board of an international union."[31]

Union leaders and members were also unenthusiastic. Some felt suspicious that their president was getting too close to management and might "sell them out." The AFL-CIO President was also cool to the move. He stated that union members are best represented when there is a clear adversarial relationship in the bargaining process.

A *Time* article concluded that:[32]

Fraser is likely to find himself torn between his responsibility to the company and his loyalties to his union members. A board decision to close a plant, for example, might be necessary to ensure Chrysler's survival but could be denounced by union workers faced with losing their jobs. Confidential information will have to be closely guarded. And many skeptics worry about any tampering with the traditional arm's-length relationship between management and labor.

Discussion questions

1. What do you think motivated Fraser's interest in a board positon?
2. Will the position enhance or degrade his power? How?
3. Is the move good politically?

Research and Development at General Rubber

Sam and Bob are highly motivated research scientists who work in the new-product development lab at General Rubber. Sam is by far the most technically competent scientist in the lab, and he has been responsible for several patents that have netted the company nearly six million dollars in the past decade. He is quiet, serious, and socially reserved. In contrast, Bob is outgoing and demonstrative. While Bob lacks the technical track record Sam has, his work has been solid though unimaginative. Rumor has it that Bob will be moved into an administrative position in the lab in the next few years.

According to lab policy, a $300,000 fund is available every year for the best new-product development idea proposed by a lab scientist in the form of a competitive bid. Accordingly, Sam and Bob both prepare proposals. Each proposal is carefully constructed to detail the benefits to the company and to society if the proposal is accepted, and it is the consensus of other scientists from blind reviews that both proposals are equally meritorious. Both proposals require the entire $300,000 to realize any significant results. Moreover, the proposed line of research in each requires significant mastery of the technical issues involved and minimal need to supervise the work of others.

After submitting his proposal, Sam takes no further action aside from periodically inquiring about the outcome of the bidding process. In contrast, Bob begins to wage what might be termed an open campaign in support of his proposal. After freely admitting his intentions to Sam and others, Bob seizes every opportunity he can to point out the relative advantages of his proposal to individuals who might have some influence over the decision. So effective is this open campaign that considerable informal pressure is placed on those authorized to make the decision on behalf of Bob's proposal. Bob's proposal is funded and Sam's is not.

From G.F. Cavanagh, D.J. Moberg, and M. Velasques (1981). The ethics of organizational politics. *Academy of Management Review* 6:369. Copyright © 1981 by Academy of Management. Used with permission of publisher and authors.

Discussion questions
1. What political tactics are used?
2. In your opinion, are the tactics ethical? Why or why not?
3. Use the decision tree (Fig. 12.2) to sort out an ethics decision. Was the decision different from your personal one? How?

REFERENCES

1. Reichman, W. and Levy, M. (1977), Personal power enhancement: A way to executive success, *Management Review* 66(3):pp. 28, 29.
2. *See* Pfeffer, J. (1981), *Power in organizations*, Boston: Pitman, for a more complete discussion of these issues. *Also see* Grimes, A. J. (1978), Authority, power, influence, and social control: A theoretical synthesis, *Academy of Management Review* 3:723–735.
3. This definition follows that used by Allen, R. W. and Porter, L. W. (1983), *Organizational influence processes,* Glenview, IL: Scott, Foresman, (1980), p. 3; *also see* Kipnis, D.; Schmidt, S. M.; and Wilkinson, I. (1980), Intraorganizational influence tactics: Explorations in getting one's way, *Journal of Applied Psychology* 65:440–442; and Schilit, W.K. and Locke, E.A. (1982), A study of upward influence in organizations, *Administrative Science Quarterly*, 27:304–316.
4. Allen and Porter, *Organizational influence processes*, p.3.
5. Allen and Porter, *Organizational influence processes*, pp. 124–25.

6. This discussion is heavily influenced by the classic works of French, J.R.P., Jr. and Raven, B. (1959), The bases of social power, *Studies in social power,* ed. D. Cartwright, pp. 150–167, Ann Arbor: University of Michigan ISR; and the later refinements and concepts of Pfeffer, *Power in organizations.*

7. *See* Kotter, J.P. (1977), Power, dependence, and effective management, *Harvard Business Review* 55(4): 125–36. Pfeffer, *Power in organizations* also has a good discussion of dependence.

8. Pfeffer, *Power in organizations* p. 106. The bases of social power.

9. French and Raven, The bases of social power. The importance of rewarding behavior is reviewed in Kerr, S. (1975), on the folly of rewarding A, while hoping for B, *Academy of Management Journal* 18:769–782.

10. McClelland, D.C. and Burnham, D.H. (1976), Power is the great motivator, *Harvard Business Review* Mar.–Apr.: 102–03.

11. Crozier, M. (1964), *The bureaucratic phenomenon,* Chicago: University of Chicago Press.

12. Pfeffer, *Power in organizations*, has a complete discussion on assessing power.

13. From *Survival in the office* by Anthony J. DuBrin. Copyright © 1977 by Mason/Charter Publishers. Reprinted by permission of Van Nostrand Reinhold Company.

14. *See* Jennings, E.E. (1971), *Routes to the executive suite,* New York: McGraw–Hill for a thorough discussion of mentors. *Also see* Schein, E.H. (1978), *Career dynamics: Matching individual and organizational needs*, Reading, Mass.: Addison–Wesley.

15. Zand, D.E. (1981), *Information, organization, and power*, New York: McGraw-Hill.

16. Adapted from Kanter, R.M. (1977), Power games in the corporation, *Psychology Today* July: 48 cf.

17. Pfeffer, *Power in organizations*, p. 97.

18 Chester I. Barnard talked about the zone of acceptance way back in 1938 in *The functions of the executive*, Cambridge, Mass.: Harvard University Press.

19. *Also see* Fast, J. (1980), *Body politics: How to get power with class,* Norwalk, Conn.: Tower Books.

20. *See* Schilit W.K. and Locke, E.A. (1982), A study of upward influence in organizations, *Administrative Science Quarterly* 27:304–316; and Mowday, R.T. (1978), The exercise of upward influence in organizations, *Administrative Science Quarterly* 23:137–156. *Also*, Porter, L.W.: Allen, R.W.: and Angle, H.L. (1981), The politics of upward influence in organizations, *Research in organizational behavior*, vol. 3, eds. B. Staw and L.L. Cummings, Greenwich, Conn.: JAI Press.

21. For a full discussion of the definitional issues *see* Mayes, B.T. and Allen, R.W. (1977), Toward a definition of organizational politics, *Academy of Management Review* 2:672–677; and Pfeffer, *Power in organizations*.

22. This definition is similar to the one suggested by Gandz, J. and Murray, V.V. (1980), The experience of workplace politics, *Academy of Management Journal* 23:237–251. Their definition is that "organizational politics is a subjective state in which organizational members perceive themselves or others as intentionally seeking selfish ends in an organizational context when such ends are opposed to those of others."

23. For answers to the rank ordering table *see* the results at the end of the references. Adapted from Madison, D.L.; Allen, R.W.; Porter, L.W.; Lenwick, P.A.; and Mayes, B.T.; (1980), Organizational politics: An exploration of manager's perceptions, *Human Relations* 33:p. 88.

24. This section based in part on Allen, R.W. Madison, D.L.; Porter, L.W.; Renwick, P.A.; and Mayes, B.T.: (1979), Organizational politics: Tasks and characteristics of its actors, *California Management Review* 22(1): 77–83; and Pfeffer, *Power in organizations*, Chapter 5. For additional tactics, *see* Kipnis, D.; Schmidt, S.M.; and Wilkinson, I. (1980), Intraorganizational influence tactics: Explorations in getting one's way, *Journal of Applied Psychology* 65:440–52.

25. Adapted from Gandz and Murray, The experience of workplace politics p.242.

26. Korda, M. (1975), *Power! How to get it, how to use it,* New York: Ballantine, p. 151.

27. *See* Pfeffer, *Power in organizations,* for a complete discussion of these issues.

28. This section is based primarily on Cavanagh, G.F.; Moberg, D.J.; and Velasques, M. (1981), The ethics of organizations politics. *Academy of Management Review* 6:363–374.

29. Cavanagh, et al., The ethics of organizational politics, p. 366.

30. Cavanagh, et al., The ethics of organizational politics, p. 369–370.

31. *Time* 19 May, 1980, p. 78

32. *Time* 19 May, 1980, p. 78.

Answers to the level of politics in business functional areas posed in Table 12.3.[28]

Function	Rank
Sales	3
Personnel	5
Marketing staff	1
Purchasing	6
Production	9
Research and development	7
Accounting and finance	8
Board of directors	2
Manufacturing staff	4

Making Decisions

PREVIEW

- Why do people and organizations make less than optimal decisions to solve their problems?

- Why must many managerial decisions be made intuitively?

- Does left-brain or right-brain dominance affect decision making?

- Why use groups for decision making when one exceptional person often makes more accurate decisions than a group?

- When should you use or avoid participative decision making?

- Why do people seem to stick by a decision even when it is obviously a poor one?

- How do you actually use decision-making techniques such as consensus, brainstorming, nominal groups, and delphi?

Preview Case: Metro Publishing's New Plant

The Decision Process: How Decisions Get Made
- Decision making and problem solving
- Identifying problems or goals
- *Perspective*: Defining Problems Using the Kepner-Tregoe Approach
- Searching for alternatives
- *Perspective*: Left-Brain, Right-Brain and Decision Making
- Evaluating alternatives
- *Perspective*: Knee-Deep in Big Muddy: Escalating Commitment to a Course of Action
- Choosing alternatives

Using Groups for Decision Making
- Why use groups for decision making?
- Disadvantages of groups for decision making
- *Perspective*: Groupthink
- Group decision effectiveness

Participation and Delegation in Decision Making
- Participation in decision making
- Delegating decisions
- When to use participation and delegation

Group Decision-Making Techniques
- Group consensus
- *Perspective*: Brainstorming
- Nominal Group Technique
- The Delphi Technique
- Which technique to use?

Summary
- Chapter review
- For discussion
- Key concepts and terms
- Suggested readings

Cases and Incidents
- Participation at Moonlight Cosmetics
- The Engineering Change

References

PREVIEW CASE: METRO PUBLISHING'S NEW PLANT

March 16, 1983: Leigh McManus, CEO of Metro publishing located in Boston, had a right to be pleased with the way things were going under her leadership. Sales had quadrupled over the past three years. Profits were up over 200 percent and would be even higher if Metro had enough production capacity to do everything in-house.

Leigh thought to herself: "We've got to build a new production plant. These subcontractors are bleeding us to death. I'm not sure where we should locate the new plant so rather than go to all the anxiety and hassle of trying to make the decision myself, I'm going to commission a task force. I'll appoint all the necessary experts, and we should get a more accurate and better decision than if I made it myself."

March 17, 1983: A letter signed by Leigh McManus appointed a seven-person task force to decide on the location for the new plant. They were given three months to complete the task and a generous budget for travel, hiring consultants, and other expenses. The task force was made up of all the interested functions—finance, production, marketing, personnel and also included an expert in law, real estate, transportation.

March through May 1983. The task force, chaired by Kevin Schultz, worked hard on their task. They visited a number of potential sites. They analyzed relative costs, advantages in transportation, and availability of the kind of manpower they would need to run the plant. Of course there was no easy agreement on the relative importance of various criteria; in fact, there was considerable disagreement and conflict. At one time they even hired a management consultant to help resolve their conflict and aid them in making a decision.

Early June, 1983. They finally resolved their differences and made their decision in favor of St. Louis, Missouri. It offered a central location, reasonably priced real estate, and a good labor pool. It was by far the most cost-effective place to locate.

June 21, 1983. Leigh was pleased with the briefing she just received from the task force. She thought to herself, "I'm pleased with the result. They did an excellent job of analysis and their decision looks good." Leigh decided that her next step would be to appoint the manager for the new plant. She wanted someone with experience with Metro; someone she knew and trusted. The only logical choice was Lloyd Webb, the present assistant production manager at the Boston plant. She called him in to her office to break the good news.

"Lloyd, are you interested in heading up our new plant in St. Louis? You would not only become a plant manager but will get the salary of one—almost double what you're now making with lots of opportunities for bonuses." Lloyd had a surprised look on his face. He replied, "Sure, it would be a great promotion to become a plant manager, and we could sure use the money, but in St. Louis? (with a slight grimace) Let me think about it and check with my wife. I'll let you know tomorrow."

June 22, 1983. Lloyd tells Leigh: "My wife is not in the least bit interested in moving to the midwest or St. Louis even at double the salary.

My kids are also rebelling. The oldest will be a junior in high school this fall. She says she would die if she had to move and leave her friends; from the intensity of her reaction I kind of half-way believe her. To keep peace in my family, I'm going to have to turn down the offer. Now if the new plant were on the east coast, or even on the west coast, I might be able to talk my family into it."

Later. Leigh thinks to herself, "What am I going to do now. The only logical choice for the job has turned it down. There's nobody else I feel comfortable with. Maybe we should go back to the drawing board and find another, more acceptable location?"

Everyone constantly makes decisions. You decided to read this chapter rather than sleep or play tennis. Leigh decided to let her subordinates make the decision about the plant location. Lloyd decided to turn down the plant managership in St. Louis. The decision process is pervasive and inevitable. Some decisions we make are good, some are bad, but we must continue to make them regardless of the outcome.

In this chapter we will analyze the basic decision-making processes for both individuals and groups with the aim of improving and sharpening our decision-making capability. We will also take a look at some common group decision-making techniques that will help us to make better decisions.

The Decision Process: How Decisions Get Made

Since everyone makes decisions, we might expect that the process would be thoroughly researched and understood. Unfortunately, this is not the case. We still have a lot to learn about decision-making processes and many issues remain unresolved. In this section, we will discuss some of the things we do know about the decision-making process using a basic model that involves identifying a problem or goal, developing alternatives, judging the alternatives, and making a choice. Figure 13.1 illustrates this basic process.

■ Decision Making and Problem Solving

Decision making is the process of thought and action that results in choice behavior.[1] Decision making differs somewhat from **problem solving**,[2] which involves a systematic process of defining the problem, gathering data, generating alternatives, making a choice between alternatives, implementing the solution, and following up as necessary (*see* Table 13.1). Although the term *problem solving* is often used interchangeably with *decision making*, we will use it to mean a more systematic, rational process that encompasses the decision-making process but adds additional steps (illustrated in Fig. 13.1). For example, some people make "spur of the moment" decisions, such as to go to the beach, without reference to the problem-solving process. On the other hand, Kevin Shultz and the task force used a problem-solving approach to generate their recommendation in the opening case.

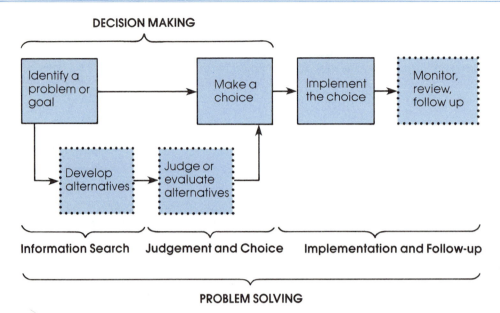

Figure 13.1. The decision-making and problem-solving process.

■ Identifying Problems or Goals

Perhaps the weakest link in the decision process is identifying and defining the problem. It is easy to misdiagnose or misinterpret the true nature of a problem. In Chapter 4, we learned how perceptions can influence and distort our view of reality. This is particularly true when it comes to problem recognition. One reason why auditors are important for organizations is that they see problems from another perspective and become good at problem identification. Values and attitudes, discussed in Chapter 3, are also important. Since attitudes are a predisposition to respond in some way to an object or event, we may find ourselves responding to a problem because of our attitude rather than the facts that exist. Two additional blocks to adequate problem exploration include:[4]

☐ Defining the Problem in Terms of a Proposed Solution

An example might be: "The problem is that we need a bigger computer." This problem definition states a proposed solution—to get a bigger com-

---

Table 13.1. Problem-solving steps.

There are a number of good problem-solving models[3] such as the one below. (Note the similarity to the model shown in Figure 13.1.)

- ■ Recognize that a problem exists.
- ■ Define the problem.
- ■ Generate possible solutions to the problem.
- ■ Evaluate alternative solutions (make judgements).
- ■ Choose a course of action (the decision).
- ■ Take action to implement.
- ■ Establish controls and follow up to make sure the problem is solved.

13.1 | *Defining Problems Using the Kepner-Tregoe Approach*

A widely employed approach to problem solving, the Kepner-Tregoe Method, states that there are several steps to recognizing and defining a problem.[5]

■ To find a problem, a manager must be alert; surveillance and inspection are needed.

■ The manager must know what the level of performance *should be* so that actual performance can be compared with it and deviations noted. Their definition of a problem is a deviation from some standard of performance.

■ If the problem is complex, it needs to be separated into subproblems, and priorities are set based upon the problem's urgency, seriousness, and growth trend.

■ The problem should be specified in terms of:[6]

What is the deviation, and what is the thing or object on which the deviation is observed?

Where is the deviation on the thing or object, and where are objects with the deviation observed?

When does the deviation appear on the thing or object, and when are objects with deviations observed?

How big are the deviations, and how many objects with deviations are observed?

puter. The real problem might be response time for customer service for which there are a number of possible solutions other than buying a bigger computer.

☐ *Diagnosing a Problem in Terms of its Symptoms*

We often tend to oversimplify a problem by dealing only with its symptoms. For example, a vice-president notes in a staff meeting that there is a turnover and absenteeism problem. As we learned in Chapter 3, these behaviors are usually symptoms of some other organizational problem that is causing dissatisfaction, such as a problem with supervisory style.

■ Searching for Alternatives

A perfect problem-solving approach would entail a detailed and complete search for relevant alternatives that might solve the problem. In some cases, however, this search for alternatives may be severely limited or nonexistent.

Bounded Rationality   **Bounded rationality** means that although people may seek the best solution, they normally settle for less than the best, because they do not have the capacity to acquire and process the complex information that would be needed for reaching the best solution.[7] People seek to bound or limit the rationality of their search process. For example, if you were in the market for a home computer, your search will probably be limited to two or three models. To gather data about the hundreds of models of home computers that are available would be a complex, full-time job; thus, you will probably bound your decision process.

13.2 | Left-Brain, Right-Brain and Decision Making

Recent evidence[8] suggests that there are differences in the way people make decisions based on whether they are oriented toward the right side of the brain (intuition, feeling, visual-spatial) or the left side of the brain (sequential, fact seeking, calculating). This raises some controversial issues for managers. Analytic, rational problem solvers, dominated by the left brain, have been accused of causing problems for organizations by overlooking unmeasurable, but important, subtleties and redefining real problems into forms that miss the point.[9] The creative, more humanistic approach to problem solving, exhibited by right-brain people, has been de-emphasized by managers. Thus managers need to distinguish between those problems that need analytic, left-brain people and those that need creative, right-brain people.

Satisficing   One form of bounded rationality is **satisficing**. "Most human decision making, whether individual or organizational, is concerned with the discovery and selection of satisfactory alternatives; only in exceptional cases is it concerned with the discovery and selection of optimal alternatives."[10] The process works something like this: "John, you don't like Applicant *A*, Mary thinks *B* doesn't have enough experience, and I don't think that *C* would fit in. Since no one has any strong feelings one way or the other about *D*, let's offer *D* the job." This decision process could result in hiring a very mediocre performer who is marginally acceptable to everyone. While satisficing and bounded rationality result in less than optimal decisions, they do serve the useful purpose of simplifying the search process. However, a manager should take care to recognize this phenomenon and try to avoid overlooking a particularly good alternative.

Intuitive Decision Making   Few decisions are made based on careful problem solving and analysis, a process called **unprogrammed decision** making. In fact, most decisions are made instinctively using a **programmed decision**-making process. For example, when you are driving a car the decision to put on the brakes is intuitive since it comes almost automatically and without reasoning. Programmed decisions are based on our past experiences and the reinforcement associated with these experiences. Years of driving experience has taught us precisely when to put on the brakes. The same type of programs often guide an experienced manager's decisions. The decision to discipline an employee, to buy an item for inventory, to sell a stock—all these may be quite intuitive for the manager.

Henry Mintzberg's classic study of managerial behavior[11] found that managers worked at a fast, action-oriented pace. Half of the activities of CEO's lasted less than nine minutes and only ten percent exceeded an hour. He concluded that executives are action-oriented and do not like reflective activities. These data support our observation that much decision making is intuitive. The fast and hectic pace of managerial jobs makes use of programmed decision making almost a necessity.

Implicit Favorite Model   It appears that many people who are using problem solving pick an implicitly favored solution early in the decision process.[12] Even though the search may be continued, decision rules and perceptual distortions are used that guarantee the implicit favorite's selection. This approach rests heavily on the concept of cognitive dissonance discussed in Chapter 3—once a favorite is chosen, reasons are found to discount the others. An example might be choice of a job. Early in the process, you may develop an implicit favorite. All other possibilities are then ruled out by criteria that insure only the favorite will win.

■ Evaluating Alternatives

If we have complete information about all the alternatives, know their value, and know the probability that various alternatives will work, evaluating the decision will be easy. But, we know that bounded rationality means we will be working with less than complete information and that through satisficing we will probably settle for less than the best.

Judgment   When we weigh alternatives, we must make a judgment about the acceptability of the possible courses of action, then make our decision. There are two aspects of judgment: expressing preferences and making predictions.[13] In the opening case, Lloyd expressed a preference not to go to St. Louis as the main reason for making his choice to decline the position. The task force made a predictive judgment since they tried to predict an uncertain future. They tried to predict construction costs, labor availability, and transportation advantages, among others.

Using Probabilities to Evaluate Alternatives   Most people in business fields have taken a course in statistics that included the study of probability. Whenever we make predictions, we are consciously or unconsciously predicting the chances of various outcomes. When we discussed motivation theory in Chapter 5, we noted that people may evelute various outcomes and have certain expectancies (probabilities) about attaining the outcomes. They are motivated (make a decision to behave) based upon these assessments. In the opening case, the task force should have gathered probabilities of getting a plant manager to relocate. Of course, bounded rationality prevented them from considering this important data.

An example of the rational use of probabilities would be a business relocation problem. If you were a business owner making a decision about opening an new outlet in the west side versus the east side of the city, you might have different probability assessments for each location alternative. If you locate on the east side, you estimate that there was a 40 percent chance that the outlet would succeed, but the potential profit is $100,000. On the west side a 70 percent chance of success, but the potential profit is only $60,000. Which do you choose?

	Ultimate Value	Probability	Expected value
East location	$100,000 profit	.4	$40,000 profit
West location	$60,000 profit	.7	$42,000 profit

■ Choosing Alternatives

The outcome of problem solving and judgment is the actual choice of which course to follow. The choice will most likely satisfice rather than maximize the outcomes of the problem-solving process. In our opening

13.3	*Knee-Deep in Big Muddy: Escalating Commitment to a Course of Action*[14]

Some people seem to get locked into a costly course of action in spite of the potential losses. Instead of cutting our losses when we find ourselves in a losing situation, we often invest more resources; we increase our commitment to a course of action. The classic example is purchasing stock. Say you paid $100 per share, but the price has now declined to $70 per share. Since you are still convinced the stock is a good buy, you invest more money at the $70 bargain price. Then when the price declines to $50, you are faced with another decision. Often, the choice is to buy again. Here's an additional example:[15]

A company overestimates its capability to build an airplane brake that will meet certain technical specifications at a given cost. Because it wins the government contract, the company is forced to invest greater and greater effort into meeting the contract terms. As a result of increas-ing pressure to meet specifications and deadlines, records and tests of the brake are misrepresented to government officials. Corporate careers and company credibility are increasingly staked to the airbrake contract, although many in the firm know the brake will not work effectively. At the conclusion of the construction period, the government test pilot flies the plane; it skids off the runway and narrowly misses injuring the pilot.

While the reasons for this phenomenon are not fully known, it appears that there is a strong motivation to justify previous decisions because we want to be seen as competent decision makers. In addition, there are strong societal norms toward consistency. Thus, we rationalize our commitment to a course of action in light of our past decisions and felt pressures from within ourselves to conform.

case, the actual choice of the task force was to relocate to St. Louis while Lloyd's choice was to remain in Boston.

Using Groups for Decision Making

Group decision making permeates our lives. We are all part of some group whether it be a family group or a work group. Sometimes there is a choice of whether to use a group, such as Leigh's decision in the opening incident. At other times there may be no choice—we must work in a group; for example, a labor-management negotiating committee. In this section we will discuss the advantages and disadvantages of groups versus individuals. In the next section, we will be discussing when groups should participate in decisions.[16]

■ Why Use Groups for Decision Making?

Greater Sum Total of Knowledge   If the problem is complex, then the resources offered by a number of people can all contribute to the solution. Gaps in knowledge of one person can be filled by another. The wide variety of skills and technical expertise, with the potential for cross-check-

Understanding Organizational Behavior

ing and verification, make groups more powerful than individuals in this case. An example might be selecting the location for a new plant. By having representatives from key areas of the company, more expertise and resources are available to help develop a better decision. Another example might be the introduction of a new piece of machinery. Engineers would provide technical input, machinists would see the problem from a more practical perspective, and a production worker could provide information about how well the new machine would be accepted from the operator's perspective.

Greater Number of Approaches to the Problem

Individuals tend to have tunnel vision. That is, they tend to see only one way of solving the problem. When several people approach a problem, each brings new insights that may result in a better solution. An engineer may see redesign as the answer, while the machinist sees that tolerances need to be changed. In addition, a comment by one person may trigger a new idea or approach from another person.

Group Decisions Are Easier to Implement

We tend to accept and support decisions that we make rather than those others make. Thus, anytime you anticipate difficulty in getting a decision accepted, group participation in the decision can be an aid. For example, if you want to introduce a new computer into your firm, it may make it much easier to do so if you involve the key people who have to work with the computer—programmers, operators, data input clerks, managers. Once these people have hashed over the advantages and disadvantages of various alternatives and reached agreement on which computer to buy, it will make it easier to implement the decision. We will discuss participation later in this chapter.

■ Disadvantages of Groups for Decision Making

Social Pressure toward Conformity

This disadvantage has received considerable attention (*see* the Perspective: Groupthink). When we studied group dynamics, we saw that there were pressures toward conformity in the group because of norms and desires for cohesiveness. Group pressures are stronger in groups that have developed a powerful sense of cohesiveness. An example might be the top-management group of an advertising firm who have worked together for years. They know each other well and feel like they are part of an effective, cohesive team. They are effective, but they have to be careful to make sure that excessive conformity does not result in groupthink and a poor decision. One way to avoid such problems is to establish the role of **devil's advocate**, someone whose task it is to question decisions, to take the other side of an issue, or to cast doubt on the decision.[17] It is also a good idea for the group leader to avoid taking a position early in the discussion of a problem.

Individual Domination

Whether a leader merges from a leaderless committee or one is appointed, the leader tends to dominate the decision-making process. If the leader happens to be an effective problem solver, then it makes little difference. If the leader tends to block others or to stubbornly persist, then the group may be ineffective. An example of this type of problem is a hard-charging junior manager at Metro Publishing, Jack Slater. Whenever Jack joins any group without a formal leader, he feels that he should be the leader. By stubborn persistence, he usually wears down his opposition. Once elected leader, he carefully prevents or puts down inputs from people who disagree with him. Thus, the decision is usually Jack's. Needless to say, the decision may not be the same one that would have been chosen with another leader. From this line of reasoning it follows that a manager should be careful who is appointed to decision-making groups; do not appoint the "Jacks" just because they volunteer every time.

Costs   It is costly to use groups for decision making. They are slower than individuals because of all the give and take that is needed to reach a decision. There are lost manhours involved, especially if production workers are used and overtime must be paid. Most of you have experienced a group-decision situation where the discussion and haggling seemed to be endless. However, this extensive discussion is often useful in the long run to resolve conflicts and make sure that all dissenting opinions are heard.

■ Group Decision Effectiveness

The process of evaluating the overall effectiveness of groups is summarized in Figure 13.2. Research has shown that group decision-making performance is generally quantitatively and qualitatively superior to the performance of the average individual in the group.[19] However, the best individual in the group is often superior to the group's performance. Thus, groups that contain a number of low-ability individuals may not perform as well as the exceptional individuals in that group. In addition, the process gains and losses must be weighted to see if group decision making is worth the cost and effort. **Process gains** may include the energizing force of working with other people, a stimulation to creativity when many different ideas are discussed, and a more careful weighing of the pros and cons of a given decision. **Process losses** involve the time and energy that must be expended to reach a decision; communications difficulties that may arise from the group's activities; and the ineffective use of group task, maintenance, and blocking roles.

Participation and Delegation in Decision Making

There are three basic ways that a manager can handle decision making: make the decision alone, allow subordinates to participate in the decision, or delegate the decision entirely to subordinates. This aspect of decision making also involves leadership style and thus serves as an introduction to the leadership process that will be covered in Chapter 14. A continuum of manager decision behaviors is shown in Figure 13.3.

■ Participation in Decision Making

Participation in decision making has been a subject for organizational writers and researchers for many years. The subject is loaded with ideological and moral connotations. Many believe that having workers participate

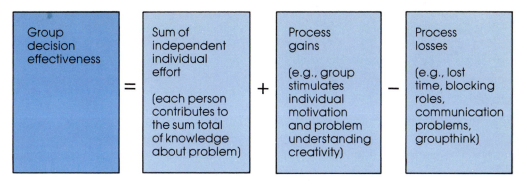

Figure 13.2. Group decision effectiveness.[18]

13.4 Groupthink

Irving Janis has coined the term **groupthink**, which means a deterioration in mental efficiency, reality testing, and judgment that results from in-group pressures. When a workgroup or policy group displays most or all of the symptoms related below, their effectiveness will be impaired and decisions will not be of good quality. The eight symptoms of groupthink are:

1. *An illusion of invulnerability, shared by most or all the members which creates excessive optimism and encourages taking extreme risks.*

2. *Collective efforts to rationalize in order to discount warnings which might lead the members to reconsider their assumptions before they recommit themselves to their past policy decisions.*

3. *An unquestioned belief in the group's inherent morality, inclining the members to ignore the ethical or moral consequences of their decisions.*

4. *Stereotyped views of enemy leaders as too evil to warrant genuine attempts to negotiate, or as too weak and stupid to counter whatever risky attempts are made to defeat their purposes.*

5. *Direct pressure on any member who expresses strong arguments against any of the group's stereotypes, illusions, or commitments, making clear that this type of dissent is contrary to what is expected of all loyal members.*

6. *Self-censorship of deviations from the apparent group consensus, reflecting each member's inclination to minimize to himself the importance of his doubts and counterarguments.*

7. *A shared illusion of unanimity concerning judgments conforming to the majority view (partly resulting from self-censorship of deviations, augmented by the false assumption that silence means consent).*

8. *The emergence of self-appointed mindguards—members who protect the group from adverse information that might shatter their shared complacency about the effectiveness and morality of their decisions.*

Irving Janis: *Groupthink: Psychological Studies of Policy Decisions and Fiascoes,* 2nd edition, pp. 256–259. Copyright 1982 © by Houghton Mifflin Company. Used by permission.

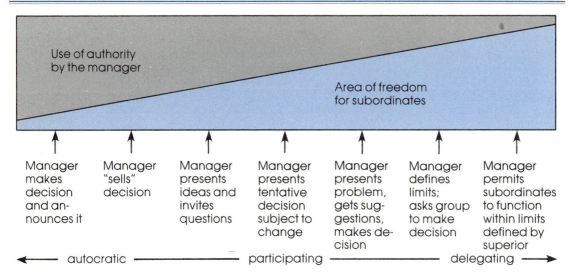

Figure 13.3. A continuum of decision-making behavior.

will cure a number of organizational ills. We will not address these issues.

While one can define **participation** in decision making in many ways, we will use it to mean the process of joint decision making by two or more parties.[20] This definition implies that all involved people contribute in some way to the decision. For example, let's say you are a manager and you want your subordinates to participate in the decision to buy a new office copier. Participation here means that you would form a group of interested employees to address the goal (purchase of a copier). You might or might not be a member of the group. If you were not a member, you would probably reserve the right to make the final decision after listening to the group's position. If you actually let the group make the decision, you are delegating—the subject of the next section. The degree of participation can range from almost none to a great deal as illustrated by Figure 13.3.

■ Delegating Decisions

When you **delegate** a decision, you allow a subordinate or group to actually make the decision. For example, if Leigh, in our opening case, had told the task force that their decision was final on site selection, that would be delegating the decision. In fact, Leigh, like most CEOs, would not delegate such a decision because the ultimate responsibility for a correct decision is hers. Thus, she will listen to the task force, and quite probably follow their advice, but she still shares in the decision. Thus, the task force was working under participative decision making, not delegation.

■ When to Use Participation and Delegation

There are a number of keys to effectively using participation and delegation. One way of systematizing the issues is the **Vroom-Yetton Model**, illustrated by the decision-tree format shown in Figure 13.4. In this section we will briefly cover the key issues involved in deciding when to use participation and delegation.[21]

Understanding Organizational Behavior

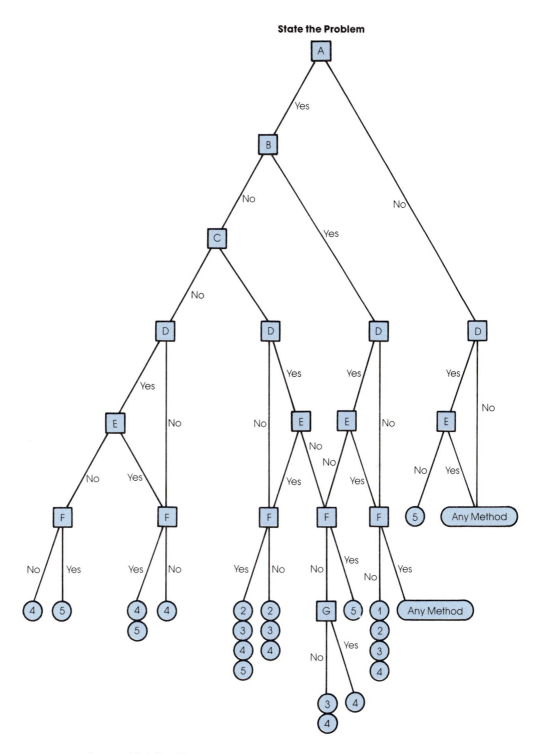

State the Problem

Figure 13.4. The Vroom-Yetton model of the group decision process.

Reprinted from *Leadership and Decision-Making* by Victor H. Vroom and Philip W. Yetton by permission of the University of Pittsburgh Press. ©1973 by University of Pittsburgh Press.

How Important Is the Quality of the Decision?

If the outcome of the decision, such as the plant location, is crucial, then the decision should not be delegated although participation may be used with final approval being reserved for the manager.

Who Has the Knowledge to Make the Decision?

If you do not have the knowledge that is needed, it is difficult to make a good decision. This goes both ways. Sometimes subordinates have knowledge of actual work processes that makes them the experts. Then, participation or delegation would be appropriate. On the other hand, if the manager or the electrical engineer is the only one with the knowledge to make the decision, then participation may not be warranted unless there is some other reason to use it, such as getting an idea accepted. If a problem needs an expert to solve it, then a group should not be used. For example, a firm may have a complex problem concerning the issue of corporate bonds. It would not make sense to use representatives from throughout the firm participate in the decision because most of them would not have the expertise needed. What is needed is a financial expert.

Is Acceptance of the Decision Critical for Implementing It?

If subordinates do not accept the decision, it may be very difficult, if not impossible, to implement it. As we have seen in the last chapter, subordinates often have a great deal of power that can frustrate implementing even the best decision.

Do Subordinates Share the Goals Associated with the Decision?

Let's say that your goal is improved organizational effectiveness, especially in terms of lower production costs. If your subordinates have a different goal, such as preserving the work standards and maintaining the social relationships with their coworkers, then participation or delegation would be futile.

Are Subordinates Likely to Agree on a Solution?

If positions are polarized between two or more groups so that a joint solution is unlikely, then participation should not be used. Say one group of employees is interested primarily in getting more overtime while another is interested in preventing overtime. These opposing positions make conflict likely and arriving at a good decision remote.

An Example Using the Vroom-Vetton Model

Jane McManos, Director of Engineering, had just heard from her boss that another division of the company, located in the Middle East, had placed an emergency request for four engineers to help with a high-priority project. Jane agreed that their help was needed and that she had the resources to meet the requirement. There was no reason why one engineer would be chosen over another. Using the Vroom-Yetton model,[22] Jane would answer *no* to question *A*, since it made little difference to her how the problem is solved as long as four engineers are chosen. The next question (*D*), "Is acceptance of the decision important?" must be answered *yes*. Question *E*, "If I make the decision alone, will subordinates accept it?" must be answered *no*. Thus the only feasible way to handle this decision is to use participative, group decision making. Let the engineers themselves work out a consensus for solving the problem of who will go.

Group Decision-Making Techniques

While there are many decision-making techniques, we will emphasize group consensus and nominal groups, with a brief explanation of brainstorming and Delphi. Consensus and brainstorming use **interacting groups** made up of people who are actively working together on a face-to-face basis with open discussion and communication. The nominal technique mixes interactive noninteractive strategies, and Delphi does not involve the direct interaction of group members.

■ Group Consensus

When committees and task forces work together to solve some problem or make some decision, they often use a technique called **group consensus**, which means that a decision or solution that is arrived at should be acceptable to all group members even though some members may not completely agree with it.[23] While complete unanimity is not the goal of consen-

| 13.5 | *Brainstorming*[24] |

This technique, developed by Alex Osborne, has been around for over forty years. **Brainstorming** is a system for creatively generating alternatives. Its strong point is that *ideation* is separated from *evaluation*. There is a natural tendency for people to immediately evaluate a proposed solution. Often, people get so bogged down criticizing and evaluating ideas that many excellent ones are overlooked. As an idea-generation technique, brainstorming may not be any more effective than the pooled efforts of a number of people working alone.[25] However, the technique is simple, widely used, easy to do, and fun. Here are the general procedures for brainstorming.

■ *State the problem*. The central problem to be addressed needs to be clearly stated in writing on a piece of paper or a blackboard. The problem should be narrowed to some manageable level. For example, brainstorming, "How can we increase profitability?" is perhaps too broad a question. A more likely question might be, "In what ways might we decrease costs on the new brake assemblies?"

■ *Rules of brainstorming*. Carefully enforcing the rules is the key to successful outcomes. Post the rules on flip chart paper so you can merely point to them to get compliance. There are four rules:

1. Absolutely no evaluation, verbal or nonverbal. Criticism is not allowed.
2. Freewheeling is welcome. The wilder the ideas, the better. No idea is too wild. An unusual idea may trigger some more feasible idea in another participant's mind.
3. Quantity is welcome and desired. The greater the number of ideas, the greater the useful ideas after evaluation.
4. Piggybacking is encouraged. Try to combine, embellish, or improve on an idea. No one should feel individual ownership for an idea.

sus, each individual should be given an opportunity to express dissent. Each must be able to agree, at least in part, with the decision. Group members should not acquiesce until they feel relatively comfortable about the decision. Here are some guidelines for helping to reach consensus:

☐ *Avoid arguing for your own position* until you have carefully listened to the positions of others. You should state your position clearly and listen carefully to others' comments about it. Try to be rational and avoid arguing for your position just because it is yours.

☐ *Do not change your mind simply to avoid conflict and confrontation.* If you cannot support a decision, state your case—stand up for what you believe. However, you should carefully explore your reasons for taking a position. Are they sound? Do others agree with them? On the other hand, you should yield to the arguments of others when they are sound and reasonable.

☐ *Try to avoid win-lose dynamics.* When the discussion reaches a stalemate, carefully evalute each position; try to search for other alternatives; or perhaps turn to brainstorming.

☐ *Avoid conflict-reducing techniques.* Majority vote or coin-tosses should be avoided, although there is some evidence that a majority vote *prior* to a group discussion may result in better decisions.[26]

☐ *View differences of opinion as helpful.* Try to establish a norm of speaking up if you differ. Since one of the major advantages of groups is the varied resources and points of view that others bring to the decision, it only makes sense to try to take advantage of this diversity.

■ Nominal Group Technique

The nominal group technique, or NGT, is a relatively new technique that involves people working together with little verbal interaction to solve problems and make decisions.[27]

How NGT Works

The group members, say seven or eight people, sit around a table in full view of each other, but they do not talk to each other at all. Instead, they spend five to ten minutes jotting down ideas on a piece of paper. After this first silent stage is completed, people share their ideas by going around the table and having people share one of their ideas at a time. The ideas are recorded on a flip chart in full view of everyone. Members continue to share their private ideas in this round-robin fashion until all ideas are reported. When sharing is completed, ideas are discussed and votes are taken to determine their importance. After the first vote, there is more discussion and then a final vote to make the decision. Table 13.2 provides a more detailed summary of what happens during the NGT process.

Advantages of NGT Over Interacting Groups

The major advantages of the nominal techniques are insuring the ideation is kept separate from evaluation, insuring balanced participation of all members and providing a systematic way of aggregating votes for decision selection. Research results[28] show NGT to be superior to interacting groups, such as a brainstorming group, in terms of generating relevant solutions, more creative solutions (because of less premature evaluation), and more broadly focused

Table 13.2. Procedures for nominal group technique.[29]

Five to nine people should make up a NGT group. A flip chart at the front of the room is used to record ideas. The six steps in the NGT process are summarized below:

1. Silently generate ideas in writing	Five to ten minutes is usually enough time for this phase. The question is posted on a flip chart at the front of the room. Participants are asked to answer the question on the chart. They are cautioned not to talk to other members or look at the work sheets of others.
2. Round-robin recording the ideas	The leader goes around the room asking for one idea from each participant and recording it on the flip chart. This goes on, round-robin fashion, until all ideas are exhausted. The chief goal of this step is to get an accurate list of ideas in front of the group to serve as a mapping of the ideas of the entire group.
3. Serially discuss the ideas	Each idea on the chart is discussed in the order it appears on the chart (serially). The leader reads each item and asks the group if there are any questions, needs for clarification, agreement or disagreement.
4. Preliminary vote on item importance	Each group member makes an independent judgment about the alternatives by rank ordering them secretly on 3" x 5" cards. The mean or average of these judgments is used as the group's decision. The NGT process may end here or the decision may be further refined through discussion and revoting.
5. Additional discussion after the first vote.	The voting patterns are analyzed and reasons examined to see if a more accurate decision can be made.
6. Final vote	The final voting occurs in the same fashion as the original vote, by secret rankings. This action completes the decision process and provides closure.

solutions. Interacting groups tend to pursue one train of discussion for long periods of time; sometimes even to the exclusion of other trains.

■ The Delphi Technique

The **Delphi technique** can be used when people cannot physically get together to make a group decision. It is a method for systematically gathering written judgments from individuals by using sequential questionnaires interspersed with summaries of results from previous responses.[30] Delphi was developed by Rand Corporation as a way of forecasting future events.[31] It takes a considerable amount of time and effort to administer; it is more costly than other group methods. The technique is particularly useful when the experts in solving a problem or making a decision cannot get together because of geography, time or other constraints.

How the Delphi Process Works   Delphi uses a series of questionnaires that begins with a rather broad question focusing on whatever needs a solution or decision. Each subsequent questionnaire uses the responses from earlier ones as its basis. The process is complete when consensus is reached or when enough information has been gathered. The Delphi takes lots of time, participant skills in writing, and motivation to complete the questionnaires and participate in the process. The process outline in Table 13.3 gives you some indication of the amount of time and effort needed to conduct Delphi.

■ Which Technique to Use?

There are no easy answers to this question. Interacting groups, especially consensus, allow for much more attention to the needs of the group and its members—it is a teambuilding experience. Brainstorming is a quick and easy way to get a number of ideas out for consideration. Nominal group technique helps get better quality decisions, but takes a bit more preparation and structure. The Delphi technique takes a long time, but can be quite useful when people cannot get together to make a decision.[32]

Table 13.3.   Process outline and schedule for Delphi.

Activities	Estimated Minimum Time for Accomplishment
1. Develop the Delphi question	½ day
2. Select and contact respondents	2 days
3. Select sample size	½ day
4. Develop Questionnaire #1 and test	1 day
a. Type and send out	1 day
b. Response time	5 days
c. Reminder time (if used)	3 days
5. Analysis of Questionnaire #1	½ day
6. Develop Questionnaire #2 and test	2 days
a. Type and send out	1 day
b. Reponse time	5 days
c. Reminder time (if used)	3 days
7. Analysis of Questionnaire #2	1 day
8. Develop Questionnaire #3 and test	2 days
a. Type and send out	1 day
b. Response time	5 days
c. Reminder time (if used)	3 days
9. Analysis of Questionaire #3	1 day
10. Prepare a final report	4 days
a. Type report and send out	1 day
b. Prepare repondents' report	1 day
c. Type report and send out	1 day
Total estimated minimum time	44½ days

Understanding Organizational Behavior

Chapter Review

■ **Decision making**, the process of thought and action that results in a choice, differs somewhat from **problem solving**, which involves such behaviors as systematic data gathering, alternative analysis, implementation, and follow-up.

■ One of the weakest links in the decision proces is identifying and defining the problem or goal. Perceptual blocks, values and attitudes, and a lack of skill in problem definition contribute to our problems in this area.

■ Our search for all the alternatives for making a decision is usually limited by our capacity to acquire and process complex information. This is called **bounded rationality**, which may be contrasted with a perfectly rational decision where all solutions are evaluated and the best one chosen. Another form of bounded rationality is **satisficing**, or choosing among the satisfactory solutions that appear rather than seeking the optimal one.

■ When decisions are made intuitively or almost automatically, they are called **programmed decisions** and can be contrasted with unprogrammed decisions, which take a lot of thought and care.

■ When we evaluate alternatives we may settle for one that satisfices, pick an **implicit favorite**, or make a careful judgment based on analysis of probabilities and other factors.

■ There may be differences in the way people make decisions based on whether they are **left-brain-oriented** (more impersonal, technical, factual) or **right-brain-oriented** (more personal, sympathetic, practical).

■ There are a number of advantages to groups. They offer a greater sum total of knowledge, more diverse approaches to a problem solution, and once a decision is made acceptance will be easier. The disadvantages of group decision making include the pressures to conform (sometimes resulting in **groupthink**), high costs, and the possibility that one or more people may dominate.

■ **Participation** in decision-making techniques can harness the advantages of the group decision process. Before using participation, consider the following questions: Who has the knowledge to make the decision? Is implementation a problem? Do subordinates share the goals of the decision? Are they likely to agree on a decision?

■ **Group consensus**, the most popular interacting-group technique, means that everyone in the group must agree, at least in part, with the decision and that all the reasons for disagreement have been discussed. **Brainstorming** is a technique that clearly separates ideation from evaluation by withholding judgment. The **nominal group** technique uses periods of working without interaction combined with discussions and voting to achieve a decision. The **Delphi** technique uses questionnaires to systematically gather written judgments from the participants. It is quite useful when experts cannot be brought together face-to-face.

For Discussion

1. How does decision making differ from problem solving?
2. Define a problem with which you are familiar using the Kepner-Tregoe approach.
3. Explain why managers do not always make optimal decisions. What impact does this have on the organization?
4. What are the major advantages and disadvantages in using groups for decision making?
5. Using the Vroom-Yetton model shown in Figure 13.4, outline the circumstances where participation should be used or avoided.
6. Compare and contrast group consensus, brainstorming, and the nominal group technique.
7. What are some examples of the types of decisions that would be appropriate for Delphi?
8. Should a manager be an autocratic or democratic decision maker?

Key Concepts and Terms

decision making

problem solving

bounded rationality

satisficing

programmed decisions

intuitive decisions

unprogrammed decisions

implicit favorite model

judgment

devil's advocate

groupthink

participation in decision making

autocratic management

delegation

Vroom-Yetton model

group consensus

brainstorming

nominal group technique

Delphi

Suggested Readings

Brandstatter, M.; Davis, J. H.; and Stocker-Kreschgauer, G., eds. (1983). *Group decision processes*. London: Academic Press.

Kanter, R. M. (1982). Dilemmas of managing participation. *Organizational Dynamics* 11:5–27.

Murnighan, J. K. (1981). Group decision making: What strategies to use? *Management Review* Feb.:133–134.

Ulschak, F. L.; Nathanson, L.; and Gillan, P. B. (1981). *Small group problem solving: An aid to organizational effectiveness*. Reading, Mass.: Addison-Wesley.

Ulvila, J. W., and Brown, R. V. (1982). Decision analysis comes of age. *Harvard Business Review* Sept.–Oct.:130–141.

Participation at Moonlight Cosmetics

Eva Gibbs, President of Moonlight Cosmetics Corporation, just finished reading an article about participation in decision making in a news magazine. She thought it sounded like a good idea and decided that participation was just what Moonlight Cosmetics needed. The next day she dictated a memo:

Participation in decision making can make a substantial improvement in our operations. Effective at once, each supervisor will include all employees who are affected by a decision in the decision-making process. Let me know if you have any problems.

Signed, Eva Gibbs

Within three months, eight of her twenty-five supervisors quit. She figured, "Good riddance. They were probably ones who couldn't adapt to a participative style."

Discussion questions
1. What decision-making process did Eva use?
2. Brainstorm some reasons why the supervisors may have left the company?
3. Evaluate the ideas you came up with in brainstorming.
4. How might Eva have handled this change differently?

The Engineering Change

The Inverse Corporation is a diversified manufacturer of component assemblies for a variety of industries. A major Inverse product line consists of passenger seat constructions for the trucking industry. Federal safety standards (FMVSS) effective in August required several major engineering changes to be incorporated into currently produced assemblies by that date. A meeting was called in June to discuss the effects of these changes.

The Meeting
Manufacturing and Production Control agreed that the changes would not cause their areas any major problems. Process and Project engineering concluded that the changes were compatible with present manufacturing facilities and would pose no appreciable obstacles. Top management assessed the changes and concluded that they would primarily affect tooling.

The tool division, represented by its chief engineer, W. Track, and his two assistant su-perintendents, were divided in their opinions of the situation. Track, recently obtained from outside the corporation to head the tool division, believed the changes were compatible with present tooling and could be accomplished for the start of production in August. His two assistants, however, disagreed and predicted a November completion date as being more realistic. They based their opinions on past tooling practices and procedures.

Sales reiterated that a November date was impossible. L. Stanley, sales chief, pointed out that competitors, who have the same type of tooling as Inverse, have committed themselves to the August date and Inverse should be able to do the same. The meeting adjourned with Inverse committed to the August completion schedule. All were in favor of the decision except the two assistant tool superintendents, H. Jones and A. Smith. The following conversation beteen Jones and Smith occurred directly after the meeting.

Smith: *"That young hot shot said he could do it but we're the ones who are actually going to do the work!"*

Jones: *"Did you hear him knuckle under to sales?"*

Smith: *"No one paid any attention to our arguments or suggestions. They acted as if we didn't know what we are talking about. We've been doing most of the work around here for the past twenty years and look who they listen to, a young outsider!"*

Jones: *"He thinks he's going to change the way we do things around here.*

Come August we'll see who is right, him or us, and believe you me it's going to be us."

After leaving the meeting Track knew he had a problem and pondered his possible solutions.

From J. V. Murray and T. J. Von der Embse (1973), *Organizational behavior: Critical incidents and analysis*, pp. 304–05. Copyright © 1973 by Charles E. Merrill, Columbus, Ohio. Reprinted with permission of publisher.

Discussion questions
1. How might Track solve this problem?
2. Which decision-making techniques would be most appropriate here and why?

REFERENCES

1. Maccrimmon, K. R. and Taylor, R. N. (1976), Decision making and problem solving, in *Handbook of industrial and organizational psychology*, ed. M. D. Dunnette, pp. 1397–1453, Chicago: Rand-McNally.

2. This usage is similar to that of Huber, G. P. (1980), *Managerial decision making*, Glenview, Ill.: Scott, Foresman. Maccrimmon and Taylor, Decision making and problem solving, do not differentiate between decision making and problem solving. they note that one may be considered to be a subset of the other depending upon usage.

3. For example, *see* Kepner, C. H. and Tregoe, B. B. (1976), *The rational manager*, 2nd ed., Princeton, N.J.: Kepner-Tregoe.

4. Huber, *Managerial decision making*, pp. 13–15. *Also see* Kepner and Tregoe, *The rational manager*, for a complete discussion of problem formulation.

5. Kepner and Tregoe, *The rational manager*.

6. Kepner and Tregoe, *The rational manager*, p. 76.

7. Simon, H. A. (1957), *Administrative behavior*, 2nd ed., New York: The Free Press.

8. Taggart, W. and Robey, D. (1981), Minds and managers: The dual nature of human information processing and management, *Academy of Management Review* 6:187–195. For a nontechnical explanation of the left-brain, right-brain concept, *see* Mintzberg, H. (1976), Planning on the left side, managing on the right, *Harvard Business Review* July–Aug.:49–58. *Also see* Ornstein, R. E. (1977), *The psychology of consciousness*, 2nd ed., New York: Harcourt, Brace, Jovanovich.

9. Leavitt, H. J. (1975), Beyond the analytic manager, *California Management Review* 17(3):5–12; and (1975) Beyond the analytic manager: Part II, *California Management Review* 17(4):11–21.

10. March, J. G. and Simon, H. A. (1958), *Organizations*, New York: Wiley, pp. 140–141.

11. Mintzberg, H. (1975), The manager's job: Folklore and fact, *Harvard Business Review* 53(4):49–61.

12. Soelberg, P. O. (1967), Unprogrammed decision making, *Industrial Management Review* 8:19–29.

13. Hogarth, R. M. (1980), *Judgment and choice*, New York: Wiley. Also see Ulvila, J. W.; and Brown, R. V.; (1982), Decision Analysis comes of age, *Harvard Business Review* (Sept.-Oct.): 130–141.

14. The title is based on Staw, B. M. (1976), Knee-deep in big muddy: A study of escalating commitment to a chosen course of action, *Organizational Behavior and Human Performance* 16:27–44. Most of the discussion is based on Staw, B. M. (1981), The escalation of commitment to a course of action, *Academy of Management Review* 6:577–87.

15. From Staw, The escalation of commitment to a course of action, p. 577, who based it on Vandiver, K. (1972), Why should my conscience bother me?, in *In the name of profit*, ed. A. Heilbroner, Garden City, N.Y.: Doubleday.

16. This section is based primarily on Maier, N. F. (1967), Assets and liabilities in group problem solving: The need for an integrative function, *Psychological Review* 74:239–249; and on Hill, G. W. (1982), Group versus individual performance: Are N + 1 heads better than one?, *Psychological Bulletin* 91:517–539.

17. *See* Herbert, T. T. and Estes, R. W. (1977), Improving executive decisions by formalizing dissent: The corporate devil's advocate, *Academy of Management Review* 2:662–667.

18. Based on Hill, Group versus individual performance.

19. Hill, Group versus individual performance.

20. For a complete discussion of these issues *see* Locke, E. A. and Schweiger, D. M. (1979), Participation in decision making: One more look, in *Research in organizational behavior*, vol. 1, ed. B. M. Staw, pp. 265–339, Greenwich, Conn.: JAI Press.

21. This discussion is based on Vroom, V. H. and Yetton, P. W. (1973), *Leadership and decision making*, Pittsburg, Pa.: University of Pittsburg Press, p. 12. *Also see* Vroom, V. H. and Jago, A. G. (1978), On the validity of the Vroom-Yetton Model, *Journal of Applied Psychology* 63:151–162.

22. Adapted from a case in Hellriegel, D.; Slocum, J. W., Jr.; and Woodman, R. W. (1983), *Organizational behavior*, 3rd ed., St. Paul, Minn.: West, pp. 415–416.

23. This section based on Hall, J. (1971), Decisions, *Psychology Today* Nov.:51 cf.

24. Osborne, A. F. (1941), *Applied imagination: Principles and procedures for creative thinking*, New York: Scribner's. (There are many later editions of this classic book.)

25. For a review *see* Maccrimmon and Taylor, Decision making and problem solving, p. 1407.

26. Hollman, C. R. and Henrick, H. W. (1972), Adequacy of group decisions as a function of decision-making process, *Academy of Management Journal* 15:175–184.

27. NGT was developed in 1968 by Andre L. Delbecq and Andrew H. Van de Ven; *see* (1971) A group process model for problem identification and program planning, *Journal of Applied Behavioral Science* 7:466–492.

28. Summarized from Delbecq, A. L.; Van de Ven, A. H.; and Gustafson, D. H. (1975), *Group techniques for program planning: A guide to nominal groups and Delphi techniques*, Glenview, Ill.: Scott, Foresman, Chapter 2.

29. *See* Delbecq, et al., *Group techniques for program planning*, Chapter 3, for more complete guidance on running a NGT meeting.

30. For more complete information on how to run Delphi, *see* Delbecq, et al., *Group techniques for program planning*, p. 87.

31. Dalkey, N. C. (1967), *Delphi*, Rand Corporation.

32. Van de Ven, A. H. and Delbecq, A. L. (1974), The effectiveness of nominal, delphi, and interacting-group decision-making processes, *Academy of Management Journal* 17: p.618.

Leadership

PREVIEW

- ■ Why aren't managers always leaders? Learn how leaders and managers differ.

- ■ How good are assessment centers for picking future leaders? Perhaps you will go through the assessment center experience.

- ■ Are taller, smarter, more active people better leaders?

- ■ What makes charismatic leaders?

- ■ What is your leadership style? People-oriented or task-oriented? Find out by filling out a questionnaire.

- ■ What is an impoverished manager? What is a 9,9 manager?

- ■ How can the maturity of subordinates affect leader behavior?

- ■ Should leaders change their style to fit the situation, use "one best style," or find situations that fit their style?

- ■ What are the built-in barriers that make organizational leadership more difficult for women?

Preview Case: The Second Lieutenant

In Search of Leadership
- The nature of leadership
- What is leadership?
- *Perspective:* Leaders Versus Managers: Is There a Difference?
- Approaches to understanding leadership

Traits and Behaviors of Leaders
- Traits of leaders compared with nonleaders
- Traits of effective leaders
- Assessment centers: Using traits and skills to select leaders
- *Perspective:* History of the Assessment Center

Social Exchange and Leadership
- Balancing rewards and benefits of an exchange
- Social exchange and power
- *Perspective:* Charismatic Leadership

Behavior of Leaders
- Ohio State leadership studies
- The Managerial Grid

Situational Approaches to Leadership
- Situational Leadership Theory
- Path-goal theory
- *Perspective:* Match the Leader to the Situation

Leadership: Summarizing What We *Do* Know
- Task-relevant expertise
- Relationship with subordinates
- Decision-making participation
- The influence of the leader
- Motivation to lead
- *Perspective:* Barriers to Female Leadership

Summary
- Chapter review
- For discussion
- Key concepts and terms
- Suggested readings

Cases and Incidents
- Lt. Kern, Revisited
- Lisa Kai

References

PREVIEW CASE: THE SECOND LIEUTENANT

Roy Kern, Second Lieutenant, United States Air Force, sat up straight at his desk and rotated 360 degrees in his government-issue executive chair, his hands firmly grasping the armrest. It was his first morning on the job as Manager of War Readiness Spares at Hunter Air Force Base. He thought to himself, "Well, you finally made it. Now's the time to put all the education to work. It's not every twenty-two year old who has sixteen people working for him; man, that's power. And, it sure is a lot of responsibility. But I know I can do it . . . ."

The telephone interrupted his thoughts. It was his boss, Lt. Col. Rosenberg, an eighteen-year veteran who seemed to know everything. Col. Rosenberg said "Roy, I know today's your first day, but we need to get going on the warehouse beautification program. I just got a call from headquarters alerting us that the Inspector General (IG) will be here next month. I want us to look good so we'll get a good rating. Why don't you talk to your NCO's (noncommissioned officers) and decide what you're going to do."

After Col. Rosenberg hung up Roy considered what to do. "Now's my chance to show the Colonel what I can do. Earlier this morning, when I toured the facilities with the NCOIC (NCO in Charge), Senior Master Sergeant Juanita Rogers, I noticed some good ways to spruce things up. We can paint the floors grey, with bright yellow lines. We can repaint the walls and ceilings from that awful green to a light blue. Boy, will things look better!"

Lt. Kern called a meeting at 11:00 o'clock for all the people who worked for him. Here's what he told them: "I just got the word from Col. Rosenberg that the IG is coming, and we have to get busy on the warehouse beautification program. Our warehouse really looks cruddy, but we can do something about it. I've decided that the best way to beautify it is to paint it. We'll paint the floors, walls, ceilings—the whole works. It will look fantastic. Since we still have to get our normal work done, I've decided that we'll do the painting over the next two weekends. Now, let's get busy and get all the supplies ready."

By the end of the week, things had gone sour for Lt. Kern. First, there had been a complaint lodged against him by a black warehouseman for violating affirmative action rules. Then the base safety officer came by and told him that he could not paint the floors. One airman, who told him he had a prior engagement for the weekend, had gone to the chaplain and complained. To top it all off, Col. Rosenberg had called him in and told him to talk to his NCO's before he did anything. His "troops" now treated him with distaste and loathing.

He said to himself, "I thought I was a leader. Where did I go wrong?"

Where did Lt. Kern go wrong? What could he have done to be a more effective leader? Does he have the right traits, characteristics, and education to be a good leader? Did he behave appropriately? Does the situation demand a different approach to leadership? Many managers in both the public and private sector experience leadership problems. We will attempt to address these problems and their solutions in this chapter.

The plan of the chapter is to cover a number of major concepts of leadership, with the goal of improving our understanding of the leadership process and thus making ourselves better leaders. We will try to understand the nature of leadership. Then we will turn to a discussion of the traits or characteristics that are associated with effective leaders. Next, we will look at the social process of leadership and the behaviors used by effective leaders. Finally, we will look at the influence of situations on leadership and then sum up what we do know about leadership.

In Search of Leadership

Does this title, "In Search of Leadership," seem strange? No topic in organizational behavior has been so thoroughly researched. There seem to be more major theories for leadership than for any other organizational topic. But, in spite of all this theorizing and research, we still have no generally accepted, comprehensive theory of leadership.[1] Thus, we are still in search of leadership.

On the other hand, all this effort has given us some insights. Each theory provides partial answers. When considered as a whole and carefully analyzed for convergence, we find that we do know something of leadership, even though we might wish for more. In this chapter we will sift through the theories to find those aspects of leadership that are useful for managers.

■ The Nature of Leadership

Leaders excite the imagination of almost everyone. Most movie themes involve some type of leader. When we think of organizational leaders, we conger up images of powerful Chief Executive Officers at the top of large corporations, of Generals in the military, of Bishops in the church, and of Senators in politics. Most of us aspire to be leaders. We, like Lt. Kern, want people to follow us, to respect us, to be influenced by us. The following excerpt illustrates our fascination with leadership:[2]

> *Leadership is a subject that has long excited interest among scholars and laymen alike. The term connotes images of powerful, dynamic persons who command victorious armies, direct corporate empires from atop gleaming skyscrapers, or shape the course of nations. Much of our conception of history is the story of military, political, religious, and social leaders. The exploits of brave and clever leaders are the essence of many legends and myths. The widespread fascination with leadership may be because it is such a mysterious process, as well as one that touches everyone's life. Why do certain leaders (Gandhi, Mohammed, Mao Tse-tung) inspire such intense fervor and dedication? How did certain leaders (Julius Caesar, Charlemagne, Alexander the Great) build great empires?*

Why were certain leaders (Winston Churchill, Indira Gandhi, the Shah of Iran) suddenly deposed, despite their apparent power and record of successful accomplishments? How did certain rather undistinguished persons (Adolf Hitler, Claudius Caesar) rise to positions of great power? Why do some leaders have loyal followers who are willing to sacrifice their lives for their leader, and why are some other leaders so despised that their followers conspire to murder them (e.g., as occurred with the "fragging" of some military officers by enlisted men in Vietnam)?

■ What Is Leadership?

Since researchers have had trouble understanding leadership, it is not surprising that it is also difficult to define. Often the definition depends more on the situation or the purpose of research than on some universal truth. It makes a difference whether you are training leaders, identifying them, or finding which behaviors are more or less effective.[3] For our purposes, we will define **leadership** as the process of influencing others toward goals.[4]

The concepts of leadership and power (discussed in Chapter 12) are closely related, since both power and leadership are concerned with the ability to bring about desired goals by influencing others. Leadership might be considered as a special case of power, where we are concerned with the relationship between leader, follower, situation, and the individual characteristics of the people involved.

PERSPECTIVE

14.1 *Leaders Versus Managers: Is There a Difference?*

How do leaders differ from managers? Or do they? Some assert that leaders, at least "great leaders" are quite different from great managers.[5] **Management** is the process of coordinating human and material resources toward objective accomplishment.[6] This definition is usually followed by a description of tasks involving planning, organizing, controlling, and motivating. It seems clear that management involves a lot of things that are not leadership.

But even when tasks are the same, there is speculation that managers may be different from leaders.[7] For example, managers are often impersonal about goals while leaders get quite emotionally involved in their goals. Managers also tend to act rationally to structure activities and limit choices whereas leaders go in the opposite direction by inspiring creativity and developing fresh approaches. Managers tend to work rather impersonally with others—they are good team players. Leaders, in contrast, are more emotionally oriented—people have strong emotional feelings toward them. In the opening example Lt. Kern might be a competent manager, but he failed as a leader.

Does this mean that if you aspire to be a manager, you cannot be a leader? Certainly not. Ideally, you would combine the two roles by striving to be both a strong manager and a strong leader. Throughout the rest of the chapter we will not make a major distinction between managers and leaders. We will assume that one of the goals of a good manager is also to be a good leader. We will also assume that not all leaders are "great leaders," but that all managers of people need to be at least competent leaders.

Understanding Organizational Behavior

Figure 14.1. The Wizard of Id: Some leaders are born.

By permission of Johnny Hart and Field Enterprises, Inc.

■ Approaches to Understanding Leadership

There are four major approaches to understanding leadership: finding out what individual traits and behaviors successful leaders possess, understanding the social exchange process between leaders and followers, observing the behaviors of effective leaders, and analyzing the situations where various types of leadership are successful. We will discuss all four, for each offers a different insight into the leadership process.

Traits and Behaviors of Leaders

Are leaders born? Are certain people predestined to be leaders? Are there certain **traits** (individual characteristics, such as physical or mental characteristics, personality, social background, intellectual ability) and **skills** (learned behaviors, such as social skills, task skills, communication skills) that all successful leaders must have? Several decades of leadership research yielded little or no evidence to support these positions. It appears that while traits are important, the possession or absence of specific traits does not guarantee success or failure as a leader.[8] However, some traits do seem to aid in leadership effectiveness in some situations.

■ Traits of Leaders Compared with Nonleaders

Early research into leadership traits focused on comparing leaders with nonleaders. Low-level relationships were found in many different areas. The research suggested that leaders possessed a number of traits and skills, although the presence of a given trait seemed to vary across situations. Some of these traits and skills are highlighted below:[9]

☐ Intelligence
☐ Alertness to the needs of others
☐ Understanding of the task
☐ Initiative and persistence in dealing with problems
☐ Desire to accept responsibility
☐ Tend to be taller, heavier, and more athletic
☐ Present a good appearance
☐ Ability to speak fluently
☐ Self-confident

Leadership

Table 14.1. Traits and skills associated with successful leaders.[10]

Traits	Skills
Adaptable to situations	Clever (intelligent)
Alert to social environment	Conceptually skilled
Ambitious and achievement-oriented	Creative
Assertive	Diplomatic and tactful
Cooperative	Fluent in speaking
Decisive	Knowledgeable about group task
Dependable	Organized (administrative ability)
Dominant (desire to influence others)	Persuasive
Energetic (high activity level)	Socially skilled
Persistent	
Self-confident	
Tolerant of stress	
Willing to assume responsibility	

Gary A. Yukl, *Leadership in Organizations*, © 1981, p. 70. Reprinted by permission of Prentice-Hall, Inc., Englewood Cliffs, N.J.

If Lt. Kern had possessed all the above traits, do you think he would have been successful? He appears to have most of them except alertness to the needs of others and an understanding of the task. Perhaps these two traits are crucial in this instance. One of the problems with trait research is that we do not know which traits are needed in a given situation. Many leadership traits and skills seem to be related to the ability to perform in a group or to attain group objectives—thus, certain traits will help a leader get things done in the group. But more than just the traits seems necessary; they must form a combination that helps the leader cope with the situation at hand.

■ Traits of Effective Leaders

More recent trait research is being conducted in a different way. Rather than comparing leaders versus nonleaders across a number of situations, we compare effective versus ineffective leaders in the same situation, or we compare the relationship between traits and leadership effectiveness. The results of these studies show stronger, more consistent results than the earlier trait studies.[11] Many of the traits and skills, illustrated in Table 14.1, are similar to those found in the earlier studies.

■ Assessment Centers: Using Traits and Skills to Select Leaders

Assessment Center Design   Much recent research has focused on using traits and skills to select leaders. At the core of this movement is the **assessment center**, a technique that uses a number of traits and skills (behaviors) to assess a person's suitability for being hired or promoted.[12] Assessment centers use a number of methods including objective tests (skills, knowledge, interests), projective tests (to measure motivation or other personality traits), interviews (to probe areas of interest), situational exercises (individual or group activities that call for behaviors similar to those of the position), and peer ratings (how well can the candidate evaluate others). Several assessors judge the performance of each candidate and make an overall selection decision.

Understanding Organizational Behavior

14.2 History of the Assessment Center[13]

The U.S. pioneer of the assessment method was the U.S. Office of Strategic Services [OSS], forerunner of the CIA. On the assumption that it takes dirty men to do dirty work, early in World War II the OSS reportedly tried recruiting some agents directly from the ranks of gangland mobs. When a number of missions were bungled, OSS officials laid part of the blame on their selection procedures. Searching for something better, they turned to the assessment method. First developed in the early 1900s by German psychologists, it had been picked up by the German military high command in the 1930s for use in choosing officers, and then borrowed by the British War Office for the same purpose.

The OSS organized the first U.S. assessment center in 1943, at a secret estate called Station S, about 18 miles from Washington, D.C. The program for that first center was developed principally by Henry Murray, the famous Harvard psychologist. By then, the service had specified somewhat more precisely the personality traits and behavioral skills it thought an effective secret agent needed. To test for them, Murray and his colleagues designed a series of simulated cloak-and-dagger situations. One required prospective spies to assume quickly and use convincingly a false identity or "cover," even under intense interrogation. By war's end, more than 5,000 recruits were processed through Station S, although no one ever really found out for sure whether the method worked.

The assessment method was essentially abandoned as a wartime relic until the mid-1950s, when American Telephone and Telegraph launched its ambitious Management Progress Study of the careers of more than 400 young executives. In order to establish a baseline measure of their abilities, AT&T industrial psychologist Douglas Bray and some colleagues developed a series of management exercises that have survived remarkably well as the core of what goes on at most of today's assessment centers. Bray [later became] director of human resources at AT&T, and under his supervision the company put nearly 200,000 employees through various assessment programs. It currently tests more than 20,000 a year at seventy different centers throughout the Bell system.

From "Measuring executive muscle" by Berkeley Rice. Copyright *Psychology Today*, 1978, 12(7), p. 99.

Do Assessment Centers Work? The assessment center has become extremely popular since its first corporate use at American Telephone and Telegraph (AT&T) in the 1950s.[14] Currently, over 1,000 organizations are using assessment centers and over 200,000 people have participated.[15] Assessment centers are good, long-run predictors of future performance.[16] Thus it seems that many organizations have found a good way to predict managerial success.

One of the top predictors of success in assessment center studies is human relations skill, in terms of the person's ability to lead a group to accomplish a task without arousing hostility (see Table 14.2). Thus, it seems logical that a social-interaction approach might help explain leadership. This is the topic of the next section.

Table 14.2. The most powerful predictors of advancement in AT&T management progress study.[7]

Trait or skill	
1. Oral Communication Skill	How good this person would be in presenting an oral report to a small conference group on a well-known subject.
2. Human Relations Skill	How effectively this person can lead a group to accomplish a task without arousing hostility.
3. Need for Advancement	How much this person wants to be promoted significantly earlier than his or her peers.
4. Resistance to Stress	How well this person's work performance will stand up in the face of personal stress.
5. Tolerance of Uncertainty	How well this person's work performance will stand up under uncertain or unstructured conditions.

From D.W. Bray, R.J. Campbell, and D.L. Grant (1974), Formative years in business: *A long term AT&T study of managerial lives.* Copyright © 1974 by J. Wiley & Sons, New York. Reprinted with permission.

Social Exchange and Leadership

Group interactions and activities are made up of a series of exchanges or transactions between group followers and leaders, called the **social exchange** process.[17] The interactions or exchanges provide rewards for both parties.

■ Balancing Rewards and Benefits of an Exchange

Since the exchange process involves weighing the costs and benefits of a transaction to see if the net result is advantageous, the relative contributions of each party are important. For example, leaders contribute their skills and efforts to help accomplish the group's goal, they coordinate the group's activities, and they reward group members. Followers, on the other hand, provide status, esteem, influence, and loyalty to their leader. If the group is successful, then the leader will maintain influence. If the group fails, it's a different story. If the failure appears to be the leader's fault, the leader will lose influence. If the fault does not seem to lie with the leader, then the leader may maintain influence.

The opening incident might be explained by social exchange theory. Lt. Kern is new. The group does not see the benefits of supporting him when the goal is negative for them, painting the warehouse. Lt. Kern has not contributed to the group's operation and welfare—there is no positive exchange of rewards between him and the group. Thus, the lieutenant is in a poor power position, but he does not recognize it and gets himself into trouble.

■ Social Exchange and Power

A social exchange approach to leadership involves the use of power and influence (discussed in Chapter 12). The leader convinces the follower that some benefit will accrue if the follower behaves as the leader wishes.[18] Because exchange theory is based on trading between parties, both should

14.3 Charismatic Leadership[19]

Charisma is a characteristic that describes leaders who by the force of their personality and abilities (a special source of power) are able to have a profound and extraordinarily strong effects on their followers. The leader and followers almost always share some common value system, ideology, or religion. Inspired, enthusiastic obedience, loyalty, and commitment are characteristics of the followers of charismatic leaders. There is a mysterious, magnetic quality to the relationship between charismatic leaders and followers.

Characteristics of charismatic leaders that distinguish them from noncharismatic leaders are dominance, self-confidence, the need for influence, and a strong conviction of the moral righteousness of their beliefs.[20] Charismatic leaders behave in the following ways:

■ *Role modeling*. The leader "role models" a value system of the followers. Often, they model self-sacrificing behavior. Thus, followers perceive the leader as competent, attractive, and successful.

■ *Image building*. Charismatic leaders actively build their image so they are viewed favorably by others. They prove their extraordinary powers to their followers.

■ *Transcendent goals*. Ideological goals with moral overtones often characterize the charismatic leader. There is a vision of what the future could be.

■ *High expectations*. By showing confidence in subordinates and having high expectations, leaders enhance a follower's self-esteem and solidify their charismatic position.

■ *Motivation*. The charismatic leader is able to arouse the motivation of followers toward accomplishing some mission. They get people involved emotionally.

incur benefits from the exercise of power. If Lt. Kern had shown the warehouse crew how they would benefit from painting (and they believed him), he might have been more successful in exercising leadership and power.

Behavior of Leaders

Another way of understanding leadership is to compare the *behaviors* of effective and ineffective leaders to see how good leaders behave. The implication here is that if we find out what behaviors effective leaders use, then all we have to do is emulate them to be successful ourselves. Before proceeding in this section, you might wish to fill out the Leadership Questionnaire in Table 14.3.

■ Ohio State Leadership Studies

The origin of the behavioral approach to leadership is the Ohio State University research program that began in the late 1940s.[21] The researchers developed a questionnaire, called the Leader Behavior Description Questionnaire (containing questions similar to the ones in Table 14.3), to measure leadership behavior. It includes items on organization, communication, recognition, integration, and coordination. Analysis of the questionnaire responses found two general factors called consideration and initiating structure. **Consideration** includes such items as openness of communication, friendliness, supportiveness, consulting with subordinates, recognition of subordinates. **Initiating structure** includes items

Table 14.3. Leadership questionnaire.[22]

Directions: The following items describe aspects of leadership behavior. Respond to each item according to the way you would if you were the leader of a work group. Circle whether you would most likely behave in the way described: always *(A)*, frequently *(F)*, occasionally *(O)*, seldom *(S)*, or never *(N)*:

A F O S N	1. I allow members complete freedom in their work.
A F O S N	2. I would stress being ahead of competing groups.
A F O S N	3. I would turn members loose on the job and let them go to it.
A F O S N	4. I would decide what should be done and when it should be done.
A F O S N	5. I would be willing to make changes.
A F O S N	6. I would ask the members to work harder.
A F O S N	7. I would trust group members to exercise good judgment.
A F O S N	8. I would schedule the work to be done.
A F O S N	9. I would consult my group before acting.
A F O S N	10. I would urge the group to beat its previous record.

Scoring: Count the number of always (A) or frequently (F) responses for the odd questions (1,3,5,7,9). Multiply this number by two and call it your *P* score; P = _____ . Now count the number of always or frequently for the even questions (2,4,6,8,10), multiply this number by two and call it your *T* score; T = _____ . Save these numbers for later interpretation.

dealing with role clarification, directing, planning, controlling, problem solving, criticizing, efficient use of resources.

You may now want to plot the scores from your responses to the questions in Table 14.3 on the scale provided in Figure 14.2. Note that the *P* score equates roughly with consideration or concern for people and the *T* score corresponds with initiating structure or concern for task.

Figure 14.2.
Consideration-
initiating structure.

Directions: Plot your *P* score on the vertical axis and your *T* score on the horizontal axis.

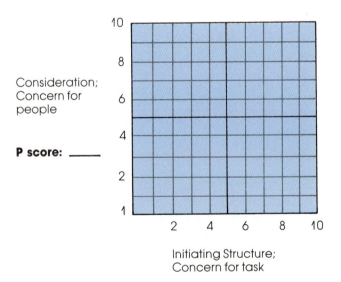

Consideration;
Concern for
people

P score: _____

Initiating Structure;
Concern for task

T score: _____

Understanding Organizational Behavior

Table 14.4. Leader behaviors and situational effects.[23]

■ The greater the pressure (deadlines, goals, controls, etc.), the more tolerance subordinates have for initiating structure.

■ When the task is enriched, consideration is not as important to subordinate's satisfaction, and initiating structure has a less negative effect on satisfaction.

■ When the tasks are routine and specified, there is a stronger relationship between consideration and satisfaction.

■ When subordinates need a lot of information and expertise from the leader, they are more tolerant and satisfied with initiating structure.

Consideration, Initiating Structure and Performance   Generally, leaders who are high on *both* consideration and initiating structure will have more satisfied and productive subordinates[23] than leaders who are low on these dimensions. The desirability of consideration or initiating structure behaviors also varies with the situation.[24] Successful leaders are flexible in their behavior. They can recognize when a given situation calls for a particular behavior. A summary of some situational effects is provided in Table 14.4. Later in the chapter we will discuss theories that consider these situational effects.

In our opening incident, Lt. Kern was probably quite high on initiating structure and relatively low on consideration. His imbalanced behavior caused problems.

■ **The Managerial Grid®**

Closely related to the Ohio State studies is the **Managerial Grid** ® (*see* Fig. 14.3), a widely used training strategy in industry.[26] The grid is based on two factors: concern for production (bottom line, profits, results) and concern for people (friendly, thoughtful, comfortable, people-oriented climate). The "concern for" does not relate directly to the amount of behavior, but to the strength of assumptions behind the leader's style. The two dimensions interact together; they are not independent. Managers are referred to as 9,1; 9,9; 1,9; 1,1. The 9,9 team manager is the ideal, while the 1,1 impoverished manager is to be avoided.

Here are some examples of how a 9,9 or team manager would handle various managerial tasks:[27]

☐ *Planning*: "I get the people who have relevant facts or stakes in the outcome together to review the whole picture. We formulate a sound model from start to completion to provide an organizing framework for integrating an entire project. I get their reactions and ideas. I establish goals and flexible schedules with them."

☐ *Organizing*: "Within the framework of the whole, we determine individual responsibilities, procedures, and ground rules."

☐ *Directing*: "I keep informed of progress and influence subordinates by identifying problems and revising goals *with* them. I lend assistance when needed by helping to remove road blocks."

☐ *Controlling*:"In addition to in-progress critiques to keep projects on schedule, I conduct a wrap-up with those responsible. We evaluate the way things went and see what we can learn from our experience and how

Leadership

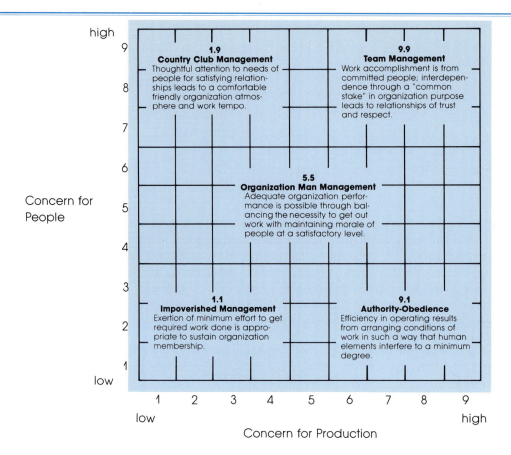

From *The New Managerial Grid®* by Robert R. Blake and Jane Srygley Mouton. Houston: Gulf Publishing Company, Copyright © 1978.
Reproduced by permission.

9,1.   In the lower right-hand corner of the Grid, a maximum concern (9) for production is combined with a minimum concern (1) for people. A manager acting under these assumptions concentrates on maximizing production by exercising power and authority and achieving control over people through compliance. This is a 9,1 orientation.

1,9.   The 1,9 leadership style is in the top left corner. Here a minimum concern (1) for production is coupled with a maximum concern (9) for people. Primary attention is placed on promoting good feelings among colleagues and subordinates.

1,1.   A minimum concern for both production and people is represented by 1,1 in the lower left corner. The 1,1-oriented manager does only the minimum required to remain within the organization.

5,5.   5,5 is in the center. This is the "middle of the road" theory or the "to-go-along-to-get-along" assumptions which are revealed in conformity to the status quo.

9,9.   Production and people concerns are integrated at a high level in the upper right-hand corner representing the 9,9 style of managing. This is the team approach. It is goal-oriented and seeks to gain results of high quantity and quality through participation, involvement, commitment, and conflict-solving.

Figure 14.3. The Managerial Grid®.

Understanding Organizational Behavior

we can apply our learning in the future. I give recognition on a team basis as well as for outstanding individual contributions."

☐ *Staffing*: "Work requirements are matched with personnel capabilities or needs for development in making decisions as to who does what."

The Managerial Grid offers a relatively simple way to view leadership that is intuitively appealing. It offers the "one, most effective style" approach to leadership, the 9,9 style.[28] In the next section we will add to the behavioral approach's power by examining how situational approaches to leadership can add to our understanding of leadership process.

Situational Approaches to Leadership

So far we have seen that certain behaviors and traits seem to relate to leadership or managerial effectiveness, but that none of these approaches presents a comprehensive picture of leadership. A **situational** approach seeks to remedy this problem by identifying situations or conditions where a particular leadership behavior or style is more effective.

We will cover two major situational approaches to leadership, the Situational Leadership theory and the path-goal theory. Another theory that has been widely researched is the Contingency Model,[29] which combines the attitudes of the leader with the situation in terms of leader-member relations, position power, and task structure to explain the effectiveness of various leaders. While space limitations prevent us from a full discussion of this rather complex model, the Perspective: Match the Leader to the Situation, addresses some of the implications of the theory.

■ Situational Leadership Theory

One of the most popular of all leadership theories is **Situational Leadership** developed by Hersey and Blanchard.[30]

Situational Leadership and the Ohio State Studies
Situational Leadership starts with the Ohio State leadership studies, which we discussed earlier in this chapter. Leader behaviors involve a combination of task and relationship behaviors (similar to the initiating structure and consideration or task and people shown in Fig. 14.2). Leadership style is the behavior pattern (high task, low relationship; high relationship, low task) that someone uses when attempting to influence the activities of others.[31] Leadership style and behavior are evaluated by the leader's followers, superiors, or colleagues—not by the leader. As we saw in Chapter 4, people's perceptions of themselves are often inaccurate reflections of their true behavior.

The key difference between Situational Leadership and the Ohio State studies and the Managerial Grid is that no single style of leadership, such as 9,9, is seen as effective, but that the effectiveness of leadership will depend upon the situation or environment. For example, in a fire department the appropriate style in an emergency would be high task, low relationship. The time pressures do not permit discussions and attention to member feelings. However, once the crisis is over, a different style will probably be appropriate.

The Situational Key: Maturity of Followers   While many environmental or situational issues are important, Situational Leadership focuses on the relationship between the leader's behavior and the maturity of the followers. Two types of maturity are seen as particularly important: job maturity and psychological maturity.[32]

Job maturity includes the extent and relevance of past job experience, job knowledge, and the degree of understanding of the job's requirements. For example, a machinist or forklift driver who has been on the job for many years and is thoroughly competent in all aspects of the job would be rated high on job maturity.

Psychological maturity involves the willingness or motivation to do something. Psychologically mature people are eager to accept responsibility, have a strong desire to achieve, and high commitment to their jobs. They have a positive self-concept and feel good about themselves and their jobs. An example might be a scientist who works independently and feels a strong internal sense of responsibility toward the task.

Subordinate Maturity and Leader Behavior   Depending upon the maturity level of subordinates, the leader will have to behave differently. For example in a situation where the followers have low maturity, such as a newly formed crew of manual workers who are generally not motivated and alienated from their jobs, the appropriate style is high task, low relationship (*see* Fig. 14.4). In our opening incident, Lt. Kern's followers probably had a high degree of task maturity and a moderate degree of psychological maturity. Thus, the best leadership style would have been high relationship and moderate to low task.

Situational Leadership and Decision Making   One important form of leader behavior, discussed in Chapter 13, was the degree of subordinate involvement in the decision-making process. Leaders can *delegate*, or allow subordinates to make the decision; they can use *participation*, or

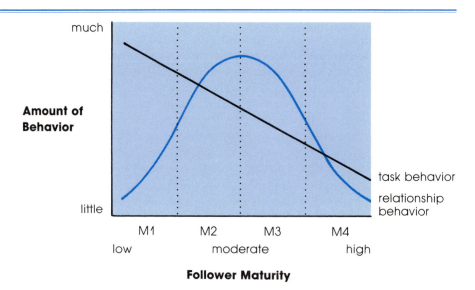

Figure 14.4.
Behavior prescriptions of Situational Leadership.

Gary A. Yukl, *Leadership in Organizations*, © 1981, p. 142. Reprinted by permission of Prentice-Hall, Inc., Englewood Cliffs, N.J.

Understanding Organizational Behavior

joint decision making; they can *sell* their decisions to subordinates even though the decision has already been made; or they can be completely autocratic, make the decision, and *tell* the subordinate what to do.[33] These four decision-making styles—delegating, participating, selling, and telling—are related to situational leadership in Figure 14.5.

Evaluating Situational Leadership   The theory makes several important contributions.[34] It focuses attention on the need for behavioral

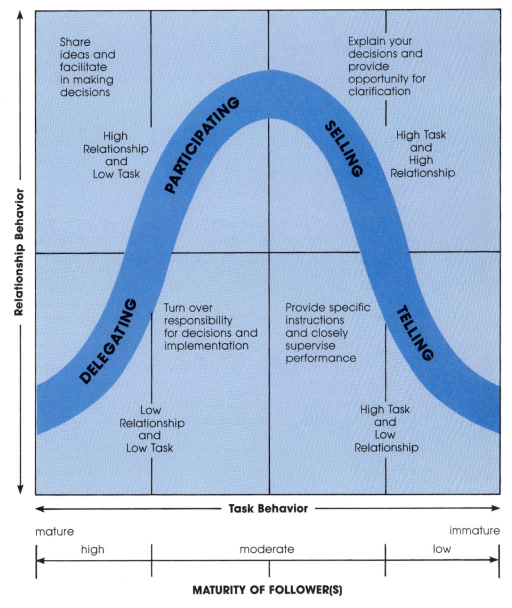

Figure 14.5. Situational Leadership and decision making.

Adapted from Paul Hersey, Kenneth H. Blanchard, *Management of Organizational Behavior: Utilizing Human Resources,* 4th ed., © 1982, p. 152 used by permission of Prentice-Hall, Inc., Englewood Cliffs, N.J. and the authors.

flexibility in different situations. It also recognizes the subordinate as the most important situational factor—we must treat subordinates differently depending on their abilities and motivation. In addition, the implication is that people may be trained and motivated so that the leadership style may evolve over time from one style to another. The final positive for the model is its relative simplicity and clear link with real, practical, everyday organizational leadership problems.

On the negative side, the theory probably ignores other important situational factors, such as the position power of the leader. In addition, there is relatively little validation research to support the theory.[35]

■ Path-Goal Theory

Path-goal theory is concerned with how leaders influence subordinates' perceptions of their work goals and the paths for attaining those goals.[36] Effective leaders help their followers achieve their goals. Examples of goals might include more pay, a promotion, a transfer to a better job, or more free time away from work.

Path-goal theory is based on the expectancy theory of motivation discussed in Chapter 5. Leaders have influence over the subordinate's ability to reach goals, the rewards associated with reaching goals, and the importance of the goals.

Leader Behaviors   There are four categories of leadership behavior: supportive, directive, participative, and achievement-oriented.[37] The first three are similar to the ones we have already discussed. **Supportive** is similar to people-oriented; **directive** is similar to task-oriented; and **participative** means that subordinates are consulted about decisions. The fourth category, **achievement-oriented** leadership, means setting challenging goals for subordinates, showing confidence in them, and continuously seeking improvement in the performance of subordinates. Whether or not each of these behaviors will be effective depends on the situation.

Situational Factors   Two major groups of situational factors are considered:[38]

☐ *Subordinate characteristics*, which are similar to those used in the Situational Leadership theory, are needs (for achievement, power, affiliation, and autonomy), the ability to do the job (skills, knowledge, and ability), and a person's personality traits (self-esteem, locus of control, authoritarianism). These personal characteristics of subordinates determine how well they will respond to various leadership behaviors. For example, someone who is high in need for achievement would work best for an achievement-oriented leader; while someone who is low in need for achievement would do best under a directive leader.

☐ *Environmental pressures* are concerned with any force in the environment with which the subordinate must cope to get the job done. Three major aspects of the environment are the task (*see* Chapter 7), the formal authority system system (*see* Chapters 12 and 15) and the workgroup dynamics (*see* Chapter 9). For example, when the task is clear, people need less supervision and participative or supportive behavior is indicated. On the other hand, if tasks are ambiguous, directive leadership may be more appropriate.

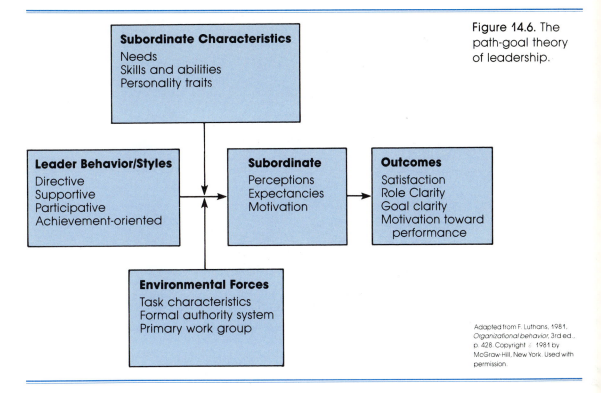

Adapted from F. Luthans, 1981, *Organizational behavior*, 3rd ed., p. 428. Copyright © 1981 by McGraw-Hill, New York. Used with permission.

Figure 14.6. The path-goal theory of leadership.

Since the situational factors are more numerous and complex than the Situational Leadership theory, more factors must be balanced, compared, and judged before a prescription can be made. The model in Figure 14.6 shows how the factors fit together in the full path-goal model.

Evaluating Path-Goal Theory   Little evidence has been accumulated on the path-goal theory. There are many variables involved, and it is difficult to simultaneously test the model. Most research to date has involved partial tests of the model, such as the effects of task structure.[39] Another issue is that the leader's role is a relatively passive one of providing guidance, assistance, coaching. This role is certainly an important one, but there seem to be many leaders who are much more active and are still quite effective. The path-goal theory, while interesting and promising, needs much more research.

Leadership: Summarizing What We *Do* Know

By now you have been exposed to a sample of the bewildering array of leadership theories. Rather than examining the weaknesses of leadership theories—and there are many—let's summarize what we do know about leadership.[40]

■ Task-Relevant Expertise

The leader's expertise in matters that are important to the group gives an important source of power. It is difficult for a leader who does not know what is going on to have influence. Leaders need skills in group process and in the technical aspects of the task. Effective leaders are able to organize and

Leadership

14.4 Match the Leader to the Situation [41]

Another situational model, developed by Fred Fiedler, takes a different approach from the ones we have discussed. Instead of leaders adjusting their behavior to fit the situation, leaders are considered to be relatively unchangeable and either must be assigned to a situation that matches their leadership style or the job must be redesigned to fit their style. Either case is called the *Leader Match* approach.

Leader Match involves identifying a prospective leader's style, finding out what situations exist in the organization, and assigning the prospective leader to an optimal leadership environment that matches his or her style. The assumption is that you need a match between the leader and the job since leadership style is relatively unchangeable. Thus, if the style does not match the situation, the leader must engineer the job to fit or find a situation more favorable to his or her leadership style.

Which is correct? Should jobs and leaders be matched or should leaders change their style to fit the situation? Most theorists seem to prefer the latter approach, but there is still controversy surrounding the issue. [42]

structure group activities; they plan, coordinate, clarify, set goals, train, summarize, and solve problems. In short, an effective leader needs to understand the group's processes and the technical aspects relating to the group's task.

■ Relationship with Subordinates

Many theories point out the importance of a leader's ability to get along with people, and particularly with subordinates. Most effective leaders treat subordinates fairly and are concerned for their needs; leaders are considerate. Feelings of trust and mutual loyalty and increased subordinate satisfaction result. However, while some level of concern is always needed, some situations may call for leaders who emphasize the task much more than emphasizing people.

■ Decision-Making Participation

While we covered participation in decision making in Chapter 13, it is also an important leadership factor. Subordinate commitment to both the decision and the leader improve when participation is used. Effective leaders use a variety of task and maintenance roles (discussed in the chapter on group dynamics) to aid in the decision-making process.

■ The Influence of the Leader

An effective leader has "clout" in all organizational directions. The leader has the ability to get things done and to influence superiors and peers to help the group. In other words, the effective leader is powerful and is thus an effective link with the world outside the group.

14.5 Barriers to Female Leadership[43]

Do women make poor leaders? Are effective female leaders more masculine? Many might answer *yes* to these myths. While more women are reaching leadership positions, there are some serious barriers to female leadership. Jean Lipman-Blumen reviewed the issue of female and male leadership in mixed-sex groups and found that:

1. "Men talk more than women." Apparently, "women, in the company of men, often feel inhibited about talking." Other leadership research shows that "those group members who are most active—including verbally active—are most likely to be perceived as leaders by other group members."
2. "Men's opinions are more likely than women's to influence the opinions of both male and female group members . . . . The resistance women encounter when offering their analyses of problems presents a serious obstacle to female leadership."
3. "Males are more task-oriented, while females are more socio-emotionally oriented."

Her research analysis concludes:[44]

Despite the many areas of conflict among the research results to date, some useful insights still may be gained from juxtaposing certain findings that have emerged:

If, in mixed-sex situations (as in day-to-day organizational life), the more active members are seen as leaders:

men are given more opportunities to talk and act; men actually do talk more than women;

men's opinions are more likely to influence the group positively and women's opinions are more likely to evoke negative or resistant reactions;

male subordinates are more likely than female subordinates to express dissatisfaction with their leader, regardless of the leader's sex; and

the most important informal groups consist of men,

then the current structure of organizations serves as a serious barrier to the acceptance of female leadership.

■ Motivation to Lead

Leaders want to lead. They enjoy the power and achievement that comes from leading. Trait research and assessment centers have shown that the desire for power and advancement are important predictors of leadership success.

SUMMARY

Chapter Review

■ While there is no single, generally accepted theory of leadership, most of us are excited by the topic and wish we could be better leaders. Leadership involves influence and is thus closely identified with power.

■ Many people believe that **management**, a term that deals with coordinating human and material resources toward goal accomplishment, is somewhat different from leadership because leaders have a more personal, emotional orientation toward their goals. An ideal manager might also be a good leader.

■ Early leadership studies, which concentrated on comparing leaders and nonleaders on a series of **traits** and behaviors, led to few consistent conclusions. Later research on traits of effective leaders has been more fruitful. Most leadership traits, such as understanding the task and desire to accept responsibility, seem to be related to getting the group's task done. **Assessment centers** have been quite successful in predicting managerial success based on a combination of traits and behaviors.

■ You can look at leadership as a process of social exchange between the leader and followers with rewards for both. Power may also be a major part of the social exchange. **Charismatic leaders** have an extraordinarily strong social power over their followers.

■ The **Ohio State leadership studies**, which focused on studying effective leader behaviors, concluded that the two most important factors are **consideration** and **initiating structure**. An outgrowth of these studies is the popular **Managerial Grid**®, which plots leader behavior on two dimensions of a grid: **concern for production** and **concern for people**. This results in various blends of behavior, such as the 1,9 country club manager; the 9,1 authority-obedience manager; the 1,1 impoverished manager; or the 9,9 team manager. This approach says there is "one, best way of leading"—the 9,9 way.

■ One of the most popular leadership theories, **Situational Leadership**, takes the dual dimensions of the Ohio State and Grid approaches and combines them with the situations, which is defined in terms of subordinate **maturity**. Thus, the best leadership style varies depending upon differences in subordinate's job maturity (ability) and psychological maturity (willingness).

■ **Path-goal theory**, a relatively new model, revolves around the leader's influence over a subordinate's goal accomplishment based on expectancy theory concepts. To succeed, a leader should vary style according to both subordinate characteristics (needs, abilities, personality) and environmental pressures (task, group dynamics, authority).

■ **Leader match** runs counter to the other situational models. It specifies that leaders should be matched to situations or that situations should be redesigned to fit the leader.

■ Effective leaders are concerned with the task and the needs of their subordinates. They use participative decision making when it is warranted, and they are motivated to seek power and leadership positions.

■ There are several barriers to successful female leadership including the tendency of women to talk less and to be more socio-emotionally oriented. In addition, men's opinions are more valued in problem-solving situations.

For Discussion

1. The Perspective: Leaders Versus Managers: Is There a Difference? points out a number of differences between managers and leaders. Do you agree with these differences? Support your postion.

2. What traits or skills seem to be associated with effective leaders? How powerful are these traits or skills?
3. How is power related to the social exchange approach to leadership?
4. Compare and contrast the Managerial Grid® with Situational Leadership. Which do you think more accurately portrays effective leader behavior?
5. What other variables besides follower maturity do you think are important for explaining leader behavior?
6. Explain how the path-goal theory of leadership works. What are its major weaknesses?
7. Which approach to leadership do you support—matching leaders to situations or training leaders to change their leadership styles for different situations? Defend your position.
8. Summarize what we do know about leadership by listing those behaviors and traits that you think are important for a leader to possess.
9. Based upon your personal experience, do you agree with the barriers to female leadership highlighted in the Perspective: Barriers to Female Leadership?

Key Concepts and Terms

leadership
traits
skills
assessment center
social-exchange process
charismatic leadership
Ohio State leadership studies
consideration
initiating structure

Managerial Grid®
Situational Leadership theory
path-goal theory
supportive leadership
directive leadership
participative leadership
achievement-oriented
   leadership
leader-match

Suggested Readings

Campbell, D. (1980). *If I'm in charge here, why is everybody laughing?* Allen, Texas: Argus Communications.

Davis, K. E. (1982). The status of black leadership: Implications for black followers in the 1980s. *Journal of Applied Behavioral Science* 18:309–322.

Martin, P. Y.; Harrison, D.; and Dinitto, D. (1983). Advancement of women in hierarchical organizations: A multilevel analysis of problems and prospects. *Journal of Applied Behavioral Science* 19:19–33.

Zaleznik, A. (1977). Managers and leaders: Are they different? *Harvard Business Review* 55(3):67–78.

Zierden, W. E. (1980). Leading through the follower's point of view. *Organizational Dynamics* 8(4):27–46.

CASES AND INCIDENTS

Lt. Kern: Revisited

Discussion questions

1. Review the opening case, "The Second Lieutenant," and apply each of the approaches to motivation (trait, social exchange, behavioral, and situational) to explaining how and why the lieutenant went wrong.

2. How could Lt. Kern have behaved so as to be a more effective leader?

3. What assumptions would you make about Lt. Kern's followers and his environment? How would these affect your decision if they were wrong?

Lisa Kai

Lisa had waited a long time for the promotion. She had just been promoted to supervisor of the New Investments Division. Although this was her first supervisory job, Lisa thought she would do well—she had the experience, education, and motivation to be a topnotch supervisor. Since she had studied organizational behavior, she knew that two problems women leaders faced were talking too little and being too concerned with people. She resolved not to make these mistakes.

Lisa told her group of seven financial technicians and three clerks that her job was to reorganize the division and make sure there were no bad investments. She said that, contrary to the policies of the previous supervisor, she would carefully and thoroughly review every recommended investment. At staff meetings, Lisa made sure that she dominated the interactions.

Five weeks after she took over, a group of three technicians cornered her after the staff meeting and told her that if she did not change her style, they were going to go to her boss and complain. They said the others felt that way, too. They had heard that in the last department, she had been very congenial to work with, but now she had turned "bitchy" and overbearing, and did not trust anyone. They just could not take any more.

Discussion questions

1. What should Lisa do now?

2. What might have been a more effective leadership style?

3. What leadership theory or theories best explains what is happening here and why?

4. Would the subordinates have acted differently if Lisa had been male?

REFERENCES

1. Yukl, G. A. (1981), *Leadership in organizations*, Englewood Cliffs, N. J.: Prentice-Hall; Bass, B. M. (1981), *Stogdill's handbook of leadership: A survey of theory and research*, New York: The Free Press; and Miner, J. B. (1982), The uncertain future of the leadership concept: Revisions and clarifications. *Journal of Applied Behavioral Science* 18:293–307.

2. Gary A. Yukl, *Leadership in organizations*, © 1981, p. 1. Reprinted by permission of Prentice-Hall, Inc., Englewood Cliffs, N.J.

3. *See* Bass, *Stogdill's Handbook of Leadership*; and Karmel, B. (1978), A challenge to traditional research methods and assumptions, *Academy of Management Review* 3:475–482.

4. This definition is similar to the one used in Barrow, J. C. (1977), The variables of leadership: A review and conceptual framework, *Academy of Management Review* 2:232–251.

5. Zaleznik, A. (1977), Managers and leaders: Are they different? *Harvard Business Review* 55(3):67–78.

6. Kast, F. E. and Rosenzweig, J. E. (1979), *Organization and management: A systems and contingency approach*, 3rd ed., New York: McGraw-Hill, p. 7.

7. Zaleznik, Managers and leaders.

8. Yukl, *Leadership in organizations*.

9. Stogdill, R. M. (1974), *Handbook of leadership*, New York: The Free Press, p. 63.

10. Yukl, *Leadership in organizations*, p. 70. *Also see* Campbell, J. P.; Dunnette, M. D.; Lawler, E. E., III; and Weick, K. E., Jr. (1970), *Managerial behavior, performance and effectiveness*, New York: McGraw-Hill.

11. Stogdill, *Handbook of leadership*.

12. Finkle, R. B. (1976), Managerial assessment centers. *Handbook of industrial and organizational psychology*, ed. M. D. Dunnette, pp. 861–888, Chicago: Rand-McNally.

13. Rice, B. (1978), Measuring executive muscle, *Psychology Today* 12(7):p.99.

14. Bray, D. W.; Campbell, R. J.; and Grant, D. L. (1974), *Formative years in business: A long-term AT&T study of managerial lives*, New York: Wiley.

15. Cascio, W. F. and Sibey, V. (1979), Utility of the assessment center as a selection device, *Journal of Applied Psychology* 64:107–118.

16. Results based on Cascio and Sibey, Utility of the assessment center as a selection device.

17. Exchange theory was developed by Homans, G. C. (1958), Social behavior as exchange, *American Journal of Sociology* 63:597–606. For the use of exchange theory in leadership, this section relys upon Jacobs, T. O. (1971), *Leadership and exchange in formal organizations*, Alexandria, Va.: Human Resources Research Organization.

18. Jacobs, *Leadership and exchange in formal organizations*, p. 339.

19. Based on House, R. J. (1977), A 1976 theory of charismatic leadership, in eds. J. G. Hunt and L. L. Larson, pp. 189–207, *Leadership: The cutting edge*, Carbondale, Ill.: Southern Illinois University Press.

20. House, A 1976 theory of charismatic leadership, pp. 193–194.

21. Stogdill, *Handbook of leadership*.

22. Abridged and adapted from the T-P Leadership Questionnaire: Seigiovanni, T. J.; Metzcus, R.; and Burden, L. (1969), Toward a pluralistic approach to leadership style, *American Educational Research Journal*, pp. 62–79.

23. *See* Kerr, S. and Schriesheim, S. (1973), Consideration, initiating structure and organizational criteria—An update of Korman's 1966 review, *Personnel Psychology* 27:555–568; and Bass, *Stogdill's handbook of leadership*, p. 592.

24. Kerr, S.; Schriesheim, C. A.; Murphy, C. J.; and Stogdill, R. M.; (1974), Toward a contingency theory of leadership based on the consideration and initiating structure literature, *Organizational Behavior and Human Performance* 12:62–84.

25. Managerial Grid ®, is the registered trademark of Blake, R. R. and Mouton, J. S. *See* their book, (1978), *The new Managerial Grid®*, Houston: Gulf. For a recent discussion of the Grid and a comparison with the Situational Leadership theory, *see* their article, (1982). A comparative analysis of situationalism and 9,9 management by principle, *Organizational Dynamics* 10(4):20–43.

26. From Robert R. Blake and Jane Srygley Mouton, *The New Managerial Grid®*. Copyright © 1978 by Gulf Publishing Company, Houston. Reproduced by permission.

27. This partial list is adapted from Kerr, et al., Toward a contingency theory of leadership, pp. 73–74.

28. Blake and Mouton, *The new Managerial Grid*.

29. Fiedler, F. E. (1967), *A theory of leadership effectiveness*, New York: McGraw-Hill; and Fiedler, F. E. and Chemers, M. M. (1974), *Leadership and effective management*, Glenview, Ill.: Scott, Foresman.

30. Hersey, P. and Blanchard, K. H. (1982), *Management of organizational behavior: Utilizing human resources*, 4th ed., Englewood Cliffs, N.J.: Prentice-Hall.

31. Hersey and Blanchard, *Management of organizational behavior*, pp. 95–96.

32. Hersey and Blanchard, *Management of organizational behavior*, p. 159.

33. *See* Tannenbaum, R. and Schmidt, W. H. (1958), How to choose a leadership pattern, *Harvard Business Review* Mar.–Apr. *Also see* the discussion of Vroom and Yetton's model of decision making discussed in Chapter 13.

34. This critique is based on Graeff, C. L. (1983), The Situational Leadership theory: A critical view, *Academy of Management Review* 8:285–291; and Yukl, *Leadership in organizations*.

35. For a recent study supporting Situational Leadership theory, *see* Hambelton, R. K. and Gumpert, R. (1982), The validity of Hersey and Blanchard's theory of leader effectiveness, *Group and Organizational Studies* 7(2):225–242. *Also see* Blake, R. R. and Mouton, J. S. (1981), Management by Grid principles or situationalism: Which?, *Group and Organizational Studies* 6:439–455; and Hersey, P. and Blanchard, K. H. (1982), Grid principles and situationalism: Both! A response to Blake and Mouton, *Group and Organizational Studies* 7:207–210.

36. House, R. J. (1971), A path-goal theory of leader effectiveness, *Administrative Science Quarterly* 16:321–39. Actually, the first path-gaol theory, a noncontingency version, was developed by Evans, M. G. (1970), The effects of supervisory behavior on the path-goal relationship, *Organizational Behavior and Human Performance* 5:177–298.

37. House, R. J. and Mitchell, T. R. (1974), Path-goal theory of leadership, *Journal of Contemporary Business* Autumn:81–89.

38. Based on House and Mitchell, Path-goal theory of leadership; Yukl, *Leadership in organizations*.

39. Fulk, J. and Wendler, E. (1982), Dimensionality of leader-subordinate interactions: A path-goal approach, *Organizational Behavior and Human Performance* 30:241–64; and Schriesheim, C. A. and DeNisi, A. S. (1979), Task dimensions as moderators of the effects of instrumental leader behavior: A path-goal approach, *Academy of Management Proceedings*, pp. 103–106.

40. Yukl, *Leadership in organizations.*

41. Fiedler, F. E.; Chemers, M. M.; and Mahar, L. (1976), *Improving leadership effectiveness: The leader match*, New York: Wiley. *Also see* Fiedler, F. E. (1965), Engineer the job to fit the manager, *Harvard Business Review* 43:118.

42. For a recent review of Fiedler's theory, *see* Strube, M. J. and Garcia, J. E. (1981), A meta-analytic investigation of Fiedler's contingency model of leadership, *Psychological Bulletin* 90:307–21. Arguments against the leader-match concept are presented in the book review of *Improving leadership effectiveness*, written by Hosking, D. and Schriesheim, C. (1978), *Administrative Science Quarterly* 23:496–505.

43. From Lipman-Blumen, J. (1980), Female leadership in formal organizations: Must the female leader go formal?, in *Readings in managerial psychology*, 3rd ed., ed. H. J. Leavitt, L. R. Pondy, and D. M. Boje, pp. 341–62, University of Chicago Press. For another view *see* Donnell, S. M. and Hall, J (1980), Men and women as managers: A significant case of no significant differences, *Organizational Dynamics* 8:60–77.

44. Lipman-Blumen, Female leadership in formal organizations, p. 344.

The Total Organization

Organizational Design and Behavior

PREVIEW

- How do you design an effective organization?

- Why should the manager ask the questions: "What is our business?" and "Who is our customer?"

- When is it better for a manager to supervise a large number of people?

- What is a tall or a flat organization? How might this structure affect you when you join an organization?

- Why is decentralization used by so many large corporations? What are the benefits?

- Are bureaucratic organizations to be avoided?

- When might you purposely structure an organization so that people have two bosses?

- Can organizations be structured to help women succeed?

Preview Case: Peak One Advertising Agency

Organizational Purpose and Objectives
- Organizational purpose
- Organizational objectives
- Purpose, objectives, and structure

Designing the Organizational Structure
- Vertical division of labor
- Span of management
- Line and staff
- Horizontal division of labor and departmentation
- *Perspective:* The Informal Organization
- Centralization and decentralization
- *Perspective:* Decentralization of General Motors
- Coordination and integration

The Organization's Environment
- Environmental uncertainty
- Technology
- Customers
- Suppliers
- Competitors
- Political-social environment
- Economic environment
- Environment and structure
- *Perspective:* Structure to Encourage Managerial Progression of Women

Types of Organizational Structures
- Bureaucratic organizations
- Functional organizations
- Product organizations
- Hybrid organizations
- Matrix organizations

Organizational Structure: Some Summary Conclusions

Summary
- Chapter review
- For discussion
- Key concepts and terms
- Suggested readings

Cases and Incidents
- Advanced Aerospace Research Laboratory
- Peak One Advertising Reorganization

References

PREVIEW CASE: PEAK ONE ADVERTISING AGENCY[1]

Adam O'Brien, President of Peak One, pondered the report in front of him from Reorganization Consultants, Inc. He thought, "Perhaps a reorganization is just what we need to put new vitality into Peak One. We're really hurting now that two of our largest clients have moved to other agencies. There must be something wrong to cause clients to leave. The consultant's recommendation will certainly tighten things up and clarify responsibilities."

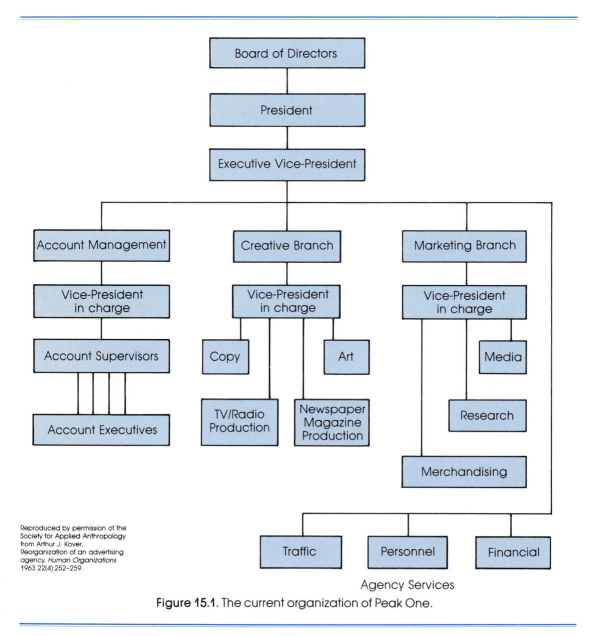

Reproduced by permission of the Society for Applied Anthropology from Arthur J. Kover, Reorganization of an advertising agency, *Human Organizations* 1963 22(4):252–259.

Figure 15.1. The current organization of Peak One.

Understanding Organizational Behavior

Adam turned to the pages marked "current organization." The organizational chart (Fig. 15.1) was the one Peak One had used for the last five years since Adam arrived. He was intimately familiar with it.

The next page gave the consultant's summary of the problems with the organization, which he already knew quite well:

1. Communication between specialists is poor.
2. Conflict exists between different account managers who compete for the specialists' time.
3. Coordination takes too much effort and energy.
4. Some clients do not get the effort they deserve and are more likely to move to another agency.

Adam then turned to the pages marked "proposed organization for Peak One." He liked what he saw (Fig. 15.2).

The Creative Branch and the Marketing Branch would be reorganized into a number of composite creative groups and marketing groups, each with a set of specialists in each area. These composite groups would work on just a few clients. The consultants listed the benefits as:

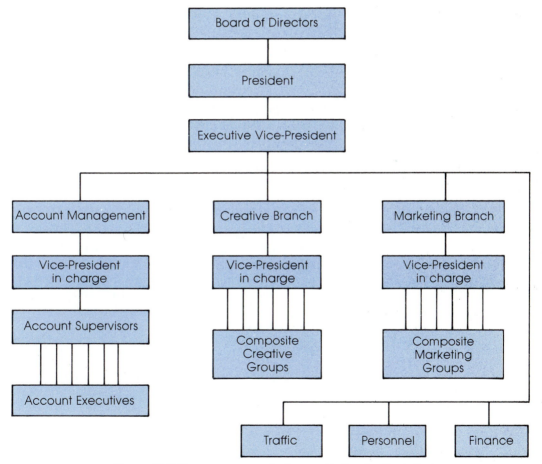

Figure 15.2. The recommended organization for Peak One.

1. More tightly integrated client service.
2. Clearer lines of responsibility.
3. Less shifting of people between clients.
4. Better coordination.
5. Faster service for clients.

The consultant's conclusion: "The net effect of the reorganization will be to create a number of small, semiautonomous agencies under the umbrella of Peak One with significantly improved responsiveness to clients and increased organizational effectiveness."

One year later. Adam sat in his office and stared at the New York City skyline. He turned to his executive vice-president, Mary McCulley, and said "Mary, this reorganization just hasn't worked out as well as we thought it would."

She replied, "I certainly agree. We have a lot better control of communications between the staff and clients, but professional communications has declined sharply and communication between members of different composite groups is almost nil. I'm afraid the result has been less challenging jobs and more feeling on the part of our people that they are being controlled. Some of our best creative people are moving to other agencies."

Adam nodded his head in agreement and continued, "The other day, I was talking to Milo Greco, our top market researcher, who said, 'Mr. O'Brien, it's getting mighty lonely since we reorganized and I moved out of the Research department. There's nobody to talk to about research. Before the reorganization, we used to talk over all sorts of things, and each one of us could learn from what the other was doing. Now I don't get a chance to talk to other professional researchers; all we talk about is sales. If we don't go back to the old way, I may have to start looking for another job.' "

Mary turned to Adam and said, "Well, shall we bite the bullet and go back to the old organization? While it had its problems, it may be the lesser of two evils."

Adam O'Brien, President of Peak One, made a rational decision to reorganize, but there were side-effects on people that produced unexpected and unintended results. In this chapter, we learn some of the basics of organizational design and some of the impacts of these designs on behavior. We will also cover the environment within which organizations must work since it can have profound impacts on the organization and its people.

Designing organizations involves many factors other than organizational structure including a number of the topics we have already covered (designing jobs and motivation systems, communication and leadership processes, group dynamics, and decision making). The systems model discussed in Chapter 1 is particularly apropos for understanding structure since the structural subsystem interacts strongly with all the other subsystems and the environment (*see* Fig. 15.3). This chapter provides a basic introduction to organizational design concepts including defining the organizational purpose and goals, principles of organizational design, types of designs, and environmental impacts on design.[2]

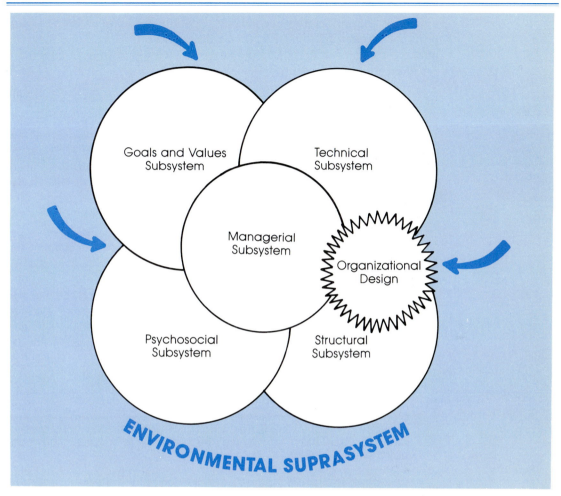

Figure 15.3. The systems perspective and organizational design.[3]

Organizational Purpose and Objectives

Organizational purpose and objectives are the overall guidelines that give meaning and direction for organizing; they provide the web that holds the organization together. Recent critiques of American management have highlighted problems in this area, especially when compared with Japanese firms.[4]

■ Organizational Purpose

The **organizational purpose** is the fundamental reason for existence of the organization. Peter Drucker, the famous management writer and consultant, points out that two crucial questions must be asked before we can understand the purpose of an organization.[5]

The first is: "What is our business and what should it be?" The answer is seldom as obvious as it seems. For example, American Telephone and Telegraph Company (AT&T) determined early in its history (between 1905 and 1915) that "Our business is service." They knew that for a regulated monopoly to survive, they needed public goodwill. However, in 1984 it appears the answer was different. AT&T divested itself from all the Bell telephone companies so that they could expand into applications of communications technology.

The second basic question is: "Who is the customer?" The answer to this question will have strong influence over objectives and goals. There may be many answers to the question with each deserving separate emphasis. For example, Boeing Aircraft Corporation sells to commercial airline companies, foreign governments, and the defense department. These three customers require different approaches and perhaps different organizational structures. This was certainly one of the issues facing Peak One in our opening case.

■ Organizational Objectives

Once the basic purpose of the organization has been determined, the next step is to translate it into objectives. An **objective** is a broad statement of a desired future condition that provides direction. An example might be "to achieve sufficient profit to finance growth and provide a reasonable rate of return to our stockholders." Although the terms *objective* and *goal* are often used interchangeably, we will define **goals** more narrowly as specific, measurable targets that we are trying to reach within a given time. For ex-

---

Table 15.1. An example of corporate objectives: Hewlett-Packard Company.

Profit	*Objective*: To achieve sufficient profit to finance our company growth and to provide the resources we need to achieve our other corporate objectives.
Customers	*Objective*: To provide products and services of the greatest possible value to our customers, thereby gaining and holding their respect and loyalty.
Fields of Interest	*Objective*: To enter new fields only when the ideas we have, together with our technical, manufacturing, and marketing skills, assure that we can make a needed and profitable contribution to the field.
Growth	*Objective*: To let our growth be limited only by our profits and our ability to develop and produce technical products that satisfy real customers needs.
Our People	*Objective*: To help HP people share in the company's success, which they make possible; to provide job security based on their performance; to recognize their individual achievements; and to insure the personal satisfaction that comes from a sense of accomplishment their work.
Management	*Objective*: To foster initiative and creativity by allowing the individual great freedom of action in attaining well-defined objectives.
Citizenship	*Objective*: To honor our obligations to society by being an economic, intellectual, and social asset to each nation and each community in which we operate.

Courtesy Hewlett-Packard Company.

ample, a goal in support of the above objective might read "to increase profit during the next fiscal year ending in July, 1985, by 10 percent." (*See* Chapter 7 for more details on goal setting.)

Types of Objectives   While objectives can vary from firm to firm, there are eight key areas where objectives are usually needed.[6]

1. ***Marketing***. Knowing who your customer is and designing the organization to serve that customer.
2. ***Financial resources***. Almost all organizations rely on financing from various sources such as bank loans or the sale of bonds.
3. ***Physical resources***. Plant and facilities, raw materials, and space utilization are important physical resources.
4. ***Human resources***. Being able to attract and keep qualified people is an important objective.
5. ***Productivity***. Effective management of resources is needed to insure productivity.
6. ***Innovation***. Creating new approaches and ideas keeps a firm from becoming obsolete.
7. ***Social responsibility***. Organizations exist within a social and political environment, thus businesses must discharge their social reponsibilities.
8. ***Profit requirements***. All the other objectives depend on profits, for it provides the financing to pursue the other objectives.

■ Purpose, Objectives, and Structure

The organizational structure should grow naturally from its purpose and objectives. If one of an organization's objectives is to encourage a creative environment where innovation will flourish, the structure must be compatible. A military-like organization with tight supervision and control would be quite inappropriate. If a human resource objective is to insure the personal satisfaction that comes from a sense of accomplishment, then the organization needs to develop structures that help reach this goal.

Designing the Organizational Structure

The **organizational structure** represents formal patterns and relationships that exist among work units or positions.[7] Organizational structure can be viewed in a number of ways: it is the framework that divides up tasks and activities; it is the formalized network of interactions for coordination; and it establishes formal authority and reporting relationships.[8] The organizational structure is usually relatively enduring and persistent. It is published in the form of an organizational chart that is widely disseminated.

In this section we will see what makes up an organizational structure and the factors that are important for organizing. We will cover the division of labor, span of management, line and staff, departmentation, centralization and decentralization, and coordination and integration. Then in the following section, we will see how these concepts are used in various organizational structures.

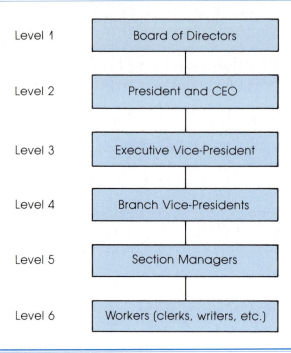

Figure 15.4. The vertical division of labor at Peak One.

Level 1	Board of Directors
Level 2	President and CEO
Level 3	Executive Vice-President
Level 4	Branch Vice-Presidents
Level 5	Section Managers
Level 6	Workers (clerks, writers, etc.)

■ Vertical Division of Labor

In all but the smallest organizations, there must be a division of labor since one person cannot do everything in an organization. There are two major ways of dividing labor, vertically and horizontally.

The **vertical division** refers to how authority, responsibility, and decision making are divided from highest levels, such as the president, to lowest levels, such as a laborer or clerk. When an organization has more vertical levels, each level of management usually makes fewer decisions since the total number of decisions must be divided among more people. For example, Peak One's original organization had at least five levels between the president and a copywriter. If the executive vice-president were to be eliminated, the number of levels would be reduced by one, or 20 percent.

■ Span of Management

One important factor to consider when dividing up labor vertically is the number of subordinates that report to a supervisor. It would be impossible for one person to supervise everyone in a large or even medium-sized organization. The number of subordinates supervised by a given supervisor is called the **span of management**, or span of control. Adam O'Brien, President of Peak One, has only one subordinate, Mary McCulley, the Executive Vice-President; thus, he has a narrow span of management. (However, in practice, many presidents share supervision with an executive vice-president with both giving orders to the various divisions of the company.) Mary, in turn, has six subordinates: account management, creative branch, marketing, traffic, personnel, and finance—a moderately wide span of manage-

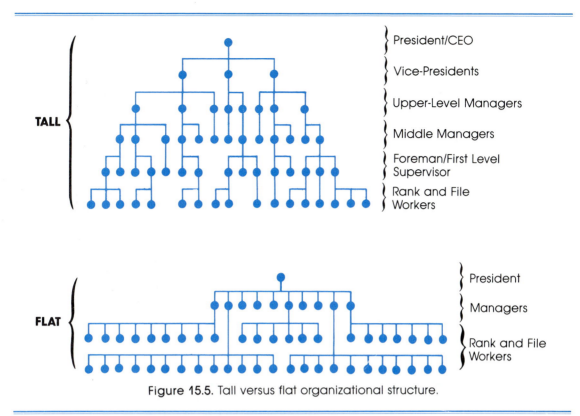

Figure 15.5. Tall versus flat organizational structure.

ment. An organization where supervisors have few subordinates is a **tall** organization; whereas, an organization where supervisors have many subordinates is a **flat** organization (*see* Fig. 15.5), provided that the organizations are the same size.

What Is an Ideal Span of Management?

Early management theorists believed that a person could not directly supervise more than five or six people because of the complexity of relationships that develop when more people are supervised.[9] However, in more recent years, this proposition has been disproved. In many situations it is quite effective for a supervisor to have many more subordinates than six[10] and there are some real psychological benefits, too. Table 15.2 shows some of the factors that need to be considered when designing the span of management.

Impact of the Span of Management

If the span is too narrow, say one manager supervising three subordinates, then it tends to result in overcontrol. Subordinates' initiative and morale are low because the supervisor spends too much time reviewing and checking their work. Narrow spans discourage delegation and participative decision making—when a boss is so close to the operation, it is easy to make all the decisions. In addition, narrow spans cost money by adding additional layers of supervision and delaying decisions as they move through numerous organizational levels (as illustrated by Fig. 15.5).[11]

Table 15.2. Factors that determine the span of management.[12]

Similarity of functions	The more dissimilar the tasks and functions, the more supervisory effort needed, and hence the narrower the span.
Geographic location	The more geographically dispersed, the narrower the span.
Complexity of functions	Highly varied and complex jobs require more supervision and a narrower span.
Nature of the personnel	The motivation and orientation of the personnel. Professional researchers will require less supervision than clerks because they are usually more committed and qualified to do the job.
Coordination and planning	The more complex the coordination and planning systems are between people, the narrower the span.

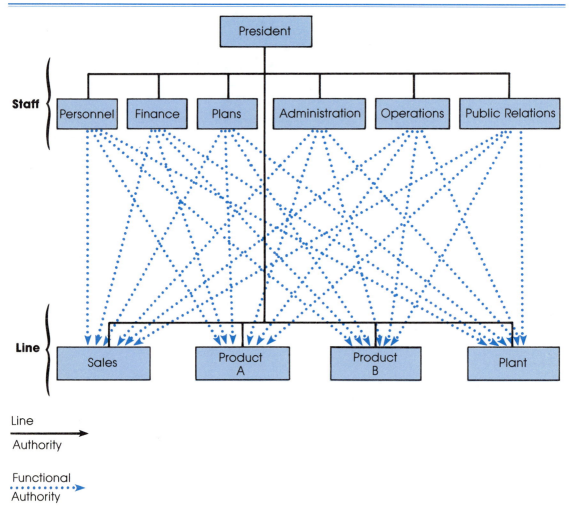

Figure 15.6. Line and staff organization.

■ Line and Staff

The line-staff concept of organization goes back thousands of years, for it originates probably with early military organizations. As it applies to business, **line** refers to those people who are involved in direct production and sales activities while the **staff** is all others (personnel, legal, administrative, public relations, finance, plans).

There are also two kinds of authority called line authority and functional authority (associated with staffs because they have functional expertise). **Line authority** is the ability to give orders because of a superior position in the organizational hierarchy. **Functional authority** is exercised by the staff when they issue orders that are concerned with their area of expertise. For example, personnel might issue an order that all job position forms must be rewritten. Even though personnel does not have a straight-line authority to direct (is not the boss) the various divisions of the company, its word is law concerning personnel matters.

Figure 15.6 graphically portrays the line-staff relationship.

■ Horizontal Division of Labor and Departmentation

The **horizontal division of labor** refers to breaking the organization down into tasks, functions, areas, or products. For example, the creative branch of Peak One (Fig. 15.7) is divided into four functions or divisions:

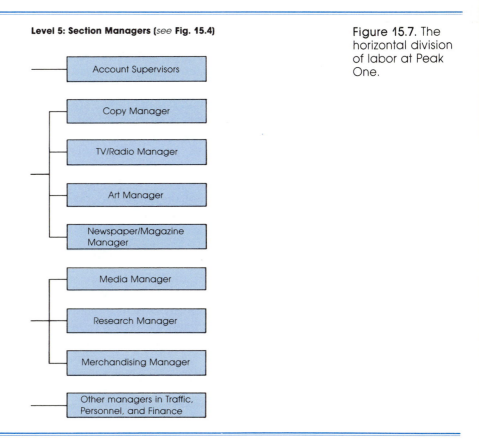

Level 5: Section Managers (*see* **Fig. 15.4**)

- Account Supervisors
- Copy Manager
- TV/Radio Manager
- Art Manager
- Newspaper/Magazine Manager
- Media Manager
- Research Manager
- Merchandising Manager
- Other managers in Traffic, Personnel, and Finance

Figure 15.7. The horizontal division of labor at Peak One.

copy, art, TV/radio, and newspaper/magazine. The process of horizontally dividing an organization is often referred to as **departmentation**, which refers to the way organizations are broken down into various departments. Departmentation is the central issue with the Peak One reorganization. Should they keep the original four divisions based on the function (copy, art) or should they develop composite creative groups with functional experts in each group?

Functional Versus Product Departmentation

The Peak One reorganization developed around the issue of how to departmentalize, by function or goal. **Functional** departments have all the people concerned with one area of expertise in the same department; for example, all art people would work in the same department. A **product** approach means that instead of being organized around the expertise of the labor, you organize around the output of that department; such as product, product group, service, markets, customers, or programs.[13] An example of a product approach is the Boeing Corporation, which includes divisions that make commercial aircraft, military aircraft, aerospace vehicles, and marine systems.

Functional departments are usually more efficient because there is less duplication of effort and there is a greater depth of expertise when problems arise. The functional approach also gives specialists a sense of belonging to people of their own kind and that their work is evaluated and controlled by other specialists. But functional departments are more likely to pursue professional or specialist objectives rather than the organization's central purpose. Product departments, on the other hand, are usually more sensitive to the needs of the product, customer, or region. They may also be easier to manage because they experience a common, unified purpose and objectives, and they are more easily held accountable for results.[14]

Our opening case involving Peak One Advertising is a good example of the problems arising from the functions versus product dilemma. Putting the specialists (researchers, copywriters), into composite groups created a product organization, where customer service and creativity were paramount. But the specialists were unhappy because there was no one to talk to; they felt isolated. They were also concerned that their boss did not understand their work and did not recognize good work when they saw it. Of course the Peak One problems might not occur in a larger organization like the Buick Division of General Motors, for it could be subdivided into functions, too.

■ Centralization and Decentralization

The concept of **decentralization** refers to the delegation or dispersion of decision making to lower organizational levels. Decentralization is not simply a function of organizational structure, it is more a function of the decision-making policies and norms for an organization. For example, we normally think of a flat organization as being more likely to be decentralized. While this may be true, it is also possible for it to be centralized. The inverse can happen when a tall organization uses decentralized decision making.

In theory, a decentralized organization could use a wider span of management since the supervisor would not have to spend as much time making decisions. We already know from Chapter 13 that participation in decisions results in higher levels of employee satisfaction. Decentralization can provide a sense of autonomy that enriches jobs. It can also provide a focal point for responsibility for performance. On the other hand, coordination and integration may be more difficult in decentralized organizations.

15.1 | *The Informal Organization*

While this chapter concentrates on structuring the formal organization, every organization also has an **informal organization**: a "network of personal and social relationships not established or required by formal authority but arising spontaneously as people associate with one another."[15] Informal organizations may be stable or constantly changing. They rely upon social relationships that are established within and between work groups. Power and politics are often the basis for the informal organization. The following organizational chart is a humorous representation of the informal organization.[16]

From J. L. Gray and F. A. Starke, 1977, *Organizational behavior concepts and applications*, p. 137. Copyright © 1977 by Charles E. Merrill, Columbus, Ohio. Used with permission.

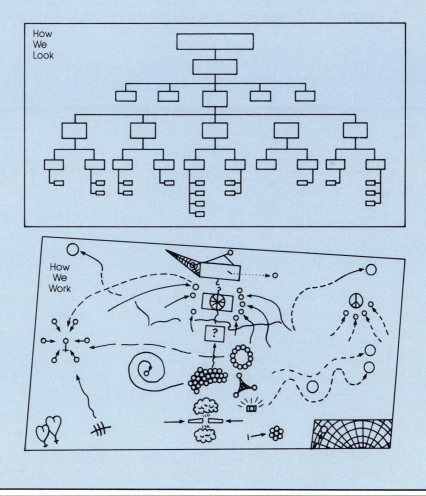

General Motors was one of the first and most famous examples of decentralization. Alfred P. Sloan, Jr., President of General Motors in the 1920s, found a number of serious problems when he took over including excessive time being consumed by administrative details and problems. He decided that decentralization was the answer. Sloan described his concept as:

. . .to divide [the organization] into as many parts as consistently as can be done, place in charge of each part the most capable executive that can be found, develop a system of coordination so that each part may strengthen and support each other part; thus not only welding all parts together in the common interests of a joint enterprise, but importantly developing the ability and initiative through the instrumentalities of responsibility and ambition—developing men and giving them an opportunity to exercise their talents, both in their own interests as well as in that of the business.[17]

As you can see Alfred Sloan understood human behavior. One of his prime reasons for implementing the decentralization concept was to better harness the motivation and ambition of his executives.

To implement decentralization, Sloan created a large number of decentralized, relatively autonomous divisions including Buick, Cadillac, Chevrolet, Oldsmobile, Pontiac, Fisher Body, AC Spark Plug, and Delco. Each division behaved as if it were a separate company, making its own decisions and creating its own revenues and profits. Of course, within each division the decision making might have been quite centralized.

The overall effects of decentralization are generally positive.[18] Employees are more satisfied, there is often higher performance, particularly for sales personnel.[19] There is also likely to be greater communication between coworkers and higher satisfaction with supervision.

■ Coordination and Integration

As organizations become increasingly complex and are organized into more and more departments, the task of coordinating and integrating everyone's effort becomes much more important and difficult. In some particularly complex industries, such as plastics manufacturing, up to 22 percent of management personnel are involved in integrating roles.[20] An **integrator** is someone who is responsible for linking and coordinating the activities of two or more departments. Integration and coordination are important in both a vertical and a horizontal direction.[21]

Vertical coordination is usually accomplished by structuring positions with the primary task of improving vertical coordination between various levels. This is often done by setting up "assistants to" (the president, the vice-president, the director) or by setting up "deputies to" (the director, the general manager, the department head). These people may have no formal line authority, but their task is to gather and disseminate information, coordinate goals, and insure everyone is headed in the direction that their boss wants.

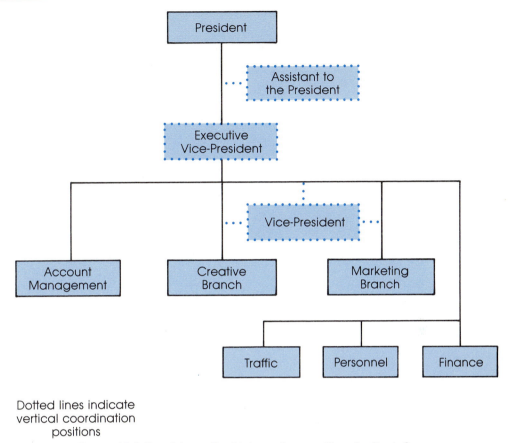

Dotted lines indicate
vertical coordination
positions

Figure 15.8. Possible vertical integration positions for Peak One.

In our opening case, the role of Mary McCulley could have been primarily vertical coordination, although her placement in the direct line of command on the organizational chart should indicate that her role involved more direction and less integration. Figure 15.8 shows how the chart for Peak One might look with the addition of several vertical integration positions.

Horizontal coordination is accomplished through several structures. Formal integrators or liaison departments may be created to help coordinate across the functional departments to insure that all work is directed toward the best interests of the company. Teams, committees, and task forces are also commonly used strategies for improving horizontal integration.

A good example of horizontal integration is often found in Schools of Business Administration. There are a number of functional departments, like accounting, management, and marketing. There also needs to be someone to integrate and coordinate the programs for undergraduates, graduates, and research. For example, the Undergraduate Director (coordinator) would be concerned with the needs and problems of undergraduate business students. Some of the concerns might be: Are there sufficient numbers of course offerings? Do schedules meet the needs of students? Is the work-

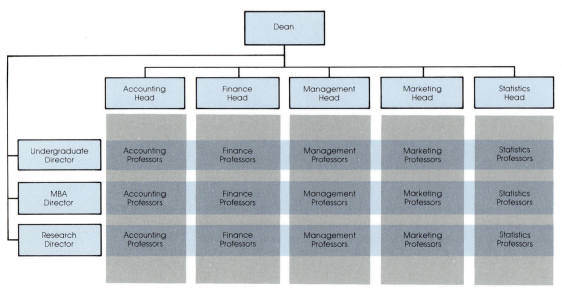

Figure 15.9. Full-time integrating roles in a business school.

From R. L. Daft, 1983, *Organizational theory and design,* p. 219. Copyright © 1983 by West Publishing Company, St. Paul, Minn. Used with permission.

load appropriate? Is the sequencing of courses correct? Figure 15.9 diagrams this type of organizational structure.

Behavior of Integrators Anyone assigned to an integrating role must have considerable behavioral skills to succeed. Integrators have little authority. They must use persuasion, expert power, and logic to accomplish their task. They must be able to communicate well, confront problems, resolve conflicts, avoid dysfunctional politics, and build organizational trust. The integrator must be able to get things done without alienating the functional departments.[22]

The Organization's Environment

All organizations operate in some external environment. The **environment** consists of all elements or factors outside the boundary of the organization that have potential to affect all or part of the organization.[23]. Pressure from the environment is an important reason for reorganization. One of the reasons that Peak One reorganized was the loss of customers (an important environmental factor).

The importance of different aspects of the environment will vary with the purpose or task of the organization. There are six components of the environment that we will consider: technology, customers, suppliers, competitors, sociopolitical, and economic.[24] The interaction of these components may create an environment with varying degrees of uncertainty. Figure 15.10 shows the impact of the environment on organizational systems.

In this section we will first discuss the issue of environmental uncertainty and then go over the components of the environment. To help inte-

Understanding Organizational Behavior

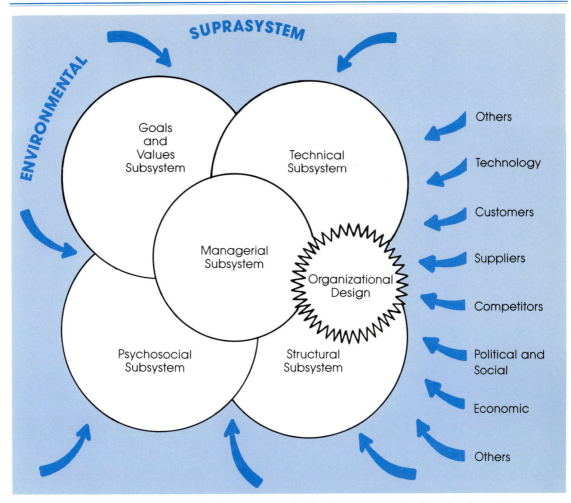

Figure 15.10. The impact of environmental factors on organizational systems.[25]

grate these concepts, we will take a look at how one corporation, Boeing Aircraft, might view their environment.

■ Environmental Uncertainty

When managers lack information about the environment, they experience environmental uncertainty. This increases the risks associated with a decision. Two elements of uncertainty are environmental complexity and the degree of environmental change.[26]

Environmental complexity refers to the number, variety, and diversity of external forces experienced by the organization. We would expect a large aircraft manufacturer to experience many complex environmental forces and thus be quite high in complexity. On the other hand an auto parts store in a large suburban community would experience low environmental complexity.

Environmental change refers to the stability or instability of the environment. Does the environment remain stable over a period of months or years or does it change almost constantly? Unexpected changes in the environment, such as an increase in the price of fuel or a change in interest rates, can cause major repercussions for Boeing. An example of a relatively stable environment might be a supermarket. The environment usually changes slowly, and there is time to plan and redesign organizational systems.

■ Technology

Technology is "the types and patterns of activity, equipment and material, and knowledge or experience used to perform tasks."[27] It involves methods, designs, machines, equipment, information, managerial techniques, and procedures. Technology can be classified in many ways:[28]

1. **Mass production** or large batch, such as automotive assembly.
2. **Craft** or small batch, such as custom suits or small boat construction.
3. **Process**, such as an oil refinery or a brewery.

Boeing's technology is extremely complex and uses large batch or assembly line and techniques. In addition, their technology is constantly changing. New fuel-saving designs in airframes and engines are being developed. Computer technology allows aircraft to take off and land in zero-visibility conditions. Organizing to harness technology is a major problem for Boeing. They need to be able to develop and respond to technological changes and yet maintain some stability in their internal organization.

■ Customers

When we discussed organizational purpose, we noted that a crucial issue is "Who is the customer?" All users of your product or service are customers, including distributors or wholesalers. Peak One was very concerned about client service—the heart of their business. Boeing has a much more complex set of customers, including major airline corporations, foreign governments, and the defense departments of the United States and other countries. These customers are just as important to Boeing as they are to Peak One. Without buyers, an organization cannot sell its product or exist.

■ Suppliers

Few organizations are completely independent. Most must rely on some type of supplier, whether it involves supplies, equipment, raw materials, or people. A large corporation like Boeing is dependent on its suppliers for subassemblies, electronic equipment, or engineering information. It is also dependent on the supply of highly qualified engineers and technicians—without them the firm could not function.

■ Competitors

Knowledge of your competition is extremely important. What deals are they offering? What new products are they developing? What new products are they developing? What are their sales approaches? How does their product or service differ from yours? How is it superior or inferior? Boeing is conscious of its competitors. If the European airbus is too successful, it might seriously threaten Boeing's success. If Boeing could convince the defense department to buy 747 aircraft instead of C5's from Lockheed, it would create billions of dollars in sales.

■ Political-Social Environment

This dimension has to do with government regulation, political attitudes toward the industry and product, and the relations with trade unions. All organizations have some dealings with the government—it is unavoidable. Boeing, being a major government contractor, has to abide by a number of additional regulations and laws. In addition, all the airline safety regulations have to be interpreted and implemented. Relations with Congress are particularly important for Boeing. When such sensitive decisions as the 747 versus the C5 are discussed and voted on in Congress, Boeing needs all the good will it can muster. Although Boeing has reasonably good relations with its own unions, the air traffic controller's strike of 1981 caused such a decline in flying hours that the demand for new aircraft began to suffer.[29]

■ Economic Environment

The general state of the economy—interest rates, inflation, unemployment, growth—all have a major impact on organizations. The recession of 1981–83 caused numerous cancellations of new aircraft for Boeing. Only last year, several people in the Pacific Northwest were considering opening a fishing tackle shop. Because of the economic conditions, especially the high interest rates, they decided not to go through with the venture. As it turns out another environmental influence (political-social) would have caused a severe threat. The courts ruled that the Indians of the Northwest are not getting their share of salmon and closed or severely restricted sports fishing.

■ The Environment and Structure

There is no simple answer to the question: "How do I best organize to cope with the environment?" Peak One reorganized for the prime purpose of better relations with their clients; yet, they ran into difficulties. Perhaps the major way to cope with environmental turbulence is to establish buffers.

Buffers are departments that deal with various aspects of the environment. They prevent the environment from interfering with the primary task of the organization, such as building aircraft. (The departments who perform this primary task are referred to as the **technical core**.) Buffer departments deal directly with the environment and prevent turbulence from reaching the technical core.[30] Examples of buffer departments are shown in Figure 15.11.

Stability of the environment is an important consideration when organizing. Generally, the more turbulent the environment, the more flexible and responsive the organization must be to effectively deal with the turbulence. This often requires departments and people who act as buffers or specialists in various environmental concerns.

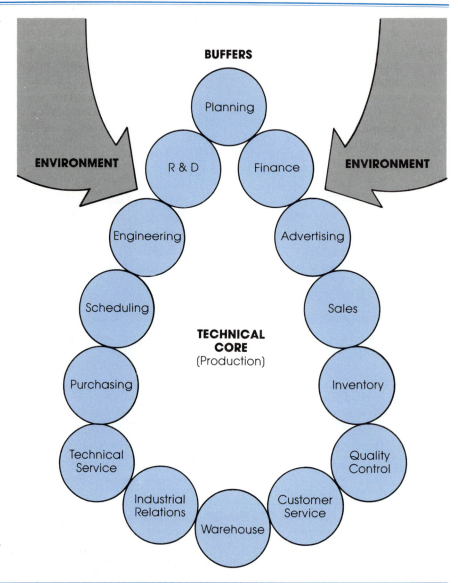

Figure 15.11. Buffer departments for coping with environment uncertainty.

BUFFERS

ENVIRONMENT

ENVIRONMENT

Planning

R & D

Finance

Engineering

Advertising

Scheduling

Sales

TECHNICAL CORE
(Production)

Purchasing

Inventory

Technical Service

Quality Control

Industrial Relations

Customer Service

Warehouse

From R. L. Daft, 1983, *Organizational theory and design,* p. 57. Copyright © 1983 by West Publishing Company, St. Paul, Minn. Used with permission.

Types of Organizational Structures

This section of the chapter provides insight into a variety of organizational structures. We will first discuss bureaucracies as a general model for large organizations. Then, we will cover examples of functional, product, and matrix organizations. An important issue to remember throughout this section is that most organizations are a blend of several structures.

■ Bureaucratic Organizations

Bureaucracy is not a type of organizational structure, but a set of characteristics that were needed for an ideal organization. Max Weber, who developed the concept of bureaucracy, felt that if the characteristics listed below were present, a more efficient and effective organization would result. Here are Weber's features of **bureaucracy**:[31]

☐ An organization that functions by the rules. It is impersonal and treats all clients alike.

☐ A systematic sphere of competence for each individual with the authority to accomplish the task.

☐ The organizational structure follows the principle of hierarchy in that compliance is not left to chance—every office has a superior one that checks on it.

☐ Rules are applied quite rationally and by people with adequate technical training. Where rules do not exist, norms become quite important.

☐ Members of the organization should be separated from the owners of the organization. Personal lives and official lives should be kept separate.

☐ Resources, including job positions, must be allocated without outside control. Favoritism is out.

☐ Administrative acts are formulated and recorded in writing, thus providing a systematic record of rule or norm enforcement.

Almost all organizations have some elements of bureaucracy. In fact, it would be hard to envision an organization that did not rely upon some rules or where favoritism is not frowned upon. In most cases effective, larger organizations will have more bureaucracy because it is need for coordination and control.[32] Figure 15.12 shows the results of research on this topic.

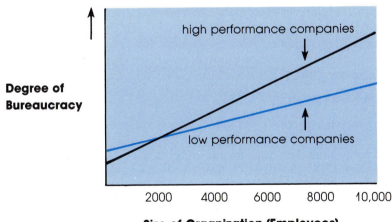

Figure 15.12. Size of the organization, bureaucracy, and performance.

Adapted by R. L. Daft from J. Child, Managerial factors associated with company performance. . . analysis, *Journal of Management Studies* 12:12–27. Copyright © 1975 by Basil Blackwell Publishing Ltd., Oxford, England.

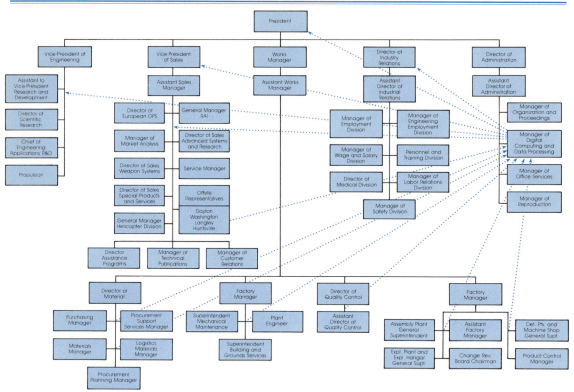

Figure 15.13. A functionally organized aerospace company showing the flow of information to and from the computer department.

From R. L. Daft, 1983, *Organizational theory and design*, p. 337. Copyright © 1983 by West Publishing Company, St. Paul, Minn. Used with permission.

■ Functional Organizations

Since functional organizations revolve around the use of functional specialists who are organized into homogeneous units, it is not surprising to see the proliferation of functional departments in a large, complex organization such as the one illustrated in Figure 15.13. The dotted lines show how computer systems impact this organization. Note how information from lower-level parts of the organization is processed, summarized, and fed to top managers.[33] This process facilitates coordination and control.

■ Product Organizations

Product structures are organized around the product, product group, service, market, customer, or programs of the organization. There are almost no pure types of product organization. Most combine at least functional and product. The organization for Levi Strauss, USA illustrated in Figure 15.14, shows this tendency. Note that there are two levels of product departmentation, one at the individual product level (Jeanswear Division) and one combining several products into a group (Group I).

■ Hybrid Organizations

We noted above that it is rare to find a pure goal-oriented or product organization. Most large corporations show a variety of structures although one may dominate. The organizational structure for the Corporate Head-

Understanding Organizational Behavior

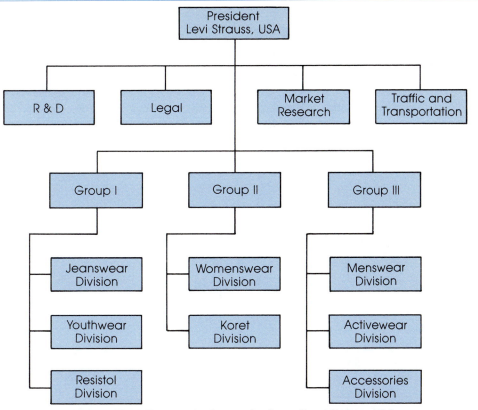

Figure 15.14. The product organization of Levi Strauss, USA.

From R. L. Daft, 1983, *Organizational theory and design*, p. 235. Copyright © 1983 by West Publishing Company, St. Paul, Minn. Used with permission.

quarters of the Boeing Company, illustrated in Figure 15.15, shows a hybrid structure. There are some traditional functional areas, mostly at the staff level, such as public affairs, industrial relations, finance, and product development. There are also product divisions, such as Boeing Commercial Airplane Company, Boeing Computer Services, and Boeing Marine Services. There are even a few geographic departments, such as Seattle Services Division, and the Washington, D.C., office.

■ Matrix Organizations

What Is a Matrix Organization?   A **matrix** organization has two reporting channels so that the same manager has two bosses. For example, an engineer may report to the chief of engineering and to the radar project manager (see Fig. 15.16). Thus, the matrix organization combines both functional divisions that concentrate on specialized, in-house resources, and on product divisions that concentrate on the output into one organization. Companies turn to the matrix design when:[34]

☐ It is absolutely essential that they be highly responsive to two sectors simultaneously, such as markets and technology.

☐ They face uncertainties that generate high information processing requirements.

☐ They must deal with strong constraints on financial and/or human resources.

Organizational Design and Behavior   **379**

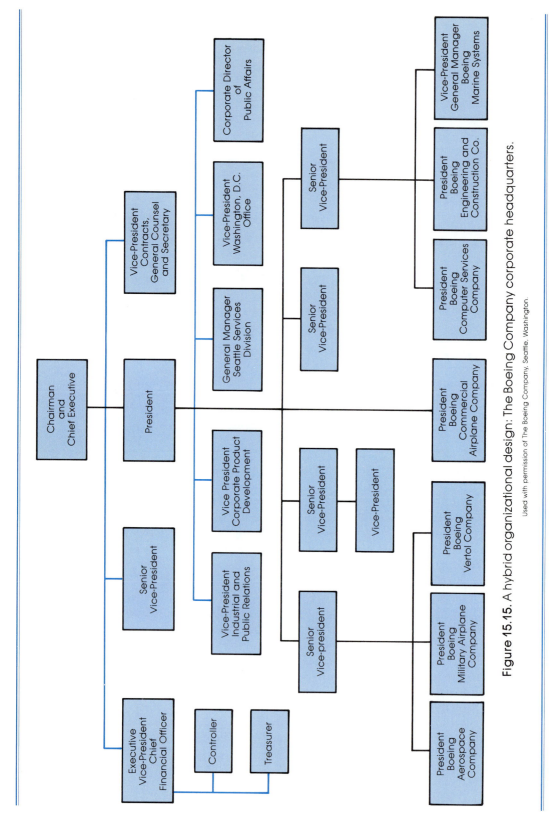

Figure 15.15. A hybrid organizational design: The Boeing Company corporate headquarters.

Used with permission of The Boeing Company, Seattle, Washington.

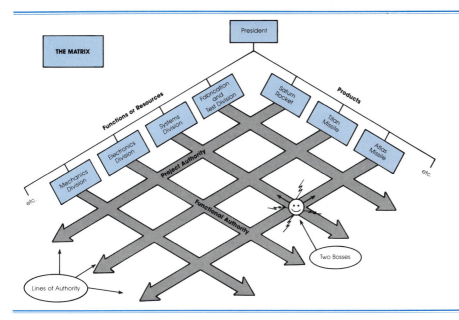

Figure 15.16. How the matrix organization works.

THE MATRIX

President

Functions or Resources

Fabrication and Test Division

Saturn Rocket

Products

Systems Division

Titan Missile

Electronics Division

Atlas Missile

Mechanics Division

Project Authority

Functional Authority

etc.

etc.

Two Bosses

Lines of Authority

Making Matrix Work   Matrix organizations must have more than just a matrix structure. There must be dual reporting, control, reward, and evaluation systems. In addition, the role of the top manager is crucial for balancing the inevitable conflicts that result from the dual-reporting structure of a matrix organization. When one boss tells you to do one thing and the other gives conflicting orders, you are torn—what do you do? The bosses of the person in the matrix must also use special skills. For example, a person who works in a geographically isolated location from his or her function may find that they are likely to be forgotten unless the boss makes an effort to provide regular feedback and recognition. Power struggles and the tendencies toward anarchy are also two frequent problems associated with matrix organizations.[35]

An example of matrix for Pittsburg Steel Company is shown in Figure 15.17. Note that the matrix does not include Field Sales or Industrial Relations.

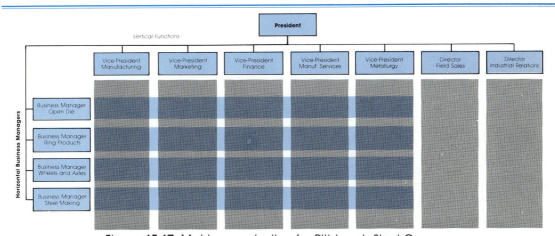

Figure 15.17. Matrix organization for Pittsburgh Steel Company.

From R. L. Daft, 1983, *Organizational theory and design*, p. 249. Copyright © 1983 by West Publishing Company, St. Paul, Minn. Used with permission

Organizational Design and Behavior

15.3 Structures to Encourage Managerial Progression of Women

In the last chapter, we discussed some of the problems women face in leadership positions, including research that shows men talk more in mixed male-female groups; men's opinions are more likely to influence both males and females; and males are more task-oriented. In addition, women generally find it more difficult to become a member of the informal managerial organization. While these problems are formidable, there are structural methods for dealing with them including:[36]

- Decentralize the organization into smaller, relatively autonomous units to give women and men a better chance to show what they can do—to perform and be measured.
- Since women have more difficulty establishing credibility when they enter organizations, they might be given more powerful symbols (corner offices) and resources (budgets).
- Women can establish their own informal organizational networks and ties so they are more involved in the organizational mainstream.
- Groups can be structured so that there is a slight preponderance of women, thus giving women a chance to perform in a more favorable situation and build a reputation before tackling mostly male groups.
- Structure opportunities for women to talk more, perhaps by making oral presentations and serving as team leaders.

Organizational Structure: Some Summary Conclusions

There are several important conclusions about structuring organizations that may help serve as a summary.

☐ *Clarify the organization's purpose.* Be sure to ask: "What is our business?" and "What should it be?" Before any organization can be designed, we must have a clear ideal of its purpose and mission. While this may seem obvious, many organizations do not experience such clarity.

☐ *Keep it simple and lean.*[37] Organizations should not overorganize. They need to adopt enough division of labor and bureaucratic characteristics to get the job done, but they should avoid going overboard. Relatively wide spans of control will save people and result in more challenge for supervisors while at the same time increasing discretion of subordinates.

☐ *Establish responsibility centers.* Large corporations can be divided into smaller product or geographic divisions and thus behave as if they were a small or medium-sized corporations. This same concept can be carried to much lower levels. Whenever an autonomous unit can be structured and its performance isolated from the total organization, there will be improved creativity, better performance, and clearer control of such units.

☐ *Stay close to your customers.* Customers are often the most important elements in business decision making.[38] If the organization gets out of touch with its customers, it is in grave danger.

☐ *Minimize environmental threats.* Organizations should not allow themselves to become hostage to a single customer, supplier, or other environmental threat. Diversification is one way to spread this risk.

☐ *Watch for changes in technology.* Careful observation of technological changes may prevent your company from being overtaken by another with the attendant danger of becoming obsolete.

SUMMARY

Chapter Review

■ Before we can organize we must have a clear sense of **organizational purpose and objectives**. The structure should then grow naturally out of the purpose and objectives.

■ **Organizational structure** is the framework that divides up tasks, activities, and responsibilities, and it establishes formal authority and reporting relationships. This dividing process, called the **division of labor**, has both a vertical and a horizontal dimension.

■ The **span of management**, an important part of the **vertical division of labor**, is concerned with the number of subordinates that report to a given supervisor. Organizations where supervisors have relatively few subordinates, and thus many layers of hierarchy, are called **tall** organizations. Organizations where supervisors have many subordinates and fewer levels of hierarchy are called **flat** organizations.

■ Most large organizations have both **line** departments and **staff** departments. People assigned to the line are concerned with direct production and sales activities while the staff is concerned with other activities, such as finance, personnel, or public relations. Different types of **authority** are associated with line and staff departments.

■ The **horizontal division of labor**, often called **departmentation**, concerns how we divide up the organization into tasks, functions, products. Two basic ways to divide are **functions** (the specialty or expertise of the department) or **product** (the output of the department; the product).

■ A **centralized** organization is one where decision making is centralized at the top of an organization. A **decentralized** organization shows more delegation or dispersion of decision making to lower organizational levels.

■ Once organizations have been divided into tasks, they must be **coordinated**. Often, an **integrator** is used to formally link the activities of two or more departments.

■ The **environment** of the organization is a crucial element to consider when organizing. The uncertainty of the environment in terms of complexity and degree of change will effect the organization's purpose and objectives and the number and type of departments that are needed to cope with environmental turbulence.

■ Important environmental impacts include technology, customers, suppliers, competitors, political-social factors, and economics. **Buffers** are people or departments that deal with environmental issues and protect the central part of the organization, called the **technical core**, from environmental threats that might decrease the core's effectiveness.

◼ While there are few pure organizational types, it is useful to understand several forms: **bureaucracy**, **functional**, **goal-oriented**, and **matrix**. These may blend together to form **hybrid** organizations.

For Discussion

1. Why is the answer not obvious to the question, "What is our business and what should it be?" Give an example of an organization that has not properly answered this question.
2. What is the difference between objectives and goals?
3. Explain how the span of management may be related to leadership and decision-making behaviors.
4. Give an example of a line and a staff position in a university organization.
5. Weigh the advantages and disadvantages of the various ways to horizontally divide up labor.
6. What is decentralization? How is it related to decision making? To power? To leadership style?
7. Explain the structures that are often used to attain coordination and integration.
8. Why is the environment so important for structuring organizations?
9. Under what circumstances might the bureaucratic organization be the most effective structure?
10. What special organizational behavior problems are created by the matrix organization?

Key Concepts and Terms

organizational structure	**decentralization**
organizational purpose	**informal organization**
objectives	**vertical integration**
division of labor	**horizontal integration**
horizontal division of labor	**environment**
span of management	**environmental uncertainty**
tall organizational structure	**buffers**
flat organizational structure	**technical core**
line and staff activities	**bureaucracy**
departmentation	**matrix organization**
functional organization	**hybrid organization**
product organization	**responsibility center**
centralization	

Suggested Readings

Duncan, R. (1979). What is the right organization structure? *Organizational Dynamics* 8 (Winter).

Galbraith, J. R. (1982). Designing the innovating organization. *Organizational Dynamics* 10:5–25.

Understanding Organizational Behavior

Kolodny, H. F. (1981). Managing in a matrix. *Business Horizons* Mar.-Apr.:17–35.

Mintzberg, H. (1981). Organization design: Fashion or fit. *Harvard Business Review* Jan.-Feb.:103–116.

Robey, D. (1982). *Designing organizations*. Homewood, Ill.: Irwin.

CASES AND INCIDENTS

The Advanced Aerospace Research Laboratory

Dr. Hans Engstrom, the newly appointed head of the Advanced Aerospace Research Laboratory (AARL), was delighted with the job. He had worked at several labs as a scientist before being selected to head the AARL. Long ago he decided that if he ever got to be a lab director he would run a "tighter" ship than the directors he had observed.

During his second week he announced two major management changes:

■ *Reorganization.* Instead of having the three assistant lab directors, each supervising ten to twelve scientists, he announced that henceforth a supervisor would not have more than four subordinates. This created another level of supervision with a number of scientists gaining the title of "Supervisory Scientist." He figured the new organization would not only result in better control, but would give added prestige to the supervisory jobs.

■ *Time and activities reporting system.* The second managerial innovation was a detailed reporting system to describe how time was spent on each task. This, he thought, will result in much better records so we can more easily justify our existence in the event of budget cuts.

Discussion questions
1. What effects do you predict from the managerial innovations in terms of satisfaction, performance, and retention?
2. What organizational structure is most appropriate for a research lab? Why?
3. What impacts might you expect from the control system? Is there a better way to control and coordinate activities?

Peak One Advertising Reorganization

Discussion questions
1. Take the opening case concerning Peak One and reorganize it into a matrix organization.
2. What do you predict the effectiveness of matrix to be?
3. What problems will possibly arise and how might they be dealt with?

REFERENCES

1. Adapted from a case presented in Kover, A. J. (1963), Reorganization in an advertising agency: A case study in integration, *Human Organization* 22: 252–259.

2. For extensive coverage of organizational design *see* Daft, R. L., (1983), *Organizational theory and design*, St. Paul, Minn.: West; and Robey, D. (1982), *Designing organizations*, Homewood, Ill.: Irwin; Mintzberg, H. (1979), *The structuring of organizations*, Englewood Cliffs, N.J.: Prentice-Hall; and Nystrom, P. C. and Starbuck, W. H., eds. (1981), *Handbook of organizational design*, New York: Oxford University Press.

3. Adapted from Kast, F. E. and Rosenzweig, J. E. (1979), *Organization and management*, 3rd ed., New York: McGraw-Hill.

4. *See* Pascale, R. T. and Athos, A. G. (1981), *The art of Japanese management: Applications for American executives*, New York: Simon and Schuster; and Ouchi, W. (1981), *Theory Z: How American business can meet the Japanese challenge*, Reading, Mass.: Addison-Wesley.

5. Drucker, P. F., 1974, *Management: Tasks, responsibilities, practices*, New York: Harper & Row.

6. Drucker, *Management*, p. 100.

7. This definition is similar to the one posed by Blackburn, R. S. (1982), Dimensions of structure: A review and reappraisal, *Academy of Management Review* 7:59–66.

8. Ranson, S.; Hinings, B.; and Greenwood, R. (1980), The structuring of organizational structures, *Administrative Science Quarterly* 25:1–17.

9. *See* Urwick, L. F. (1956), The manager's span of control, *Harvard Business review* 34(3):39–47.

10. *See* Koontz, H. (1966), Making theory operational: The span of management, *The Journal of Management Studies* 3:229–243.

11. For reviews *see* Dalton, D. R.; Todor, W. D.; Spendolini, M. J.; Fielding, G. J.; and Porter, L. W. (1980), Organizational structure and performance: A critical review, *Academy of Management Review* 5:49–64; Oldham, G. R. and Hackman, J. R. (1981), Relationships between organizational structure and employee reactions: Comparing alternative frameworks, *Administrative Science Quarterly* 26:66–82; and Cummings, L. L. and Berger, C. J. (1976), Organizational structure: How does it influence attitudes and performance?, *Organizational Dynamics* 5(2):34–49.

12. Koontz, Making theory operational.

13. Jelinek, M.; Litterer, J. A.; and Miles, R. E., eds. (1981), *Organizations by design: Theory and practice*, Plano, Texas: Business Publications.

14. *See* McCann. J. and Galbraith, J. R. (1981), Interdepartmental relations, in *Handbook of organizational design*, ed. P. C. Nystrom and W. H. Starbuck, New York: Oxford University Press. *Also see* a classic article discussing these issues: Walker, A. H. and Lorsch, J. W. (1968), Organizational choice: Product vs. function, *Harvard Business Review* Nov.-Dec.

15. Davis, K. (1981), *Human behavior at work: Organizational behavior*, 6th ed., New York: McGraw-Hill, p. 329.

16. Gray, J. L. and Starke, F. A. (1977), *Organizational behavior concepts and applications*, Columbus, Ohio: Charles E. Merrill, p. 137.

17. Curtice, H. H. (1972), General Motors organization, philosophy, and structure, in *Management: A book of readings*, 3rd ed., ed. H. Koontz and C. O'Donnell, p. 343, New York: McGraw-Hill.

18. For a review *see* Cummings and Berger, Organizational structure. *Also see* Duncan, R. (1979), What is the right organization structure?, *Organizational Dynamics*, Winter: 59–80.

19. Ivancevich, J. M. and Donnelly, J. H., Jr. (1975), Relation of organizational structure to job satisfaction, anxiety-stress, and performance, *Administrative Science Quarterly* 20:272–280.

20. Lorsch, J. W. and Lawrence, P. R. (1972), Environmental factors and organizational integration, in *Organizational planning: Cases and concepts*, eds. P. W. Lorsch and P. R. Lawrence, Homewood, Ill.: Irwin and Dorsey.

21. For a more complete discussion of horizontal and vertical integrating roles *see* Daft, *Organizational theory and design*, Chapter 6.

22. Lawrence, P. R. and Lorsch, J. W. (1967), The new managerial job: The integrator, *Harvard Business Review* Nov.-Dec.:42–51.

23. Daft, *Organizational theory and design*, p. 42.

24. Duncan, R. B. (1972), Characteristics of organizational environments and perceived uncertainty, *Administrative Science Quarterly* 17:313–327.

25. Systems model based on Kast and Rosenzweig, *Organization and management*.

26. Jurkovich, R. (1974), A core typology of organizational environments, *Administrative Science Quarterly* 19:380–394; and Thompson, J. D. (1967), *Organizations in action*, New York: McGraw-Hill.

27. Gillespie, D. F. and Mileti, D. S. (1977), Technology and the study of organizations, *Academy of Management Review* 2:p.8.

28. Woodward, J. (1965), *Industrial organization: Theory and practice*, London: Oxford University Press. *Also see* Randolph, W. A. (1981), Matching technology and design of organizational units, *California Management Review* 23:39–48.

29. For more information *see* Fischer, D. W. (1983), Strategies toward political pressures: A typology of firm responses, *Academy of Management Review* 8:71–78.

30. Thompson, *Organizations in action*.

31. Adapted from Weber, M. (1947), *The theory of social and economic organization*, New York: Oxford University Press.

32. Child, J. (1977), *Organizations*, New York: Harper & Row.

33. *See* Daft, *Organizational theory and design*, Chapter 8, for a discussion of the impact of computers on organizational structure.

34. Summary from Davis, S. M. and Lawrence, P. R. (1978), Problems of matrix organizations, *Harvard Business Review* 56(3):p.134.

35. Davis, S. M. and Lawrence, P. R. (1977), *Matrix*, Reading, Mass.: Addison-Wesley. *Also see* Kolodny, H. F. (1981), Managing in a matrix, *Business Horizons* Mar.-Apr.:17–35.

36. Based on Lipman-Blumen, J. (1980), Female leadership in formal organizations: Must the female leader go formal?, in *Readings in managerial psychology*, 3rd ed., eds. H. J. Leavitt, L. R. Pondy, and D. M. Boje, pp. 354–355, Chicago: University of Chicago Press.

37. Several of these points were made by Daft, *Organizational theory and design*, pp. 503–505. Also see Peters, T. J., and Waterman, R. H. Jr., (1982), *In search of excellence*, New York: Harper & Row.

38. Daft, *Organizational theory and design*, p. 502; and Peters and Waterman, *In search of excellence*.

Organization Change and Development

PREVIEW

- Did you know that even chief executives sometimes have trouble changing their organizations? Find out why and what can be done.

- When is creating dissatisfaction desirable?

- Which change factor do you think is most powerful: a manager's expectations or the nature of the change innovation itself? The answer may surprise you.

- Why is participation in the change process one of the most powerful tools for managers?

- How can force-field analysis help you sort out complex changes?

- Why do people sometimes revert back to their original behaviors in spite of all your efforts to change them? Find out what you can do to prevent this problem.

- What is organization development, and why is it so popular with companies? Does it really work?

PREVIEW CASE: GREAT PACIFIC SHIPBUILDING

Mallory Webb was the third chief executive of Great Pacific Shipbuilding in the past four years.[1] Great Pacific was such a big money loser that the President of Meganational Conglomerates, owner of Great Pacific, told him this was going to be the last chance for the corporation. If it could not be turned around by the end of next year, then Meganational would cut their losses and liquidate it.

Great Pacific was poorly managed. It had plenty of business but was plagued by duplication of effort and lack of responsiveness to its customers. Previous CEO's had known these problems and tried to "shake up" and reorganize the company. Somehow nothing ever seemed to change—there was always some reason why change could not be done.

Mallory, a successful manager with a good track record, had also tried to make changes. He ran into the same roadblocks and became frustrated, knowing that if he could not succeed at Great Pacific his career as a chief executive would be over. He decided to seek the aid of Douglas Nelson, a Northwest University professor, who is an expert in organizational change and development.

After several lengthy discussions, they decided on a strategy using a systematic change process. Here's what they did:

Getting ready. They worked together to figure out who the "stakeholders" were—those key people who might have a stake in the success or failure of the change. The group included most of the major line and staff executives, about sixteen people. Mallory appointed them to a planning team and asked them to join himself and the consultant at a three-day offsite workshop at the Meganational Retreat Center at Lake Wilderness. Doug interviewed each of these executives in preparation for the workshop to find out how they felt about the performance of Great Pacific.

The Offsite Workshop. Mallory began the meeting by "laying it on the line" that performance is low and there may be a threat to the very existence of Great Pacific. He stated his objective of figuring out how to turn around the business and make it profitable once again. Then Doug fed back the recurring themes from the interviews, which centered around widespread dissatisfaction with organizational performance.

During the week, the group worked to analyze the organization. They considered the basic purpose and mission of Great Pacific. They asked, "What is our business and what should it be?" They asked, "Who is the customer?" After extensive problem-solving sessions using a technique called Force-Field Analysis (to be discussed later in the chapter), they decided on reorganization as their major change strategy. A transition team was appointed (one person from each major line and staff division) to help implement the planning group's ideas.

Organizing the Transition. The day after they returned, Mallory wrote a memo to all division chiefs summarizing the results of the workshop, announcing the transition team, and setting the date for a company-wide management meeting to discuss the new organizational

Understanding Organizational Behavior

structure. The transition team put the finishing touches on the new design, including detailed statements of strategy and purpose for the new structure. They developed a detailed transition plan outlining time schedules, responsibilities, and methods. The transition team met frequently with the planning group, including several, one-day offsite meetings.

Top Management Support. Mallory continued his involvement and strong support for the changes that the planning group had developed, for he agreed with the plan and had been a major influence in its formulation. He attended transition group meetings from time-to-time to find out what was happening and to show support and concern. In private, he confronted several people who were resisting and sought their support. He was also careful to insure that rewards, such as promotions, went to people who were enthusiastic supporters of the change.

Executing the Plan. During the next four months, the reorganization took place just as the transition team had planned. Several times during the period, questionnaires were used to find out how things were going and whether the employees saw any problems. When problems were uncovered, they were addressed, and the new structure was fine-tuned.

Results. The change was effective. Performance improved and both managers and employees were more satisfied with Great Pacific. Profits were in the black within six months, assuring the survival of Great Pacific and enhancing Mallory's record as a chief executive.

Managing the change process is one of the most important aspects of a manager's task. Effective change management often makes the difference between a highly successful manager and a mediocre or poor one. Mallory's predecessors had all failed to change Great Pacific and as a result faded into managerial obscurity. Mallory's success will lead to other challenging positions. In this chapter, we will provide some of the keys to understanding and managing the change process. We will also discuss organization development, an effective change strategy that concentrates on organizational behavior issues.

The Change Process

To **change** is to move from one state or condition to another state or condition. While change is constant and inevitable, it does not always occur in the direction a manager wants it to go. Every CEO at Great Western wanted a positive change in organizational performance; only Mallory was successful in achieving this goal. The key reason for his success was an understanding of the change process. Change was carefully managed and directed toward the desired goals using a total systems perspective.

There are many pressures on managers to change. Thus, planning and executing change is one of the major tasks of managers who are working in the managerial subsystem. Some of the pressures toward change and resistance to change are shown in Figure 16.1.

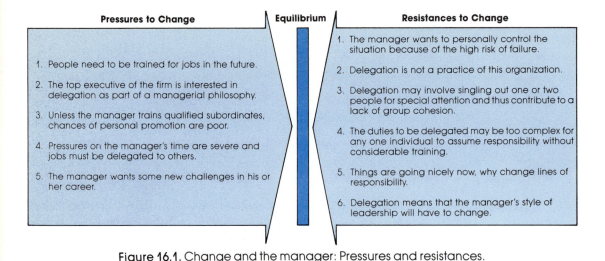

Pressures to Change	Equilibrium	Resistances to Change
1. People need to be trained for jobs in the future. 2. The top executive of the firm is interested in delegation as part of a managerial philosophy. 3. Unless the manager trains qualified subordinates, chances of personal promotion are poor. 4. Pressures on the manager's time are severe and jobs must be delegated to others. 5. The manager wants some new challenges in his or her career.		1. The manager wants to personally control the situation because of the high risk of failure. 2. Delegation is not a practice of this organization. 3. Delegation may involve singling out one or two people for special attention and thus contribute to a lack of group cohesion. 4. The duties to be delegated may be too complex for any one individual to assume responsibility without considerable training. 5. Things are going nicely now, why change lines of responsibility. 6. Delegation means that the manager's style of leadership will have to change.

Figure 16.1. Change and the manager: Pressures and resistances.

■ A Systems Perspective of Change

Since organizations are systems made up of a number of subsystems existing within the environmental suprasystem, we would expect that the change process would affect all systems.[2] For example, Mallory's predecessors at Great Pacific thought that all they had to do to change the organization was to change the structure by managerial edict. They failed. Mallory's approach considered the entire system, with particular attention to the psychosocial subsystem including power relationships, communication, group dynamics, and motivation. By structuring the groups into planning groups and task forces, Mallory was able to get people involved, motivated, and directed towards the change.

Changing pay systems, computer systems, performance appraisal procedures, structures, supervisors, or working hours, all have impacts on the organization. For example, a new performance appraisal system designed to get more accurate records for assignments and promotions will affect motivation, conflict, group dynamics, and other aspects of the organization.

■ Equilibrium and Change

Since change involves moving from one state to another, change means that the **equilibrium** of the system is affected—the forces acting upon the system have become imbalanced and **disequilibrium** has been created. Before Mallory's arrival at Great Pacific, previous CEOs had been unable to break the equilibrium; no matter what they tried, things remained the same. Thus, an important part of the change process is recognizing that the force of inertia is great and that something may be needed to force the system into disequilibrium before change can happen.

If change involves moving from the current state to a desired state and to do this a change in equilibrium is needed, then one can look at the change process as unfreezing, moving or changing, and then refreezing in the desired state.[3] Figure 16.2 graphically depicts the change process.

Understanding Organizational Behavior

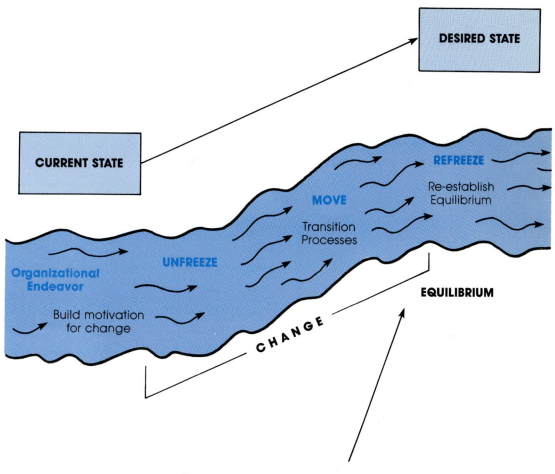

Figure 16.2. The change process.[4]

■ Overview of the Change Process

Organizations move along in a state of equilibrium transforming inputs into outputs (organizational endeavor). Then someone or something comes along and creates the motivation to change because of dissatisfaction with the current state. This process of creating a need for change is called **unfreezing**. Once the system is unfrozen, it can be changed—hopefully in the direction planned by the manager—into a new and desired state. This part of the process is called **moving** or changing. It involves a number of processes that make the change more effective. Finally, when the desired state is reached, the system must be **refrozen** at this new level; equilibrium must be reestablished.

Now that we have covered an overview of the change process, we will discuss each aspect of the process: unfreezing, changing or moving, and refreezing.

Organizational Change and Development

Unfreezing: Getting Ready for Change

Many of the problems associated with change concern the forces against unfreezing; the forces for maintaining the equilibrium or status quo. We will discuss two major problems, resistance to change and power and political dynamics, and then what to do about them.

■ Resistance to Change

Perhaps the overriding cause of resistance is fear; fear of the unknown; fear that needs would not be met. People resist change for a number of reasons:[5]

Interference with Need Fulfillment　If people's security, social, esteem, or other needs are threatened, resistance will be great. Even such relatively minor changes as relocating people may disrupt social relations or status relationships and arouse great resistance.

New Learning May Be Needed　It takes a lot of effort to find new and different ways to manage the environment when the status quo changes. For example, if the change is a new boss, an employee must learn the new boss' idiosyncracies and desires. A new organizational structure means that you have to learn who to go to with a problem; where to go to get things done.

Vested Interests　People who have power have a vested interest in the status quo. A manager whose department is threatened with a merger with another will resist to maintain the current position.

Comfort with the Status Quo　People like stability and may have invested a great deal of effort in the current system. The present system may be rewarding, easy, and certain. Change often creates anxiety and at least temporary discomfort. People generally prefer positive reinforcement of the present system over the punishment, even though short-term, that may result from a change to a new system.

Impaired Feelings of Self-Control　Change, especially if imposed by management, often reduces feelings of self-control and autonomy. These feelings may be de-enriching, dissatisfying, or even threatening. A faculty member who has been writing textbooks is told that writing texts is not sufficient to get promoted; articles must also be published in professional journals. This results in an experienced loss of autonomy.

Group Norms　As we noted in Chapter 9, norms are powerful determiners of behavior. Norms generally support the status quo. For example, a change in work standards may result in a violent reaction from the members of the involved workgroups.

Ideological Objections　The person may be against the change for ideological reasons, such as the change's relationship to human rights, war, or status of women. For example, a manager may resign rather than support

Understanding Organizational Behavior

a planned acquisition of a subsidiary in South Africa because of opposition to apartheid.

■ Power and Politics

Power and politics are particularly important when it comes to change. Whenever you unfreeze a situation you are, in fact, tearing down or destroying the old system and creating a new one. The increased ambiguity that results is likely to increase political and power-oriented behavior as people jockey for position in the new state.[6] If the change is opposed by powerful factions, as it was at Great Pacific, then there is little likelihood of successful unfreezing without some strategy to motivate the factions to action. When Mallory created the planning group that included all the important "stakeholders," he was forcing the power coalitions to join in designing the change; thus they were unfrozen.

■ Strategies for Unfreezing

Arouse Dissatisfaction with the Current State
Sometimes dissatisfaction already exists and this step is not needed. But if the organization is complacent and content, as Great Pacific may have been before Mallory's arrival, some act is needed to jolt the organizational members into a dissatisfied state. Mallory did this by telling them that Great Pacific would be closed if they could not improve organizational performance. This strategy of highlighting deficiencies in organizational performance or functioning is the most common way of unfreezing. Since data is particularly useful for justifying discrepancies, it is an important aid in creating a belief that the present state is unsatisfactory and needing correction.[7]

Active and Strong Top Management Support
If top managers are not supporting the change or just giving it "lip service," then unfreezing is unlikely.[8] Lack of top management support also means that middle management is also unlikely to be firmly committed to the change. Top management pressure may be enough in itself to unfreeze the organization, especially if the CEO has considerable power. A top manager's expectations can have a powerful influence (see the Perspective: Expectations and Change). But in many cases, top management support is not sufficient, as was the case at Great Pacific where various organizational power centers were resisting change.[9]

Use Participation
Perhaps the single most powerful technique for aiding the change process is participation in planning and decisions surrounding the change. People tend to support what they have developed. If some outside group or person tries to introduce change, people resist—the "not invented here" syndrome is at work. Participation builds ownership for the change and heightens motivation to make the change work.[10] Participation also helps communicate what the change is about and provide information about the circumstances surrounding the change.

In the preview case, Mallory used participation by having both a planning group and a transition team. Each involved different levels of the organization and built ownership and commitment to the change.

| 16.1 | *Expectations and Change*[11] |

An important element in the success or failure of any change effort is the expectations of the parties. If the manager who is making the change expects success and the other participants believe it will succeed, then it seems plausible and even likely that the change will be successful. This raises an interesting question about the effects of any innovative organizational change: Are the results due to the innovation itself or due to the manager's expectations that the innovation will succeed? A field experiment was designed to test this issue.

The study involved four plants of a large nonunionized clothing patterns manufacturer that was implementing a job enrichment plan to improve productivity and to help ward off a union organizing campaign. The research was designed to find out the relative effects of the innovation and the effects of top manager's expectations about the results of change efforts.

Managers at two of the plants were told that a job redesign change would result in higher productivity while the managers of the other two plants were told that the aim was to improve employee relations. Results showed that the manager's expectations were a more powerful predictor of outcomes than the form of the innovation itself. When managers expected higher productivity, that outcome resulted; when they expected better employee relations, that is what happened.

The conclusion of the research is that managerial expectations surrounding a change may be more powerful in explaining the results than is the innovation itself. Thus, expectations may result in a self-fulfilling prophecy.

Build in Rewards   Since people are motivated to behave in ways that are rewarding, a key to unfreezing is to tie rewards to the change. For example, use recognition, praise, status symbols, or even bonuses to get people involved in the change. In addition, if you can show how the outcomes of the change will create long-term rewards, be sure to make these linkages clear. Mallory used both rewards and punishments (private verbal reprimands) to help with the change at Great Pacific. He also made it clear that the change was necessary to insure they had permanent employment.

Use Force-Field Analysis   One technique that is useful for identifying resistance to change is called **Force-Field Analysis**.[12] The notion here is that there are both driving and resisting forces that tend to keep the situation in equilibrium. If these forces can be clearly identified, then a manager or task force can work on the resisting forces to try to get the equilibrium to move to a new level. The length of the arrows represents the power of each force, just as if it were a mathematical vector. Increasing driving forces, while sometimes effective, is usually much weaker than removing restraining forces because increased drive often tends to be offset by increased resistance (*see* Fig. 16.3 for an example of this technique).

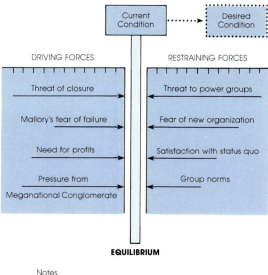

Figure 16.3. Force-field analysis for Great Pacific Shipbuilding.

Current Condition ┄┄→ Desired Condition

DRIVING FORCES | RESTRAINING FORCES

Threat of closure → ← Threat to power groups

Mallory's fear of failure → ← Fear of new organization

Need for profits → ← Satisfaction with status quo

Pressure from Meganational Conglomerate → ← Group norms

EQUILIBRIUM

Notes

1. Length of the arrow indicates the strength of that vector—driving or restraining.

2. Always try to remove restraining forces rather than increasing driving forces.

Moving: The Change Itself

Once resistance has been overcome, we move into the change itself—the **transition** or movement from one state or condition to another. Some changes are instantaneous, like a new parking plan effective on Monday. Others take much longer, like the conversion of an accounting system from manual to computer records. Regardless of how long the transition lasts, it must be managed. We will discuss four aspects of the moving phase: establishing goals, using leverage points, structuring the transition, and maintaining communication.

■ Establish Clear Goals

Once people are unfrozen, they want to know where to move. Goals provide a clear picture of what you want. They provide the blueprint for action, and they communicate what you want the future condition to look like. A written statement explaining the goals and purposes of the change should be widely disseminated to all who are involved in the change.[13] A statement that is developed through participation is desirable. In the Great Pacific example, Mallory made sure that everyone knew the goal of the change: to make the business profitable by the end of next year.

■ Use Leverage Points

Our systems perspective says that there are multiple impacts of the change—it permeates many organizational systems. Every possible point in the system that will help create the change must be utilized. That is where **leverage points** come in because this term refers to any point in the orga-

16.2 | *Overcoming Resistance to Change: A Classic Experiment*[14]

Just after World War II, the Harwood Manufacturing Corporation, which employed mostly women who made pajamas, was having trouble implementing a change that would increase production. There was a strong norm that production should not exceed sixty units per hour. There was also considerable resistance to changing jobs because of the time need to get fully up to speed on a new task.

To help unfreeze the workers, an experiment was set up where total participation (all group members) was used in two groups: representative participation (elected or appointed person represents the group) in one group and no participation for a control group. Participation took the form of explaining the need for change in terms of costs and of having the group approve a plan to achieve the objectives and take the actions needed to effect the change.

Immediate improvements were seen in the groups using total participation and somewhat slower improvements for the group that used representative participation. Learning new techniques occurred much more rapidly in the participation groups and efficiency improved more rapidly in the participation groups. In addition, the quit rates were much lower for these groups. The control group production remained low during the whole time of the experiment. Thus, participation greatly facilitated the change.

A follow-on experiment used participation on the control group with the same improved results. The researchers concluded that by using group participation, resistance to change could be reduced or eliminated.

nization that serves to reinforce and support the change. For example, the change at Great Pacific involves changing procedures and rules, job descriptions, and reporting relationships. Training is also an effective leverage point for clarifying what needs to be done and why it needs to be done, thus creating a smooth transition.

■ Develop Management Structures for Change

Someone or some group needs to be the focal point for the change. This **transition manager** or **transition task force** develops a transition plan that specifies the resources for the transition, the timetable, transition management strategies (pilot projects, consultants), and control mechanisms to insure the change is proceeding as planned. The transition is often easier if the transaction manager is not closely identified with either the present state or the future state. This means that the manager will be perceived as impartial and without a high personal stake in either the new or old state. In addition, the transition manager should be selected because he or she has the clout to mobilize the resources needed, has the respect of top management, and has effective interpersonal skills.[15]

The types of structures that may be used for transition management are shown in Table 16.1.

Table 16.1. Transition management structures.[16]

■ *CEO as the transition manager.* If the change is very important and is not so time consuming that it becomes unmanageable, then the CEO may elect to be the transition manager. In the early unfreezing stages of change, the CEO often takes personal charge as Mallory did in the opening example.

■ *Appoint a transition manager.* Someone may be appointed as the temporary project person for the change. This person serves a role that is very similar to a product person's role in the matrix organization we studied in the last chapter. The transition manager's job is to keep all activities oriented toward the change goals and to surface problems that need resolving. The person that is appointed may be either a functional expert, a line manager, or someone who is a charismatic leader who can marshal considerable confidence and trust of colleagues participating in the change. An example of this later category is when a university president selects one of the most esteemed and respected professors to effect a change in the university's calendar.

■ *Appoint a task force.* This is one of the most popular and effective transition structures because you involve all the constituencies that are concerned with the change on the transition team. This is the approach used by Mallory in our preview case. The reason this approach works so well is that it allows participation of all concerned parties in the change.

■ *Normal hierarchy.* Managers are given the additional task of carrying out the change. This approach has the advantages of the task force, and it involves management personnel in the change itself. This is often a good strategy since the managers will have to live with the change and should have a hand in designing it.

■ Maintain Open, Two-Way Communication

The last major step in transition is to make sure that communication channels are open so that problems and concerns can be resolved with haste and so that we will know whether the change is taking place as planned. Data can be collected through interviews, observations, open forums, reports, company records, or other sources. Without communication and followup, the CEO may be surprised, or even horrified, that a change that was ordered was not accomplished. One reason for these "unexpected surprises" is that "bad news" is avoided, especially when there is no reporting system that forces people to surface it.[17]

Refreezing: Making the Change Stick

If the change has been properly managed, refreezing in the new state of equilibrium should be relatively easy because people will be motivated to adopt the new state and management mechanisms will insure that it is easy to do. However, there are still a few key points to consider when refreezing: building success experiences, rewarding desired behaviors, building social bonds, and developing structures for institutionalizing the change.

■ Build Success Experiences

Success is a very powerful positive reinforcer. If the new system works well, people will be motivated to adopt it. This means that care must be taken to make sure that the change will actually work as planned, without major defects problems. A good strategy for extremely difficult and complex changes is a piece-by-piece or incremental implementation so that one small success can build on another. It may also mean that the problems that are tackled under the new system are the ones that are likely to be successfully resolved.

For instance, assume that a firm has decided to use quality circles to improve its quality and productivity (*see* the Perspective: What Are Quality Circles?). The circle facilitator makes sure that the problems that are initially undertaken are ones with a reasonable chance of success, thus insuring reinforcement and refreezing of the experience of using quality circles.

A success experience can sometimes be created by using **pilot projects**, trying out a change in one workgroup where the change has a high probability of success. Say that the manager of a large division believes that job redesign is a good strategy for improving the organization. The manager knows that while six different sections have volunteered to try the job redesign, there is a much greater probability of success in two of them. The change strategy is to use these two sections as a pilot project. The success of the pilot efforts may encourage job redesign throughout the division. But pilot projects do not always work as planned. The rest of the division may see the pilot groups receiving special attention while they do not, resulting in increased resistance to change.

16.3 What Are Quality Circles?[18]

Quality circles are small groups of volunteers who meet periodically to identify, analyze, and solve problems related to product quality or other issues.[19] These meetings normally involve about one hour per week. Circles investigate problems, recommend solutions, and take actions when they have the authority.

The concept of quality circles originated in Japan in the 1950s based on American quality control techniques. However, they emphasized the involvement of workers in the entire quality process rather than using quality control technicians as is commonly practiced in the United States. Quality circles have been enormously successful in Japan with over a million workers participating.

The strategy of quality circles is to make every member a quality control technician so that he or she can analyze problems using a number of problem solving techniques. This means that the first step in the process is extensive training for circle leaders who, in turn, train the circle members. The leader is normally the workgroup supervisor of the circle. In fact, the circle process is designed to use the regular and normal chain of command; the hierarchy is not bypassed.

Once their training is complete, circles may select or be assigned a problem to solve. They use various techniques to identify the problem, such as a cause-and-effect diagram, which graphically identifies all possible causes that may result in the target effect (i.e., a defective part). Once the problem is clearly identified, they develop solutions and present these solutions to management through normal channels. The presentation process itself is emphasized as a way of providing recognition and perhaps job enrichment for circle members. Rewards may or may not be given for implemented ideas.

■ Reward Desired Behavior

Refreezing the change should employ good behavior management techniques discussed in Chapter 6. Desired behaviors should be positively reinforced and undesirable behaviors—usually those associated with the old situation—should be ignored (extinguished) or punished. While this strategy seems obvious, many organizational changes keep on rewarding people for the old behaviors rather than the new behaviors.

For example, a supply manager was inadvertantly guilty of such behavior. A large complex supply activity was being converted from manual records to computer files. But, there were numerous problems in the computer records that caused out-of-stock conditions. When this happened on some items, like typing paper or pens, it was quite embarrassing to the supply manager. Several of the manager's subordinates, who had been supply clerks under the old system, continued to keep manual records on these "hot" items in their desk drawers. Whenever the manager needed to know something about a hot item, they would be consulted and then praised for their good work. The manager did not realize that the old system was being positively reinforced and thus the change was not being refrozen.

■ Build Social Bonds

While building social bonds is not applicable to all types of change, it certainly is whenever group dynamics are disrupted. Organizational structure changes, physical location changes, or shift changes, all have the potential for disrupting established social and group relations. During this time it is often good strategy to get the group to work together on some common problem—to do teambuilding (*see* Chapter 9 and Reference 20). Social interactions, such as office parties, may also facilitate building social bonds.

■ Develop Structures to Institutionalize

Often a structure that helps solidify the change can make the difference between success and failure. To illustrate, two companies send their employees to training on quality circles. Upon their return, one company relies on the individual managers to develop and support the quality circles, while the other company establishes a quality circle section, headed by a full-time facilitator. Needless to say, the first company's program never got off the ground while the second company's efforts were quite successful because they had established a structure to institutionalize the change.

■ Making Change Work

The problems, processes, structures, and dynamics we have discussed all interrelate within the organizational system. All must be considered if change is to be effective. At each step, unfreezing, moving, or refreezing it is possible to "blow it" and revert back to the original state. Thus, vigilance must be constant until the change is firmly refrozen. In the next section we will see how the change process is often systematized using the concept of organization development.

Organization Development

The roots of organization development (OD) go back over thirty years to such people as Kurt Lewin (who developed the notions of unfreezing, changing, and refreezing), Douglas McGregor (of Theory Y fame), and Robert Blake (one of the developers of the Managerial Grid®).[21] These people and others developed OD as a way of applying behavioral theories to solve organizational problems. Over the years OD has continued its growth and its orientation toward solving organizational problems. It is certainly an important way of changing and improving organizations that involves many of the change strategies we have already discussed.

■ What Is Organization Development?

While there is no definition that everyone agrees upon, we will define **organization development** (OD) as a process of planned organizational improvement that is sustained for a relatively long period and employs behavioral science technology.[22] This definition is quite broad. It includes almost everything relating to applied behavioral science from quality of work life strategies, transactional analysis, quality circles, teambuilding, to weekend sensitivity training.

While people generally agree on some aspects of the definition, many go further in limiting the definition of OD. The following dimensions are often considered essential or at least important for defining OD:

☐ *Organization wide*.[23] Some feel that by definition OD should focus on the entire organization, not just part of it. In practice, most organizations are too big to tackle all at once, so one part is often the focus. However, the systems perspective would say that change in one part may affect the others so an organization-wide perspective is needed.

☐ *Managed from the top*.[24] Others feel that OD must have the total commitment, involvement, and support of top management. While this is certainly desirable, it may be possible to conduct OD in lower levels of the organization where top management is not involved at all.[25]

☐ *Using action research*. Action research, which we will discuss in detail later in the chapter, involves gathering data on organizational problems and then taking action based on the data to solve the problems. One could argue that there are some OD strategies, such as transactional analysis or goal setting, that may not involve action research. However, many consider action research to be an essential element of the OD process.

It is difficult to capture the essence of OD in a definition for there are many aspects of the OD process that are important, but not universally applicable. For instance, many OD activities (often called interventions) focus on working with and developing intact formal workgroups. In addition, OD practitioners are often tied to a set of humanistic assumptions and values, like collaborative management, the importance of individuals, congruence between individual and organizational goals, and the desirability of authentic, open, interpersonal relations.[26] Another way to get the flavor of OD by highlighting how it differs from other techniques is provided in Table 16.2.

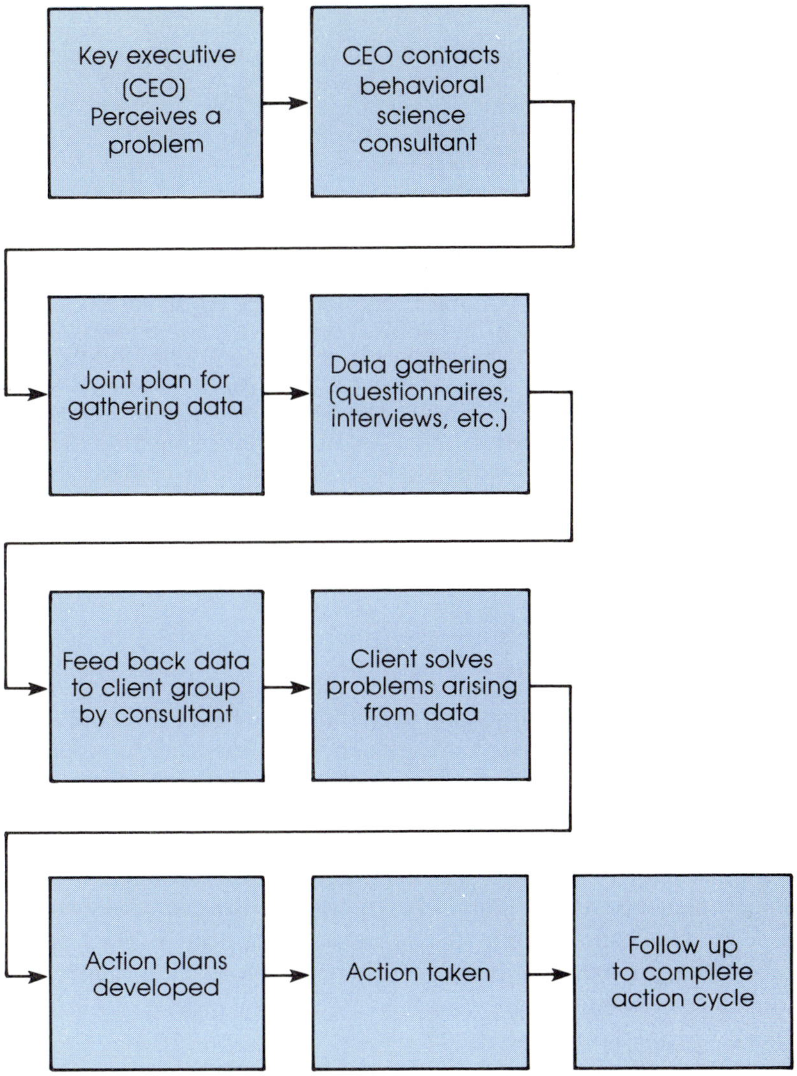
Key executive (CEO) Perceives a problem
CEO contacts behavioral science consultant
Joint plan for gathering data
Data gathering (questionnaires, interviews, etc.)
Feed back data to client group by consultant
Client solves problems arising from data
Action plans developed
Action taken
Follow up to complete action cycle

Figure 16.4. The action-research process for OD.

Table 16.2. How OD differs from other techniques.

- An emphasis, although not exclusively so, on group and organizational processes in contrast to substantive content.
- An emphasis on the work team as the key unit for learning more effective modes of organizational behavior.
- An emphasis on the collaborative management of work-team culture.
- An emphasis on the management of the culture of the total system.
- Attention to the management of system ramifications.
- The use of the action research model.
- The use of a behavioral scientist-change agent, sometimes referred to as a "catalyst" or "facilitator."
- A view of the change effort as an ongoing process.

Wendell L. French, Cecil H. Bell, Jr., *Organization Development: Behavioral Science Interventions for Organization Improvement*, 2nd ed., © 1978, p. 18. Reprinted by permission of Prentice-Hall, Inc., Englewood Cliffs, N.J.

Table 16.3. Data-gathering techniques.[27]

- **Polling.** This technique simply floats a question and provides some scale to respond to. For example, a manager may say, "How optimistic are you that we can complete the contract on time? Use a scale where 1 is very pessimistic and 10 is very optimistic." The manager then counts the poll, posts them on a blackboard or chart, and discusses what they mean.

- **Sensing.** This technique is a little more structured. The manager may or may not be present depending on how threatening that presence might be. Groups of five to seven respond to an open-ended question such as, "What kinds of things are getting in the way of you doing your job more effectively?" A recorder captures the responses on flip-chart paper for later consolidation and review.

- **Questionnaires.** Questionnaires are widely used to measure such things as job satisfaction. They can also be used effectively if they are tailored to the situation and have open-ended questions. The trouble with questionnaires is that they can cover only a limited number of topics, and it is difficult to decipher the relative importance of different problems. Nevertheless, they are cheap and when you have a large number of people to cover, perhaps the only feasible way.

- **Interviews.** Whenever feasible, this is probably the favorite data-gathering method of OD consultants because it is possible to get a better feeling for problems, and it is more likely that some unexpected problem may surface. However, interviews cost more, both in consultant time and in time of the interviewee.

■ Action Research

Action research is the process of gathering data, feeding back the data to the clients, problem solving or dealing with issues that arise from the data, developing action plans to resolve the problems, and following up to see that the action has worked as planned (*see* Fig. 16.4).[28] Action research is a way to find out what problems may exist and then deal effectively with the changes that are needed to solve them. Consultants are often involved in action research because an impartial third party is more likely to get accurate data than an insider with an "axe to grind." However, there are strategies, such as the confrontation meeting (*see* the Perspective: The Confrontation Meeting) or brainstorming (*see* Chapter 13), that can generate data without a consultant.

■ Gather Data for Diagnosis

The first step in action research is to find out what is going on so that a situation can be diagnosed or defined. Gathering data can be done in a number of informal and formal ways. Simply observing what happens is the first step. Are people cheerful? Efficient? Helpful? Watch for nonverbal cues that might indicate problems. The next step, covered earlier in Chapter 8, is to listen carefully and objectively. Listen for meaning. Probe when needed. Obviously, an outsider can elicit freer responses than someone inside the organization. Formal ways of gathering data include polling, sensing, questionnaires, and interviews. Each is briefly discussed in Table 16.3.

■ Feedback Data to Clients

The next step in the action-research process is to summarize the data in some usable form for the clients. Incidentally, we have not addressed who is the client, an important issue. While there is disagreement here, many feel that the client is the workgroup or entire group from which the data were gathered.[29] The data are normally summarized into themes or

16.4 The Confrontation Meeting

A confrontation meeting is an OD design that can be accomplished in one day. It is usually conducted by the senior manager (CEO) of the target organization. It has seven phases.[30]

■ *Phase 1: Climate setting*. The CEO sets the climate for the meeting by stating the objectives and making it clear that people are free to express their concerns openly. This phase will take about one hour.

■ *Phase 2: Data gathering*. The total group is divided into heterogeneous groups of seven to eight people each. No boss and subordinate should be together and each group should contain people from every functional area. Top managers usually meet in a separate group so they will not inhibit communication. The group is given some question to address such as "What obstacles are getting in the way of achieving higher productivity?" or "What is the single most important problem facing you as a manager?" Each group elects a recorder and presents its results to the entire group one hour later.

■ *Phase 3: Information sharing*. Each reporter writes the group's data on newsprint and tapes it to the wall. The reporter then orally presents the results to the group. After all the data have been reported, the leader or members suggest themes or categories that seem to summarize the major issues. This process usually takes at least one hour.

■ *Phase 4: Priority setting and action planning*. The group decides which theme or problem it will work on. Then the entire group divides into subgroups based upon their formal workgroup assignment (i.e., all salespeople would be in one group headed by the sales manager). These functional groups discuss the problem and decide what action they are willing to take to correct the problem. In addition, they highlight problems that must go to the top management team for resolution. This phase takes about an hour and fifteen minutes.

■ *Phase 5: Organization-level action planning*. When the total group reconvenes, each functional unit reports its commitment to actions to the total group. In addition, the groups indicate which items they believe should be addressed first. Top management reacts to the recommendations and makes commitments and decisions (setting targets, assigning task forces, providing resources). This phase will take one to two hours.

■ *Phase 6: Top management team follow up*. Immediately after the confrontation meeting, top management decides when it will follow up on the actions that were agreed upon.

■ *Phase 7: Progress review*. A two-hour follow-up meeting is held with the total group four to six weeks later.

problems that come up during data collection. These are displayed on flip-charts or some other method so the entire group can see them.

■ Problem Solve, Action Plan, and Follow Up

The clients absorb the data and review it to more clearly define their problems. Once the problems are clearly defined, they are often placed in priority order. Then one is chosen for solving; one that there is a reasonable chance of success. The group goes through the process of weighing alternatives, generating solutions, and evaluating data before finally reaching a consensus on the problem's solution. Next follows the **action plan** that spells out who will do what and when. It sets responsibilities for action. A follow-up meeting is scheduled for a few weeks or months hence to see if actions are proceeding as planned.

■ Great Pacific Shipbuilding as an OD Example

Can our preview case be used as an example of OD? Let's see how well it fits the OD and action-research model. It began when the CEO contacted a consultant who was an expert in organizational change (and probably OD). Together they developed a strategy for involving the right people (the stakeholders) and gathering data about performance through interviews. The next step, in what you will recognize as an action-research process, was an offsite, three-day retreat. The consultant fed back the data that he had gathered, and the group spent the rest of the retreat working on important issues that were raised. The problem-solving process resulted in a recommendation and action plan to reorganize and create a transition team. Actions were taken by the CEO and the transition team to make sure that the action plan was proceeding as desired. Follow-up was accomplished by several offsite, one-day workshops. The Great Pacific case is indeed a good example of OD in action.

■ Effectiveness of OD

OD has been widely used in industry, hospitals, churches, military organizations, city governments, Indian tribes, and many other types of organizations. But has it been effective in improving organizational effectiveness? The research evidence[31] has not been encouraging, but it is muddied by the very nature of OD—a broadly focused organizational change strategy. The shear number of processes and outcomes that may be affected by OD is staggering. Since almost everything in an organization is potentially affected by the OD process, it is not surprising that the outcomes are difficult to capture with normal experimental procedures that rely on measuring two or three variables and hoping the remaining ones are constant. Perhaps a more optimistic view would be that OD has been growing over the past generation to a point where most major corporations have some type of internal OD effort.

SUMMARY

Chapter Review

■ Since a change in one subsystem will affect other subsystems, a systems perspective is essential for effective change management. The concept of **equilibrium** is also important since change always involves creating **disequilibrium** so that we can move from one state to another.

■ People resist change and are hard to unfreeze because change affects their need fulfillment, their vested interests, or their feelings of self-control. People may also resist because group norms oppose the change, because they feel comfortable with the current state, or because of their ideological opposition to the change.

Understanding Organizational Behavior

■ Power and politics are important when changing an existing system or creating a new one, thus "**stakeholders**" need to be identified and involved in the change.

■ Major strategies for **unfreezing** include arousing dissatisfaction with the current state, gaining top management support, and using participation.

■ Once resistance has been overcome, the **movement** or **transition** from one state to another must be managed by establishing clear goals, using leverage points, developing a structure for the change, and opening up communication channels.

■ **Refreezing**, making change stick, is easier if the change is successful and positively reinforced. Care should be taken to extinguish old state behaviors, strengthen social bonds, and develop the proper structures for the new state's institutionalization.

■ **Organization development** (OD) is a process of planned organizational improvement sustained over a relatively long period of time and using behavioral science technology. It differs from other change strategies because it emphasizes intact work teams, focuses attention on behavioral processes, makes extensive use of collaborative management, uses action research as its central method, and pays close attention to systems ramifications.

■ **Action research**, a cornerstone of many OD efforts, involves gathering data from a client, feeding the data back to the client, problem solving on surfaced issues, developing action plans, and following up at some later date. While OD enjoys widespread use in organizations, it is relatively unproven through empirical research. One possible reason may be the sheer number and complexity of variables that may be affected by OD.

For Discussion

1. Explain why the change manager must consider the systems ramifications of change.
2. Why do people resist change and what can be done to reduce this resistance?
3. How do expectations and the self-fulfilling prophecy relate to the change process?
4. Explain why even powerful managers must pay careful attention to strategies for unfreezing resistance to change.
5. Pick a problem in implementing change with which you are familiar and make up a Force-Field Analysis chart similar to the one shown in Figure 16.3.
6. What are transition structures and how are they used?
7. Describe the major strategies for refreezing a change.
8. Using the example of implementing quality circles (the Perspective: What Are Quality Circles), indicate which actions are needed to carry out the entire change process in terms of unfreezing, changing, and refreezing.
9. What makes organization development different from other organizational change activities such as management development or quality circles?
10. Explain how the action-research process works.

Key Concepts and Terms

change process
equilibrium
unfreezing
transition
Force-Field Analysis
leverage point
transition manager
quality circles

pilot project
institutionalize
organization development
collaborative management
action research
diagnosis
data-gathering techniques
confrontation meeting

Suggested Readings

Ackerman, L. S. (1982). Transition management: An in-depth look at managing complex change. *Organizational Dynamics* Summer; 46–67.

Burke, W. W. (1982). *Organization development*. Boston: Little, Brown.

Kanter, R. M. (1983). *The changemasters: Innovation and productivity in the American corporation*. New York: Simon and Schuster.

Krell, T. C. (1981). The marketing of organization development: Past, present, and future. *Journal of Applied Behavioral Science*. 17: 309–323.

Tichy, N. M. (1982). Managing change strategically: The technical, political, and cultural keys. *Organization Dynamics* 11: 59–80.

CASES AND INCIDENTS

Shift Change

There are eight employees in the Reliability Test Laboratory. The laboratory performs a quality control function by testing random samples of daily production for physical characteristics. Until January of this year, the employees had worked from 6:30 A.M. to 3:00 P.M. each day. Don Kuntz, a Reliability Engineer, was in charge of the major product line tested in the lab and held the secondary responsibility of managing the lab. As a result, the lab employees were relatively unsupervised.

In mid-December when it became evident to top management that Kuntz was overworked in this dual capacity, David Barnes was advised that he would become foreman of the lab effective January 1. Barnes had previously worked in an office adjoining the lab as a non-supervisory member of the Reliability Engineering Department.

When Harry Boyles, supervisor of Reliability Engineering, advised Barnes of his new assignment he also cautioned him that employees were not working between 6:30 A.M. and 8:00 A.M. Don Kuntz had worked from 8:00 A.M. until 4:45 P.M. in order to handle his engineering responsibilities, and as a result, the lab had been unsupervised early in the shift. To combat this, Boyles had decided to change the hours for all lab employees to 8:00 A.M. through 4:30 P.M. effective January 1. Boyle also informed Barnes that the lab employees had already been informed of the change.

On January 1, when Barnes was introduced as the foreman of the lab, reporting directly to Kuntz, the change in working hours became effective. The change in working hours met with drastic reaction. The men had worked the same shift (as in all the production areas) for an average of twenty-three years each, and immediately began requesting consultation with their union representatives in order to fight the shift change. They were told that such action was legitimate, according to the labor agreement. Next, the group began a work slowdown in protest. After approximately two weeks, Charles Turner approached Kuntz with the comment, "we know that the shift was changed because we weren't working before 8:00 A.M. If you will return the shift to the original time, we will promise to begin work promptly each morning." Kuntz told him that management was pleased with the new arrangement and had no changes in mind.

One of the policies of the company was that safety glasses were to be worn at all times in the lab area; however, Kuntz had been quite lax in enforcement of this rule and Barnes had been told by Boyles to remedy the situation. He relayed this message to the group and everyone wore their glasses the first day until about 4:00 P.M. The group had gathered around a table to the rear of the lab, and Barnes noticed the absence of the glasses as he approached the table. He reminded the group to wear the glasses and they all responded except for Turner who replied, "Why doesn't Kuntz wear his safety glasses over there in his office;" Barnes replied that it was necessary to wear the glasses only around the moving machinery in the lab. Turner responded, "I won't wear my glasses unless Kuntz does." With this, several other employees removed their glasses. Barnes then told Turner, "You are suspended for the balance of this shift and one day, with no pay."

The next day there were five employees absent from work.

From J.V. Murray and T.J. Von der Embse (1973), *Organizational behavior: Critical incidents and analysis*, pp. 288–89. Copyright © 1973 by Charles E. Merrill, Columbus, Ohio. Reprinted with permission.

Discussion questions
1. What factors seem to cause this resistance to change?
2. How might the change process be better designed for success?
3. What should Barnes do now?

Seahaven City

Seahaven City is a medium-sized town in the Northwest United States with a population of about 150,000. The new City Manager, Barbara Young, observes a great deal of waste and inefficiency in the government services for Seahaven. In addition, the recession in the building industry has reduced tax receipts by 24 percent. There is a serious problem with where to get the money to run the city when the reduced budget is activated next quarter.

All city employees, including the department heads, are civil service and cannot be fired or demoted. There are currently 1,950 employees in Public Works, Fire, Police, Water, Electric, Administration, and Personnel.

Discussion questions
1. What change strategy would you use if you were Barbara Young?
2. How would you go about unfreezing the situation?
3. How might OD be used as a change strategy?
4. Diagram the action-research process that might be applied in this case.

REFERENCES

1. Based on a situation presented by Nadler, D. A. (1981), Managing organizational change: An integrative perspective, *Journal of Applied Behavioral Science* 17: 191–211; however, names, places, and events have been changed.

2. For complete coverage of systems theory in relation to change, *see* Katz, D. and Kahn, R. L. (1978), *The social psychology of organizations*, 2nd ed., New York: Wiley; and Alderfer, C. P. (1976), Change processes in organizations, *Handbook of industrial and organizational psychology*, ed. M. D. Dunnette, pp. 1591–1638, Chicago: Rand-McNally.

3. Based in part on the ideas of Lewin, K. (1947), Frontiers of group dynamics, *Human Relations* 1: 5–41.

4. Model adapted from Lewin, Frontiers of group dynamics; and Nadler, Managing organizational change.

5. Many of the ideas in this section come from Zaltman, G. and Duncan, R. (1977), *Strategies for planned change*, New York: Willey; and Nadler, Managing organizational change.

6. Nadler, Managing organizational change; and Tichy, N. M. (1982), Managing change strategically: The technical, political, and cultural keys, *Organization Dynamics* 11: 59–80.

7. Nadler, D. A. (1977), *Feedback and organization development: Using data-based methods*, Reading, Mass.: Addison-Wesley.

8. Zand, D.E. and Sorensen, R. E. (1975), Theory of change and the effective use of management science, *Administrative Science Quarterly* 20: 532–545.

9. Lee, J. A. (1977), Leader power and managing change, *Academy of Management Review* 2: 73–80.

10. Nadler, Managing organizational change. *Also see* Kanter, R. M. (1982), Dilemmas of managing participation, *Organizational Dynamics* Summer: 5–27.

11. King, A. S. (1974), Expectation effects and organizational change, *Administrative Science Quarterly* 19: 221–230.

12. The origin of this technique is Lewin, K. (1951), *Field theory in social science*, New York: Harper & Row. It is widely used by organization development consultants; *see* Fordyce, J. K. and Weil, R. (1979), *Managing with people: A manager's handbook of OD methods*, 2nd ed., Reading, Mass.: Addison-Wesley.

13. Nadler, Managing organizational change.

14. Coch, L. and French, J. R. P., Jr. (1948), Overcoming resistance to change, *Human Relations* 1: 512–532.

15. Beckhard, R. and Harris, R. T. (1977), *Organizational transitions: Managing complex change*, Reading, Mass.: Addison-Wesley; and Ackerman, L. S. (1982), Transition management: An in-depth look at managing complex change, *Organizational Dynamics* Summer: 46–67.

16. Based on Beckhard and Harris, *Organizational transitions*, pp. 47–48.

17. Nadler, Managing organizational change.

18. For details on quality circles, *see* Ingle, S. (1982), *Quality circles master guide: Increasing productivity with people power*, Englewood Cliffs, N.J.: Prentice-Hall; Yeager, E. (1980), Quality circles: A tool for the 80s, *Training and Development Journal* 134: 60–62. For a research review *see* Wood, R.; Hull, F.; and Azumi, K.; (1983), Evaluating quality circles: The American application, *California Management Review*, 26:37–53.

19. Munchus, G., III (1983), Employer-employee based quality circles in Japan: Human resource policy implications for American firms, *Academy of Management Review* 8: 255–261.

20. Dyer, W. G. (1977), *Teambuilding: Issues and alternatives*, Reading, Mass.: Addison-Wesley; *also see* Liebowitz, S. J. and Meuse, K. P. (1982), The application of team building, *Human Relations* 35: 1–18.

21. *See* French, W. L. and Bell, C. H., Jr. (1972), A brief history of organization development, *Journal of Contemporary Business* summer: 1–8.

22. For a discussion of definitional issues *see* Huse, E. F. (1980), *Organizational development and change*, 2nd ed., St. Paul, Minn.: West; French, W. L.; Bell, C. H., Jr.; and Zawacki, R. A., eds. (1983), *Organization development: Theory, practice, and research*, 2nd ed., Dallas: BPI; Burke, W. W. (1982), *Organization development*, Boston: Little, Brown; and Beer, M. (1980), *Organizational change and development: A systems view*, Santa Monica: Goodyear.

23. Beckhard, R. (1969), *Organization development: Strategies and models*, Reading, Mass.: Addison-Wesley.

24. Beckhard, *Organization development*.

25. Beer, M. and Huse, E. (1972), A systems approach to OD, *Journal of Applied Behavioral Science* 8: 79–101.

26. French, W. L. and Bell, C. H., Jr. (1978), *Organization development*, 2nd ed., Englewood Cliffs, N.J.: Prentice-Hall, p. 18.

27. For more information about data collection techniques, *see* Fordyce and Weil, *Managing with people*.

28. This definition is similar to the one used by French and Bell, *Organization development*, p. 88. *Also see* Frohman, M. A.; Sashkin, M.; and Kavanagh, M. J. (1976), Action-research as applied to organization development, *Organization and Administrative Sciences* 7: 129–142.

29. See French and Bell, *Organization development*.

30. Beckhard, R. (1967), The confrontation meeting, *Harvard Business Review* 45: 153–154.

31. For reviews *see* Porras, J.I., and Berg, P.O. (1978), The impact of organization development, *Academy of Management Review* 3: 240–266; Nicholas, J. M. (1982), The comparative impact of organization development interventions on hard criteria measures, *Academy of Management Review* 7: 531–542; and Armenakis, A. A.; Bedeian, A. G.; and Pond, S. B., III (1983), Research issues in OD evaluation: Past, present, and future, *Academy of Management Review* 8: 320–328. For a more supportive study, *see* Porras, J. I.; Hargis, K.; Patterson, K. J.; Maxfield, D. G.; Roberts, N.; and Bies, R. J. (1982), Modeling-based organizational development: A longitudinal assessment, *Journal of Applied Behavioral Science* 18: 433–446.

Organizational Culture and the Quality of Work Life

CHAPTER 17

PREVIEW

- Why is it that some organizations seem to be vibrant and alive while others stagnate? Find out how culture may explain this phenomenon.

- How can corporate heroes help instill values and improve performance?

- What is the climate of your organization? Fill out a questionnaire to find out.

- What is Theory Z? How does it relate to Japanese management?

- Can organizational culture be changed?

- What factors make up a good quality of work life?

- How do companies go about improving quality of work life?

- What organizational changes does the future hold?

Preview Case: Columbine Airlines

Organizational Culture
- The nature of culture
- *Perspective*: Instilling Organizational Values in Japan
- *Perspective*: What Makes an Organizational Hero?
- Organizational climate
- Type Z organizational cultures
- A critique of Theory Z
- Organizational culture and management

Quality of work life
- What is quality of work life?
- What makes up quality of work life?
- *Perspective*: Applications of QWL Strategies
- Quality of work life activities
- Making QWL innovations work

Organizations of the future
- *Perspective*: The Contractual Organization: For Fees, Not Wages

Summary
- Chapter review
- For discussion
- Key concepts and terms
- Suggested readings

Cases and Incidents
- The New Chief Executive
- Eli Lilly

References

PREVIEW CASE: COLUMBINE AIRLINES

When the extensive federal regulation of the United States airline industry was relaxed in the late 1970s, Columbine Airlines saw their chance to expand into a really first-class airline. While Columbine had a good reputation in the Rocky Mountain area, they were not well known in other parts of the country.

Barbara Pike, age forty-two, took over as President of Columbine five years ago after the founder of the airlines, Jonathan Pike, her grandfather, died. Barbara carries on the traditions of the company that are evident from the company slogan: "We care."

Barbara's goal for Columbine is to make it the best airline in America, and perhaps in the distant future, the best airline in the world. She defines "best" in terms of best service, quality, and safety. No United States airline seems to exhibit the kind of care for customers that some overseas airlines, such as Singapore Airlines or Cathay Pacific Airlines, lavish on their customers. She intends to change all that.

Luckily, Columbine is already on its way toward becoming a top airline. Most of the reason for its success is that the firm's employees share the company value of service and caring because that is how they are treated. Her grandfather had considered the airline's workforce to be more like partners than employees. Never in the twenty-five-year history of the company had anyone been laid off because of a business slump. If problems arose, workers *and* management went on a reduced work week or even took pay cuts rather than put anyone out of work.

There is a climate of mutual trust at Columbine between management and employees. Communication is open, easy, and informal. Whenever an important decision is made, employees have an input. Innovations and creativity are encouraged and improvements are rewarded through a variety of incentive and profit-sharing programs. Almost all employees display a strong loyalty for the company.

Perhaps the paramont reason for Columbine's success is shared organizational values, beliefs, goals, and philosophy. Everyone believes in what the company is doing and provides strong support for the direction it is moving.

While every aspect of managing people in organizations is important, when they are all combined, they make up the organizational culture—perhaps the major determinant of effectiveness and quality of working life for organizational members. Columbine Airlines, and many other successful enterprises, has a culture that reinforces the organization's goals.

In this concluding chapter, we will see what elements make up the organizational culture and how it relates to quality of working life. Then we will turn briefly to some future forms of organization that may be an outgrowth of cultural change.

Understanding Organizational Behavior

Organizational Culture

Organizational culture consists of all the shared beliefs, behaviors, and symbols (including language) that are characteristic of an organization at a given time.[1] The concept of culture is broad and encompasses all of the organizational subsystems we have covered so far in this text. Culture describes how everything meshes together to form the organization's essence—its personality.

In this section we will discuss the major dimensions of culture and then turn to the interrelationship between culture and organizational climate. Finally, we will discuss the Type Z culture that is displayed by many successful American companies.

■ The Nature of Culture

While culture encompasses the entire organizational milieu, there are three aspects that seem particularly important: values, rituals, and heroes.[2]

Organizational Values

In Chapter 3, we defined values as broad, general beliefs about some way of behaving or some end state that is preferred by the individual.[3] **Organizational values** are defined in the same way except that the end states are those that are preferred by the organization and shared by organizational members rather than those held by a single individual. Cultures of successful organizations see a good match between individual and organizational values.

An organization's values provide its philosophical direction. Slogans often reflect these shared values. For example. Columbine Airlines slogan, "We care," reflects a high value on providing caring, excellent service to customers and at the same time a concern for employees, too. Other examples of these shared values[4] might be Caterpillar's "Twenty-four hour parts service anywhere in the world," which indicates a great concern for prompt worldwide customer service; and DuPont's "Better things for better living through chemistry," which reflects a commitment to innovation as a prime value.

Many authors attribute Japan's success to the shared values held by everyone in the organization.[5] Japanese organizations spend a great deal of time and effort socializing and instilling values in their employees (*see* the Perspective: Instilling Organizational Values in Japan).

Rituals

A second aspect of organizational culture is the nature of the symbolic actions it takes, its rituals. **Rituals** include many different types of symbolic actions such as ceremonies, shared leisure and play, and behavior patterns, For example, the people who work in the home office of Columbine Airlines get together on the first Saturday of each month for a beer bust. Practically everybody attends and has a good time. In a university, the members of the math department get together for jogging every day at lunch, rain or shine. Staff meetings are another example of ritualistic activities. The number of meetings held, the time, the setting, the seating arrangement, the attendees, and the conduct of the meeting all are influenced by rituals.[6]

Instilling Organizational Values in Japan

The Japanese take the initial orientation of employees very seriously for they see it as a way to permanently instill organizational and work values. In addition to the usual technical training, new employees also receive spiritual training aimed at developing their values.

One example of how this training is accomplished is an endurance walk of twenty-five miles.[7] The first nine miles are covered with everyone walking together as a single body. For the next nine miles people walk in squads and for the last seven miles they must walk alone and in silence. The first nine miles passes pleasantly with everyone conversing and joking. During the second nine miles competition develops between the squads and the pace quickens, resulting in blisters and stiff muscles. For the final segment, people walk single file and in silence—the excitment was gone and each individual was alone. People become very aware of their aches and pains. To finish the walk requires great persistence and spiritual strength, representing an ability to accept responsibility in the face of hardship, a value that is highly prized in Japanese organizations.

Other strategies are aimed at instilling a sense of teamwork in people who have worked primarily as individuals while in school. One training technique is to form new employees into teams who are required to actually produce one of the company's products.[8] This task forces people to work together to get their job done and illustrates the value of teamwork.

Heroes   Most successful organizations have their **heroes**.[9] The heroes may be someone living, such as the high regard that Columbine Airlines has for Ed Carlson (a very successful chief executive at United Airlines); or it may be for some historical person like Jonathan Pike (founder of Columbine), who was extremely influential in building the airline from nothing. Heroes reinforce the organization's cultural values by making success seem human and attainable, providing role models, symbolizing the company to the outside world, and setting a performance standard that motivates achievement.

Situational heroes (*see* the Perspective: What Makes an Organizational Hero?) serve to humanize success by publicizing the results obtained by high-performing organizational members. For example, a million-dollar club may be formed with membership linked to generating $1 million worth of sales within a given period. People who make this goal are rewarded with bonuses or a trip to the South Pacific or Europe. These people are then seen as heroes by other organizational members.

Mary Kay Ash, who founded Mary Kay Cosmetics, is an example of an organizational hero. She provides a role model for others to emulate. At General Electric the hero is Thomas Edison, an inspiring role model for engineers and scientists. The exceptional performance of heroes sets high standards for organizational members and thus motivates performance.

In this section we have covered only three dimensions of culture—organizational values, rituals, and heroes. There are many other organizational processes that have a significant impact on culture, including: communication, group dynamics, decision making, power, leadership, and change.

17.2 | *What Makes an Organizational Hero?*[10]

There are two types of heroes, visionary heroes and situational heroes. **Visionary heroes** have a broad philosophical influence on the organization, they light the way for all employees. In contrast, **situational heroes** inspire people with an example of their day-to-day success.

A visionary corporate hero is driven by the ethic of creativity. The hero inspires employees throughout the firm. Visionary heroes often differ from managers, who are driven by the ethic of competition, or a desire to win the game. However, it is certainly possible for a hero to also be a manager. Thomas Watson, the head of IBM for many years, is an example of a hero-manager.

There are three characteristics of visionary heroes. First, they were right about something, such as a new product, marketing strategy, or organizational strategy; they succeeded in a big way. Second, they are persistent; they do not give up easily even in the face of considerable resistance. Third, they have a sense of personal responsibility for the continuing success of the organization.

Situational heroes are made because of some interaction between personal motivation and characteristics and organizational goals that create a winner. An example might be the article in IBM's corporate magazine, *Think*, which indicates that a salesperson in Seattle has just completed thirty years of membership in IBM's Hundred Percent Club (those people who sold 100 percent of their quota for the month).

Many of these dimensions are included within the concept of organizational climate, the topic of the next section.

■ Organizational Climate

One way to measure the organizational culture, at least in part, is by evaluating its **organizational climate**, which consists of the way people perceive their organizational environment.[11] As with culture, so many different factors make up the organization's climate that no single, universally applicable list of factors may be possible.[12] What is important in one organization or even one part of an organization may not be important in another.[13] To aid you in understanding climate, you may wish to complete the questionnaire in Table 17.1.

If you fill out the questionnaire in Table 17.1, you will note that there are a number of factors that seem to be important determiners of organizational climate across many different organizations.[14] These factors correspond to the five factor scores in the Organizational Climate Questionnaire.

1. *Individual autonomy*. The amount of individual freedom, initiative, and responsibility that a person possesses.
2. *The degree of structure imposed upon the position*. The amount of direction, supervision, rules and procedures, and objectives associated with the job.
3. *Reward orientation*. The promotions, praise, pay, and other rewards including the fairness of the rewards.

Organizational Culture and the Quality of Work Life

Table 17.1. Organizational Climate Questionnaire

Directions: The following are types of behaviors that may occur in organizations. Using the scale below, mark the number that corresponds to the way you perceive your organization behaves in each situation.

1	2	3	4	5
It makes a great effort to do this	It tends do this	I do not know what it would do	It tends to avoid doing this	It makes a great effort to avoid this

____ 1. This organization allows people a great deal of freedom to determine how to do the job.
____ 2. The pay here is fair and equitable.
____ 3. This organization will "screw you" if you are not careful.
____ 4. There are many rules and regulations in this organization.
____ 5. This organization really cares about its employees.
____ 6. Innovation and initiative are encouraged around here.
____ 7. Promotions in this organization are based on politics.
____ 8. There are detailed standards for most tasks in this organization.
____ 9. Employees are often asked to participate in important decisions in this organization.
____10. There is a great deal of criticism in this organization.

Scoring: The first scoring step is to correct several reverse-scored items. For Questions 3,4,7,8 and 10 the score must be converted using the following table:

Your Score	Corrected Score
1	5
2	4
3	3
4	2
5	1

Now add the scores as indicated below:

1. Autonomy, question 1 + 6   _____ (range 2 to 10)
2. Structure, question 4 + 8   _____ (range 2 to 10)
3. Rewards, question 2 + 7   _____ (range 2 to 10)
4. Caring, question 5 + 10   _____ (range 2 to 10)
5. Trust, question 3 + 9   _____ (range 2 to 10)
6. Total Organizational
   Climate Score   _____ (range 10 to 50)

A low score (10 to 25) indicates a very supportive organizational climate. A high score (35 to 50) indicates a hostile climate.

4. *Consideration, warmth, and support*. The degree of care for employees evidenced by the organization and supervisors.
5. *Trust*.[15] The degree to which employees feel they can make themselves vulnerable to the organization without having that vulnerability abused.

An organization such as Columbine Airways will probably have a supportive organizational climate. We already know from the introductory case that the organization seems to really care about its employees, they express consideration and warmth. We might also surmise from the data that an atmosphere of trust prevails because of the way layoffs are avoided even under adverse business conditions. As you might expect, Columbine also has an excellent reward program where people are paid fairly and equitably with bonuses for outstanding performance. One aspect of Columbine that runs somewhat counter to their otherwise supportive climate is that there are many rules and regulations required by the government that take away some of the autonomy in the job. However, this is not a serious problem since most employees feel that it is simply a "fact of life" for the airline industry.

■ Type Z Organization Cultures

During the past several years there has been considerable concern about the ability of American organizations to compete with the Japanese. Analysis of Japanese management generally concludes that there are a number of cultural reasons for Japan's success.[16] William Ouchi has studied this process and asserts that there are also a number of American firms that operate in much the same fashion as Japanese firms—he calls these Type Z organizations .

Ouchi classifies organizations into the three types shown in Table 17.2. **Type A** organizations display the typical pattern of most American firms: high rates of mobility, self-reliance, and individual responsibility. Because of high turnover of employees, there is little long-term concern for employees. **Type J** organizations are typical Japanese companies with lifetime commitment to employees, consensus decision making, slow promotion, and high concern for employees. **Type Z** organizations are American organizations that share some of the same types of concern for people and commitment to long-term goals as do Japanese organizations.

A model of Theory Z, such as the one shown in Figure 17.1, predicts such outcomes as cooperation, intimacy, closeness, trust, autonomy—all aspects of organizational climate. In addition, both Type J and Type Z organizations have a strong sense of corporate values, goals, and culture; there is a cohesion and sense of togetherness.[17] This cultural combination is predicted to result in improved satisfaction, a heightened sense of autonomy, and increased production.

Table 17.2. Type A, Type J, and Type Z organizations.

Type A (American)	Type J (Japanese)	Type Z (Modified American)
Short-term employment	Lifetime employment	Long term employment
Individual decision-making	Consensual decision-making	Consensual decision-making
Individual responsibility	Collective responsibility	Individual responsibility
Rapid evaluation and promotion	Slow evaluation and promotion	Slow evaluation and promotion
Explicit, formalized control	Implicit, informal control	Implicit, informal control with explicit, formalized measures
Specialized career path	Nonspecialized career path	Moderately specialized career path
Segmented concern	Holistic concern	Holistic concern, including family

From W.G. Ouchi and A.M. Jaeger (1978), Type Z organization stability in the midst of mobility, *Academy of Management Review* 3:308, 311. Copyright 1978 by the Academy of Management Review. Reprinted by permission.

Figure 17.1. Model of Theory Z.

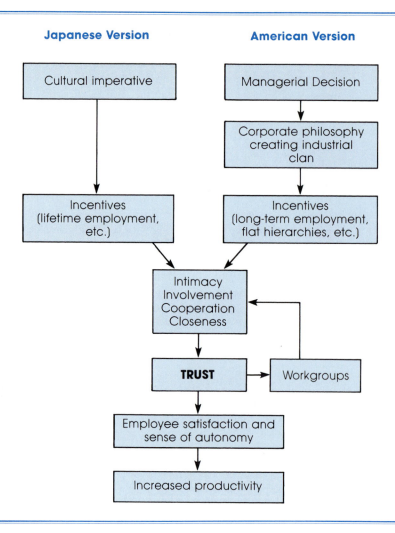

Japanese Version

American Version

Cultural imperative

Managerial Decision

Corporate philosophy creating industrial clan

Incentives (lifetime employment, etc.)

Incentives (long-term employment, flat hierarchies, etc.)

Intimacy Involvement Cooperation Closeness

TRUST

Workgroups

Employee satisfaction and sense of autonomy

Increased productivity

When we look for examples of Type Z organizations, we find many of them already existing. Often listed are IBM, Hewlett-Packard, Rockwell, Eli Lilly, and Intel.[18] Columbine Airlines, in our opening example, might also join such giants as Delta and United Airlines as Type Z organizations. Note that all these organizations have a reputation for excellent performance.

■ A Critique of Theory Z

Since Theory Z is quite new, it is not surprising that little research has been done to test it. There is some research support for the notion that Theory Z-type organizations have flourished in Japan.[19] Problems with Theory Z seem to center around whether or not it can be widely employed in modern American society with our individualistic values.

There is also the question of whether American workers would tolerate slow evaluation and promotion and less specialized career paths. These parts of Theory Z are certainly quite different from the actual practices of many organizations, including some that have been categorized as Type Z.

Understanding Organizational Behavior

Another concern centers around our ability to change organizational cultures. Ouchi suggests a strategy for going from Type A to Type Z (*see* Fig. 17.2). We know from our discussion of change in the last chapter that unfreezing is often difficult. This is especially true for the organization's culture.[20]

Organizational Culture and Management

One factor that always seems to be associated with well-run companies is an effective organizational culture.[21] A distinctive culture exerts a powerful influence on managerial behavior and on the strategies of the organization. It provides the sense of direction and values for all members of the organization. In addition, an organization with a supportive organizational climate has a culture that should enhance the quality of work life of organizational participants, the topic of our next section.

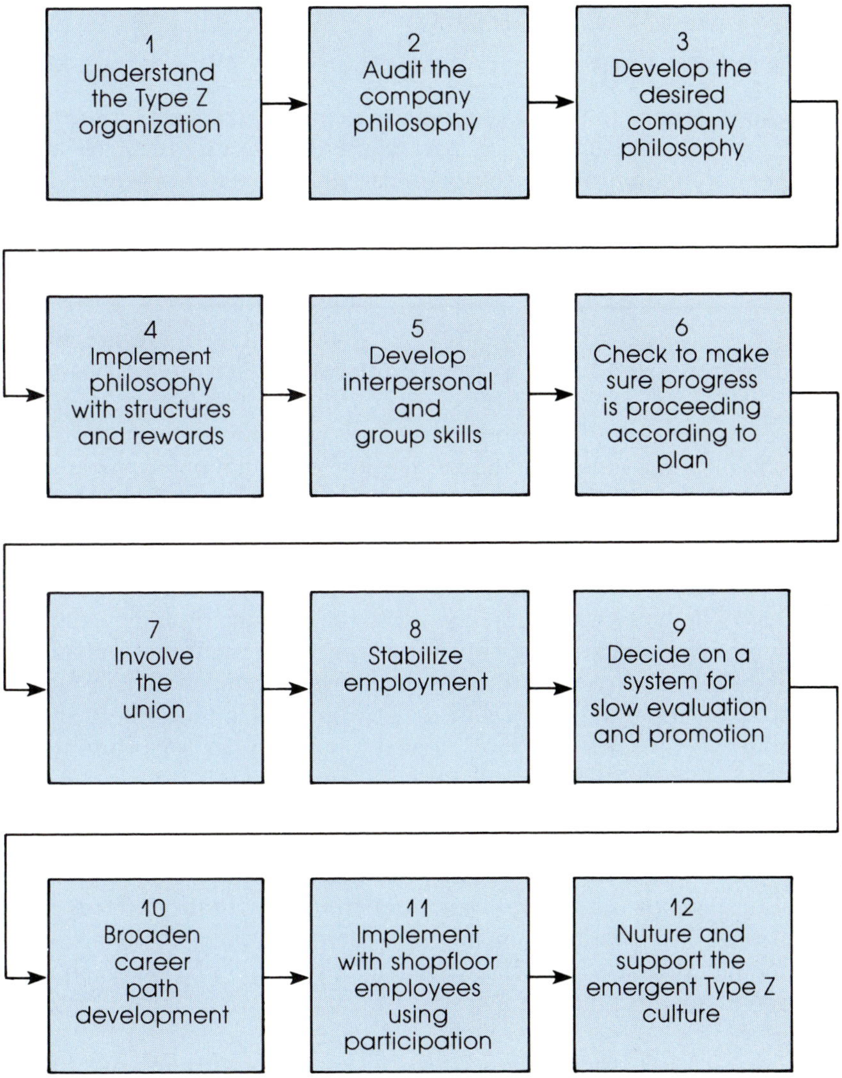

1 Understand the Type Z organization
2 Audit the company philosophy
3 Develop the desired company philosophy
4 Implement philosophy with structures and rewards
5 Develop interpersonal and group skills
6 Check to make sure progress is proceeding according to plan
7 Involve the union
8 Stabilize employment
9 Decide on a system for slow evaluation and promotion
10 Broaden career path development
11 Implement with shopfloor employees using participation
12 Nuture and support the emergent Type Z culture

Figure 17.2. Going from Type A to Type Z.[21]

Quality of Work Life

Quality of work life (QWL), a concept that developed around 1970, is a reflection of the organization's culture.[23] In this section, we will review the meaning of QWL, examine the criteria that result in high QWL, and discuss how to successfully implement QWL innovations.

■ What Is Quality of Work Life?

The meaning of QWL is quite vague. Numerous organizational improvements bear the QWL label including: incentives plans, job enrichment, sociotechnical systems, and quality circles. Since all of these strategies aim at improving the individual employee's well-being, perhaps they are all concerned with improving QWL. We will define **quality of work life** as a concern for the impact of work on individual's well-being as well as for improving organizational effectiveness.[24] The focus of QWL is on outcomes for the individual—how work can cause people to be better rather than how people can do better work.[25]

■ What Makes Up Quality of Work Life?

Another way to define QWL is to review the criteria that make QWL good or poor. Five criteria are particularly important: adequate and fair compensation, opportunity to use human capacities and to grow, social integration in the workplace, constitutionalism in the work organization, and the relationship of work to the total lifespace.[26] These are explained in the following paragraphs.

Adequate and Fair Compensation   While there are no clear standards for adequate pay, it is nevertheless quite an important influence over QWL and quality of life in general. Without sufficient pay, it is difficult to go beyond physiological and safety needs to achieve esteem, growth, and self-actualization. Equitable and fair pay are important determiners of motivation and job satisfaction (*see* Chapter 5). People who are inequitably treated are generally dissatisfied with their jobs and experience low QWL.

Opportunities to Use Human Capacities and Grow   This criterion has to do with the design of work so that it is an enriching experience. The work itself needs to provide opportunities for autonomy, responsibility, and feedback (*see* the discussion of the Hackman-Oldham model in Chapter 7). People want to be able to use valued skills and abilities and learn new ones. People are also interested in opportunities for promotion and growth coupled with reasonable job security.

Social integration in the Workplace   The nature of interpersonal and group relationships is quite important. People need to belong, to fulfill their social needs. An organization offers the opportunity to form support social relationships and friendships. It offers the potential for a sense of community. It is also important that the organization be relatively free of prejudice and sexual harassment.

Constitutionalism in the Work Organization   High QWL organizations are concerned about the rights of employees. The right to privacy, due

Understanding Organizational Behavior

17.3	*Applications of QWL Strategies*

"An important minority of the Fortune '500' companies are attempting some significant work improvement projects," says Richard Walton, an QWL expert who closely follows what industry is doing towards changing QWL.[27] Some of the leaders include General Motors, Procter and Gamble, Exxon, General Foods, TRW, Cummins Engine, and Citibank.[28] In Sweden, Volvo has also been a leader in QWL efforts centered around sociotechnical improvements.[29]

An example of how one of these firms, General Motors, has used QWL is illustrated by their project at Tarrytown, New York, which focused upon management-labor cooperation to improve both plant effectiveness and QWL.[30] Most of the 3,800 employees were involved in planning and problem-solving processes with a heavy emphasis on participative management. Costs of the QWL program of about $1.6 million were offset by gains in productivity and quality. For example, Tarrytown went from one of the poorest plants in terms of quality to one of the best. In addition, absenteeism was reduced from over 7 percent to between 2 and 3 percent. Grievances declined from over 2,000 to 32. The conclusion at Tarrytown is the QWL worked.

process, equity, and free speech are all important. Individuals want to be respected.

Work and the Total Lifespace   The interaction of work with family, friends, and geographical location are also important. Does the work demand so much that it interferes with family and leisure activities? Is there so much stress and pressure that health suffers (*see* Chapter 11)? The interaction between the organization, the family, and the community are increasingly important concerns of QWL.

■ Quality of Work Life Activities

There are four general types of QWL activities: participative problem solving, work restructuring, innovative reward systems, and improved work environments.[31] These activities are discussed in the following paragraphs.

Participative Problem Solving   Participation in decision making (discussed in Chapter 13) has often taken the form of some type of **labor-management cooperative groups**.[32] More recently, quality circles (workgroup level people who solve problems relating to quality and other issues; *see* Chapter 16) have become a popular strategy.[33]

Work Restructuring   The strategy here is to change the nature of work by redesigning the task to be more interesting, challenging, and growth-related. Such changes as job enrichment and sociotechnical system designs (discussed in Chapter 7) apply here.

Organizational Culture and the Quality of Work Life   423

Innovative Reward Systems

Pay systems that stimulate creativity, innovation, and improved sharing of rewards are another key approach. Perhaps the best example here is use of the **Scanlon Plan**, which entails tying financial incentives to organization-wide productivity. A committee of workers and managers is formed to stimulate increased productivity, and a philosophy of participative management is the central focus.[34] Monthly bonuses are paid to everyone in the plant based on increased labor productivity that is obtained through problem-solving approaches to improving production.

Improving the Work Environment

The strategy here is to improve the tangible working conditions by changing working hours, physical conditions, or rules. Such innovations as flexitime (described in Chapter 7 and Reference 35) are often used. Another way to rearrange working schedules is **job sharing**, a strategy where two people share the same job.[36] Each fully qualified person works part-time, and the people divide the responsibilities and benefits of one full-time job. This allows people who want to work, but do not wish to work a full workweek, to be meaningfully employed.

Another strategy for improving the work environment involves redesigning the physical facilities of the workplace to be more pleasing, safe, and comfortable.[37] Many companies are responding to this aspect of QWL—witness the beautiful surroundings of Weyerhaeuser's corporate headquarters shown in Figure 17.3.

Figure 17.3.
Weyerhaeuser headquarters, Federal Way, Washington.

Courtesy of Weyerheuser Company.

■ Making QWL Innovations Work

Unfortunately, QWL efforts do not always work. One recent study examined the long-term effects of QWL projects that had been initially successful. They found that at the end of five years "only *one third of the change programs* exhibited some reasonable level of persistence."[38] The others either no longer existed or they were declining in importance. One reason for the demise of these efforts is that they were never institutionalized, which means that that patterns of behavior did not become part of the daily, persistent functioning of the organization.[39] Fortunately, there are some strategies that may help institutionalize the innovations (*see* Chapter 16 for other suggestions).

Training   While initial training efforts are usually good, follow-on training may be dropped and new organizational members ignored. Where inadequate training exists, the innovations are less likely to be institutionalized.[40] The key is to conduct regular training sessions to make sure everyone knows what behaviors are associated with the QWL efforts.

Commitment   People who are commited are motivated to continue the behaviors associated with the QWL innovation. People seem to have a stronger commitment if they voluntarily choose to participate in the program.[41] They also are more committed if they perceive a need for the program.[42]

Rewards   When improvements in productivity, quality, or other tangible benefits accrue, rewards need to be shared equitably. It is unwise to assume that employees will be satisfied solely by intrinsic rewards.[43] Another issue is whether rewards are linked with performance. Based upon our knowledge of motivation (Chapter 5), we would expect that rewards will be more motivating and will cause more persistent interest in the QWL effort if they are tied to performance.

Diffusion   The issue here is how widespread or diffused the QWL innovation is. If it applies only to a small portion of the organization, it is less likely to persist because "we-they" relationships develop that result in intergroup conflict and competition.[44] If lower-level managers are involved (such as in a job enrichment project), but middle-level managers are left out, they will be likely to resist the innovation and "sandbag" it at the first opportunity.

The preceding concepts give ideas for how QWL efforts can be institutionalized. However, it is not easy to accomplish such changes for QWL efforts often involve a basic change in the organization's culture. For example, participative management strategies abound within QWL techniques. An organization with an authoritarian culture will find it extremely difficult to implement them. In spite of these difficulties, organizations of the future must cope with an increasingly complex environment and much stiffer international competition. Thus, an organizational culture that harnesses the creativeness of its members may be the key to organizational effectiveness and survival.

Organizations of the Future

Effective management of an organization's culture is certainly one of the critical elements for coping with the rapidly changing environment of the 1980s and 1990s. The Type Z culture will become more widespread. Managers will become even more concerned with managing human resources.[45] In addition, new ways of working with unions will develop so that more collaborative cultures emerge.[46] Organizations will realize that high performance and high QWL can go "hand-in-hand." Thus, more collaborative, participative cultures will be the norm.

Organizations of the future will place more emphasis on developing a clear sense of organizational purpose and philosophy.[47] But they will also need to develop better systems for maintaining these key aspects of culture during the transition of one chief executive to the next.[48]

We may also see a major shift in the way work is organized. More emphasis may be placed on team approaches, where people work together in relatively autonomous groups to accomplish the task.[49] It is possible that teams may become so autonomous that they are treated like independent subcontractors (*see* the Perspective: The Contractual Organizations: For Fees, Not Wages).

In conclusion, there will be many changes in organizations that help to cope with environmental change and the competition created by the increasing internationalization of business activity. Emphasis on product quality will become increasingly important. We may also expect employees to demand that organizations place more emphasis on QWL issues. This changing world of work is certainly an exciting place for the manager of tomorrow.

PERSPECTIVE

17.4 | *The Contractual Organization: For Fees, Not Wages*[50]

Charles Handy foresees major changes in organizations of the future. People may work more like contractors with greater self control and less alienation. Here is how he describes the "contractual organization:"

Wages are paid for time spent, input. Fees are paid for work done, output. The professional gets a fee; the worker a wage. Fees are more liberating for the individual, avoiding the hierarchical relationships detested by the Greeks and allowing work to be done at a person's own pace in his or her own way. More and more organizations are realizing that they can contract out a lot of the work to be done without forfeiting control. No longer, with electronic controls, do you have to bring everyone into one shed in order to control their work. The controls can go on line. Mini-electronics puts the factory in the bedroom, with an automatic sewing machine, or at least in a community workshop where sophisticated equipment could be on hire. The new businesses that are springing up increasingly rely on high-technology contracted work. If Marks and Spencer can contract out their manufacturing and still control it, why not others? If hamburger chains can franchise distribution, why not others?

Understanding Organizational Behavior

Chapter Review

■ **Culture** describes how everything meshes in an organization. Three important aspects of culture are **organizational values**, which provide philosophical direction; **rituals**, which includes behavior patterns, ceremonies, and shared leisure activities; and **heroes**, who serve to reinforce organizational values and provide role models.

■ Corporate heroes may be either **visionary**, those who are driven by the ethic of creativity and have broad organizational impact; or they may be **situational** heroes, people who serve to inspire because of their day-to-day success.

■ **Organizational climate** is the way people perceive their organizational environment. Several important aspects of climate include: individual autonomy, the amount of structure imposed on the position, reward systems, consideration, and trust.

■ **Type Z** organizations are American firms that share some of the concern for people and commitment to long-term goals that characterize Japanese organizations, **Type J**. Typical American firms, called **Type A**, exhibit high rates of mobility and are centered around individual effort and achievement. **Theory Z** predicts improved organizational climate because of a corporate philosophy that creates closer links between the individual and the organization.

■ **Quality of work life** is concerned with both the individual employee's well-being and improving organizational effectiveness. QWL consists of adequate and fair compensation, opportunities to learn and grow, effective social integration in the workplace, protection of individual rights, and a good interaction between work and the total lifespace.

■ QWL activities have been conducted in a wide variety of organizations. They usually involve four general types of activities: participative problem solving, work design, innovative reward systems, and improving the work environment. Long-term success of QWL efforts is doubtful unless the changes can become institutionalized or a part of the day-to-day functioning of the firm. Aids for institutionalizing include thorough training, building commitment, establishing effective rewards, and obtaining widespread **diffusion** of the innovation.

■ Organizations of the future will be more concerned with managing their culture and developing organizational philosophies and goals. Managers will emphasize both excellence in performance and high QWL. We may see a shift in the way work is organized from individualistic to a more group-centered approach that may even involve contracting.

For Discussion

1. Describe the factors that make up an organization's culture. Based on your experience, give two contrasting examples of organizational culture.
2. Give an example of an organizational hero. Was this person a visionary or situational hero?

3. Compare and contrast organizational climate with organizational culture.

4. Explain the difference between Type A, Type J, and Type Z organizations. Which one would you prefer? Why?

5. Using the model for going from Type A to Type Z shown in Figure 17.2, explain how it fits with Lewin's model of the change process (unfreezing, changing, refreezing) discussed in Chapter 16. Do you see problems? Explain.

6. Describe an organization with a high quality of work life and a low quality of work life.

7. How can the QWL process be made more effective?

8. Do you agree that the organization of the future may be a contractual organization? Why or why not?

Key Concepts and Terms

organizational culture	Type J organization
organizational values	Theory Z
rituals	quality of work life
heroes	commitment
organizational climate	diffusion
Type Z organization	institutionalization
Type A organization	contractual organization

Suggested Readings

Deal, T.E., and Kennedy, A.A. (1982). *Corporate cultures*. Reading, Mass.: Addison-Wesley.

Mares, W.J., and Simmons, J. (1983). *Working together: From shop-floor to boardroom*. New York: Knopf.

Miles, R.E., and Rosenberg, H.R. (1982). The human-resource approach to management: Second-generation issues. *Organizational Dynamics* Winter; 26–41.

Nadler, D.A., and Lawler, E.E., III. (1983). Quality of work life: Perspectives and directions. *Organizational Dynamics* Winter; 20–30.

Schwartz, H., and Davis, S.M. (1981). Matching corporate culture and business strategy. *Organizational Dynamics* Summer; 30–48.

CASES AND INCIDENTS

The New Chief Executive

Richard Chan, the new CEO, faced a tough problem at Associated Electronics, a manufacturer of precision test equipment. Sales were declining because Associated had failed to expand their international operations in spite of the forecasted decline in the domestic market. In addition, the previous CEO, Victor York, had been a hard taskmaster who had alienated all the younger engineers and sales-people. Turnover rates were high and absenteeism was a problem.

Perhaps the worst problem was that technology was by-passing them. The Japanese had entered the market and already had a substantial market share. Associated's major American competitor, Hewlett-Packard Company, had developed a number of innovations that had put them on the cutting edge. Hewlett-Packard also had a strong international division.

Internally, there are a number of management problems, including poor communication, intergroup conflict, poor decision making, and a general low level of motivation.

Discussion questions

1. What should Richard Chan do to resolve these problems?
2. If the culture needs changing, how should he go about it?
3. What changes would need to be made to improve the organizational climate?

Eli Lilly

The following are excerpts from an interview with Richard D. Wood, CEO of Eli Lilly, a large pharmaceutical manufacturer with net sales of over $2 billion.

How would you describe the traditions and values that were carried over from the time Lilly was a family business?

■ *Well, I think a lot of traditions have been kept in the company, and I think our present management has always felt an obligation to continue them because we think they serve the company very well. As we look at the world today and on down the road, they stand out as sound, valuable influences that are and will be important to the way the corporation operates. The key one relates to people and the importance that was always placed on the industrial relations aspect of managing the business; I guess this translates into a belief that people really are what makes the corporation and the business. You need the best quality people that you can find, and you need to motivate them, pay them well, and treat them fairly—with respect and with equity. This means promoting people on the basis*

of merit, rather than other elements that sometimes creep into the picture.

What is the Lilly style of managing?

■ *I would say it's basically the team approach. I think it's carried out in a very positive way—we want every piece of the business that is concerned with an issue to have a part in the decision-making process. And we want to get a consensus on the proper course of action, which means that each participant will have an opportunity to contribute to that decision.*

Are there any concluding remarks?

■ *I would like to point out the one thing that makes Lilly unique, and that's the atmosphere in our company—an atmosphere you might not find in many organizations. I think our employees in the company understand the conditions under which we operate and they respect them—and I think they also respect the honesty and integrity of management in the decision-making process, particularly as it applies to them as individuals. And if we can maintain that kind of feeling in that kind of atmosphere, ev-*

erything else will fall into place. Pretty good formula, I think.

Discussion questions

1. Does Eli Lilly appear to exhibit Type A or Type Z behavior?
2. How would you characterize the organizational climate at Eli Lilly?
3. Can you detect a clear philosophy for this organization?

REFERENCES

1. This definition is similar to the one used by Pettigew, A. W. (1979) On studying organizational cultures, *Administrative Science Quarterly* 24: 570–581; Harris, P. R. and Moran, R. T. (1979), *Managing cultural differences*, Vol. 1, Houston: Grid; and Sathe, V. (1983), Implications of corporate culture: A manager's guide to action, *Organizational Dynamics*, 12(2):5–23.

2. Deal, T. E. and Kennedy, A. A. (1982), *Corporate culture*, Reading, Mass.: Addison-Wesley.

3. Based on Rokeach, M. (1968), *Beliefs, attitudes, and values*, San Francisco: Jossey-Bass.

4. Deal and Kennedy, *Corporate culture*.

5. Pascale, R. T. and Athos, A. G. (1981), *The art of Japanese management*, New York: Simon and Schuster; and Ouchi, W. G. (1981), *Theory Z*, Reading, Mass.: Addison-Wesley.

6. Deal and Kennedy, *Corporate culture*.

7. Rohlen, T. P. (1974), *For harmony and strength*, Berkeley, Ca.: University of California Press.

8. Clutterbuck, D. (1978), Down to earth training for graduate recruits, *International Management* May: 45–47.

9. Based on Deal and Kennedy, *Corporate culture*.

10. Based on Deal and Kennedy, *Corporate culture*.

11. Schneider, B.; Parkington, J. J.; and Buxton, V. M. (1980), Employee and customer perceptions of service in banks, *Administrative Science Quarterly* 25: 252–267.

12. *See* Jones, A. P. and James, L. R. (1979), Psychological climate: Dimensions and relationships of individual and aggregated work environment perceptions, *Organizational Behavior and Human Performance* 23: 201–250.

13. *See* Powell, G. N. and Butterfield, D.A. (1978), The case for subsystem climates in work organizations, *Academy of Management Review* 3: 151–157; and Drexler, J. A. (1977), Organizational climate: Its homogeneity within organizations, *Journal of Applied Psychology* 62: 38–42.

14. Campbell, J. P.; Dunnette, M. D.; Lawler, E. E., III; and Weick, K. E. (1970), *Managerial behavior, performance, and effectiveness*, New York: McGraw-Hill.

15. *See* Zand, D. E. (1972), Trust and managerial problem solving, *Administrative Science Quarterly* 17: 229–239; and Barnes, L. B. (1981), Managing the paradox of organizational trust, *Harvard Business Review* Mar.–Apr.: 107–116.

16. Ouchi, W. G. and Jaeger, A. M. (1978), Type Z organization: Stability in the midst of mobility; *Academy of Management Review* 3: 305–314; and Ouchi, *Theory Z*.

17. Marshland, S. and Beer, M. (1983), An evaluation of Japanese management: Lessons for U.S. managers, *Organizational Dynamics* Winter: 49–67.

18. Ouchi, *Theory Z*, p. 31.

19. Sullivan, A critique of Theory Z.

20. Allen, R. E. (1976) Changing corporate culture, *Sloan Management Review* Spring.

21. Swartz, H. and Davis, S. M. (1981), Matching corporate culture and business strategy, *Organizational Dynamics* Summer: 30–48.

22. Adapted from Ouchi, *Theory Z*, Chapter 5.

23. For a review of the origins of QWL, *see* Nadler, D. A. and Lawler, E. E., III (1983), Quality of work life: Perspectives and directions, *Organizational Dynamics* Winter: 20–30. *Also see* (1973) *Work in America*, Cambridge, Mass.: MIT Press; Davis, L. E. and Cherns, A. B., eds. (1975), *The quality of working life*, New York: The Free Press; and Hackman, J. R. and Suttle, J. L. (1977), *Improving life at work*, Santa Monica: Goodyear.

24. This definition is based on Lawler, E. E., III (1982), Strategies for improving the quality of work life, *American Psychologist* 37: 486–493; and Nadler and Lawler, Quality of work life.

25. Nadler and Lawler, Quality of work life, p. 26.

26. This section is adapted from Walton, R. E. (1973), Quality of working life: What is it?, *Sloan Management Review* Fall: 11–21.

27. Walton, R. E. (1979), Work innovations in the United States, *Harvard Business Review* 57: p. 91.

28. Walton, Work innovations in the United States. *Also see* Mares, W. J., and Simmons, J. (1983), *Working together: From shopfloor to boardroom*, New York: Knopf.

29. Gyllenhammar, P. G. (1977), *People at work*, Reading, Mass.: Addison-Wesley.

30. Guest, R. H. (1979), Quality of work life—learning from Tarrytown, *Harvard Business Review* 57.

31. The categories and the discussion are based on Nadler and Lawler, Quality of work life.

32. *See* Fuller, S. J. (1980), How quality-of-worklife projects work for General Motors, *Monthly Labor Review* July: 37–39; Bluestone, I. (1980), How quality-of-worklife projects work for the United Auto Workers, *Monthly Labor Review* July: 39–41.

33. Yeager, E. G. (1981), The quality control circle explosion, *Training and Development Journal* Apr.: 98–105; and Wood, R.; Hull, F.; and Azumi, K., Evaluating quality circles: The American application, *California Management Review*, 26:37–53.

34. Driscoll, J. W. (1979), Working creatively with a union: Lessons from the Scanlon plan, *Organizational Dynamics* Summer: p. 61.

35. Ronen, S. (1981), *Flexible working hours*, New York: McGraw-Hill.

36. Frease, M. and Zawacki, R. A. (1979), Job sharing: An answer to productivity problems?, *Personnel Administrator* Oct.

37. Steele, F. I. (1973), *Physical settings and organization development*, Reading, Mass.: Addison-Wesley; and Holahan, C. J. (1978), *Environment and behavior*, New York: Plenum.

38. Goodman, P. S. and Dean, J. W., Jr. (1983), Why productivity efforts fail, in *Organization development: Theory, practice, and research*, rev. ed., eds. W. L. French, C. H. Bell, Jr., and R. A. Zawacki, Plano, Texas: Business Publications.

39. This definition is similar to the one used by Goodman and Dean, Why productivity efforts fail.

40. Goodman and Dean, Why productivity efforts fail; Nadler and Lawler, Quality of work life.

41. Goodman and Dean, Why productivity efforts fail.

42. Nadler and Lawler, Quality of work life.

43. Walton, R. E. (1980), Establishing and maintaining high commitment in work systems, in *The organizational life cycle*, eds. J. R. Kimberley and R. H. Miles, San Francisco: Jossey-Bass.

44. Goodman and Dean, Why productivity efforts fail; Nadler and Lawler, Quality of work life. *Also see* Walton, R. E. (1975), The diffusion of new work structures: Explaining why success didn't take, *Organizational Dynamics* Winter: 3–21; and Walton, R. E. (1977), Successful strategies for diffusing work innovations, *Journal of Contemporary Business* Spring: 1–22.

45. Miles, R. E. and Rosenberg, H. R. (1982), The human-resource approach to management: Second-generation issues, *Organizational Dynamics* Winter: 26–41.

46. Greensberg, P. D. and Glaser, E. M. (1981), Viewpoints of labor leaders regarding quality of worklife improvement programs, *International Journal of Applied Psychology* 30: 157–175.

47. Vaill, P. B. (1982), The purposing of high performing systems, *Organizational Dynamics* Autumn: 23–39.

48. Pickhardt, C. E. (1981), Problems posed by changing organizational membership, *Organizational Dynamics* Summer: 69–80.

49. Miles and Rosenberg, The human-resource approach to management.

50. Handy, C. (1980), The changing shape of work, *Organizational Dynamics* Autumn: p. 31.

GLOSSARY

abililty The skills and knowledge that make it possible for a motivated person to perform.

absenteeism The number and duration of absences from work of an employee or group of employees. Often expressed as a percentage of total available working hours.

achievement motive Concern with pursuit of excellence, accomplishing unique goals, and achieving high levels of performance and efficiency.

achievement-oriented leadership Behavior that encourages subordinates to set challenging goals, show confidence in subordinates, and continuously seek improvement in subordinates' performance.

action-research The process of gathering data, feeding back the data to a client group, problem-solving issues that arise from the data, developing action plans to resolve problems, and following up to see that actions have worked as planned.

active listening Empathetic listening used when someone else owns a problem and needs to work through its solution.

acute episodic stress Stress caused by intense, relatively infrequent events with relatively brief physiological effects but long-lasting psychological effects.

Adult ego state That part of a person that seeks knowledge, gathers facts, analyzes data, and organizes and tests reality.

affiliation motive Concern for social relationships, such as friendship, love, and approval.

assessment center A technique that uses a number of traits and behaviors to assess a person's suitability for being hired or promoted.

attitude Tendency to react in a favorable or unfavorable way toward some object, person, group, or idea.

authority The right to order or ask others to do what you want them to do.

autocratic management A domineering manager who makes decisions without consulting employees.

autonomous workgroups Another term for self-managing workgroups.

autonomy The degree of freedom surrounding the work.

aversive Unpleasant, repugnant, or disgusting.

avoidance A strategy of conflict resolution that relies upon avoiding a confrontation with the hope that the conflict will defuse itself.

behavior An observable, tangible act done by someone.

behavior modification The process of changing behavior by managing the consequences that follow some behaviors.

belief A personal conclusion about what is true or not true or what is beautiful and not beautiful about the world.

biofeedback Using information about pulse, breathing rate, and blood pressure to provide feedback to enhance relaxation.

blocking roles The roles played by group members that are concerned with opposition or blocking of the group's goals.

bounded rationality The ability to seek and choose rational decisions is limited or bounded by our capacity to acquire and process complex information.

brainstorming A technique for creatively generating and evaluating ideas.

buffers   Departments or people whose task is to deal with the environment and thus buffer the technical core of the organization.

bureaucracy   A form of organization that is oriented toward impersonal rule enforcement, systematic spheres of competence for members, fair allocation of resources, and written records.

burnout   A state of mental, emotional, and physical exhaustion that results from working with people and complex organizations over an extended period of time in emotionally draining situations.

centralization   Centralized decision making and control.

change   To move from one state or condition to another state or condition.

charismatic leadership   Leadership by force of personality and abilities that has a profound and extraordinary effect on followers.

charting   The use of some type of graph or chart to monitor behavior over time.

chief executive officer (CEO)   The senior manager in the firm who is responsible for the overall operation of the organization; usually, the CEO is also the president.

Child ego state   That part of personality that is concerned with impulses, feelings, and uninhibited release of emotions; not related to age.

chronic stress   Stress that is encountered relatively frequently as part of the day-to-day workload and task.

circadian rhythm   The twenty-four hour cycle of the body involving changes in heartrate, metabolism, sleep cycles, and urine flow.

coacting workgroups   People who work together as a group but whose tasks are relatively independent from one another.

coalition   An alliance or union between two or more people.

coercive power   The ability to order someone to do something backed up by force or punishment.

cognitive dissonance   When two attitudes, beliefs, or behaviors conflict or are inconsistent with each other.

cohesiveness   The attractiveness and hold that a group has for its members. The strength of the members desire to remain in the group and be committed to the group.

collaborative management   A management style that obtains the involvement of employees in the management of the organization

competition   Two or more people or groups seeking to gain the same thing that the others are seeking.

complementary transaction   When a message that is sent to a specific ego state gets the predicted or expected response.

compromising   A strategy of conflict resolution that involves bargaining and negotiations.

conflict   The perception that one's needs, concerns, or desires are being frustrated or are about to be frustrated.

conformity   The degree of adherence to the group's norms.

confrontation meeting   An OD strategy that is designed to diagnose organizational problems and take action to resolve them.

consequence   The outcome that follows some behavior, such as a reward or punishment.

consideration   The concern of a leader for the followers, including friendliness, supportiveness, open communication, recognition.

contingencies of reinforcement   The systematic management of the S-O-B-C model of behavior modification so that behavior changes in the desired direction.

contingency approach   An approach to management that is based upon using situational effects to explain and predict behavior.

contractual organization   An organization that is structured so that employees are treated as independent contractors with fees being paid for work done.

control group   A group in an experiment that is not exposed to the experimental treatment.

cooperation   Working together to achieve mutual goals.

cooptation Making people whose support is needed members of the group so that they will support the groups norms, values, and goals.

correlation A statistical method of showing a relationship between two variables. Correlation coefficients range from -1.0 to $+1.0$. Zero correlation means no relationship while a positive or negative number of 1.0 means perfect correlation.

crossed transaction A message that is addressed to one ego state but receives an unexpected response from another ego state that disconfirms the person's position.

decentralization The delegation or dispersion of decision making to lower organizational levels.

decision making The process of thought and action that culminates in choice behavior.

defense mechanisms Strategies and techniques that are used by an individual to reduce anxiety and frustration and protect self-esteem.

delegation Allowing subordinates or groups to make a decision on their own.

Delphi technique A method for systematically gathering written judgments from individuals by using sequential questionnaires interspersed with summaries of results from previous responses.

departmentation The process of breaking down the organization into units or departments.

dependent variable An end result that is caused by some independent variable.

devil's advocate Someone whose role is to question decisions and take the opposing view on a decision.

diagnosis Determining what the problem is using data gathering or analysis techniques.

differentiation The degree that departments differ from one another, both structurally and emotionally.

diffusion The spreading of innovation; particularly QWL projects.

directive leadership Leaders who are more concerned with the task; with initiating structure.

division of labor The way that tasks are divided among organizational members.

efficiency Accomplishing the job with a minimum expenditure of effort and materials.

ego state A consistent pattern of feeling, thinking, and experience that is related to a corresponding consistent pattern of behavior. The three ego states are Parent, Adult, and Child.

encoding The process of making the message of the sender into a form that can be recognized by the receiver.

environment The environment consists of all the elements or factors outside the boundary of the organization; such as, customers, suppliers, politics, economic conditions, and national culture.

equilibrium A state of balance because of opposing forces.

equity theory The process of explaining how individuals compare their rewards and efforts with others and perceive fair and equal treatment or inequity.

E.R.G. theory A theory of motivation that builds upon Maslow's hierarchy of needs. It involves only three needs: existence, relatedness, and growth.

expectancy theory A theory of motivation that attempts to explain why people choose various paths that will lead to need satisfaction.

expectations Anticipation that an event or behavior will lead to outcomes.

experimental research A researcher manipulates the situation or events and controls the research environment to establish causality of the experimental treatment.

expert power Power derived from expertise on a subject. Others are influenced because of perceived superior knowledge.

extinction Ignoring or doing nothing following some behavior.

extrinsic rewards Rewards that come from sources outside the individual; rewards from others.

feedback   Any kind of returned information from a source; a response to a sender's message; clear and direct information about job outcomes and job performance.

field of experience   The totality of one's past experiences, personality, and self-concept.

fight-or-flight response   A reaction to a stressor that prepares the body for fighting or fleeing by increasing the heartrate or pumping adrenalin into the body.

fixed interval schedule   A fixed amount of time passes between rewards.

fixed ratio schedules   A reward is given after a fixed or specified number of responses.

flat organizational structure   An organization with few levels between the highest and lowest person in the organizational hierarchy; wide spans of control.

flexitime   A system where employees can choose their own work schedules—especially arrival and departure times—within certain limits.

forced compliance   Applying pressure to get someone to voluntarily behave in a way he or she do not want to, thus creating dissonance and changing his or her attitudes.

force-field analysis   A technique for identifying the driving and restraining or resisting forces associated with a given change.

forcing   A method of conflict resolution that involves the use of power or coercion to resolve a conflict.

frustration-regression   That part of E.R.G. theory which states that people who are continually frustrated in satisfying a need will regress to seeking satisfaction of a lower need.

functional departments   Structuring based on placing people with the same expertise in one department.

games   Recurring patterns of behavior that are aimed at some predictable outcome or payoff that is usually associated with a negative life position.

goal acceptance   Whether or not goals are accepted by the employee.

goal clarity   The degree of specificity and clarity possessed by the goals.

goal difficulty   The level of challenge or difficulty of the goals.

goal setting   The process of developing, negotiating, and formalizing targets that an employee is responsible for accomplishing.

goals and values subsystem   That part of the organizational system that is concerned with beliefs, attitudes, goals, and values of the organization and its members.

grapevine   All informal communication within the organization.

group   A collection of individuals who have interactions with one another toward some common goal or purpose.

group consensus   A decision process where all group members can accept the decision even though they may not completely agree with it.

groupthink   The tendency for a group to have reduced reality testing, mental efficiency, and judgment because of ingroup pressures.

growth-need strength   A moderator of the job enrichment process; the need to develop, grow, experience new skills, and be challenged.

halo effect   A general impression that causes one or more characteristics to be used to evaluate a person on other characteristics.

heroes   People that are held in high regard by members of an organization. They may be visionary heroes, who have broad philosophical impact on the organization, or they may be situational heroes, who inspire others through day-to-day success.

horizontal division of labor   Breaking down and organizing into tasks, functions, products, or areas; departmentation.

horizontal integration   People, groups, or departments whose purpose is to coordinate the activities of functional departments.

hygiene factors   Factors that are similar to extrinsic rewards: pay, supervision, rules and regulations, working conditions.

idiosyncratic credits   Deviance that is tolerated because an individual has accumulated credits for being a good group member and conforming to group norms over a long period of time.

I-message   A way of confronting problems that involves making a statement composed of three elements: behavior, tangible effects, and feelings.

implicit favorite model   The decision model which states that people pick an early favorite in the decision process and even though they continue to evaluate alternatives they have already chosen an implicit favorite solution.

impression management   The process of controlling the images and perceptions that other forms about us.

incentive pay   Pay that provides a motivation to produce or perform.

independent variable   The causal factor in research.

inequity   The ratio of outcomes to inputs is perceived to be unfair when compared with those of some other person or group

influence   The process of producing intended effects in individuals, groups and organizations.

informal organization   A network of personal and social relationships that arise spontaneously as people associate with one another.

informational listening   A listening process that consists primarily of the transmission of information from a speaker to a listener.

ingratiation   Making a conscious effort to increase another's liking of the ingratiator.

initiating structure   The concern of the leader for task; such as directing, planning, controlling, problem solving.

institutionalize   To make a new condition part of the normal day-to-day, persistent operation of the organization.

integration   The process of coordinating and integrating the diverse activities that are created by the division of labor of differentiation.

interacting group   A workgroup where all members must complete the task before the product is done. Also, a group that communicates openly during the group process.

intergroup conflict   Conflict between two groups.

interpersonal conflict   Conflict between two people.

interpersonal listening   A listening process that involves an interaction between the speaker and the listener.

intervention   Any action that intervenes in an organizational process; a term often used by OD practitioners.

intragroup conflict   Conflict within a group.

intrapersonal conflict   Conflict within an individual.

intrinsic rewards   Rewards that come from within the person or from the job itself.

intuitive decisions   Decisions that are habitual and automatic; programmed decisions.

job characteristics   Those characteristics that are needed for an enriched job; including skill variety, task identity, task significance, autonomy, and feedback.

job characteristics model   A model of the enrichment process that predicts certain outcomes if jobs are enriched.

job design   The deliberate, purposeful planning of the job including all its structural and social aspects and their effect on the employee.

job engineering   Maximizing the efficiency of the job through time and motion studies and man-machine interfaces.

job enlargement   Adding more tasks to the job for variety.

job enrichment   The process of making jobs more interesting, meaningful, and challenging by using the proper blend of job characteristics.

job rotation   Doing different jobs to add variety, or for training.

job satisfaction   The degree of pleasurable or unpleasurable feelings that one has toward a job or job experiences.

leader-match approach   An approach to leadership which states that leaders should be matched to the situation or that situations should be redesigned to fit the leader.

leadership   The process of influencing others toward goals.

left-brain functions   The left brain (of a right-handed person) controls the analytic, systematic, sequential, and verbal functions.

leverage point   Any point in an organization that serves to support and reinforce a change.

line activities   Activities that affect the direct production and sales of an organization.

locus of control   The degree of which a person feels that his or her life is controlled by self or internally versus by the environment, fate, or chance, or externally.

maintenance roles   Those roles performed by an individual or group that are concerned with maintaining the interpersonal relationships of the group.

management   The process of planning, organizing, controlling, and leading the efforts of organizational members toward goals.

management by objectives (MBO)   A managerial process where superiors and subordinates jointly identify common goals, define areas of responsibility, measure progress, and assess results.

Managerial Grid®   A model of leadership that considers the interaction of concern for people and concern for production on a grid and classifies leaders according to their location.

managerial subsystem   That part of the organizational system that is concerned with coordinating, planning, controlling, and leading.

Maslow's hierarchy of needs   A theory of motivation that states that needs are arranged in a hierarchy. When a given need predominates, it will motivate until satisfied; then another higher-level need will take over.

matrix organization   An organizational structure with dual reporting channels so that the same person has two bosses, a functional one and a project or product one.

merit pay   Pay that is tied to performance appraisals.

messages   The thoughts, images, feelings, ideas, and facts that are transmitted from one person to another.

motivation   The process that causes behavior to be energized, directed, and sustained.

motive   The state of tension within an individual that arouses behavior directed toward satisfying some goal; see need.

need   A tension created by some psychological or physiological deficiency that arouses an individual to try to satisfy that need.

negative reinforcement   The removal of an unpleasant or aversive stimulus that results in an increase in behavior.

nominal group technique (NGT)   A decision-making system using a structured group meeting where people work in the presence of others but without interaction with them.

nonverbal communication   Any conscious or unconscious signal, other than a verbal one, that communicates. Typically, nonverbal signals include eyes, face, body posture, hand movements, dress, and spatial relationships.

norms   Rules of behavior and expected ways of behaving that have been accepted as legitimate by members of the group.

objective   A broad statement of a desired future condition that provides direction.

operant conditioning   The management of behavior by altering environmental events and the consequences that follow behavior.

organization   A system that coordinates people, jobs, technology, and management practices to achieve goals.

organization development (OD)   A process of planned organizational improvement that is sustained for a relatively long period of time and employs behavioral science technology.

organizational behavior   The study of the human aspects of organizations, including individual behavior, group behavior, and their interaction with organizational structure, culture, and processes; with the goal of improving organizational effectiveness.

organizational behavior modification   The application of behavior modification strategies to organizational situations.

organizational climate   The way people perceive their organizational environment; including such aspects as autonomy, structure, rewards, consideration, and trust.

organizational culture   The shared beliefs, philosophies, values, behaviors, and symbols (including language) that characterize an organization at a given time.

organizational politics   Seeking selfish ends to enhance or protect the self-interest of individuals or groups.

organizational purpose   The fundamental reason for the existence of the organization.

organizational structure   The formal patterns of relationships that exist among work units or positions; the way tasks are divided between organizational members, the rules and procedures for accomplishing these tasks, and the authority and responsibility relationships that exist between people in the organization.

paralinguistics   The study of the vocal part of a message, including such aspects as range, resonance, tempo, control, intensity, and pitch.

Parent ego state   That part of the personality that is concerned with limits of behavior, prejudices, critical behaviors, and nurturing; concern for what should and ought to be done. Developed from observing parents and other authority figures.

participant observer   An academic researcher who becomes a member of an organization so that behavior can be observed in a natural way.

participation in decision making   The process of joint decision making between two or more parties.

participation leadership   Leaders who allow subordinates to participate in decision making.

paternalism   Treating employees as if they were children and the manager or company is the parent.

path-goal theory   A model of leadership that considers the leader's ability to influence the subordinate's goal attainment. The model considers both leader behaviors and situational factors.

perception   The process of organizing and interpreting environmental inputs that are obtained through our senses.

personality   A set of relatively stable personal characteristics and tendencies that determine our thoughts, feelings, and actions in combination with the social and biological pressures of the moment.

piece-rate pay   Paying on the basis of the number of units or pieces that are produced.

pilot project   Trying out a change by implementing it in only part of the organization.

positive reinforcement   The application of a pleasant or desirable outcome following some behavior that results in an increase in future behavior.

power   The ability to bring about outcomes that are desired through the use of influence.

power balancing   Each use of power tends to be offset by a counter use of power; power is normally in a state of equilibrium.

power motive   Concern with controlling and influencing others.

powerlessness   Perceived feelings of a lack of power.

problem-ownership model   A strategy for approaching interpersonal problem solving by using active listening or I-messages depending upon who owns the problem.

problem solving   A systematic method of defining the problem, gathering and evaluating data, generating alternatives, making a choice between alternatives, implementing the solution, and following up as needed.

process   The study of how and why activities, results, or states happen; procedures for carrying out a sequence of activities within a system.

process losses   Losses in group effectiveness because of communication, conflict, role behaviors, or other factors.

product form of organization   An organization that is structured around the output, product, product group, service, market, customer, or program.

productivity   The output of goods or service per worker.

programmed decisions   Decisions that are habitual and automatic; intuitive decisions.

psychological filters   The filters within a person's mind that distort, block, or change sensory inputs based upon personality, attitudes, values, needs, and past experiences.

psychological positions   The way a person feels about self and others, usually translated into four quadrants: *I'm OK, you're OK; I'm OK, you're not OK; I'm not OK, you're OK; and I'm not OK, you're not OK.*

psychosocial subsystem   That part of the organizational system that is concerned with individual and group behavior of people working together.

punishment   The application of an unpleasant or aversive outcome that causes a decrease in behavior.

qualitative research   Research that is based upon observation or authoritative opinion.

quality   The defects per unit produced.

quality circles   Small groups of volunteers who meet periodically to identify, analyze, and solve problems related to product quality or other issues.

quality of work life (QWL)   Concern for the impact of work on individual's well-being as well as improving organizational effectiveness.

realistic job preview   Giving prospective employees a realistic picture of the positive and negative aspects of the job.

refreezing   Making sure that an equilibrium is established for the new condition after change.

relaxation response   The slowdown of the body's heartrate, metabolism, breathing; opposite of the fight-or-flight response.

reliability   The degree to which the research instrument or design yields consistent results time after time or question after question.

responsibility centers   Autonomous subparts of the organization that have more or less total responsibility for their product or function.

reward power   Influence obtained by the ability to reward people with money, recognition, promotion, status, and other similar outcomes.

right-brain functions   The right hemisphere (for right-handed people) controls the intuitive, visual-spatial, sensuous, and holistic functions.

rituals   Part of an organization's culture consisting of symbolic actions; such as, ceremonies, leisure and play, and other behavior patterns.

role   Set of behaviors that are expected when a person occupies a certain position in an organization or in life.

role ambiguity   Uncertainty and lack of clarity surrounding the role to be performed.

role clarification   Open discussion of role expectations to clarify roles and reduce stress.

role conflict   Incompatible messages and expectations concerning the roles to be played.

role overload   Expecting someone to perform too many jobs or roles at one time.

satisfaction   The process of seeking acceptable alternatives rather than optimal ones.

Scanlon Plan   A financial incentive plan that involves sharing cost savings and using participative management techniques.

schedules of reinforcement   The timing of rewards or other outcomes following behavior. Ratio schedules involve a certain number of desirable responses, while interval schedules are concerned with the time interval.

schmoozing   Allowing groups to socialilze, to talk, use the telephone, and fool around.

selective perception   The process by which our minds select or allow certain inputs to predominate.

self-actualization A need that indicates desire for self-fulfillment and reaching potential.

self-concept The totality of an individual's thoughts and actions with reference to himself or herself as an object.

self-fulfilling prophecy When expectations about ourselves or others result in behavior that causes the expectation to come true.

self-managing workgroups Groups who are given autonomy over many aspects of their jobs; including, job design, goal setting, rewards, and member selection.

sensing systems The systems used to perceive; including visual, auditory, taste-smell, touching, and orienting.

shaping Using behavior modification techniques to gradually change behavior as desired.

situational leadership theory An approach to leadership that combines relationship behavior and task behavior and their interaction with the maturity of followers.

skills Learned behaviors; such as social skills, task skills, and communication.

skill variety Doing a number of different things; using valued skills and abilities.

S-O-B-C model A model for understanding the behavior modification process, which involves the stimulus (S), the person (O), the behavior (B), and the consequences (C).

social exchange process The interaction or exchanges between people who are members of a group, including those between a leader and the follower.

social loafing The possible tendency of individuals to produce less when working in the presence of others because they feel less pressure to perform.

socialization The process of learning the norms, values, and behavior patterns of a group or organization.

sociotechnical systems Designing the jobs and organization so as to optimize the relationship between the technical system and the social system.

span of management The number of subordinates that report directly to a supervisor.

staff activities Activities that support the primary purpose of the organization, such as personnel and legal.

status An individual's rank of worth within a group as determined by the individual's behaviors, attributes, characteristics, and possessions that are valued by that group.

status incongruence When status characteristics are inappropriate for the position in the group.

status symbols The possessions—clothes, office, voice—that reflect a person's relative status in a group.

stereotype A generalization about a class or group of people.

stimulus An environmental cue that elicits behavior.

stress A response, physical or psychological, to an external event that places special physical and psychological demands on a person and causes a deviation from their normal functioning.

stressor A stimulus condition that results in the response of stress.

structural subsystem That part of the organizational system that is concerned with rules, procedures, structures, reporting relationships, authority and responsibility.

superordinate goal An overall goal that transcends all others.

supportive leadership Leaders who show a great deal of consideration for their followers; leaders who are people-oriented.

survey research Using questionnaires to gather data about some issue that is of concern to the manager.

system An organized, unitary whole made up of interdependent subsystems and delineated by identifiable boundaries.

tall organizational structure An organization with many levels of hierarchy between the highest and lowest person; narrow spans of control.

task identity Doing the whole task or job from beginning to end.

task roles   Roles performed by an individual or group that are concerned with getting the job done.

task significance   The meaningful impact of the task on the organization and other people.

team   A group of people who must work together in a collaborative way to achieve the group's goals.

teambuilding   A strategy for improving the ability of teams to work together in an effective way, with a heavy focus on identifying and solving problems.

technical core   The primary task of the organization, such as production.

technical subsystem   That part of the organizational system that is concerned with knowledge, processes, techniques, and facilities that are used to transfer inputs to the organizational system into outputs.

technology   Types and patterns of activities, equipment, materials, knowledge, and expertise needed to accomplish the task.

theory   A way of relating how concepts, variables, or things relate to one another.

Theory X   An assumption that people are essentially lazy, dislike work, and must be coerced and controlled to be motivated to perform.

Theory Y   An assumption that people are self-directed, have the capacity for imagination and innovation, and that they seek responsibility.

Theory Z   A model that predicts that the proper corporate philosophy and human resource management systems will create a climate of intimacy, involvement, cooperation, and trust with long-term positive effects on satisfaction and performance.

third party   A person who acts as a facilitator to resolve problems or conflicts between two other people.

traits   Individual characteristics of a person; such as physical characteristics, personality, and intellectual ability.

Transactional Analysis (TA)   A theory of personality and human behavior that focuses on psychological positions, games, and transactions between people. It may also refer to that aspect of TA that is concerned with analyzing transactions and chains of transactions and their associated ego states.

transition   Movement from one state of equilibrium to another.

transition manager   A person, group, or unit that is responsible for planning and executing a change.

turnover   The proportion of employees who leave or quit.

Type A behavior   Behaviors that exhibit a chronic, incessant struggle to achieve more and more in less and less time. Often involves aggressiveness, hostility, anger, a sense of time urgency, and an achievement orientation.

Type B behavior   Behavior that does not include Type A behavior. Easy-going, nonaggressive, with little sense of time urgency or achievement orientation.

Type Z organization   An American organization that shares some of the same concerns for people and commitment to long-term goals as do Japanese organizations.

ulterior transaction   A hidden message that always involves more than two ego states.

unprogrammed decisions   Decisions made after careful problem solving and analysis.

valence   The desirability of a given outcome for a specific individual.

validity   The degree to which the research design, data, collection method, and instrument measure what they are supposed to measure.

value   A broad, general belief about some way of behaving or some end state that is preferable to the individual.

value programming   The process by which values are formed.

variable interval schedule   A variable amount of time passes (based on some average) between rewards.

variable ratio schedule   Rewards are given after a person performs the behavior a variable number of times.

vertical division of labor   The way authority, responsibility, and decision making are divided between the highest and lowest levels of the organization.

vertical integration   People, groups, or departments whose purpose is to co-ordinate between different levels in the organization.

vicarious reinforcement   Experiencing the rewards of others as if they were your own.

Vroom-Yetton model   A systematic, decision-tree approach to evaluating when to use participative decision making.

win-lose model   The outcomes that result from competition and cooperation; including, win-win, win-lose, and lose-lose.

zone of acceptance   The area of behavior where people will be likely to ac-cept the use of power.

INDEX